NORSE
SEA-
ROUTES

LAND
under the
POLE
STAR

Northward ye would extend
Your sway o'er realms of cold;
Pleasing this is to all good men,
King beneath the lodestar!

(From Sturala's kvad, *or lay, composed for King
Håkon Håkonsson after Greenland had become
part of the Norwegian realm,* Leiðarstjerna
(lodestar) was an old Norse word for Pole Star.)

The author aboard the *Benedicte* off the coast of Greenland

HELGE INGSTAD

LAND
under the
POLE STAR

A Voyage to
the Norse Settlements of Greenland
and the Saga of
the People that Vanished

Translated from the Norwegian by
NAOMI WALFORD

ST. MARTIN'S PRESS

NEW YORK

To the memory of my father

OLAV INGSTAD

CONTENTS

LIST OF ILLUSTRATIONS

Plates 1–46 appear between pp. 32 and 33

LIST OF ILLUSTRATIONS

☒☒☒☒☒☒☒☒☒☒☒☒☒☒☒☒☒☒☒☒☒☒☒☒☒☒☒☒☒☒☒☒

PREFACE

THE journey described in this book was made in 1953 by my wife, my-self and Harald Botten from Fosnavåg, in a small motor-boat named *Benedicte*. Our object was to learn more of the old Norse settlements founded in Greenland by Eirik the Red in about A.D. 1000. We covered 2,500 nautical miles, and made many trips inland over the mountains to home-steads at the very fringe of the inland ice.

Into this account I have woven the saga of those remarkable Norsemen who colonized a remote Arctic island, remained there for about 500 years and then mysteriously disappeared. The Norse people who lived in Greenland in the Middle Ages are referred to throughout as Norse Greenlanders, to distinguish them from the Greenlanders of today.

My grateful thanks to the many people who have helped me, either in connection with my expedition or with the preparation of this book, have been rendered elsewhere. The one to whom I owe most is Anne Stine, my wife, who endured the hardships of this enterprise without a murmur. Her help has been invaluable, not only on the journey but in the writing of this book.

My Greenland expedition and the conclusions I drew from it led me to make five more expeditions, this time to North America, in 1960–64, when the site of a Norse settlement was discovered and excavated at L'Anse au Meadow, on the northern tip of Newfoundland. Carbon dating from about A.D. 1000 confirmed my theories that Norsemen discovered the New World at about this time, and that Leiv Eiriksson and other Norsemen had their headquarters in Newfoundland. An account of these later expeditions is given in the sequel to this book.

HELGE INGSTAD

I ERIC THE RED

ABOUT a thousand years ago a remarkable fleet set sail from north-west Iceland, consisting of twenty-five ocean-going Viking ships. Aboard them was a variegated throng of men, women, children, cattle, sheep, horses, pigs and dogs. Quarters were cramped, for the cargo took up a great deal of room; and a very mixed cargo it was. It included bales of hay for the livestock, dried fish, dried meat, cheese and butter, farming tools, household implements, tents, hunting gear, weapons – in short, everything essential to existence in those days. All these goods were covered with hides and lashed firmly down. Cattle lowed, horses stamped, and children clung to their mothers, who stood by the gunwale of the heeling vessel, gazing back at Iceland as it sank slowly beneath the horizon.

The atmosphere on board was heavy and subdued, for these people were emigrants. Their goal was an entirely new country: Greenland. Under the taut, square sails the fleet was heading for drift ice and glaciers.

This expedition was one of the greatest Arctic enterprises of all time; as many as six hundred people may have taken part in it, under the leadership of that most outstanding figure Eirik the Red (Eirik Raude). Fourteen of the ships arrived; the rest either foundered or had to turn back. Are Frode in his *Íslendingabók*[1] – a work dating from about 1130 – tells us that this event took place 'fourteen or fifteen winters before Christianity was introduced into Iceland': that is, in A.D. 985 or 986. From Frode's book we gain an almost first-hand account of the discovery and settlement of Greenland; he gives as his source his uncle Torkel Gellison, 'who remembers a long time back.' Gellison had been to Greenland himself, and obtained his knowledge from one who had sailed with Eirik the Red on his voyage to the new country. These Norsemen not only struck root in that remote Arctic land: they later headed even farther west, and discovered North America. The Greenland community lasted for about 500 years, and then mysteriously disappeared.

Before speaking in greater detail of Eirik the Red and the colonization of Greenland, it will be as well to set the historical scene of his achievement.

He lived at the end of the Viking period, that age of expansion in the history of the North which lasted from about A.D. 800 to the beginning of the eleventh century, and of which he was a most typical figure. The Viking voyages began as minor piratical raids on the coasts of England and Scotland, and developed into great armed expeditions that aimed at conquest and settlement in foreign lands. The causes of this sudden migration are not easy to determine. Farmland may have been scarce in the home country; social conditions, and last but not least the craving for adventure, no doubt played their part. Far, foreign shores became a realm where young men from the North could win riches and honour.

Swedes headed mainly for countries in the east; Danes went to England where they founded a great kingdom, to France and other lands farther to the south. But it is above all the expeditions of the Norwegians and their descendants the Icelanders that are of interest, because so many of their vessels ploughed the northern seas and because they made the history of Greenland a part of their own.

The coastline of Norway is a very long one, and the sea was the ancient and familiar highway of her people. Far and wide they sailed, without compass, and made their landfall. Generations of experience had taught them to build a vessel that was a marvel to behold as she clove the seas with her square sail set, and today the slender lines of the Gokstad ship* in the museum in Oslo testify to their mastery of the art of shipbuilding.

The main outward route was *Vestervegen*, the Western Route, from the west coast of Norway to the Shetlands, Orkneys or Hebrides. From there the course might continue southward, usually along the west coast of England to the Isle of Man, Ireland or France, and occasionally farther, into the Mediterranean and on to Istambul (Miklagard). Norwegian Viking kingdoms were founded in the Orkneys and Hebrides, in Scotland, Northumberland, the Isle of Man and Ireland, where Dublin was the royal seat. Professor Haakon Shetelig writes in this connection: 'Throughout the century, from Harald Hårfagre to Olaf Trygvason, a considerable part of the British Isles was virtually Norwegian territory, offering free access to travellers, traders and emigrants from both Norway and Iceland, although no political links existed between the Viking settlements and the homeland.'[2]

As evidence of this we find a great number of Norwegian place-names on the coasts of Scotland, England and Ireland, besides burial-places and rune-stones. On the Isle of Man certain elements of the old Norse legal systems are in force to this day.

The 'Islands of the Western Ocean' – the Faroes, Orkneys and Shetlands – had a special status: they were not reckoned as foreign territory, but as the Vikings' own, by right of earlier settlement. What happened to the few Irish hermits who had settled in the Faroes and Iceland is not known. The Islands

* This ship was excavated in 1880 from a burial mound in south Norway. It measures 24 metres in length, 5 in width and 1·7 in depth (80 ft. by 16 ft. by 5 ft. 8 in.).

of the Western Ocean acquired special importance as gateways to the south.

It is said that Iceland was discovered by Gardar the Swede and the Norwegian Nadodd; this would have been about the middle of the ninth century. Here too Irish hermits were living at that time: those strange men who journeyed to the ends of the earth to worship their God. The majority of the immigrants were Norwegians from either west Norway or the Western Isles and Ireland, though there was also a Celtic element.

Often it was the chiefs who crossed the seas, with kinsfolk, servants, thralls and all that belonged to them, and they seized large domains. But peasants too found their way to the new island. In Iceland Norwegian speech and law prevailed, but the country soon became a free state, and in A.D. 930 the people established their own *Althing* (parliament) and their own legal code.

To this period also belongs the Norwegian Ottar's voyage of discovery eastward along the north coast of Norway to the region bordering the White Sea: Bjarmeland. The geographical work commissioned by Alfred the Great in about 890 gives an absorbing account of this journey and of conditions in northern Norway. Other chiefs followed in Ottar's wake and from trade in the White Sea acquired valuable goods such as walrus tusks, furs and so on.

These expeditions, then, did not always spell war; their purpose was also the discovery of unknown countries, followed by colonization or commerce.

In many ways the Viking period meant a great deal to Norway and Iceland. These were countries with strong traditions where law, social order and the literary arts were concerned, but they lay in a cultural backwater. Now the European influence washed in like a fresh tide: commerce and shipping flourished, new customs were adopted, poetry and other arts received stimulus from abroad, and a people that until then had believed in Thor and Odin and the power of fate, and for whom honour won in battle was the highest honour of all, now learned of a new and gentle god: the White Christ.

Such in brief is the background to Eirik the Red's achievement. It is important to examine the colonization of Greenland in its wider perspective, and particularly in relation to Norwegian expansion westward to the Shetlands, Orkneys, Faroes and Iceland. The discovery and colonization of Greenland and the voyages to North America came as the climax to a long process of development: the Western Route had been followed through to the end.

Eirik the Red[3] was born in Jaeren, a coastal district of Norway, in about A.D. 950; that is, shortly after Harald Hårfagre had welded Norway into a single kingdom, and during the reign of Håkon the Good. The flat farming region in the south-west differs from most other parts of the country. No skerries protect its shores, and the open horizon was ever before men's eyes.

Many of the mightiest families of the Viking period lived here in Rogaland. The saga of Eirik the Red tells us: 'There was a man named Torvald ... Torvald's son was called Eirik Raude. Father and son sailed from Jaeren to Iceland because of a slaying.'

When Torvald and Eirik came to Iceland the best land had been taken, and conditions were fairly stable. Up and down the country powerful men ruled as *godar* (chiefs), each over his own domain. The majority of the people were heathen, and this was the harsh period of family feuds described two hundred years later by the saga-writers. Blood-vengeance was law, and even minor offences were enough to bring about a violent clash.

Eirik and his father had to make their way to the remote north-west coast to find land fit to settle on. They chose Hornstrendene and called their farmstead Drangar. This was a bleak region of wild hills and snowfields facing the Arctic Ocean, where at times drift ice swept in and piled up along the coast; and it was far from any other human habitation. Stock-raising brought in a little, no doubt, but fishing and hunting of seal and other game were essential to survival. The struggle for existence must have been hard indeed, but the fact that Eirik learned to maintain life in conditions so similar to those of Greenland undoubtedly proved of great value to him later on.

Then Torvald died. Eirik married the strong-willed Tjodhild, whose family also came from the west of Norway, and were descended from the kings of Hordaland. This was a fortunate marriage, for the bride had powerful kinsmen in Iceland.

Eirik moved south to Hvamsfjord, at the head of the great Breidafjord, where Tjodhild's family lived. Here in Haukadal he received some land and built the homestead named Eirikstad. Some of the most renowned of Iceland's settlers lived in this part of the fjord; a number of them were wealthy chiefs, with numerous thralls and followers. Many had travelled far and wide, often to Norway, where it became the custom for kings to take Icelanders into their courts as skalds.

Beside the long fire on winter evenings the possibilities of discovering and colonizing new lands were constantly discussed. It was not long since Iceland itself had been a new land, so that the prevailing spirit and outlook here were those of a pioneer community. Stories were told of seafarers, driven westward by gales, who had seen new shores and strange things. At times imagination played so great a part that it was hard to distinguish fact from fiction, as for example in the case of Are Mársson, who drifted to Whiteman-land or Great Ireland, where he was baptized by chiefs in white garments. That strange land was said to lie six days' sail west of Iceland! There was also the simple and more credible account of the Norwegian Gunnbjørn who, driven westward by storms, found some islands which he named after himself. This was about the year 900. It is hard to say just where these islands may have been, though the indications are that they lay in the Angmagssalik region of east Greenland. Gunnbjørn later settled in Breidafjord, in Iceland, where his descendants remained, so his story carried especial weight.

Eirik listened. Much of all this was new or only vaguely known to him, for he had lived long in isolation in the remotest part of the country; and what he now heard of the blue coasts in the west fired his heart.

But these Breidafjord folk were fierce and fiery, and their swords sat loose in the scabbard. Eirik had fallen into dangerous company, and was soon in trouble. His thralls had started a landslide over the homestead of Valtjofstad, and were slain by Eyolf Saur. Eirik promptly retaliated by killing both him and Holmgange-Ravn, was brought to trial and sentenced to leave Haukadal.

He moved to the south of the Hvamsfjord, took possession of the islands cf Brokøy and Oksnøy, and set about building his third home. At this time he had lent his bench timbers to one Torgest of Breidebolstad, and these were of considerable value in an almost treeless land. When he claimed them Torgest refused to hand them over; Eirik therefore went over and took them. Fighting broke out and a number of men were killed, including two sons of the house.

The case came up for trial in the spring of 982 at the *Thing* or council meeting at Torsnes, farther down the fjord, and many attended. Eirik's friends rallied to his support, including Vigastyr who spoke in his defence. The sentence was outlawry, though for how long a term we do not know.

Eirik's enemies now set off in search of him, but he stayed in hiding until with the help of his friends he had fitted out a ship for a long voyage. He assured them that he would do as much for them should need ever arise, and he kept his word. Several of them later came to Greenland, where he helped them to settle.

Eirik the Red's saga states in spare and telling words: 'He said he meant to seek the land that Gunnbjørn ... had seen when he was driven westward over the ocean and found Gunnbjørn Skerries. He said that if he ever found this land he would come home again to his friends. Then Eirik sailed out to sea from Snaefellsjøkel.'

Eirik headed westward and sighted the east coast of Greenland, at a point probably a little to the south-west of Iceland. Skirting the belt of drift-ice southward, he rounded the southernmost point of Greenland and sailed northward along the west coast. Here he found what he had been seeking.

Much of this unknown coast must have looked familiar to him: the off-shore islands, the deep fjords, the whales, seals and birds. The seaboard is bare enough, but experience in their own country told him and his men that the best land would lie at the head of the fjords. Great was their joy as they sailed in and beheld green slopes where not only grass grew, and osiers the height of a man, but where even dwarf birch covered the sides of some of the valleys.

Eirik remained in west Greenland for three years, and explored the country systematically from Cape Farewell in the south to, apparently, as far north as Vesterbygd. He spent the first winter on Eiriksøy (Eirik's Island) in Austerbygd: this was an island off Eiriksfjord. In the following spring he moved up Eiriksfjord to a place where later he built his manor house Brattalid, and settled for good. His keen eyes had discovered the finest land in west Greenland. That summer he sailed north to Vesterbygd and named many of the places there.

He seems to have wintered that year on islands in the south. Next summer he again headed northward along the west coast (though some say the east) to Snefjell and into Ravnsfjord; here he believed that he had penetrated farther inland than the head of Eiriksfjord. The third winter he spent on Eiriksøy again.

Then he returned to Iceland, where men must have marvelled to behold his weatherbeaten vessel sail in towards the homesteads of Breidafjord.

During his three years in the western ocean he had discovered and explored a whole new country. Now his ambition was to colonize it, and for this he had to arouse interest among the people. His flair for publicity prompted him to call this country Greenland, for people would feel more inclined to go to a place if it had an attractive name.

The news spread through Iceland like a prairie fire. People flocked to Eirik to learn more of this new land in the west, and no doubt he had sketch-maps to show them. In sailing they would risk their lives; they would have to cut themselves off, sell farm and property, and part from those they knew and loved. But in those days the race was young; and for those who owned little, or were driven to the wall in family feuds, the choice was not hard. In every one of them burned the longing for adventure; every one of them dreamed of sailing in towards the blue coastline of a virgin land.

Now in many places a great bustle began: there were ships to be built or repaired, farms to be sold, and such equipment and goods obtained as were needful for starting life in a new country. There were contracts to be made with those who stayed and those who came, not forgetting the chiefs who, with their respective followings, were to receive certain well-defined estates. All this was more complicated than a military or trading expedition, for room must be found on board for women, children, thralls, livestock and much else.

At length all was ready, and one day in the late summer of 985 or 986 the fleet of twenty-five heavily laden vessels stood away to the westward, towards some of the most dangerous of all known waters. After weeks at sea, now tossed hither and thither by gales, now cruising warily forward among ice-floes, fourteen ships headed in to the coasts of west Greenland. The rest, as we saw, either sank or had to turn back.

Now at last the voyagers stepped ashore on to firm ground – the ground of the new land where they were to build their homes. Animals were let out to graze and children to play, while the women cooked over camp fires. The men scanned the countryside with expert eyes, rejoicing in the rich pasture, the untouched piles of driftwood that through the years had accumulated on the beaches, and at the sight of seals and birds and the herds of wild reindeer grazing on the heights. Egil Skallagrimsson's saga gives in a few words a picture of this time: ' ... a man might bring down his quarry where he would, for all creatures were placid and unafraid ... knowing nothing of man ... '

The chiefs with their following went each to his own fjord, and then the best site for the chief homestead had to be chosen. Of the settlement period in Iceland the saga tells us that for this the custom was to cast overboard a post of the high seat, and build the house near the place where it was washed up.

Individual claims had to be staked. In Iceland the methods had varied: barked posts might be driven into the ground, or marks carved in the rock, or coins left here and there, and one settler is reported to have carried fire round the boundaries of the land he took. As the flow of settlers increased stricter rules had to be applied, to prevent any individual laying claim to a disproportionate area of land. Oddly enough the Icelanders appealed to the Norwegian king Harald Hårfagre to lay down these rules. He decreed that no one might take more land than his ship's crew could walk over, bearing fire, in the course of one day. For women the limit was the distance they could cover on a spring day with a two-year-old heifer.

What methods the immigrants to Greenland used is unknown, but no doubt they were guided by experience in Iceland, being all too familiar with boundary disputes between neighbours; and there are indications that they marked out the land with cairns. A great number of such cairns have been found in the old settlements. Yet they may well have used fire too, for in fire there was magic.

The chiefs took possession of large areas, often that surrounding a whole fjord. The Icelandic Settlers' Book (*Landnámabók*) tells us: 'Eirik the Red took Eiriksfjord and lived at Brattalid, and at his death was succeeded by his son Leiv [the discoverer of Vinland, North America].'[4] There follows a list of ten other chiefs, each of whom took a fjord in Austerbygd, while others are mentioned as having journeyed farther, to Vesterbygd.

In many respects the method of land-allocation would have been similar to that of Iceland, each chief distributing shares to kinsmen and friends and others. Those who stood lowest in rank in this aristocratic society – freedmen and the like – received the poorest land, sometimes in remote areas, and a number of them were probably tenant farmers, as in Norway and Iceland. The colony was the kingdom of the chiefs.

The saga records that Eirik *took possession* of Greenland. It is not easy to say just what this implied, but conditions were somewhat different from those in which Iceland was colonized, and the extent of the settlement depended entirely upon the contribution made by each chief. Here it was Eirik the Red who had not only discovered the country but explored it, and organized the whole migration. We cannot estimate the extent of his power, but the sagas indicate clearly that he assumed the position of leader from the very beginning.

Eirik the Red had completed his task. He must have been a remarkable man: proud and pugnacious, but farseeing; and the magnitude of his achievement testifies to exceptional qualities of leadership.

II THE PEOPLE STRIKE ROOT

WHEN news of the successful landing and settlement in Greenland spread through Iceland, the Islands of the Western Ocean and Norway, a fair number of the inhabitants were impelled to emigrate too. We may well marvel at the daring of these folk, who set sail with all their possessions in open ships across those perilous seas, to found a new home. The King's Mirror (dating from about 1250), which gives much important information about the Norse Greenlanders, also tells us something of their mental attitude.

> Thou wouldst fain know why people journey to that land [Greenland] at such peril to their lives. It arises from the threefold nature in man. One part is the desire to vie with others, for it is the nature of man to go whither there is great danger and to win praise and renown thereby. Another part is the desire for knowledge, for it is man's nature also to seek out and behold those things which have been told him. The third is the desire to gain possessions.[1]

In Greenland, gaining possessions meant not only increasing flocks and herds, but also, and to a greater extent, acquiring profits from hunting. To people who were hunters almost to a man, the abundance of game held special attraction. It brought them not only food but also trade. Walrus tusks, hides, furs, down, blubber, etc., fetched high prices in the European markets; and it was with exuberant hope that the people set out on the great adventure.

The stormy ocean was dangerous enough, but worse than anything was the drift-ice. A powerful current from the polar basin sweeps southward along the east coast of Greenland, carrying with it huge masses of ice, as well as icebergs split from the glaciers. This current rounds the southernmost tip of Greenland and runs northward again along the west coast, off the land where Eirik and his people had their settlements.

At times the ice may be favourable, leaving channels and patches of open water where ships may pass. At other times it is very different, and presents grave dangers even to the shipping of our own day. Off the west coast of Greenland pack-ice may form a barrier all the way to Godthåb, the site of

Vesterbygd, and ancient sources suggest that drift-ice presented as many difficulties then as it does today.

At first there was no doubt a steady flow of immigrants, with occasional waves of newcomers after trading vessels had reached Norway or Iceland with especially valuable cargoes of walrus-skin, walrus tusks, hides, pelts, down and so forth.

Who were the first settlers? Mainly Icelanders. Chroniclers show more interest in the chiefs who sailed with Eirik the Red than in the ordinary farmers, women and thralls, of whom we hear little.

Norwegians also made the voyage to Greenland, naturally enough, and settled there. Living conditions were much the same as those they were used to on the west and especially the north-west coast of Norway. The country possessed a fleet of ships that plied constantly between Norway, Iceland, the Hebrides, Orkneys and Shetlands, and elsewhere. Eirik and other voyagers to Greenland had kinsmen in Norway, which was favourably situated for trade with the new colony, and soon it became customary to take the direct route between Norway and Greenland.

Norwegian kings took a great interest in the new country, the first of them being St Olav, at the beginning of the eleventh century. Many of the great men of Greenland became guests of the kings, and maintained close relations with them. Leiv Eiriksson visited Olav Trygvason[2] at Nidaros and was well received. He was given the task of promoting Christianity in Greenland, and returned there accompanied by a priest.

From these facts it is evident that quite soon after the first settlement the people of Norway must have had a good knowledge of Greenland, and we hear of vessels leaving Norway for that colony as early as the year 990 or so.

When in A.D. 1000 Leiv Eiriksson had discovered Vinland (North America) and was returning to Greenland, he came upon a ship wrecked on a reef. She belonged to Torer, a Norwegian,[3] who had his wife with him. Leiv rescued the fifteen people on board and brought them into Brattalid in Eiriksfjord, and it was after this incident that he was given the nickname of The Lucky.

The first explicit mention of a trading vessel in Greenland dates from 1061; she was Norwegian. Many Norwegian chiefs appear to have sent such vessels from quite early times. Commerce led to increased interest in the new country, and as emigrants could travel aboard these merchantmen we may take it that Norwegian emigration to Greenland began fairly soon.

The link between Greenland and Norway was later strengthened, and not by trade alone. The Church of Greenland came under the See of Nidaros, and the country itself became subject to the Norwegian Crown; thus bishop, priests, commissioners and others must also have crossed the ocean. We may assume that there were immigrants from the Orkneys, Shetlands and Faroes as well. The direct route from Bergen to Greenland often brought ships near these islands, and many a time they must have put in there to seek shelter from gales, or for other reasons, as Norwegian fishing-vessels bound for Greenland do to this day. One such immigrant was the Christian from the Hebrides who sailed to Greenland with Herjolf, the founder of the great Herjolfsnes estate in south Greenland, at the time of the first settlement. It is strange to hear of such a man seeking to dwell among heathen in that remote region of the Arctic. Perhaps he was some kind of missionary. His passage must have been a rough one, to judge by the poem he made about the Northern Ocean and its mighty seas:

> God the sinless I pray,
> Save my voyage from danger;
> Lord of Heaven on high
> Guard Thou my ways.

While on a voyage to Norway Leiv Eiriksson was driven off course and landed in the Hebrides. He stayed there for a time and fell in love with Torgunna, a lady of high birth. She conceived by him, and on his departure he gave her a gold ring, a Greenland cloak of wadmal and a belt. The child was named Torgils and later, it is said, went to Greenland.[4]

The newcomers found themselves in possession of a strip of land along the southern part of the west coast of Greenland. To the east it bordered the inland ice, that vast shell that covers the major part of the island to a height of 3,000 metres (10,000 ft.), and to the west the Davis Strait and drifting pack-ice. Here are weather-beaten islets, deep fjords and mighty mountain masses with snowfields and valleys, but also more level areas; a multitude of lakes and flashing rivers bring life to the landscape. In places the land has shaken off the yoke of the inland ice that once covered it all, while elsewhere mighty blue-green glaciers thrust right out into the sea.

The sea-coast is bleak enough, for here the winds and the cold air off the drift-ice exert their full force. But the land at the head of the fjords is often surprisingly fertile, yielding grass, brightly coloured flowers, angelica, juniper and willow, and in the best places alder as well, and dwarf birch. The vegetation closely resembles that found at tree-line level on the Norwegian ranges. Although the southern tip of Greenland lies at roughly the same latitude as Oslo, an Arctic climate prevails; yet in the places where people built their homes conditions were suitable enough.

At Nanortalik, the meteorological station near Herjolfsnes, the southern part of the former Norse colony, the mean temperature for the warmest month (July) is recorded as 6·2° Centigrade, and for the coldest (January) 5·3° below zero. These figures relate to the period 1884–1925.

At Godthåb, which lies in the northern part of the Norse region, the recorded July average is 6·5° C., and the February average 10·1° C. below zero, the average for the year being 1·9° C. below zero. Maximum and minimum temperatures for the year are given as 15·7° C. and 22·2° C. below zero. These figures relate to the period 1876–1925.

In both these regions the temperature is below that necessary for corn-cultivation, but allows of a relatively abundant growth of grass. In many places conditions are good for livestock, especially sheep. The best areas are at the head of the fjords, but records here are incomplete.

The climate, though somewhat harsher than immigrants from Iceland and Norway were accustomed to, offered no surprises, and to the northern peoples of those days living-conditions must have been good, not only as regards pasture but above all because of the exceptionally plentiful game both at sea and on land.

Of the two settlements, Austerbygd in the south was the better; it extended from Herjolfsnes near the southern tip of the country to about latitude 61½° N. Farther north came uninhabited coast, and then round Ivigtut a lesser settlement, often known as Mellombygd. Vesterbygd lay farther in-land, round the group of fjords east of Godthåb, at about 64° N. The dis-tance from the northern end of Austerbygd to the south of Vesterbygd is about 240 nautical miles. A seventeenth-century account gives it as: 'six days rowing with a crew of six in a six-oared boat'.[5]

In time the most fertile areas were put to full use, especially those at the head of the fjords. There also the chiefs had their dwellings: Brattalid, Hvalsøy, Gardar and others. Herjolfsnes was an exception, being situated on the coast. Inland areas too were exploited; and here we find Vatnahverfi with some fifty homesteads. Elsewhere there are small enclosures far up among the hills in the reindeer country. Some farms lie in incredibly remote spots, at the very fringe of the inland ice, and in exploring the ancient Norse settlements one receives a strong impression that dwellings were built in almost every place where it was at all possible to survive.

The most easterly of the Norse buildings lies on the Lindenow fjord, on the east coast. This was apparently a hunter's hut. On the west coast the settlements extend, as we said, as far as the Godthåb area. Farther north than that no ruins have been found, but there are signs that Norsemen went there either on hunting-trips, or to trade with Eskimoes, or on voyages of exploration. Among the most important of these indications is the remarkable rune-stone that was found on the island of Kingigtorssuaq, at about 72° 58′ N.

The learned Icelander Bjørn Jónsson states that Austerbygd possessed 190 homesteads and Vesterbygd 90:[6] 280 in all. From other ancient manuscripts[7] we learn that in Austerbygd there were twelve parish churches and two monasteries, and in Vesterbygd four churches. The following summary

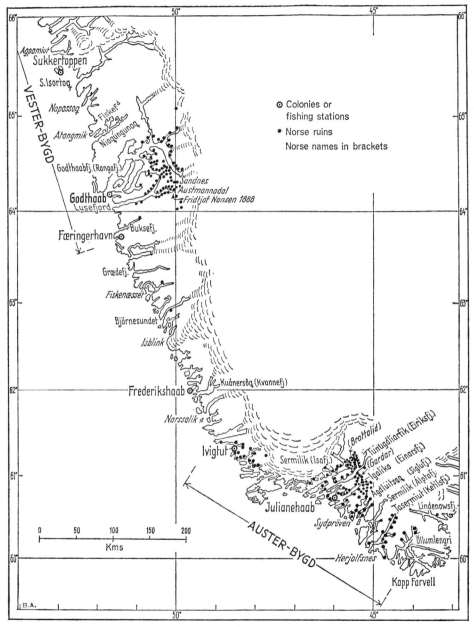

South-west Greenland, showing the old Norse settlements of Auster- and Vesterbygd.
Black dots indicate the ruins of farms, churches and religious houses.

23

shows the number of farms, churches and monasteries which are known at present:

(1) *Austerbygd*
    (*a*) The central area in the south:
                    185 farms   14 churches   2 monasteries
    (*b*) Mellombygd (Middle Settlement):
                    22 farms   0 churches   0 monasteries

(2) *Vesterbygd*   71 farms   3 churches   0 monasteries

         Total   278 farms   17 churches   2 monasteries

Rather more homesteads have been found in Austerbygd than Bjørn Jónsson mentions, while it seems that in Vesterbygd about twenty dwellings still remain to be discovered. As regards the churches, more have been found in Austerbygd than are named in the sources, and this is probably because some of them were small family chapels or chapels-of-ease. Three parish churches have still not been found: those of Aros (or Vik), Gardanes and Isafjord. In Vesterbygd only one (Hóp) is still undiscovered.

It is difficult to assess the size of the population. The King's Mirror, written in the thirteenth century, observes: 'If Greenland had lain nearer to other countries it might have been called the third part of a diocese.' But we can deduce little from that. A colony comprising 278 homesteads, 17 churches, two monasteries and a bishop's seat indicates a fair-sized population. Local conditions have a bearing on this. The stern struggle for existence on so many fronts necessitated a larger number of able-bodied men and women on each homestead than would have been required in places where food was easier to come by. Up there in the north it was not only stock-raising but fishing, hunting and trapping that took many of the farm-hands a long way from home.

Later I shall go into this more fully; for the present I say no more than that these homesteads comprised a considerable number of rooms. When estimating the population we should remember that at places such as the chief's manor at Brattalid, and Gardar, the seat of the bishop, at least a hundred people must have lived, and no doubt a great number also on other large estates, such as Hvalsøy, Herjolfsnes, etc. In general I believe that at the most flourishing period of the settlements the population was more numerous than is usually estimated, and I would suggest that it amounted to between four and five thousand,* that is to say an average of from 14 to 16 people per farm, which is by no means excessive for that way of life.

* The number is usually reckoned at about 3,000. Finnur Jónsson allows for 20 people to a farm and puts the total population at about 9,000.

When in about A.D. 1000 the Norsemen came to Greenland another race was living there: the Eskimoes. In the course of time these Eskimoes had wandered across from the west – from Siberia, Alaska and northern Canada – following the coasts and the string of Arctic islands in the north. They crossed to Greenland by the narrow Smith Sound or from points near it. Some made their way farther north, and stayed there; others went to the east coast. But the most natural way and the one taken by most of them led southward along the west coast of Greenland. In time they arrived at the southernmost point of the country, rounded it and went on up the east coast as far as the Angmagssalik region. But all this happened very slowly, almost by chance, and over a long period of time.

A Norwegian ethnographer and archaeologist, the late O. Solberg,[8] believed that the Eskimoes must have come to Greenland long before, in prehistoric times. He found little support for this theory, but recent digs in Greenland have confirmed it. According to the Danish archaeologists Helge Larsen and Jørgen Meldgaard[9] there were at least five separate Eskimo immigrations. The very oldest of the cultures have been found to the north, in Peary Land, while so far as the east and west coasts are concerned the oldest is the Sarqaq culture, which may date from about 500 B.C.

But Greenland resembles a continent in extent, and it was long before Norsemen and Eskimoes made contact with one another. In Are Frode's *Íslendingabók*, dating from the first half of the twelfth century, it is recorded: ' ... in both the east and west of the land they found dwellings and fragments of boats and implements, from which they perceived that the people who lived there were of the same kind as those of Vinland, whom the Norse Greenlanders call Skraelings.'[10]

It appears from this that at that time the immigrants had still not encountered any Eskimoes; but by the end of the twelfth century they had met them, for *Historia Norvegiae*[11] says of the period that Norsemen hunting in the north had come upon some little people whom they called Skraelings. This account is consistent with the fact that the Norsemen had regular hunting-grounds far to the north of the settlements, to which they sailed every year.

Not until the fourteenth century, however, did the Eskimoes move south in any numbers, towards the settled areas. This is evident from the finds made by the Danish archaeologist Therkel Mathiassen,[12] first at Inugsuk near Upernavik at about 73° N., and then elsewhere farther south along the coast. He revealed what is known as the Inugsuk culture, which shows strong Norse influence and had a highly developed kayak civilization. The Inugsuk people (Thule Eskimoes) came from Canada to Greenland in about A.D. 1100, moving down the west coast and round to Angmagssalik in the east.

Some of them settled in Austerbygd, and there was a time when Eskimoes and Norsemen were neighbours.

*

Our knowledge of the Norse community in Greenland is based on a varied collection of sources. Most of them have been collated in the work entitled *Grønlands Historiske Mindesmaerker* (1838–45). Yet it amounts to little enough when we reflect that Norsemen lived in that country for five hundred years. Irreplaceable manuscripts have been lost, but we may still hope that a few more will turn up and throw light on what is still obscure.

It may be useful at this point to summarize the main features of the history of the Norse Greenlanders.

The great colonizing expedition led by Eirik the Red took place in 985 or 986. His people built their homes, raised livestock, fished and hunted.

The boldest of them sailed westward on voyages of discovery, and North America was discovered by Leiv Eiriksson in about the year 1000.

Most of the first settlers were heathen, but in about 1000 Christianity began to spread among them. In 1126 the people had their own bishop, and from 1153 the Church of Greenland came under the authority of the Archbishop of Nidaros in Norway.

Relations with Norway became increasingly important, and trade was carried on mainly through the port of Bergen. In 1261 the Greenlanders gave their allegiance to King Håkon Håkonsson of Norway, and their country became part of the Norwegian realm.

In the fourteenth century the Norse Greenlanders made real contact with the Eskimoes who had migrated southward along the west coast.

From this time onward, contemporary sources tell us less and less about these people in the west. Sea-communications, always uncertain, dwindled almost entirely away. There may have been a number of reasons for this: the Black Death, Norway's weakened state and the union with Denmark must have had a good deal to do with it.

The last bishop of Greenland whom we know with certainty to have lived in the country was Alf, who died in 1377. Bishop Anders may have been there in 1406.

It is between 1406 and 1410 that we last hear anything definite about the Norse Greenlanders, when a ship from Norway berthed for the winter at Austerbygd. Icelandic annals mention among other things a wedding in Hvalsøy church, but give no hint that anything was amiss with the Greenland community.

Then the curtain falls.

However, in the frozen soil of Herjolfsnes churchyard clothes of European cut have been found, indicating that there must have been Norse people living in Greenland as late as 1500 or thereabouts.

At the end of the sixteenth century the coasts of Greenland were rediscovered by Martin Frobisher, John Davis and James Hall, and William Baffin; others followed, including whalers. But we hear nothing of any meeting with Norse Greenlanders. Then in 1721 the Norwegian Hans Egede arrived – the 'apostle of Greenland' – convinced that he would find people of his own race. But it soon became clear that the Eskimoes were now in sole possession of Austerbygd and Vesterbygd, and that not a single representative of Norse stock remained.

What fate overtook these people, after five hundred years?

III LANDFALL

T HE motor-boat chugged through heavy seas along the west coast of Greenland at about latitude 61° N. Sunlight lay on the sea, the islands and the drifting icebergs. In the east the mountain ranges stood out sharply against the blue of the sky, and now and then we caught a glimpse of the inland ice.

The boat was the *Benedicte*, and her crew apart from myself consisted of my wife Anne Stine, and Harald Botten, a young seaman from Sunnmøre in west Norway, whence so many vessels sailed for Greenland in ancient times. Our craft was of the dory type, a twenty-eight-footer, but very sturdy. Moreover, she was well known in the west of Norway for, during the war, that old Viking Ole Solbjørg took her from the Faroes to Norway, where under the very noses of the Germans he captured two of his own fishing-boats and slipped away with them to England.

After a ten days' voyage from Norway in a fishing-boat it was wonderful to be one's own master at last and to potter about along the coasts of Greenland as we chose.

Not that the crossing lacked interest. In ugly seas, or when drift-ice came by, my thoughts often went back to those who crossed these waters so many hundred years ago, in open boats. Tossing for weeks, sometimes months, to reach Greenland – and how many of their vessels were smashed by breakers or ice!

There were the Faroes, where we went ashore, and where we found much to remind us of our kinship with the inhabitants. This land was colonized in the ninth century. To behold its strangely riven islands with their dark-green grass, their flicker of birds and the blue seas smashing against their cliffs, was an unforgettable experience.

We looked at Kirkjubø, the royal farmstead, where King Sverre lived as a child; at the great cathedral that was never finished, and at the beautiful church of St Olav down by the water where, when gales lash the sea, fish are sometimes flung in through the windows.

Yet perhaps what struck me most forcibly was the continuance of the old customs which elsewhere belong to past history. Here the ancient dances and ballads are still performed with real fervour; and other deeply-rooted traditions too bring one a whiff of the Middle Ages. Like Greenland, the Faroes were subject to Norway both as a tributary and as an ecclesiastical province, and ships from Greenland are believed to have called at these islands; so it is only reasonable to suppose that the inhabitants of both countries were in close touch with one another.

Creeping forward among mighty icebergs that glided north with the current, we scanned the coast. There it was that the Norsemen dwelt for so long, and where today ruins of churches, monasteries and farms bear witness to this strange colony. So far we could see only the naked side of the land, where vegetation was sparse, and stunted by cold winds from the Davis Strait; but behind it, we knew, lay a green countryside, somewhere at the foot of the inland ice.

The plan was to cover the greater part of the ancient Norse settlements. First we would visit Austerbygd, and then continue northward to Vesterbygd, that vast complex of fjords east of Godthåb. Finally we meant to go still farther north, to the old Norse hunting-grounds known as Nordrsetur (Holsteinsborg, the Disko district, etc.) and see as much as we could before the winter ice closed the fairway. It would be a long and probably arduous journey for we should have to be continually cruising in and out of deep fjords, as well as crossing the hills on foot to reach the remote inland farms.

My object in making this journey was to see for myself the essential parts of the country where the Norse Greenlanders lived and worked; for, having spent many years among Arctic Indians and Eskimoes I knew how essential it is, in forming any assessment of Arctic peoples, to have first-hand knowledge of their living-conditions; far more so than in regions where life is easier.

In this case I was faced with many questions of a special kind, connected with stock-breeding, hunting, fishing, housing, shipping, trade, drift-ice, climate, Eskimoes and much else. I was also convinced that useful comparisons could be made with conditions in various parts of west Norway, the starting-point for those who emigrated either to Iceland or to Greenland in ancient times, and where many of the old ways were preserved until far into our own age. If during our journey we made any discoveries, such as unknown ruins and so on, it would be all to the good; but it was not our main purpose.

There it was – Eiriksøy, Eirik's Island! Some mighty icebergs had gone aground on the shore there, and the sun struck sparks from their blue-green mirrors. Here it was that Eirik the Red wintered about a thousand years ago. The saga says: ' ... and the third winter he was on Eiriksøy, off the mouth of Eiriksfjord.' He was in exile then, but filled with the rapture of the explorer and with bold plans for the colonization of this vast country.

We altered course and steered due east, into that deep, magnificent fjord, the spray flying from our bows.

On the north side of the mouth of the fjord is a promontory: a kindly stretch of low land at the foot of a towering crag, and here we glimpsed the modern Greenlanders' Narssaq (plain), which we were to visit on our way out. There and elsewhere in the neighbourhood are ruins of Norse settlements and of Dyrnes (Hardsteinaberg) church. In Ivar Bårdsson's old *Description of Greenland* we read: '... Divrenes [Dyrnes] church is the largest parish church in Greenland, and it lieth upon the left hand as we sail into Ericksfiord ...'[1]

Before travelling farther, I must say something about ancient topography. Our knowledge is drawn from sagas and ancient manuscripts. Thus Bjørn Jónsson and Arngrimur Jónsson (1568–1648), in their copies of old documents, have given us particulars of many churches, fjords, etc. Of these Ivar Bårdsson's *Description* is not the least important.

Ivar Bårdsson was a churchman of Bergen. In 1341 he received a mandate from Bishop Haakon to go to Greenland on Church business. He may have re-visited Bergen in 1344, but until 1364 the greater part of his time was spent in Greenland. He is said to have been for many years the bishop's deputy at Gardar, and this must have been between 1348 and 1368, when Greenland was without a bishop.

The description was originally written in Old Norse, and was most likely taken down from Ivar's verbal account. All that survives of it are copies in Danish and other languages.* The Danish translation dates from the beginning of the sixteenth century. It is easy enough to find errors and obscurities in this ancient work, but they are trifling compared with much that is undoubtedly accurate. On our journey we used Bårdsson's fourteenth-century *Description* as a guide-book. It not only gave us information, but conveyed the very spirit and atmosphere of those old times.

The outer end of Eiriksfjord is flanked by steep mountains, including the magnificent Nunarsarnaq, on the north side. About halfway up the fjord the character of the landscape changes: in the south the hills drop down to the narrow isthmus between Eiriks- and Einarsfjord. From here it is only a short distance by land to Gardar, the bishop's seat, and the meeting-place of the *Thing*, or parliament.

Before us now the inner end of Eiriksfjord came in sight: one of the most fertile areas in the country, where more houses were built than anywhere

---

* One translation of 1594 is by William Barents, the rediscoverer of Svalbard. This is of particular interest here in that Ivar Bårdsson's *Description* includes navigational instructions relating to Svalbard. According to Icelandic annals, that group of islands was discovered by Norsemen in 1194.

else. And soon, on the gentle slope running down to the shore we glimpsed a luxuriant expanse of green: an old Norse field. Here a house once stood – a house of stone and turf, with a grass-grown roof – where generations of Norsemen lived and toiled and died.

Ahead of us glistened a belt of drifting floes and bergs which looked like a solid barrier, but we managed to nose our way through. Most of this ice was from the Koroq fjord, where a glacier was calving.

Eiriksfjord now bends due north and becomes narrower. To the south, on the opposite side, the mighty summit of Igdlerfiksalik soars into the sky. Ivar Bårdsson[2] calls it Burfeld, from Old Norse Burfell. Daniel Bruun climbed it in 1894 and found the ruins of two huts, probably look-out posts. Certainly this peak commands a tremendous view of fjords, valleys, glaciers and mountains.

Large areas of Eiriksfjord may be ice-bound in winter. In the 'twenties the ice often lay from October to May, though now, in this milder period, conditions may be different. Icebound fjords were a common but very important factor in the life of the Norsemen here. Boats had to be beached and other means of transport substituted. Sea-going ships would hardly have been laid up on the inner fjords; they would have been left far enough out for the hunters to reach open water early in the spring, either for seal-hunting among the offshore islands or for longer voyages to the north.

In places such as the narrow part of Eiriksfjord, the ice must have brought neighbours on opposite shores nearer together, as in Norway; they could go visiting in sleighs behind their brisk little horses.

Evening was drawing on; a rising wind whipped the fjord and the boat rolled heavily. Our first goal was Eirik the Red's homestead Brattalid, on the western shore, but there is no harbour near it, and for the present we had to seek shelter on the opposite side and drop anchor there.

Blue-black clouds pierced by the red light of the setting sun chased over the heights, and one of the peaks seemed on fire. Just behind us and all round the end of the fjord, ancient homesteads once lay side by side, with boats on the shore, stock grazing, men and women busy about their work and children at play; while along hard-beaten tracks between the farms wayfarers came and went on horseback.

Somewhere here was Stokkanes, whose first owner was Eirik's friend Torbjørn Vivilsson and his daughter Gudrid. The Fosterbrothers' Saga, of about 1025, tells of a new owner and some dramatic events:

'Skuf owned a farm at Stokkanes; it lay on one side of the fjord and Brattalid on the other. A man by name of Bjarne lived with Skuf; he was a sensible man, well liked, and skilled in many things, especially as a smith. They owned the place jointly and agreed well together.'[3]

At that time Tormod Kolbrunarskald had come to Greenland to avenge the death of his fosterbrother. He lived at Brattalid with Torkel, the son of Leiv Eiriksson, who by then was dead. There was to be a great Christmas banquet and Torkel had ale brewed, to win prestige; for drinking-parties were rare in Greenland.

Here the saga adds a vivid little touch: 'Skuf and Bjarne spent Christmas at Brattalid, and they took household gear with them, to lend: vessels and clothes of the kind that were usual at that time.' No doubt these were simple enough things – soapstone pots, horn spoons, wooden ladles and dishes, woven cloths to hang on the walls, etc., with perhaps one or two especially costly items from Norway, for Skuf had recently returned from Nidaros.

So the Stokkanes folk sailed across the fjord, from near our anchorage, to Brattalid, to celebrate Christmas. When they came back they carried a killer on board: Tormod Kolbrunarskald, a member of St Olav's bodyguard.

Night fell over Eiriksfjord. Anne Stine had turned in and Harald and I were doing a few last jobs on deck when suddenly we heard splash after splash alongside. It was too dark to see what was happening, but Harald cried, 'Salmon!' Seizing a rod I tossed out the spinner. The fish took it, but behaved rather oddly for a salmon, rushing furiously back and forth and refusing to rise. 'What *are* you doing?' shouted Anne Stine from her sleeping-bag. 'I'm into a salmon,' I replied nonchalantly. '*No!*' she exclaimed, coming to the hatchway to admire her husband playing this noble Arctic fish.

I wrestled with the creature for a long time; it was powerful, and stayed stubbornly below, while the reel sang merrily. At last I got it up, under went the net, and on the deck thrashed – a large cod.

We were soon in the thick of a shoal of great cod that splashed all round the boat: in the thick, that is, of something that must have been of prime importance in the life of the Norse Greenlanders. Cod have their spawning-grounds far up many of the big fjords, often near the most populated parts of the ancient Norse settlements, so that in places the people had fish at their very doors – always supposing the climate was as it is today.

Before turning in I stood for a while looking out over Eiriksfjord. Ranges and hills melted into the grey of night, and an iceberg glided by. How beautiful a country these Norsemen had! It was their home; they knew every bay, every river, every peak, and all the land- and sea-ways that led to seal, reindeer, driftwood – or the bishop.

In the course of centuries these places acquired names that grew from the people's lives – and many names there must have been. But there was one with a special ring to it – the oldest and finest: Brattalid, the house of Eirik the Red. It lay there opposite us, across the fjord, and we were going there at dawn.

Anne Stine caught red char near the ruins of the Foss homestead, which was probably the property of the Norwegian king.

above: Greenlander in his kayak. *below:* The *Benedicte* which carried us about 2,500 sea-miles up and down the coasts of Greenland. She was a 28-footer; no beauty, but a sturdy craft.

above: Ponies grazing by old Norse ruins near Eiriksfjord. The slope immediately below and to the left was the site of Brattalid, Eirik the Red's manor-house, *below:* The ruins of Brattalid church, just below the great house.

Aerial photograph of Herjolfsfjord and its immediate surroundings, in the most southerly part of Austerbygd. Beside the inlet marked with a white arrow (*centre*) lay the manor of Herjolfsnes and a church. Ships from Norway often made this their first port of call after their long voyage across the North Atlantic.

West Greenland types of today. *below, left:* 'King' Amos, leader of the people of Gardar and a descendant of the Norwegian Anders Olsen.

above: Ruins of the byre at Brattalid. Partitions between stalls consisted of a flat slab of rock or the shoulder-blade of a whale. *below:* Harald Botten and Filimon the Greenlander in a canvas boat at the head of south Strømfjord. Harald was a fine seaman and a delightful companion.

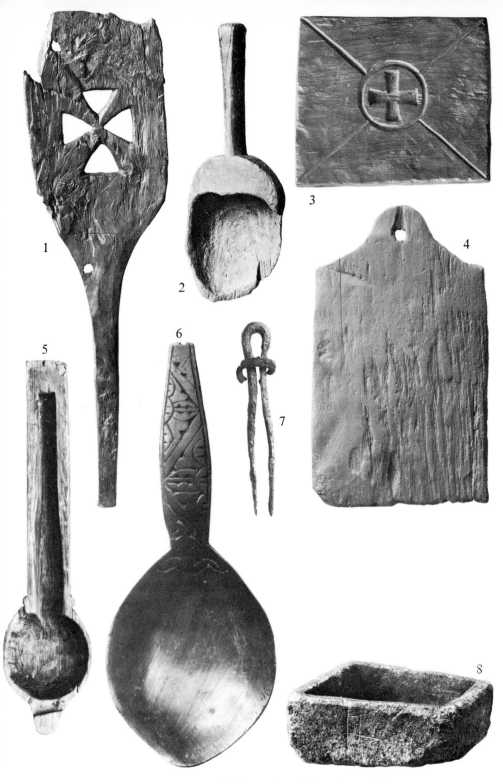

From Sandnes, Vesterbygd: 1. Wooden implement for stirring whey and the like. 2. Wooden scoop. 3. Wooden platter. 4. Wooden chopping-board. 5. Wooden spoon-case. From Austmannadal: 6. Ornamented horn spoon. From Brattalid: 7. Tweezers. (Photographs: National Museum of Copenhagen.)

☒☒☒☒☒☒☒☒☒☒☒☒☒☒☒☒☒☒☒☒☒☒☒☒☒☒☒☒☒☒

IV   BRATTALID

GREEN hillsides streaked with patches of red sandstone and a river winding and glittering down to a plain by the sea-shore – such was our first impression as we headed in. And so inviting is this place that our first involuntary thought was: 'How good to live here!' Yes, Eirik the Red knew what he was doing when he chose it for his home.

We dropped anchor off the shore of a wide plain which in the old days, no doubt, was the parliament- and market-place. The sun had just risen above the mountains and the air was transparently clear.

It was the modern age that met us first as we stepped ashore. There were some little houses on the slopes, and beyond them we saw grazing cattle and a few fine Iceland ponies with light-coloured manes and shaggy forelocks. A pig waddled away, and somewhere a cock was crowing. Next we came upon a vegetable garden, a potato-patch and a smiling old man who spoke nothing but Eskimo. The leader here was said to be called Erik Raude Fredriksen.

These people are the Greenlanders of today who have settled in this historic place, which is known now by the Eskimo name of Qagssiarssuq, or The Little Valley. Here as everywhere in west Greenland the inhabitants are of very mixed race, but their language and basic characteristics are Eskimo. There are about one hundred and thirty-five of them; they live by stock-raising, fishing and some hunting, and make use of the ancient Norse en-closures and paddocks, both here and elsewhere. Their animals consist of about 6,000 sheep, 11 cows, 3 pigs, 37 horses, some poultry and a dozen Scottish sheep-dogs. Their farming is not very efficient – they are too easy-going by nature for that – but they make a fair living.

This gives us some idea of the potentialities of the country, which cannot have altered much since Eirik the Red's cattle and sheep and horses grazed among these hills. But of course in those days the land was exploited to a far greater extent.

We walked down to the river that rippled so merrily away through grass and buttercups to the sea. Ten or twelve women were working here; the elder ones stood at the water's edge boiling and washing fleeces in big cauldrons. Young girls came running up and carried the wool to a grassy slope where, laughing and chattering, they spread it out to dry.

Not far from the river we saw some massive ruins dating from the days of earlier inhabitants, the Norse Greenlanders. At that time too girls must have carried raw wool up to those same slopes, dreaming as girls will when the river ripples and the sky is high and the wool dazzling white upon the green grass. But those girls lived hundreds of years ago and their lives are a closed book.

We felt at once that this had been a place of great importance in the old days: the home of many people and large herds of animals. Ruins of some sixty buildings still exist: churches, farms, byres, barns, storehouses, boundary walls, wells and other structures. The buildings are mainly concentrated in two areas: the more fertile of these lies to the north and comprises a small plain by the shore and the slopes above it. Here there were two farms, and a river that has cut a deep channel formed the boundary between them. North-west of these, and rather more than a quarter of a mile from the shore, lay a little hill-farm. A fourth homestead was situated on a larger plain to the south.

Originally the whole of this area must have formed one estate, and the owner would have lived in the big house near the church to the north. A chief such as Eirik needed plenty of room, and would not care to be crowded by his neighbours. But in course of time the estate must have been subdivided, and there are distinct traces of boundary walls. These walls were built of stone or turf, some being as long as two hundred metres (220 yards).

It is difficult to determine the original size of the home pastures. For one thing, the sea has engulfed some of the land, which has sunk between 17 and 20 feet since the Norsemen settled here. Also much of the soil has been swept away in storms. We can merely deduce, from the remains of byres and other buildings, that the grassland was extensive.

Now for Brattalid itself. It lies exactly as one would expect Eirik the Red's homestead to lie: a little way up the slope and sideways on to the fjord. What a view he had! From here we look over the ruins of the old church and far across the water, where scattered drift-ice glitters in the sun. No ship could come in unobserved by someone on the place. To the south great Burfell soars into the blue.

Much of what we read in the ancient records came to life as we stood here by the ruins, with the green slopes and the blue fjord before our eyes. Eirik's sons were Leiv Eiriksson, who discovered Vinland (North America), Torstein who settled in Vesterbygd and died there, and Torvald who made the voyage to Vinland and was killed by either Eskimoes or Indians. There was also his daughter Freydis who married Torvard, of the great Gardar estate on Einarsfjord, later the seat of the bishop. It is said that she was

34

haughty and wilful and that she took her husband – an inferior man – for his money. She too made the Vinland voyage.

Leiv Eiriksson inherited Brattalid on the death of his father, and from him it descended to his son Torkel. We know a little too of later owners. In the first half of the eleventh century the Icelander Skald-Helge,[1] storm-tossed, came to Greenland, where he married the widow at Herjolfsnes. Later he moved to Eiriksfjord, and eventually to Brattalid, as the Law-man of the country.

In about 1123 Sokke Toresson was chief at Brattalid.[2] It is recorded in *Flatøyboka*: 'There was a man named Sokke, son of Tore, who lived at Brattalid in Greenland. He was a respected man with many friends, and his son Einar was gifted and full of promise. Both father and son wielded great power over the Greenlanders as rulers in the land.' Later I shall tell how Sokke summoned his people to a *Thing* and established a bishopric with the help of the Norwegian king Sigurd Jorsalfare.

Then we have Ivar Bårdsson's account,[3] dating from the middle of the fourteenth century, from which we learn that the Law-man of the country usually lived at Brattalid. It seems likely that Bjørn Jorsalfare[4] stayed there in the 1380s as judge and revenue officer of Eiriksfjord.

Other scraps of information have come down to us, some of them of a dramatic kind. The *Flóamanna saga*,[5] which is somewhat imaginative, tells of Torgils Orrabeinfostre who sailed to Greenland in about 1001 and lived at Brattalid until he quarrelled with Eirik the Red. It seems that a polar bear came to the place and that he killed it with his sword. It was about this time that Leiv Eiriksson saved the Norwegian Torer and his crew from shipwreck. Torer and his wife, as was mentioned earlier, were invited to stay at Brattalid, and the rest were lodged in farms round about. During the winter they were visited by a severe sickness, and many died.

It is from the first period of the settlement that we have our most colourful account.[6] In about the year 1000 two Icelandic ships put in at Eiriksfjord, each with a crew of forty. One belonged to Torfinn Karlsevne. Eirik and a number of farmers rode down to the vessels and did some trade with them; he then invited the ships' companies to stay at Brattalid for the winter. They carried all their wares to the homestead, and are said to have lacked neither storehouses nor any other thing that they needed.

But as Christmas-time approached Eirik grew gloomy, and when Torfinn asked what the matter was, he replied, 'I fear lest when you go elsewhere it may be said that never did you have a worse Yule than with Eirik the Red.' What irked him was that he could offer no Yule-ale to his guests.

Torfinn then gave him all the grain and malt he wanted, and a magnificent entertainment was prepared such as was unknown in that needy country. When the festival was over, Torfinn asked for the hand of the beautiful

Gudrid (Torstein's widow), and the marriage took place that same winter, at Brattalid. The celebrations were talked of far and wide. The saga tells us: 'There was great joy at Brattalid that winter, with gaming and the telling of sagas, and other diversions ... There was much talk also of visiting Vinland the Good, and it was said that a voyage thither would bring in much gain, since the country was so fertile. Karlsevne and Snorre made their ship ready to sail for the new country when spring came.'

In one way and another it becomes clear that Brattalid was the meeting-place of the country's leading men through the ages; only Gardar, the bishop's house, could vie with it in this respect. From Norway and Iceland as well as from the Greenland settlements men came to Eirik the Red's homestead, to trade and exchange news; and here great men assembled for feasting. Brattalid was also the starting-point for the most important expeditions to North America.

The ruins of the homestead show us first that there was a great hall. Outside this lay a long-shaped area, apparently covered in, at the south-east end of which was an impressive well-head built over a spring. The other end faced a group of five rooms connected by a passage. Outside the buildings is a vast midden, which shows that the place was inhabited for a very long time. In 1934 Poul Nørlund and Mårten Stenberger[7] carried out a dig here and elsewhere in the Brattalid area. Some of their finds and deductions will be mentioned later.

The hall is one of the oldest Norse buildings ever found in Greenland, and no doubt it dates from Eirik the Red's day. Here it stood, fairly and firmly on the slope, with its massive stone walls and turf roof, like a face turned towards the fjord: a worthy dwelling for the foremost man in the land.

This is the 'long-house' of the Viking period. The style of building has its early origins in Norway, and it is of special interest that in the south-west of that country, where Eirik the Red and his ancestors came from, the long-house can be traced back to the days of the migration. Emigrants carried the style out to Iceland and the Isles of the Western Ocean, and last it reached the Arctic.

The massive walls of the hall were of stone and turf and about 1·5 metres (5 ft.) thick. The door was in the middle of the long side facing the fjord, and here the walls had a thickness of more than three metres (10 ft.). Thus the entrance forms a passage, and is paved with flagstones. The room inside is 14·7 metres long by 4·5 wide (about 49 ft. by 15 ft.). The floor is of beaten sand and earth. Immediately opposite the door there was a large cooking-place, and there were open fires here and there about the floor.

The construction of the roof is unknown, but it may have been supported by upright posts, and there is reason to think that flat slabs of sandstone were

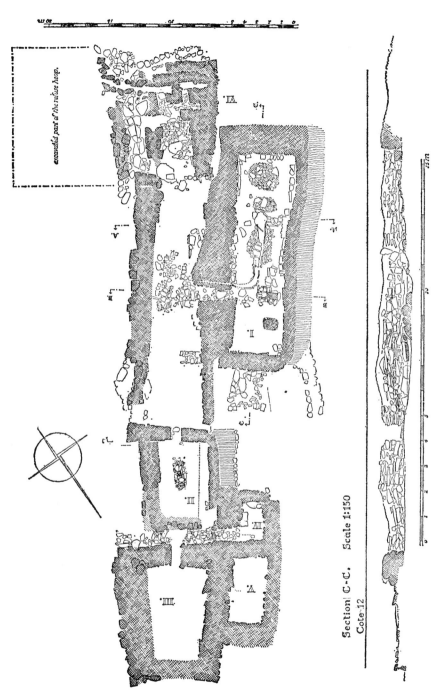

Section C-C. Scale 1:150

Cote-12

Ground plan of Brattalid, home of Eirik the Red. I. Hall, the oldest part. Channel and pool for running water are indicated here, also fire-places. II—V denote later additions (Ganghus or passage-houses). VI. Well. (National Museum, Copenhagen)

excavated part of the refuse heap.

laid under the roofing-turf. As in Norway, light was admitted through the smoke-hole in the roof, but there must also have been small window-openings through which one could survey the valley and the fjord. This was essential.

A remarkable feature is that water was 'laid on'. It comes from a little spring under the rear wall, and runs along a gully to a basin in the middle of the floor. From there the channel continues parallel with the long sides of the room and then bends and runs away under the wall by the door. It is paved with flat stones and was presumably covered over to prevent fouling of the water.

What was the reason for this arrangement? Poul Nørlund and Mårten Stenberger cite two examples from the Icelandic sagas which are of relevant interest.[8] The *Sturlungasaga* relates that when Rafn and his men were to attack Myrar farm, they first diverted the course of the river that led into the house. The farmer realized that they meant to set fire to the place and begged for mercy. In *Hardar Saga Grimkelssonar* we hear that the owner led a stream into the house at the approach of his enemies.

This may provide an explanation for the Brattalid water-system, though it may also have been devised simply to save work indoors; or it may have been combined with some necessary drainage. Traces of such indoor channels have been found in other buildings, like the one discovered by C. L. Vebaek while excavating an old homestead at Narssaq at the mouth of Eiriksfjord.

Many interesting finds have been made in the hall and in the midden outside, such as bones of reindeer, walrus, seal, whale and domestic animals; and from these we learn a good deal about the Norsemen's diet. Many fragments of soapstone cooking-pots, bowls and lamps have been discovered, also about twenty spindle-whorls and a number of weaver's weights. Other objects include barrel-staves, knives, a whetstone, draughts and chessmen, and an iron spearhead thrust between stones in the wall.

These things tell their own story. As in Norway and Iceland the great hall was the place where most of the house-folk gathered when not at work out of doors. In the Edda poem 'Rigstula' we find a description of the yeoman's hall as it was in the Viking period. A man and a woman sit there, he with his carving, she with her spinning-wheel. When the guest enters, food is offered him there: 'Full bowls she set before him; roast veal was the finest dish.'

Evening in the great hall of Brattalid. The long fire is ablaze down the middle of the room, and throws flickering light on the black stone walls. Slowly the smoke rises up through the vent, and all round there are people, some seated on roughly hewn benches of driftwood, others on stools or reindeer-skin. The air is smoky, and there is a pungent smell of blubber and hides.

Here and there pronged soapstone lamps are fixed into the walls; their wicks, floating in blubber, bear a kindly little flame.

Many of the women are busy carding, spinning and weaving. The loom is upright and quite small, and the warp is stretched by a row of soapstone weights. The weavers' work is endless, for cloth is needed not only for clothes, sails, tents and so on, but also for barter when the Norway boat comes in. Other women are busy stitching and dressing hides, while children romp and play near by.

The men are busy with their own work; some are repairing harness or tools, others harpoons, fishing-tackle, arrows and bows or bear-spears. One perhaps has an Arctic fox hung up by the hind legs; he slits the skin carefully and pulls it off.

Some are idle. Two men sprawl on a reindeer skin under a lamp – they're in another world; they're playing chess. The chessmen are finely carved from walrus-bone. Others chat: their talk ranges from hunting and distant places to a pretty girl at a near-by homestead; now and then some salty jest sets laughter ringing down the hall.

It's getting late. One after the other the members of the household lie down on the benches along the wall, or on the floor, and roll themselves up in sheepskin or reindeer hide. The fire dies. An old woman kneels down by it and scrapes together the embers, which she shovels carefully into a little stone-lined hole in the floor. Then she blows out the blubber lamps ...

But this great room was also the banqueting-hall, and magnificent feasts were held in it down the ages. Many great men sat at the long table, and many marvellous tales were told there. Eirik the Red himself once occupied the high seat: a massive, weatherbeaten figure ...

But no feast ever outdid the celebrations at Brattalid when the long-awaited ship from Norway arrived, possibly for the first time for years. As the great sail glides in through the drifting ice far out at the mouth of the fjord, feverish activity begins in the homestead. Women sweep and tidy, boil and roast. The long table is pushed into the middle and laid with cups and platters of wood and soapstone. The finest wall-coverings of picture-weaving are brought out from the chests and hung up, and the girls fly out to the storehouse to fetch stacks of butter, cheese, dried meat and other provisions of the very best.

But the lads jump on to horses and tear off with the message token, which will be carried on from farm to farm, and up to the remotest huntsman's hut in the hills, bringing the most joyful news of all: the ship from Norway is in!

V GREEN HILLSIDES BEYOND THE ICE

IT is a real experience to wander over the level land by the water, and up the slopes, looking at the many ruins that tell us how people ordered their lives in the old days. Some ruins have been excavated, others remain buried: a mystery.

A little way below Brattalid there once stood not only a church but also a large farm-building. It was about 53 metres (180 ft.) long, but quite narrow, comprising three byres, two barns and other accommodation less easy to identify. One can see the care that was taken to protect the cattle from winter cold, for the walls are of stone and something like a metre and a half (5 ft.) thick, and outside them is a turf bank.

The internal width is not quite four metres (13 ft. 4 in.) and yet two rows of cows stood here. Their stalls are divided from each other by flat stones set edgeways and driven into the walls, and in one place the shoulder-blade of a whale has been used as a partition. The floor is mostly flagged, and in the middle is a stone-paved gully. The entrances are long and narrow, to prevent the entry of too much cold air. Indeed, the place is so well insulated that unless an odd chink was left here and there the animals must have gone very short of oxygen.

Most of the Norse cattlesheds in Greenland were built on this pattern. The animals were terribly crowded, even allowing for the fact that they were smaller than those of today.

We crossed the river and climbed the steep slope to the ruins of the neighbouring homestead, which stands by itself on a level stretch of ground overlooking the fjord. Here there was no hall, but eight rooms linked by a passage-way, and the house is of a later type. A little farther on we came upon the ruins of a byre and barn, of which the details remain remarkably distinct. Especially noteworthy is the paved entry which is 7·5 metres (25 ft.) long by only 60 cm. (2 ft.) wide, and crooked at that. It is a marvel that the cows could squeeze through it.

In the barn a remarkable find has been made: a piece of pierced soapstone on which is engraved the outline of a hammer, Thor's emblem. This probably dates right back to Eirik the Red's time, when heathendom still prevailed.

*

Thor's hammer engraved in a piece of soapstone

It was a fine summer day, and we could see far and wide; in the transparent air the blue of the fjord, the distant mountains and the glaciers seemed to have drawn nearer. Around us lay a lush meadow where long-stemmed buttercups grew in sweeps that looked like yellow brush-strokes against the green. As we stood there beside the old byre, a gleaming black raven came hopping towards us, up to the neck in buttercups. There was something purposeful about him, as if he had been awaiting us and was hurrying to be on time. He was quite tame and came right up to me, with his head on one side and an observant look in his eye. All at once he bounced down the long entry into the byre, and on from stall to stall, glancing back at us now and again, as if to make sure that we were following. He seemed to have made it his task to show us every detail of the building. Finally he hopped up on to the ruins of the barn where the stone with Thor's hammer carved on it had been found, and sat there for a while, hunched and thoughtful. Then, in a moment, he was gone.

This was an odd way for a raven to behave. I remembered how often the Greenland legends mention ghosts: was this Eirik the Red re-visiting the old places?

There are traces of many kinds of enclosures. Some of the pens were large, and were probably used when the sheep were rounded up in autumn. There are remains of stone and turf walls, some barely visible; yet at one time they were probably eight feet high, as in Iceland, to protect the home fields from wind and blown sand.

Faint traces of such a wall run down the slope towards the bay where we had dropped anchor, and here the gales had swept large areas bare of soil. This plain was in all likelihood the first parliament- and market-place in the country, as Poul Nørlund and Mårten Stenberger pointed out[1]; later the *Althing* was held at Gardar on the neighbouring fjord.

We can still see the remains of stonework pertaining to the 'booths' or roofless huts of those attending the *Althing*; there are also hearths, and along this part of the shore there were no doubt a number of different kinds of buildings, vanished now; for when the land sank the sea washed a great deal away. We may be sure that there were boathouses there, fishing-huts, storehouses and much else.

As the time of the *Althing* approached, people poured into Brattalid, riding, rowing or sailing. Farmers made for their booths and pitched the tent-roof over the stone walls. The parliament met, the laws of Greenland were proclaimed and lawsuits heard. But the assembly was far more than this: it meant a holiday for people who had endured a hard and often lonely existence in the wilds. Now they met not only their friends but also new people with new ideas, and it was a relief to be able to talk to someone.

Here boy met girl, and later on, it might be, they would go off together to build their own home in the wilds. Here sagas were told; there were games, dancing and wrestling-matches, and also bartering. A hunter from the far north in need of iron for spear- and arrow-heads might bring walrus-tusks in exchange, while a man from inland could offer reindeer-hide in return for seal-blubber.

Among the most important things was the telling and hearing of news. Everyone had something to relate about his part of the vast country, whether an ordinary, everyday incident or some more important event that stirred men's minds: a tussle with a polar bear, it might be, a shipwreck, or a voyage to an unknown coast.

Afterwards, when all had returned home, the story would be told and told again. Years passed, people died, but the tradition lived on, and new youngsters sat listening to it by the long fire on winter evenings. In course of time the story would be trimmed and shaped and become crystallized in form and content – and a new saga was born.

Although the Brattalid folk raised cattle and other animals on quite a large scale (as we saw from the size of the buildings and enclosures and from the fine grazing in the hills), fishing and hunting were at least equally important. Besides great numbers of cod, the fjord waters yield catfish and lumpfish. In spring masses of capelin come in, so that in places one can scoop them out with a landing-net.

Magnus Degerbøl[2] has examined the animal-bones found at Brattalid, and they have much to tell us. More than half are the bones of seal, especially the Greenland seal. The hunters went out in search of them among the skerries, where they had their spring and autumn haunts. They also caught large whales and polar bears, which, in earlier times at any rate, may have come into the fjords with the drift-ice. The legend that Torgils Orrabeinfostre killed a polar bear quite near Brattalid may be founded on fact. Bones of walrus have been discovered too, which means that the hunters must have

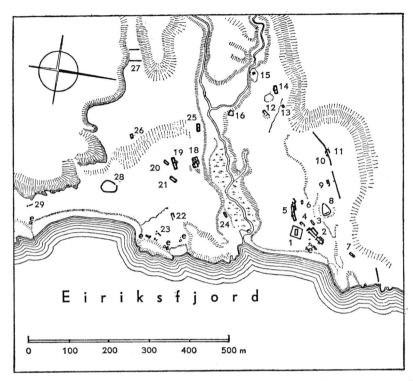

Map of the northern area of Brattalid. 1. the church. 2. homestead or manor-house of Brattalid. 3. storehouse. 4. ? storehouse. 5. byre and barn. 18. neighbouring farm. 19. byre. Remaining numbers indicate ruins of storehouses, outbuildings, byres, sheepfolds, etc. The Tingvoll or parliament-place is not shown, as it lay outside this area and to the left.
(National Museum, Copenhagen)

made long voyages to the north. Other bones show that reindeer provided much of the settlers' food, as did hare, grouse and seabirds.

The horses at Brattalid, like the cattle and sheep, were small – about 12 or 13 hands (127 cm.) – that is, they were no larger than the horses in the North some hundreds of years B.C. No doubt they remained out all the year round, as they do today. The faithful dog also found its way to Greenland. Bones of a big, long-legged dog have been found at Brattalid, and those of some smaller breed on other farms. Dogs would have played an essential part in the rounding-up of animals in the hills; the large breed may have been something like a Scots collie, and the smaller a Norwegian deer-hound. Watch-dogs must also have been kept.

The people apparently smelted their own iron from bog-ore, and at the extreme south of the estate there are remains of something that may have been a forge. A few iron objects have been found, including sickles, knives, a pair of pincers and frost-nails. No doubt the Eskimoes have since removed many such things from this centrally placed homestead.

Among other interesting finds we should mention combs, bone needles, part of a whetstone, sled-mountings of whalebone, and various soapstone objects such as ladles and oil lamps of the same type as the Norwegian ones of the Viking period. Then there are the wooden things, such as barrel-staves, scoops, etc., no different from those used on Norwegian and Icelandic farms right down to our own day. Their tools were axe, knife and probably some sort of lathe; there is nothing to show that plane or saw was used.

Almost everything was home-made, and only a few imported articles have been discovered, as for instance a decorated iron hasp, probably from a chest; the kind of chest in which women kept their finest clothes, their most precious needlework, weaving and other things of value.

Anne Stine came running in excitement. 'Come and look,' she said. Obediently I followed her to a ruin, where she told me to peer through the chinks. From within, a heap of skulls grinned at me, surrounded by other bones. All were contained within a sort of chest formed by stones.

Eskimoes had buried their dead here; it was not unusual for them to use a Norse building for a tomb. The skeletons probably date from the seventeenth century, long after the Norsemen disappeared and before Hans Egede re-introduced Christianity to the country.

Nearer the shore are dwellings of a later date, showing that a number of Eskimoes wintered there. Tradition has it that many of them starved to death, and in one of the houses the skeletons of a whole family still lie on the sleeping-benches. For people who raised no livestock, or who were not careful to build up reserves of food, wintering at the head of a fjord was a risky business. For these seal-hunting kayak-people the outer coast was a far safer place during the cold season.

We looked in vain for the cave where Tormod Kolbrunarskald hid after slaying the powerful Torgrim Trolle, to avenge his fosterbrother.[3] We saw some birch-scrub, but also a number of big tree-roots, which showed that large mountain birch trees had once grown in these parts. Conditions are favourable enough for us to assume that a considerable part of the Brattalid slopes were wooded when Eirik the Red came to the country.

Copsewood near a homestead was wealth in Greenland; it provided material for tools, as well as charcoal for the smelting of bog-ore. Without it, people had to make do with driftwood. Woodland also meant fodder for livestock. So it came about that generation after generation despoiled the land of trees until they had deprived themselves not only of useful material but also of a wind-break for the home fields.

44

We walked uphill to the north-west to look at the 'Fjellbygd'[4] or hill settlement, as it is often called, and had not gone far before the landscape took on a new character: the river foamed down through a ravine, and farther on there were rocks, fertile slopes and pools.

Of the Fjellbygd little remains: just a small farmhouse standing by itself among the rocks, about 500 feet above sea-level. There are a number of out-buildings and a midden, all indicating that this was a permanent dwelling. It seems likely that it belonged to Brattalid; as sheep and horses were left out all the year round the 'lord of the manor' would certainly have had people living up among them in the hills.

On the way back we came down the slope immediately behind Brattalid. A little way above it there is a terrace with some scattered stones on it, perhaps the remains of a barn, and here we paused for a moment to enjoy the view over the settlement and the fjord. In the foreground eight Iceland ponies were grazing, brown with white manes, while two little foals frolicked about. Evening was coming on; the sun rode the mountain ridge, and the long clouds were fringed with red. Peace lay over the river and the green fields of the valley.

At such an hour, long ago, smoke would have been rising from Eirik the Red's massive, turf-roofed long-house; his people would be coming home from field and pasture, unhitching the horses and putting away their primitive tools, while in the great hall the women hastened to bring out the sour milk, dried meat and fish. Through the narrow entrance the men filed in to take their place in the great room, where the evening light slanted down through the smoke-vent.

A sudden rushing sound made us look up: it was the raven. He flew directly over us with heavy wing-beats, heading for the dark fells.

A passage in Ivar Bårdsson's *Description of Greenland* runs: 'There, farther up the fjord, stands Leijder [Brattalid] Church, which owns everything round the head of the fjord, even to the other side of Burfjell. Everything beyond Burfjell belongs to the Cathedral. There lies a great homestead called Brattelede, where the law is wont to dwell.' From this we may appreciate the strong position held by the Church of Greenland in the middle of the fourteenth century.

We stood by the ruins of the old church, on the plain near the water, a little below Brattalid homestead. Only the foundations are left, built of massive, well-hewn stones. Round the church runs the churchyard wall. There is something familiar about the whole layout and one is reminded of the ancient stone churches of Norway.

The building is rectangular with an inside measurement of 12·5 by 4·5 metres (about 41 ft. 8 in. by 15 ft.), and had two entrances. In the middle there must have been a hearth, for there is a hole in the floor lined with flat stones; and no doubt a little warmth was welcome when the winter day was cold and the sermon long.

Whatever there may have been of ornament in the church has long since vanished, but we may suppose that the chiefs of Brattalid took care that this important church should be fittingly adorned – so far as their modest materials allowed. Tapestries on the walls, perhaps; an altar-picture in relief, some soapstone carvings, and a few costly treasures brought at one time or another from Norway, such as an altar cloth and holy water stoups. The font was no doubt of soapstone. Most probably the skin of a polar bear lay on the cold earth floor for the priest to stand or kneel on, as in Nidaros Cathedral.[5]

The churchyard wall remains in astonishingly good repair after all these centuries. No doubt it held the same profound significance here as in Norway and Iceland: within it the ground was sacred, and damned to all eternity was he whom the priest denied burial there. The Gulating law, written down in about 1150, decrees that everyone who dies shall be carried to the church and buried in holy ground, except for malefactors, traitors, murderers, thieves and suicides; these were to be buried at high-water mark, 'where sea and green turf meet'.[6]

How old is the church? It seems likely that church-building in Greenland was influenced chiefly by that of Norway. In Norway rectangular stone churches became usual towards the end of the thirteenth century; Brattalid church may therefore date from about 1300.

Practically nothing of importance was found in this church, except the following, uncovered by G. F. Holm:[7] partly melted lumps of bell-metal or light bronze, lumps of slag and pieces of carved soapstone, indicating that the building must have been destroyed by fire.

Beneath it, as elsewhere in Greenland, remains of an older church have been found; and it was indeed the custom among Norsemen to erect any new church on the site of an old one.

The saga tells us that Eirik the Red's wife Tjodhild embraced the new faith, and built a church 'not too near the houses'. Eirik the Red remained heathen: Thor and Odin were mighty enough for him. Tjodhild cannot have been very easy to deal with, for she refused to lie with him so long as he remained unconverted. And this, says the saga, was displeasing to Eirik.

Where was this church of Tjodhild's? The phrase 'not too near the houses' need not indicate any great distance, for Norse domestic chapels often formed part of the cluster of farm-buildings. We should also remember that the old Norwegian–Icelandic law very rarely allowed a church to be moved. In the Icelandic *Grágás* it is stated: 'Every church shall stand upon the place where it was consecrated, unless prevented by landslide, flooding, underground fire or violent streams and the like.'[8] If moving became necessary, there were strict and detailed rules for the exhumation of all skeletons and re-interment in the new churchyard: 'They should begin to dig at the uttermost ends of the churchyard and seek bones as they would seek for money ...'

It was thus reasonable to assume that Tjodhild's chapel once stood on the site of the old church. But in 1961 a Greenlander accidentally discovered a site a little farther away, where the remains of a small building about 15 square metres (50 square ft.) in area have been excavated, as well as bones from a number of skeletons. This may have been Tjodhild's chapel.

A number of tombstones were found in the churchyard, and on one of them a large cross was cut. There were also traces of many burials, such as bones and pieces of woollen cloth in which the deceased had been shrouded. One burial was in the church, where a skeleton was found among fragments of a coffin. But owing to the coarse, gravelly nature of the soil everything was in a bad state of preservation.

The finest discovery was a little grave surrounded by handsome stones; it was only 1·43 metres long (about 57 inches). On the headstone runes had been carved the words 'Ingibjørg's Grave'. Simple but telling words that speak to us of sorrow and of a little girl who once played around Brattalid. The brevity of the inscription brings it all alive. Her first name was memorial enough: everyone knew Ingibjørg.

On a sunny summer's day, about as warm as it would have been in the Norwegian mountains, we left Brattalid and made for the head of Eiriks-fjord, so as to gain a general picture of the dwellings and living-conditions in that area.

Soon we came upon one ruin after another, some of them those of quite large farms. They lay not only on either side of the inner arm of the fjord but also in a level valley leading from Eiriksfjord to the fjord of Sermilik in the west.

So numerous in their day were the homesteads and people of Eiriksfjord that the chief must have held a strong and influential position in parliament and elsewhere. The largest of the homesteads lay at the entry to this valley, at a place called by the Eskimoes Qordlortoq, and might almost be compared with Brattalid in size. There was a main dwelling-house with a great number of outbuildings. Near by runs a salmon river, said to be one of the best in the district.

Quite close to the homestead Poul Nørlund and Mårten Stenberger have identified a small church, as well as another similar one farther up the valley.[9] It had an internal measurement of about 3·5 by 2·25 metres (11 ft. 8 in. by 8 ft. 4 in.). The churchyard wall was almost circular, which is exceptional in Greenland, where it is usually rectangular. These little places were presumably domestic chapels.

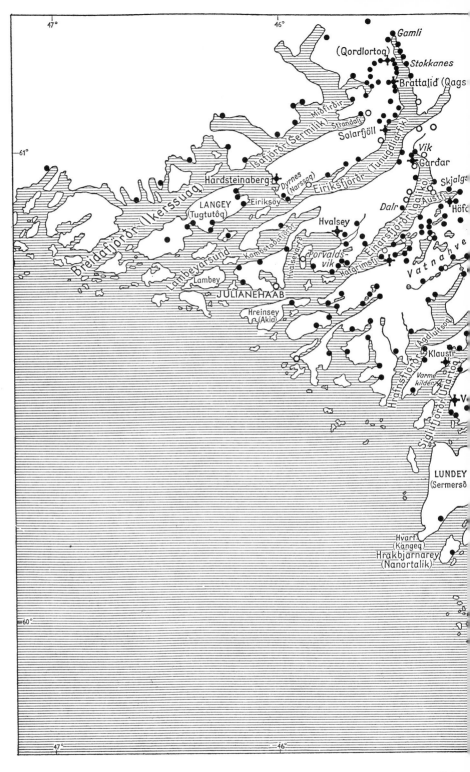

Gamli

(Qordlortoq)

Stokkanes

Brattalið (Qags

Miðfirðir

Sermilik   Strandafj

Ísafjörðr   Solarfjöll

61°

Eiríksfjörðr (Tunugdlarfik)

Vik

Garðar

Hardsteinaberg   Dyrnes   Skjalgs

(Narssaq)

LANGEY   Eiríksöy   Dalr   Höfð

(Tugtutôq)

Hvalsey   Austri

Kambstaðafjörðr   Vatnahve

Lambeyarsund   Hvalseyarfj   Þorvalds-   Hafgrimsfj

Lambey   vik

Breiðafjörðr (Ikerssuaq)   JULIANEHAAB

Hreinsey

(Akia)

Klaustr

Hrafnsfjörðr

Varme   Útartoq

kilder

V

Sigtfjörðr

LUNDEY

(Sermersö)

Hvarf

(Kángeq)

Hrakbjarnarey

(Nanortalik)

60°

47°   46°

Map of Austerbygd, omitting the most northerly area which w

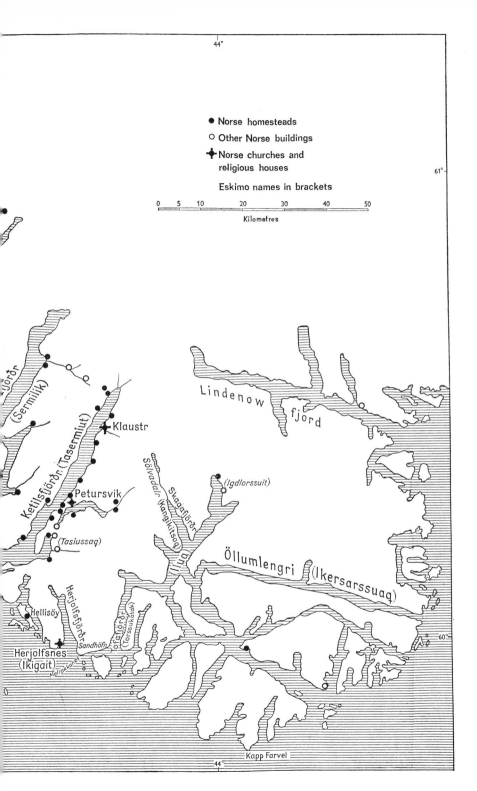

Norse homesteads
Other Norse buildings
Norse churches and religious houses
Eskimo names in brackets

0 5 10 20 30 40 50
Kilometres

61°

44°

Lindenow fjord

Klaustr

(Igdlorssuit)

Sölvadalr (Kangikitsoq)

Skagafjörðr

Pmavik

Petursvik

(Tasiussaq)

Ketilsfjörðr (Tasermiut)

(Sermilik)

jörðr

Öllumlengri (Ikersarssuaq)

Herjolfsfjörðr

Hellisöy

Sandhöfn

Herjolfsnes
(Ikigait)

Melrakkanes

Eiríksfjörðr (Torssukátak)

60°

Kapp Farvel

44°

nown as *Mellombygd* or *Middle Settlement* (see p. 261)

Qordlortoq marks the beginning of the valley leading to Midtfirdir (Sermilik); a pleasant valley in which many fine inland farms were situated. A salmon river runs through it, and on its gentle slopes grow beds of osier, harebells and daisies. To the north, in striking contrast, wild crags soar into the sky, with black gorges and precipices over which the river hurls itself to the depths below.

The first man to investigate the ruins in these parts was the Norwegian Aaron Arctander,[10] in 1777. He records in his diary that in the course of only a few hours he caught sixty 'salmon' (Arctic char) in the river.

From the inner extremity of Eiriksfjord a broad valley runs north; beyond it, blue-green glaciers glisten between the mountain peaks. Here too there is a fine salmon river. North-east of its mouth lies the site of a medium-sized Norse dwelling-place, which may be the one mentioned in the Foster-brothers' Saga:

'Up under the icefield in Eiriksfjord dwelt a man called Gamle. He was poor and lived apart from other folk, but he was a great fisherman. His wife's name was Grima. She was a notable woman with knowledge of many things; a good physician also, and learned in the ancient arts.'

It was to their house that Tormod Kolbrunarskald was brought by his friends after being severely wounded. When his enemies came after him and began searching the farm for him, he was saved by Grima's black arts. She was in league with the god Thor, and had a large image of him carved on a chair-back.

Arctander speaks of fine grasslands beside the salmon river at the fjord's end and mentions that on the north-eastern side there is a considerable birch wood – considerable by local standards, of course. In choosing the name Greenland for the new country, Eirik spoke no more than the truth: the luxuriance of the vegetation in such sheltered places is quite extraordinary. There are osier-beds, various kinds of grass and moss, angelica, bachelor's button, lady's mantle, harebells, dandelions, saxifrage, daisies, sorrel, scurvy-grass, fungi, rose-root, crowberry, whortleberry, juniper, fern, convolvulus and much else.

During the Arctic summer, so rich in sunshine, plants grow almost visibly, and the flowers have bright colours and sweet scents. In the winter they do not wither as in the south, but most often remain green beneath the snow, with buds all ready to lift themselves to the sun when spring comes again. There is little time, for summer is short, and all must be brought to fruition before it ends.

There are more than four hundred kinds of plant in Greenland, of which perhaps six were introduced by the Norsemen of old time.[11] The seeds probably came with the fodder that was brought over for the livestock.

We noticed some old cairns, and were to see more later. Eskimoes and whalers also raised cairns, but many were built by Norsemen, who perpetuated this old Norwegian–Icelandic custom. In some cases these cairns formed boundary-marks between estates. Others marked a route across country or gave a bearing to those at sea. There were also cairns on hilltops, where men climbed to get a view of the drift-ice and perhaps to light beacons as a warning when trouble was brewing. Finally, certain cairns and other collections of stones will have had a quite particular significance, as for example the three cairns on Kingigtorssuaq Island far to the north, where the famous rune-stone was found.

We headed out into the fjord in the same sparkling weather. Anne Stine lay sunning herself on deck as if she were on the Riviera. Behind us the green slopes of Brattalid receded as the desolate mountains below the inland ice stood forth above them.

We came to Narssaq (plain) at the mouth of the fjord: an evenly-sloping headland under the mighty mountain Qaqarssuaq. Here is a colony that has grown very considerably in recent years. About seven hundred Greenlanders now live here, in little houses dotted about the plain. Modern fishing has given them their livelihood: first and foremost prawns, but also cod, halibut, sea perch, etc. They also hunt seal. There is a prawn-cannery, and an abattoir where the local sheep are slaughtered.

In the old days the name of this place was Dyrnes; it is a fertile area where a number of Norse dwellings were built. But since the dawn of the modern age much has been destroyed. Some farms that once lay about two and a half miles to the north also belonged to this settlement, and ruins of a church have been found: no doubt Dyrnes church, which is believed to be identical with Hardsteinaberg.

There are indications that the Narssaq area, Dyrnes (-ness) itself, was an important place. The home fields and the hill-pastures were good, and it lay near the fishing-grounds and the offshore islands: the haunt of seals. There was also a good harbour. It was a place where seafarers would naturally put in, whether outward bound from either of the fjords, or sailing up and down the coast, and the inhabitants must have been in constant touch with the outside world.

This is of particular interest in view of the remarkable discoveries made only a few days before our arrival. We met K. N. Christensen, the manager, who told us of them.

Some Greenlanders were fetching soil from a large mound under which a Norse ruin was buried. They dug a deep hole down to a stone wall, where they came upon a piece of quartz crystal, and a stick, on three sides of which a number of runes were carved. The following year the ruin was excavated by C. L. Vebaek,[12] who found among other objects a wooden sword,

51

arrowheads of both iron and bone (Viking-period type), and a worn slab with marks and some holes, reminiscent of an old bearing-dial. This farmstead turned out to have water 'laid on', like Brattalid.

The most remarkable find was the rune-staff (see Plate 8, top): one of the most interesting Norse finds yet made in Greenland. Various other runic inscriptions had been discovered, in which, as one might expect, the later or 'younger' alphabet was used. But these runes were inscribed in an older form: the Norwegian–Swedish alphabet which was the forerunner of the later. This has more characters and in some cases different ones, and went out of use in Norway in about A.D. 1000.

Erik Moltke, who has given a provisional interpretation,[13] states that this is certainly the oldest runic inscription known from Greenland, and that it was carved there; this he deduces from the B and R characters, which are peculiar to Greenland. It presumably dates from the time of Eirik the Red.

The content is no less interesting. On one side of the staff a complete 16-character runic alphabet is carved. On the second there are secret runes: mystic signs imbued with magical powers. On the third side is an inscription which according to Erik Moltke runs: 'Bibrau is the name of the maiden who sits in the blue.'

We walked up to the ruin, which is a long mound overgrown with grass. A deep hole had been dug in the black earth, and we could see part of the stone wall near which the rune-staff had been found. The place is well situated on the slope, commanding a wide view over the islands and the drifting ice.

Here, long ago, a man sat bent over this staff, carving these runes. Each character was formed with care, for this was an important matter. He wrote not as we write, seeking only to give clear expression to his thoughts; these signs came from the gods and had magic in them. The runes stem from the ruling powers, says the Edda, and in them dwell the forces of life itself.

The Norse Greenlander of Dyrnes must have been well versed in the mysteries, for he knew even the secret runes. With a skilled hand he carved them – and there they remain, occult and strong.

I looked out over Eirik's Island, where he wintered about a thousand years ago. It lies not very far off shore, and it would be strange if he did not cross over to Dyrnes more than once, to hunt there and survey the good land. But now fog was gathering out there among the islands, the mighty icefields vanished in the greyness, and a cold breath swept in from the sea.

An Arctic land, harsh and full of danger when the forces of nature turn against mankind – when the gale roars in and ships whirl in a welter of boiling seas and shattered ice; when hunting fails, when ice and snow cover the grazing-lands and threaten the livestock with starvation. Here powerful runes are needed.

'Bibrau is the name of the maiden who sits in the blue.'

VI OF HOMES AND MEN

AMAN walks up the hillside, wading through osier-beds, stiff grass and willow-herb, and pausing continually to look about him. He has a view over the fjord and the snug harbour where the ship lies at anchor, and the plain where tents have been pitched and the people are gathered. He turns aside, crosses the slope to the very foot of the cliff, and then back again at a higher level. He walks slowly, using his eyes, and then halts uncertainly: where shall he build the homestead?

For days now he has been roaming in search of a good site. He has been into the hills; the pasture there was rich and he saw the tracks of many reindeer. He has been along the shore and found some good heaps of driftwood. He has tried for salmon in the river and gone sea-fishing, and has seen both seal and whale. He knows that almost the whole of the slope running down to the bay can be turned into fine enclosed pastures. His house should stand on a piece of level ground at the top of the slope – but is there any water?

Then he spies a patch of tall-stalked angelica: a juicy plant that grows in damp soil. He walks over to it, beats the grass aside and finds a spring, whose waters ripple down a tiny channel. Swiftly he returns to his chosen site, paces it along and across, and marks the four corners with stones. There he will build his house; just so shall it stand above the home fields, facing the fjord.

Going a little way down the slope he takes flint and steel and sets fire to grass and moss; and soon a sea of flame sweeps over the hillside. At once there is a stir in the camp below, and men, women and children come flocking up the hill. They know that he has made up his mind: it is here that they are to build their new home.

Now follows a busy time. Some clear the scorched slope of brushwood, roots and stones. Others follow, loosening the soil with primitive wooden picks and spades, not digging deep but making sure that the ashes are buried, so as to serve as manure. Big stones are left where they lie; they will hold the heat of the sun and keep off the night frost.

Above, the settler and some of the best-skilled farm-hands have begun to build. Their only materials are stones, turf and a pile of driftwood timbers for roof-trusses and so forth. Two shaggy little ponies haul sled-loads of stone over the rough ground. Women, young people and children bring up turf –

more and more turf. Even tiny children help with this, getting very tired and very dirty, but happy to be building a real house, just like the grown-ups.

And then one day the house stands there at the top of the slope, snug and welcoming under its turf-covered pitched roof, with its long side facing the sea. The youngsters swarm inside while their mother follows with the household belongings. She puts each thing in the place where it is always to be kept: the soapstone cooking-pot, the barrel for sour milk, the wooden scoops and ladles, the loom, the bale of wadmal, the sewing things and the clothes.

Outside the settler is busy hewing boards for benches from a balk of driftwood. Then suddenly he pauses in his work and looks up: the first smoke is rising, swirling gently to the sky.

This is only the beginning of a settler's work; next he must build byres, barns and enclosures. Plenty of tasks await him on the farm, by the fjord and in the hills. But now he has a home – a shelter in that chill land – and everything else will get done in time.

In Greenland the struggle for existence was so hard that it was especially important to have more than one means of livelihood (i.e., hunting and fishing as well as farming). The varied forms of activity engaged in over a wide area naturally influenced the siting of the settlements. We have seen that most of the homesteads were built at the head of the fjords, where the vegetation was richest, but many people went inland. The largest of the inland settlements was the beautiful Vatnahverfi, where the farms lay beside lakes abounding in fish. The bleak sea-coast was ill suited to stock-raising, and few Norse houses are to be found here, though the offshore islands were important as hunting-grounds.

The size of the houses varied very much. Large estates such as Brattalid, Hvalsøy, Gardar and Herjolfsnes had many outbuildings of different kinds, and often a church. Probably the fjord-chief built these places. There were also medium-sized farms and some small ones, inhabited perhaps by servants or tenants.

In building their farms the Norsemen had always two particular considerations to bear in mind: the cold and the difficulty of obtaining fuel.

At first, of course, there was a wealth of accumulated driftwood on the beaches – tree trunks that had drifted from Siberian rivers across the Arctic Ocean – but obviously these stocks were soon exhausted. After that there was only the scanty day-to-day flotsam to fall back upon, and this was usually too precious to burn. Sound wood was needed for boat-building, furniture and household implements, harpoon-shafts and other things, and this was obtained mainly from timber washed up by the sea.

The most important fuel was what could be gathered from the ground: birch, crowberry, osiers, juniper and so on. And when the immediate neighbourhood had been stripped of this, men had to go farther afield. No doubt much of it was brought in by boat, and in some places turf was used, but good peat hags are rare in Greenland, the peat being thin and of poor quality. Sheep-dung, beaten hard in the byres, was probably used too, as in Iceland, and also fishbones. There is evidence that in the smithies the bones of animals provided fuel. Last but not least, seal and walrus blubber were important both for heat and light. The fuel problem was always a difficult one, and became worse as time went on and the best patches of birch scrub were cut down.

For this reason the settlers paid great attention to insulation. They were familiar with their building-materials, turf and stone, for these were used on the west coast of Norway, in Iceland and the Faroes, though in a slightly different manner. In Greenland the façade of the main building was often built entirely of stone, with a wall of turf inside. The other walls would have a stone foundation, but were constructed of slabs of turf arranged in a regular pattern. The houses must have had pitched roofs (pointed gable-ends of stone have been found in a ruin at Undir Höfdi in Einarsfjord), and the rafters were of driftwood or birch. Chinks were stopped up with turf or sometimes clay, and in only two instances is mortar known to have been used: Hvalsøy church and a small building at Gardar.

Other outbuildings were of stone or turf, or both. Apart from structures designed to house animals, there might also be a bake-house for cooking, cheese-making, etc.; also storerooms, forge, steam-bath-house and the like. One type of storehouse was peculiar to Greenland, and may be seen on many of the farms. It was built of stone without any form of mortaring, and often stood on a tall vertical stone or rocky outcrop, so as to be inaccessible to dogs or foxes. In these people must have kept things which required good ventilation: presumably hides, furs, dried meat, etc.

It seems that cellars were also used; these were dug into the permanently frozen ground and served as refrigerators.

At the time of Greenland's colonization, the 'long-house' of the Viking period was the usual type in Norway, and emigrants to the Shetlands, Orkneys, Faroes and Iceland perpetuated the style in the new country. In its original form the long-house had only one room, and the hall at Brattalid is an example of this ancient pattern. Another hall is the one by Hvalsøy church, and here holes in the floor have been found, to take the posts that supported the roof. There are similar halls at Herjolfnes and the episcopal seat of Gardar, the latter being larger as one might expect.

We have a glimpse of the Icelandic hall in one of the sagas. We learn that Olav Pål[1] sailed to Norway, was given timber by Håkon Jarl and returned home: 'That summer Olav built a guest-hall that could be heated, and was larger and handsomer than any seen before. Famous tales were painted on the wall-planks and on the roof. These were so well done that people thought them finer than hangings.'

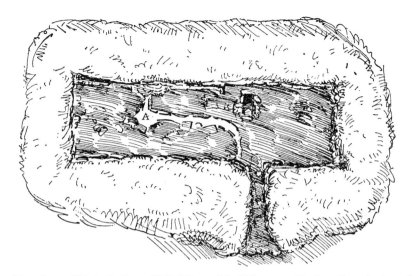

A long-house. This is the Great Hall of Brattalid which presumably dates from the time of Eirik the Red. It measures 16 × 5 metres (53' 6" × 13' 4") and was massively walled with stone and turf. Through it ran a man-made channel of running water which included a pool (A). (National Museum, Copenhagen)

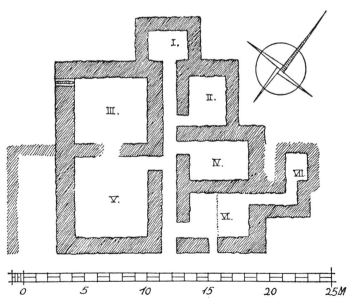

Passage house, Austerbygd. (National Museum, Copenhagen)

The Greenland long-house might have several rooms, and a good example of this is the great house of Sandnes, in Vesterbygd (see illustration on page 273). The door was in the middle and often opened into a passage, such as may be seen in Norwegian farms today. In Iceland the door was at the gable-end.

There was also another type of dwelling-house: the passage-house (*gang-hus*). The front of this was relatively short, and rather small rooms lay on either side of a passage leading in from the main entrance. Here too the most important outbuildings were separate from the dwelling.

The third type, the 'central house', was different again. This too was a passage-house, but dwelling, byre, forge, barn and bath-house, etc., all formed part of one structure, linked together by passages between the rooms: a fortress against the cold. The rooms were often numerous and small. Such a building has been found in Austmannadal, in Vesterbygd, right up under the inland ice; it was excavated by Aage Roussell and proved to have about twenty-one rooms (see page 58).

An interesting feature of the 'central house' is that the cowshed was often at the heart of the building. Thus not only did the animals keep warm, but their warmth spread to other rooms, providing a sort of central heating. Such a dwelling was also more economical in building-materials and made work easier in winter, when one could tend the livestock without going out into the cold.

The chief advantage of both passage-house and central house was that the small, sheltered rooms needed little fuel; they could be kept fairly warm with blubber-lamps.

Neither of these types of house is known to have existed in medieval Norway or Iceland; the first of them dates from the later period in Iceland. But excavations have been relatively few there, and the same is even truer of the west and north-west coast of Norway.

The chief and the wealthy yeoman had thralls and farmhands who could collect fuel enough for long-house and banqueting-hall, and no doubt they also owned the hillsides, where there was plenty of dwarf birch. For the general run of settlers it was different. If fuel was scarce, rooms must be small; and they would have shown a remarkable lack of common sense if they had not arranged a means of communication between them: that is to say, a passage.

An existence based on stock-raising, hunting and fishing meant that activity had to extend over a wide area; consequently a large number of people were attached to every big farm. As among Eskimoes and Arctic Indians, the hard struggle for survival could be fought better by a group of people than by individuals. Many exacting tasks had to be carried out, often simultaneously.

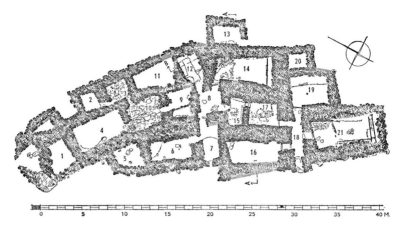

Central house, Vesterbygd. Living-rooms, byres, storerooms, etc., are all built together. There are about 21 rooms in all. (National Museum, Copenhagen)

There was first the work in and about the homestead itself: tending of live-stock, milking, butter- and cheese-making, spinning, weaving, tanning, making of clothes and shoes, cooking, building up plentiful stocks of dried fish, dried meat, blubber and other things for the winter, breaking new ground, manuring, erecting boundary walls and outhouses, shipbuilding, iron-forging, collecting fuel, etc. If the farm were isolated and near the sea, enough hands had to be available to haul up a big boat.

Next there was the work away from the homestead – at sea or inland. Gathering winter feed for the stock took many men far afield, in addition to the collection of driftwood, bog-ore, eggs, down, berries, angelica, etc. Fishing in fjord, river and lake was as important as hunting and trapping. Reindeer-hunting went on all the time, but especially in autumn when the animals were fat. Many men had to spend a long time in the hills if they were to bring home enough meat, and the same was true of seal-hunting, not only in the fjord areas but right out among the islands, where Greenland seal and hooded seal made their seasonal migrations. There were also voyages to be made to Nordrsetur, those rich hunting-grounds far north of the settle-ments, where a skilled hunter could find walrus-tusks, bearskins, blubber and other valuable things. Finally, there were duties in connection with the church, or the clergy.

It was said of Skallagrim, an enterprising settler in Iceland, that his wealth 'had many legs to stand upon', and in Greenland too it was essential to work in many different ways for one's livelihood. Additional labour must have been necessary, and it seems more than likely that many farms which were at first believed to have been independent were in fact attached to some large estate, in the feudal manner. The chiefs distributed land among their kinsmen and friends, and in return demanded help from them and from tenants, as well as from their own housefolk. A number of chiefs brought thralls or slaves with them when they arrived: men and women captured on Viking raids. Thralls were chattels: clothes, shelter and food was all they were entitled to, and their owner had absolute power over them. Aud the Sharp-witted, who came to Iceland from the Islands of the Western Ocean, had a king's daughter of Irish extraction as slave-woman for her own daughter, and it is a fact that the prosperity of the rich yeoman farmer of Iceland was largely based on the labour of his thralls.

The *Flóamanna* saga, in its account of Torgils Orrabeinfostre's arrival in Greenland,[2] shows that his party numbered thirty-five, including twelve thralls of his own, and doubtless some belonging to one of the other men who accompanied him. And although the *Flóamanna* saga is not always reliable, it is likely to be accurate on such a practical matter as the equipping of an emigrant ship with the necessary labour for a household in a new country.

There is good reason to think that a considerable number of thralls were brought to Greenland in the course of time, and it is interesting to note that anthropological study of skeletons found there indicates a Celtic element.[3]

But the ordinary farmer too needed many people to help him, and he could not afford to buy thralls or even perhaps to hire help. It seems likely that in such cases more than two generations continued to live on the homestead and share the work. Sons and perhaps also daughters with their children lived with their parents, the father being head or ruler of the household.

This patriarchal system was usual in Norway, in the Iceland of the saga-period, the Scottish Highlands, Ireland and the Slav countries. As late as the beginning of the eighteenth century we learn of Norway: 'At that time the household consisted of five married couples with their children, amounting in all to twenty-seven or thirty persons, eating from the same dish and drinking from the same cup. The father of the family ruled them all.'[4]

Here we note a deeply-rooted characteristic of the Norse people: their strong sense of ancestry and their inbred attachment to the ancestral homestead.

VII PASTURE BELOW THE INLAND ICE

IN all that concerned livestock the Norse settlers followed the old northern tradition that was rooted in the Stone Age. Conditions in Greenland were very similar to those in Iceland and much of Norway, and although the average temperature was somewhat lower in this Arctic land, and special precautions had to be taken, stock-raising in the main followed the familiar pattern.

Developments in the Greenland of our own century enable us to appreciate many of the problems that faced the Norsemen. The Greenlanders of today are hunters by nature and tradition, but the supply of game has dwindled so disastrously of late that the inhabitants have had to take to other means of livelihood: fishing and stock-breeding. The idea of putting potential pasture-land to use was no new one; Hans Egede and Anders Olsen introduced it in the eighteenth century, but only in modern times have their plans been realized to any great extent. The enterprise has meant a breach with the past, and a completely new mode of life for a race of nomads with the fire of the hunter in their veins. Sheep-stations have been established in the Julianehåb district and by the Godthåb fjord, with a slaughter-house at Narssaq.

The project is now well under way, and the people are making use of the grazing on many of the old Norse infields, Eskimo grounds and hill pastures. Round Julianehåb – the major part of the old Austerbygd – there are today about 20,000 head of sheep (divided into 250 flocks), that is to say 4 sheep to every one of the 5,000 inhabitants; 100 head of cattle, 90 Iceland ponies and 1,800 chickens.

The sheep are mainly of the Icelandic breed. A full-grown animal yields about 2 kilograms (4½ lb.) of wool. The ewes are milked, and their milk is exceptionally nourishing. These sheep stray far into the hills and it may take two or three weeks to round them up, in June for shearing and in the autumn for slaughtering. They thrive well on the rich summer pasture.

Most of the sheep and horses are left out all the winter. Cattle are kept in their stalls from October to May, except for occasional short periods in good weather. The winter fodder comes mostly from the old Norse meadowland, and is supplemented by fish-offal, capelin and seaweed. Little is done to increase the yield of the home fields, and what manuring is done is of a random kind.

Altogether it may be said that sheep-raising in Greenland has prospered surprisingly within a short time, which speaks well for the potentialities of the country. The Greenlanders of today are of course better off in this respect than their predecessors in the old days, when pasture-land was exploited to a far greater extent. On the other hand they are beginners at the game, and through the centuries the infields have greatly deteriorated. It is estimated that with better use of the land the number of sheep may be increased to 85,000 head. This prospect is the more interesting in that it throws light on the past.

The numerous sheep-pens, many of them large, are a clue to the size of the flocks kept. Cattle-raising too was carried on on a large scale – far larger than today. The number of stalls in the byres that have been found show that a medium-sized farm kept about five cows and a large one from fifteen to twenty, while big estates like Brattalid and Gardar had even more.

But if there was one type of animal that the settlers understood and valued, it was the horse. In Iceland, those handsome, sturdy little ponies were indispensable, for riding, pack-carrying and draught. It was quite a usual thing for people to ride hundreds of miles through lava-country and swift rivers, over mountains and icefields; and thanks to the ponies winter forage could be brought from far away. The chiefs of saga days attached great importance to having the best horses, and in heathen times such animals were often buried in their master's grave. A horse was the best present that any man could give his friend, and stallions were pitted against each other in horse-fights. In Norway too the horse played an important part during the Viking period and the Middle Ages.

Horses would be quite as useful in Greenland as in Iceland and Norway, so there is every reason to suppose that they were bred there. Few of their bones have been found, and Poul Nørlund[1] does not believe that horses were very numerous, as most of the transport would have been by boat. Against this it must be remembered that the Catholic faith held horses to be unclean animals, unfit for food, so that their carcases would not have been brought home; they may indeed have been dumped in some place specially reserved for animals that died from natural causes. If so, we would not expect to find many of their bones in the middens. There are large areas of the country where horses would have been invaluable: for example in carrying home winter forage from far away in the hills. And why should not the settlers have had great numbers of them? They were useful, and could survive all the year round in the open. Indeed, as in Iceland, they would be likely to multiply all too quickly if left on their own.

As for goats, no doubt a certain number were kept for the sake of the cheese, but sheep were more profitable from the point of view of meat and wool, and surely far outnumbered the goats.

In the course of the five hundred years during which the Norsemen inhabited this Arctic country, the law of natural selection must have operated among their animals. The result was a particularly hardy strain, able to endure hunger and cold in the manner of the huskies and wild animals of the Arctic. This was an important advantage to the settlers, as it enabled them to leave their horses and sheep in the open all the year round. Only cattle and a few other animals of special value were housed during the winter.

The shepherds, of course, would have remained with their flocks, and were no doubt helped by sheep-dogs. In winter it would have been impractical, if not impossible, for them to come right down to the settlement for supplies and to visit their families; their homes had to be in the hills. There too they could cultivate an extra crop of hay, for use in an emergency. Those members of the family who were not tending the sheep could hunt reindeer or fish for salmon.

Most of the stock – cattle, sheep and horses – were of course let out to grass on the rich pasture of the hills in summer, but they could not have derived full advantage from it if they had had to come back to the homestead every evening for milking. Everything points to the likelihood of their having been shielings up in the hills where milking, cheese-making and other dairy-work could be done. Hitherto it has been thought that there were no shielings in Greenland, because the farmhouses in the hills there were much bigger than the shielings in Norway, which were intended only for use in summer. But it is natural to suppose that the dwellings built in the hills by the rich farmer, or by a number of smaller farmers jointly, served a dual purpose: sheep-tending in winter and dairy-work in summer.

Autumn was a busy time, for then the sheep were rounded up over wide areas and driven down to the homestead for slaughtering. No doubt everyone in the settlement helped with this, combing the hills under the direction of the most experienced man; many of them probably on horseback. At last the animals were driven in to the great fold at Brattalid, Gardar or elsewhere. People from all over the district would gather there, for everyone owned some sheep in the flock. It was a joyful occasion, almost a festival, as the beasts streamed down from the fells. Once in the fold they were sorted out according to ear-marks, and there was much else to be done; but the work went merrily, for the sheep – the wealth of the hills – were safely home, and in fine condition.

Manuring was important so far to the north. It had long been practised in Norway and became general in Iceland too. Among the valuable objects in the Oseberg ship, in which the ninth-century Queen Asa was buried, was a wooden dung-fork. In many parts of Norway and in Iceland the method known as *grindgang* was used. In spring, before the new growth appeared, movable pens were set up in the home fields, into which the cows were driven after milking. Week by week these pens were shifted until the whole area had been dunged. This very practical method may well have found its way to Greenland.

The home fields were never ploughed. The most important farm implement, apart from sickle and scythe, was the very primitive spade of reindeer horn and wood. It was thus something of a problem to get the dung properly spread and crumbled, so as to be of maximum benefit to the soil and not interfere with mowing. Perhaps the method used was one that I have heard of in north Norway, where birch-twigs were tied together in big bundles, weighted with stones and dragged over the manure.

Seaweed and fish-offal may well have provided additional fertilizer, in the old Norwegian–Icelandic fashion.

On my way among the Norse settlements I came upon ditches and dams designed to carry water to the fields. Such a system was most noticeable at Gardar, but there is every reason to think that the old Norwegian method of irrigation was widely practised in Greenland as it was in Iceland. Often a stream or river ran quite close to a farm, and it was then a simple matter to run a leat across to the cultivated land. In the regions where most of the Norsemen settled the climate is dry, and in some places the soil yielded very little. Irrigation worked wonders, not only by increasing fertility but by so strengthening the vegetation that it could withstand the onslaught of the föhn winds.

Where mountain streams were used for irrigation, valuable minerals were washed into the soil. Such streams are often grey with fine dust from rocks and stones, and contain phosphorus, potash, lime and sometimes nitrogen.

Another way of bringing moisture to the soil in a dry climate is one I have seen practised in Lesja, Norway. Fences are set up across the fields to catch the snow in drifts. These drifts lie well on into the spring, and soak the ground with thaw-water. This method would have been useful in many parts of Greenland.

The relatively small home fields yielded valuable hay, but it was the outlying land that was the real basis of stock-breeding. There sheep and horses grazed all the year round, and the other animals in the summer, and from there much of the winter feed was collected.

In Iceland, moss, leaves, scurvy-grass, angelica, seaweed, etc., were gathered to supplement the hay. People rode long distances to fetch it, often in large parties.

On many Norwegian farms the yield from outlying land was at least as important as that of the home fields. When the mowing was over people set out over lowland and fell to gather forage of various kinds: grass from the meadowland of the shielings, from marshes and from between stones and stumps everywhere; and rushes from the meres. Some of this harvest was stored in primitive outbuildings, but most of it was stacked. Leaves were collected in great quantities, often in steep places where horses could not go, so that the 'sheaves' had to be carried by men. In some places moss-gathering was the most important activity; reindeer moss and Iceland moss were among the kinds most in demand.

I have spoken in some detail about forage-gathering in the mother-countries Iceland and Norway, because until quite recently the old Viking methods survived there, and because this is a question which must have been of equal importance to the people of Greenland. There forage must have been collected on the shore, in the valleys and in the hills, and presumably included grass, sandwort, ferns, osier, juniper, birch leaves, seaweed, reindeer moss and Iceland moss. Much of this was by no means bad feeding-stuff. A chemical analysis at the Agricultural College of Norway shows that 3 kilograms of air-dry reindeer moss (*Caldonia Rangiferina*), containing 14 per cent water, is equal to one fodder unit: i.e., one kilogram (2·2 lb.) of barley.

Harvesting the country in this primitive way required laborious effort by many people. In Norway mowing and gathering might take eight weeks, and a working day of from sixteen to twenty hours was not unusual. The same was true of Iceland. Fish and fish-offal provided valuable feed, and occasionally whale-meat and blubber. Cattle and horses thrive on this food.

At the radio station on Bjørnoya (74° 13′ N.), shortly before the war, there was a Nordfjord horse called Blakka which for many years lived chiefly on raw birds, raw eggs and polar-bear meat, and indeed preferred them to hay when this was available. Blakka was never so happy as when he was taken out on to the ice to bring home a polar bear, for he knew that he would be given the carcase. For weeks he lived and throve on the frozen meat. He would go out in all weathers throughout his many winters in the Arctic, and he developed a long, thick coat. I may mention that the Yakuts who migrated northward to Siberia and settled there fed their horses and cattle to a large extent on meat and fish.

The following account from Erik Hansen Schønnebøl's *Description of Lofoten and Vesteraalen*, of 1591, gives a graphic picture of how people coped with the problem in a part of north Norway which was surely bleaker and more barren than Austerbygd in Greenland:

There is neither field nor meadow to any of these farms. Not a handful of corn is sown, and almost all they reap is a little grass, enough

left: Gravestone from Brattalid churchyard. *right:* Gravestone from Herjolfsnes. The latter bears the inscription: HER HUILIR HRO[AR] KOLGRIMS: S[ON]. (Here lies H. K.) (Photograph: National Museum of Copenhagen.)

above: Bathing in the warm springs of Siglufjord, while icebergs float by. The temperature was 41° C. *below:* Lars Øye in Faeringehavn with his tame eaglet.

Various implements: 1. Wooden spade, Sandnes. 2. Head of sledgehammer,
Vatnahverfi. 3. Ice-crampon, Brattalid. 4. Awl, Sandnes. 5. Hasp, Brattalid.
6. Knife with wooden handle, Sandnes. 7. Spade of reindeer-horn, Sandnes.
8. Whetstone, Brattalid. (Photographs: National Museum of Copenhagen.)

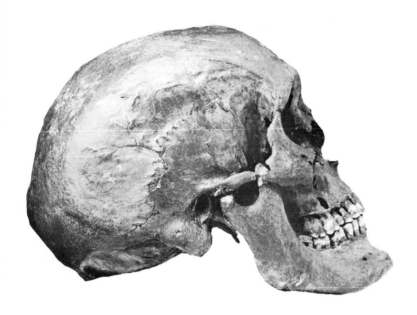

above: Skull of a man, Gardar. Characteristically Nordic in type, with a capacity of 1400 c³. (Photograph: National Museum of Copenhagen.) *below:* Summer in Vesterbygd.

above: Arched window in east wall of Hvalsøy church. *below:* Man's skeleton discovered in the north-east chapel of Gardar cathedral. With it was found an episcopal ring of gold, and a crosier, handsomely carved from walrus tusk. Probably the remains of Jon Smyrill, King Sverre's fosterfather (see p. 186). (Photographs: National Museum of Copenhagen.)

Scene from Vatnahverfi, the land of lakes. The saga relates that Hafgrim took possession of land in Hafgrimsfjord and Vatnahverfi in about the year 1000. (Photograph: Geodetic Institute, Copenhagen.)

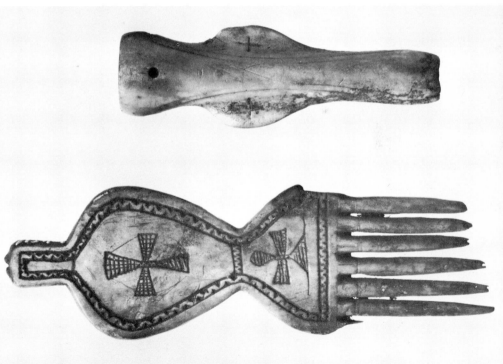

above: Storehouse in Torvaldsvik built on a high rock out of reach of foxes and dogs. *below:* Needle-case and comb of walrus tusk engraved with crosses, from the east coast of Greenland. These objects were found on an Eskimo site near Scoresby Sound. (Photograph: National Museum of Copenhagen.)

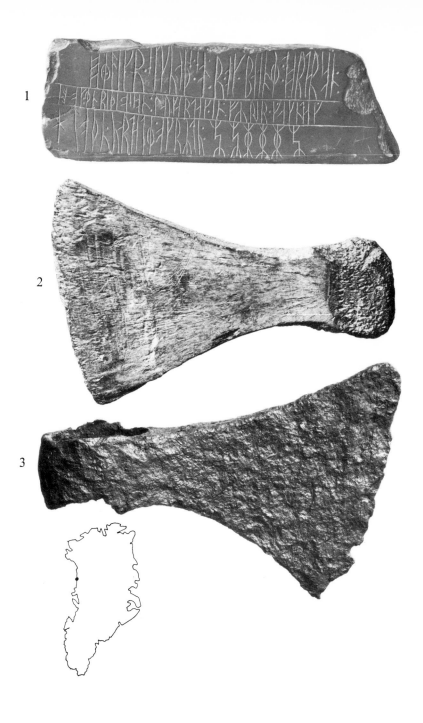

1. Runestone from Kingigtorssuaq, found at 72° 57′ N. On it is inscribed: 'Erling
Sigvatsson, Bjarne Tordsson and Eindride Oddsson raised these cairns on the
Saturday before Rogation Day and runed well.' 2. Axe of whalebone from
Sandnes in Vesterbygd. 3. Iron axe from Austerbygd. (Photographs: National
Museum of Copenhagen.)

to support five or six cows; yet their beasts are fed and kept throughout the winter for the most part on *molle*: that is to say cods' heads, seaweed and the backbones of fish. All this is ground up together and is known to everyone here as *molle*.

How much winter-feed did a milch-cow need in those days? Sigurdur Sigurdsson believes that in the saga period in Iceland it amounted to about 500 kilograms (1,100 lb.) of hay. Her annual milk-yield he puts at 1,100 kgs. (2,420 lb.). In Iceland in 1937 the yield was 2,600 kgs. (5,720 lb.).

In assessing the state of livestock in Greenland we should bear in mind that throughout the Middle Ages it was customary to keep a greater number of cows than conditions warranted. This resulted in a very poor milk-yield in winter, while towards spring the animals had often become so emaciated and wretched that they could hardly stand. The 'spring-pinch' was something that most farmers had to contend with in the old days.

Stock-raising in the Arctic involves risks of many kinds. The winter of 1948-9 gave us an example of how abrupt climatic changes may lead to disaster.

In January severe cold set in, with blizzards from the north. Then came a warm south-easterly wind that melted the snow. Again the wind swung round to the north, bringing bitter cold, and the half-thawed snow froze, covering the countryside with an icy crust which prevented the animals from digging down through the snow to graze. They made for the fjord, and numbers of them lost their footing on the icy cliffs and fell into the sea. Some sought shelter behind stones and hill-sides, but gales swept in and buried them in drifts so that they suffocated. Many reached the shore in their search for seaweed; to do that they had to jump down from an icy ground and were unable to climb back. A great number were drowned, others ate too much of the salt seaweed and died of poisoning. In all, 10,500 sheep perished, of which 4,000 were from Brattalid and as many more from Gardar: that is to say, half of all the stock in the Julianehåb district.

It should be added that most of them could have been saved if the Gardar people had not sent away their big motor-boat; for with that and a few lighters the animals could have been picked up along the shore. Such disasters would also be greatly lessened if the Greenlanders of today took care to arrange shelter for the stock and make forage-dumps here and there in the hills. But they have the improvidence of the hunter in their blood. For the Norsemen stock-raising was an ancient trade, and they set about it more methodically, as we have seen.

Summer too can be cold enough to cause famine among the animals. At other times there may be a plague of caterpillars that strip the greenery over wide areas, as happened in 1932.

Wild beasts were another scourge, and necessitated a constant watch on the stock. Arctic foxes made off with the lambs, and eagles were even more of a menace. From time to time wolves might wander in. There are no wolves in west Greenland today; in the last century two were recorded, but the numbers of reindeer have so greatly diminished that wolves find it hard to survive there now. It must have been very different in the old days, when herds were numerous.

The polar bear haunts the drift-ice, but it may stay on land for long periods, especially when it scents food. In earlier times there were many more of them than there are today. Hunters now pursue them over large areas of both the east and the west coast, and their quarry has little chance of escape. Bears' bones have been found in a number of Norse ruins. When such a beast scented livestock and went hunting over the outlying pastures, the settlers were in real trouble.

Having just written this, I see in the paper that in the Norwegian communes of Trysil and Engerdal over a thousand sheep have been killed by bears in the course of the last few years. This modern example is enlightening. So important was it to get rid of such sheep-killers that the Norse Greenlanders instituted a bear-toll: that is to say that any man who slew a bear was entitled to a contribution from every householder.

But the greatest danger of all was a slower and more insidious one: the reckless stripping of copse and scrub and heather. Much fuel was needed, not least for the smelting of bog-ore, and there was a chronic shortage of wood. Besides this, leaves were harvested for fodder, and the livestock added to the damage by nibbling the tops of dwarf trees and stunting their growth. Thus men destroyed the protection essential to the other vegetation, and winds and drifting sand eroded the soil or buried it.

Stock-breeding in the Arctic was carried on in the teeth of many difficulties; but the settlers were experienced men who in general contrived to restrict damage to the minimum. Disasters to flocks and herds were as well known in Norway, and certainly in Iceland, yet there men struggled on against misfortune and won through. And surely the Norse settlers of Greenland were as dauntless, and as tough.

VIII LIVING OFF THE COUNTRY

I N the summer of 1123 the Norwegian Ketil Kalvsson came to Greenland to trade. He was of the famous Ringnes family of Hedmark and related to the Norwegian royal house. When he and his men landed to lay in provisions for their homeward voyage they came upon a secret underground cellar. In it were: '60 carcases, close on 500 kgs. [1,100 lb.] of butter and a quantity of dried fish'.[1]

The King's Mirror mentions the making of a 'great deal of butter and cheese'. This took place during summer and autumn; in the winter, on starvation diet, the animals yielded little or no milk. It was therefore essential that calving and lambing should occur during the spring. It is likely that ewes were milked as well as cows; this was the practice in Iceland, where in famine years ewes' milk was of vital importance. There a full-grown ewe yielded from 40 to 50 litres (9 to 11 gallons) of milk; and it is far richer both in nourishment and vitamins than cows' milk.

Butter was rancid, being made without salt. Part of the milk was made into a sort of fermented curd or junket. Remains of vats for the storage of milk have been found on many Norse farms. Butter was not only a food, but also currency and an export. In Iceland rent was paid in butter, and up to 15,000 kgs. (30,300 lb.) were delivered annually to each of the two episcopal seats.[2] No doubt a considerable amount of butter went to the Greenland bishop's house of Gardar likewise. And here it was of particular importance that the butter should be rancid, for it kept much longer than the salted kind. The Norse Greenlanders might have to store their export butter for a very long time, owing to the uncertainty of sea-communications, and Eggert Olafsen declares that sour butter would keep 'for twenty years and more'.[3]

In Iceland a certain amount of salt was extracted partly from seaweed (black salt) and partly from sea water, but this was an extravagant process in a country so short of fuel. Both there and in the Faroes people made do with little or no salt. Fish was dried, and so was meat, which was often smoked; and no doubt the same was done in Greenland. Absalon Pederssøn Beyer states[4] that besides iron and other wares the bold seamen of Hardanger sold salt in Greenland, but it is clear that so small and uncertain a supply could not have gone far.

The King's Mirror says: ' ... but concerning that matter you spoke of, whether there be any corn grown there [Greenland], I believe folk have but little help from that. Yet some there are, chiefly among those that are held to be of the better and richer sort, who sow in the hope of a crop. But most people in that land do not know what bread is and have never seen it.'

These are clear, unequivocal words which are appropriate to conditions today. In a few places at the head of the fjords a little barley may ripen, if the weather is exceptionally good, but that is all. Querns have been found at the bishop's house and on some of the other large homesteads, but there may be a number of reasons for that. In Norway such things were put to many uses, and in Greenland they may have served to grind sandwort, fishbones, moss, roots and the like.

In the Iceland of the saga period a certain amount of gardening seems to have been done, while in Norway, in the days of the Vikings, turnips, cress, apples and angelica were cultivated. In Greenland today many people have plots where turnips, carrots and other vegetables of fine quality are grown, so it is likely that in the old days too there were such gardens, especially round monasteries and churches.

A large number of wild plants were used as food by the Norsemen; sagas and later writings make it clear that Icelanders, Faroese and Norwegians had a wide knowledge of such herbs and their relative food-values. Even the apparently meagre plant-life in the valleys and hills had something to offer – berries, mosses, roots, stems, small leaves and such – while the sea provided weed which was useful not only as fodder, manure and fuel but also as human food.

This intimate knowledge of wild plants must be based on a very ancient tradition, such as we find among Eskimoes and Indians. It was a knowledge won by successive generations in their ceaseless struggle for survival, and every source of nourishment was exploited to the full. In northern lands, where there was often a shortage of food, these wild herbs formed a valuable supplement, and not only in times of famine; to a greater or lesser extent they formed part of the daily diet.

I will confine myself to mentioning only a few of the wild plants used by Norwegians and Icelanders for food in the old days. They are to be found also in Greenland, and no doubt were put to the same use there.

Iceland moss (*Cetraria islandica*). This was eaten in Iceland and Norway[5] up to our own day, and it is still used as pig-food. In Iceland especially this moss formed an important element in the diet, and great quantities of it were collected every year. It was made into porridge or gruel. In Norway, with the addition of flour, it was also made into bread.

Angelica (*Archangelica officinalis*), mentioned in the old Norwegian–Icelandic laws, was cultivated as a pot herb in both countries, and according to N. Lid[6] there were angelica-gardens at Voss in Norway as late as the 1920s. A cultivated strain was evolved of which the stem, instead of being a hollow, thin-walled tube, contained a marrowy tissue, with only an irregular little canal up the middle.

A rich plot of wild angelica was regarded as a great asset to an estate in old times. Both stalk and root were eaten. Of the root Eggert Olafsen says: 'It is buried in earth until the winter, and is then eaten raw on dried fish, with milk, cream or butter.'[7]

In south-west Greenland angelica is abundant in certain places, and is found as far north as Disko Bay. The Eskimoes are very fond of it.

Sandwort (*Elymus arenarius*). This is a wheat-like plant found on beaches or sand-dunes, where one would think it impossible for anything to grow. It is quite common in both Norse settlements. Eggert Olafsen[8] gives us a detailed eighteenth-century description of how the 'wild corn' of Iceland was used. It was threshed, dried over the fire, ground in a hand-quern and then made into porridge or flat-bread, or eaten raw with cream or milk. The gathering and transport of this plant involved much work: forty pony-loads were needed to make one barrel of flour. The straw was used for thatching or forage.

Dulse (*Rhodymenia palmata*). This is a dark-red, flat-bladed kind of sea-weed containing nutritious, digestible, nitrogen-free substances. It has been used in Norway and Iceland from early times, and is mentioned both in sagas and law-books. In Iceland it was washed, dried and often eaten with fish and meat; and it was so highly valued that it was used in barter for butter, wool, meat and hides.[9] This seaweed is also used by Eskimoes.

Willow-herb (*Epilobium angustifolium*). In the old days people in many countries made flour of the root,[10] and it grows in profusion round the old Norse ruins of Greenland.

Other edible plants to be found there, which were used in Norwegian and Icelandic households, are: stonecrop (*Sedum roseum*), silverweed (*Potentilla anserina*), mountain sorrel (*Oxyria digyna*) and scurvy-grass (*Cochlearia officinalis*).

In Greenland there are also great quantities of crowberries and whortle-berries, some cranberries, and juniper berries which in the old days were used medicinally.

According to ancient accounts from Norway and Iceland, the gathering of wild edible plants was carried out annually and methodically, as part of the farmer's work. A certain quantity was aimed at: enough to last for a great part of the winter. Up to the end of the last century it was the custom in Iceland for the people to set out in companies and ride far and wide to collect angelica, dulse and other plants, camping out in tents on long journeys into the mountains and to distant coasts. Boys and girls went too. It was hard work, but a festival, and we may suppose that this same tradition continued in Greenland.

The ale and mead that flowed so abundantly in the North throughout the Viking period and the Middle Ages was scarce enough in Greenland, and Eirik the Red himself, as we saw, was vexed at being unable to offer his seafaring guests a drink. In Bishop Pål's saga[11] we find an amusing account of how Bishop Smyrill of Greenland taught his people to make wine from crowberries, according to a recipe given him by King Sverre. On the whole it was perhaps just as well for the Norsemen of Greenland that there was little or no alcohol to be had in the country; for spirits were surely the cause of many of the long and bitter family feuds in Norway and Iceland.

The diet of the settlers was simple but wholesome, and varied enough to keep them free of any deficiency-disease.

The Norse Greenlanders mastered the art of smelting iron from bog-ore. This process had been known in Norway centuries before Christ, and in the Viking period there was a great increase in production. Iron was forged not only for home use but for sale. The smelting was done far up in the valleys of the high ranges, as is evidenced by many traces of furnaces, slag-heaps, charcoal, etc., found there.

When Norsemen emigrated to Iceland they continued this work in the new country. The usual method in the North was generally speaking as follows: The ore was collected from bogs and fired in a funnel-shaped pit dug in the ground and lined with clay. On either side were two bellows placed at an angle to each other. Dry wood mixed with charcoal was burnt in the pit, and bit by bit the ore was added. The iron was then extracted, but was still so impure that the slag had to be hammered out of it. The result was a serviceable though rather soft iron.

The Fosterbrothers' Saga[12] says of Bjarne of Stokkanes that he forged a broad axe for Tormod Kolbrunarskald according to the latter's instructions: 'It was hammered right out to the edge, and there was no inlaid edge of steel. It was an axe with a bite.' Ruins of many simple smithies have been found on the homesteads, including Brattalid (southern farm), Gardar,[13] Sandnes and an inland farm in Austmannadal. Sledge-hammers and tongs have also come to light. Anvils appear to have been of stone.

Slag undoubtedly originating from smelting has been discovered as well. So far no pits have been found, but these must certainly have been near the place where the hammering-out was done, as it would have been pointless to bring lumps of half-finished iron all the way from Norway. And bog-ore is not hard to find in Greenland.

Iron-production required a great deal of work, including that of charcoal-burning, which was a whole process in itself. All in all, iron-smelting in

Greenland must have caused serious inroads on the sparse woodland, which as we have seen was continuously depleted for other reasons. Iron was doubtless scarce enough on this Arctic island, but it is difficult to assess just how scarce, for throughout many long ages the Eskimoes have raked through the ancient ruins and collected anything that might be of use to them. Presumably a certain amount of iron was imported; for both the King's Mirror and Absalon Pederssøn Beyer speak of this.

Of the most important iron tools that have been found in the Norse settlements of Greenland may be mentioned: axes, knives, scythes, billhooks, smith's tongs, sledge-hammers, sheep-shearers, chisels, awls, steel for fire-kindling, and spearheads.

The old Greenlanders were undaunted by the dearth of iron. They were resourceful; they made do, and with an excellent substitute: *bone*. Many articles made of walrus-, whale- or reindeer-bone have been found among the ruins, such as: axes, arrow-heads, spades, sledge-runners, needles and even a padlock.

Another important material was soapstone, which was to be found in both Auster- and Vesterbygd. Cooking-pots, oil-lamps, bowls, troughs, weaving-weights and many other things were made of it. Fragments from churches show that it was used also for decoration. In Norway the soapstone industry had been long established, so that the Greenlanders' work was based on an ancient tradition. Indeed, so highly skilled were they in this field that one may question whether they did not outdo their masters.

Driftwood, as we have already seen, was a material of vital importance. Numbers of useful things were made from it, such as bowls, cups, ladles, plates, fish-slices, etc. Some of the objects were turned, which shows that the Norse Greenlanders must have contrived to construct some sort of lathe.

Driftwood also came in handy for the making of looms. These were presumably vertical frames propped against the wall, and the women stood to work at them. We have no means of knowing whether they produced picture-weaving, but it seems likely that they would have continued in this old tradition from Norway and Iceland. The commonest dye-lichens grew in west Greenland, such as litmus or rock-moss (*Parmelia saxatilis*), which yielded a brown dye. Then there was 'corkin' (*Ochrolechia tartarea*). This was fermented with urine and gave a fine light-red colour. Both these lichens were widely used in the Middle Ages, and considerable quantities were exported to England from Norway.[14]

At the time of the settlement, the Norse Greenlanders' ships – sometimes quite large ones – were built in Norway, and occasionally in Iceland. As time went on the Greenlanders were forced to build their vessels of driftwood, and such vessels were necessarily smaller. Icelandic annals of 1189[15] tell us that Asmund Kastanraste sailed from Greenland to Iceland in a ship that was held together with wooden pegs and the sinews of animals (whale-bone?). Torfinn Karlsevne's saga[16] tells of boats that were greased with 'seal-tar', which presumably means boiled seal-blubber. Norwegian skills in shipbuilding found their way to Arctic islands; and later I shall be speaking of a find that furnishes proof of this.

For tanning leather the Norse Greenlanders may have used the same materials as in Iceland: a solution of meadowsweet, bearberry, heath or birch-bark; perhaps also tormentil (*Potentilla erata*), which played so great a part in the tanneries of the Faroes, Orkneys, Shetlands and Norway (among the Lapps).

Above: *spindle-whorls of soapstone.* Below: *mould for making spindle-whorls, with runic inscription reversed.*

The materials these Arctic people had at their disposal were simple indeed. There is something moving about the reindeer-horn spades, the worn knives with the walrus-tusk handle, the whalebone axe, the sheep-clippers and the horn spoons, which were all kept in carved wooden cases or hung on wooden pegs; these things speak of folk who toiled for their very lives and treasured what few valuables they possessed.

Yet it would be wrong to regard their implements as inadequate. We must regard them in the light of another age than ours and against the background of inherited techniques by which, like Eskimoes and Icelandic and Norwegian hill-farmers, they could achieve the most incredible things with the work of their hands.

IX FISHING AND HUNTING

W E passed a small boat that rocked at the mouth of a fjord: a Greenlander was fishing. No sooner did he cast his line than he got a bite
and he hauled in a ceaseless succession of struggling cod. He was
wading in them. Between the skerries we caught a glimpse of trawlers out on
the banks, and knew that they were sweeping in catches that would soon fill
their holds.

There is a wealth of fish in Greenland waters today, especially of cod;[1] but
it was not always so. Off west Greenland the sea-temperature is on the
borderline of what fish can tolerate, and a fall of only a few degrees is
enough to drive the cod elsewhere.

We are now in a period of higher sea-temperatures and milder climate on
land than has been known for a long time, and this is true not only of Greenland but of other Arctic regions as well. The warm spell set in about 1920
and has enormously increased the numbers of cod and other kinds of fish.
Those that hitherto have been rare visitors, such as torsk and ling, now find
their way to the coasts of Greenland; and at the same time the truly Arctic
breeds that prefer cold waters, as for instance the Arctic cod and halibut,
have moved farther north.

A corresponding change has occurred among whales and seals. Thus the
ca'ing whale has begun to appear off west Greenland, while the white whale,
narwhal, ringed seal and other large sea-creatures have gone north. This
means that the inhabitants of the south-west coast of Greenland, where the
Norsemen lived, can no longer find enough seal and have taken to fishing
instead.

There were similar warm periods in the last century, but the cold ones
were longer and the supply of fish diminished. This fluctuation must be
taken into account when estimating the possibilities of fishing and seal- and
whale-hunting in the days of the Norse Greenlanders.

Old sources make occasional mention of fishing in the Middle Ages, the
most important being the fourteenth-century account by Ivar Bårdsson who
for twelve years was the leading churchman in Greenland. He states that
there were 'all manner of fish, and more than in any other country'.[2] Yet
even then there were 'black years', and one such is mentioned in Eirik the

Red's saga,[3] when those who went out caught little, and some did not return.

Certainly the dearth of fish must have made life harder, yet we should remember that the colder water attracted more seal and other creatures of the high Arctic to take their place.

I have spoken chiefly of cod, which was the most plentiful, but in the fjords and among the skerries there are other kinds of fish, such as rose-fish, catfish, halibut, herring, lumpfish, etc. Capelin was of special importance; in spring shoals of them come inshore, followed by the cod. Capelin are easy to catch and provide excellent food for man, livestock and dogs. In addition to all these, of course, there were the freshwater fish, chiefly Arctic char (*Salmo alpinus*). Only in one or two of the rivers are real salmon to be found.

It is not clear what the Norse Greenlanders used for nets. They may have made them of sinew, strips of whalebone or wool. Certainly they used hooks, and perhaps also salmon-spears.

In Ivar Bårdsson's *Description*[4] the expression 'sailing to islands' is used. This has a genuine ring, and was no doubt the popular expression for the seasonal hunting among the skerries, which took place chiefly in autumn and early winter, when the Greenland seal were fat, and again in summer when the hooded seal were at their best. It is of special interest that hunters were active on the skerries at the time when ice was forming in the fjords. In the early part of the autumn seal-hunting was presumably combined with the hunting of reindeer, which were numerous on many of the offshore islands.

A cheerful, lively time it must have been when boats from many homesteads put out through the drift-ice, manned by vigilant hunters. The black seal is sighted – and like lightning the harpoon streaks out. Towards evening weary men row in to the old camp with a heavy load of carcases in tow. Fires are lit; there arises the pungent smell of seal-meat roasting on the spit, while the hunting men discuss today's bag and the prospects for the morrow.

Both the finds that have been made and local conditions in general show that hunting was at least as important as stock-raising, if not more so. The same was true of many Norwegian homesteads in the Middle Ages.

For a long time the Norse Greenlanders had the Greenland seal (*Phoca islandica*; season: September–December, moving north) and the hooded seal (*Cystophora cristata*; season: May–June, moving south) to themselves. But in the fourteenth century the Eskimoes began their southward migration in earnest, and it was on these hunting-grounds among the offshore islands that competition between kayak-people and Norsemen was fiercest.

Ringed seal (*Phoca hispida*) were also hunted, but most of these gathered north of the settlements. Another species is the common seal (*Phoca vitulina*). These prefer a milder climate and are seldom found in great numbers, but

are valuable game. Today they are rare in Greenland, for they come ashore
to breed and change their coats, and so have fallen an easy prey to the rifle.

In the old days there must have been a good many of these common seal
in Greenland. A seal-rookery was a very valuable part of an estate, and as
the power of the Church increased it acquired such hunting-grounds; we
hear that the See of Nidaros owned a number of seal-rookeries, and there are
indications that a similar custom prevailed in Greenland. Harpoons were no
doubt used, but in Norway and Iceland traps were also laid inland, or they
were caught in nets. The Gulating Law[5] mentions this, and in the Icelandic
law-book *Grágás*[6] the net used is said to have been 'twenty meshes deep'.

In those days considerable quantities of other large sea-creatures frequented the coasts of Greenland, such as the bearded seal, rorqual, cachalot,
Greenland whale, humpback whale, walrus, narwhal, beluga whale, porpoise,
ca'ing whale, etc. Their migrations took them regularly along the coast and
sometimes into the fjords. Many sought the drift-ice and colder waters north
and east of the settlements, and we shall consider these in more detail later
in connection with the long voyages to distant hunting-grounds. Evidence of
the abundance of Greenland whale, walrus and the like in earlier times may
be seen in the intense whaling activity that began in the seventeenth century
off the north-west coasts, and continued for two hundred years.

For the Norsemen, harpooning whale was an old-established art. The
older Gulating Law[7] has two chapters on whaling-regulations and is explicit
on the subject of whale-hunting. The King's Mirror[8] gives detailed descriptions of various species of whale found in the Arctic Ocean, displaying a
knowledge of these creatures such as could have been acquired only through
generations of hunting. The Norwegian Ottar's remarkable ninth-century
account of his voyage of discovery to Bjarmeland, on the White Sea, makes
it clear that in those days the people of north Norway were familiar with
walrus-hunting. We hear in the Fosterbrothers' Saga that the Norse Greenlanders had harpoons, and it is possible that they also used poisoned arrows[9]
when hunting whale, as on the west coast of Norway. Walrus were sometimes harpooned or, when they came ashore in great numbers, were speared.
Probably many people banded together when shoals of ca'ing whale and
beluga came in, and the catch would have been shared out according to set
rules, as among Eskimoes and the Faroese.

Such animals were valuable in many ways, not least as a source of blubber
for food and light, and for export. The meat was eaten by both men and
stock. Skins, bones and whalebone had many uses and considerable commercial value, especially walrus- and narwhal-tusks.

At the time of the colonization of Greenland, the people of Norway and
Iceland were experienced bear-hunters. In Iceland polar bears often came

inland from the pack-ice along the shore, and Norwegian fisherfolk must have encountered them on their northerly voyages. In Norway there were also numbers of land bears. It was customary to attack them with spears, and Norwegian seal-hunters and trappers of Svalbard still hunted them in this way down to the end of the last century.

The people of Greenland caught polar bears alive and sent them to Norway. The sagas give many instances of this: the Norse Greenlander Einar Sokkeson[10] brought a live polar bear to Sigurd Jorsalfare in exchange as it were for a bishopric, and Kolbein the Norwegian[11] took one to King Harald Gille. There is also a long and absorbing account – which later became a folk-tale in the North – of the Icelander Audun,[12] who brought a live polar bear to show the Norwegian King Harald Hårdråde, and afterwards presented it to the Danish king.

It has been argued that a number of structures in Greenland were bear-traps.[13] This is unlikely, both because it is very difficult to build a strong-enough trap and because a grown bear cannot be tamed. If a live polar bear was wanted, the hunters would have been more likely to catch the cubs after the mother had been killed, preferably while swimming.

So usual a thing was it to catch these bears alive that the Icelandic law-book *Grágás*[14] contained ordinances on the subject. A man owning a tame polar bear was to treat it as a dog and pay compensation for any damage it did. And any man harming a tame bear, unless it was guilty of some fault, had also to pay compensation. By law it was permissible to eat bear-meat, but not that of any other 'claw-animal'.

The catching of sea-birds was another important activity, and in many places along the coast there are auks, eiderduck, guillemots, puffins, etc., though the true haunts of such birds are for the most part to be found farther north. The Norsemen must certainly have collected down, which was a valuable export. And in Greenland there was one bird that was especially valued because it was easy to catch, and that was the great auk. It had a black back and a white belly, and a white patch in front of the eye, and resembled the little auk, though it was considerably larger. Its wings were too narrow for flight. It is now extinct.

Among the land-animals of Greenland the reindeer held a special position. Throughout the ages this remarkable beast has been of inestimable value to many northern peoples, and was indeed of vital importance to the inhabitants of northern Europe when, tens of thousands of years ago, the inland ice was slowly disappearing. It was vital also to the Stone-Age men of the Norwegian mountain plateaux, to Siberian tribes, to the Eskimo tribes of Alaska and Canada, to the North American Indians and to many hill-dwellers in Norway throughout the Viking period and the Middle Ages. Even today there are a few races that are noted for reindeer-hunting, including the

Chippeway Indians north-east of the Great Slave Lake in northern Canada, and the Nuniamut Eskimoes in Alaska. I lived among these people for many years and know just what the reindeer can mean to primitive races: it supplies them with practically all the necessities of life. Such examples enable us to appreciate its value to the Norsemen of Greenland.

There must have been great numbers of reindeer in west Greenland during the Norse period, not only in Auster- and Vesterbygd, but also in the extensive regions round the fjords and at the fringe of the inland ice farther north, as far as Upernavik. The pasture is good, and it is significant that the Greenland deer is larger than the Norwegian variety.

Down to the middle of the last century there was still an abundant head of deer, but when the Danish Greenland Monopoly began trading in skins and antlers a great slaughter began. In 1839 alone about 37,000 animals were shot, and Henry Rink[15] states that in the period 1845–9 about 25,000 deer were killed annually. Between 1838 and 1855, 462,588 reindeer were shot. Even before that time the toll taken must have been heavy: Hans Egede arrived in the country in 1721, and after a while bow and arrow gave place to firearms.

Reindeer in the Julianehåb district (Austerbygd) were exterminated about a hundred years ago, while even in the Godthåb area (Vesterbygd) and regions farther north their numbers are very greatly diminished.

Eskimo history too indicates the existence of great numbers of deer; for although Eskimoes hunted mainly seal and walrus, many of them had a 'land-side' as well. With the approach of summer it was usual for them to set off in companies up the rivers and lakes to the reindeer haunts inland. They used kayaks and occasionally women's boats, sometimes carrying them for long distances across country.

Rink[16] tells us that certain groups were mainly deer-hunters, and hunted seal only to get enough blubber for their lamps.

For people who, like the Norse Greenlanders, were largely dependent on reindeer, the herd migrations were of great importance, for in the course of these the animals appear in large numbers and are easy to take. The annual migrations of the deer – like those of the seal – help us to a deeper understanding of the Norsemen's way of life.

Wherever reindeer are found in their natural state they have clearly defined routes which they follow in search of pasture. In north Canada[17] they head in spring for the Arctic coast, where some swim out to the islands to calve. In the autumn they return in great masses southward towards the forests. In north Alaska[18] they make similar migrations, as also in some parts of Siberia, while in north Norway the domesticated deer move in much the same way. There is every reason to think that the migration of the wild deer in west Greenland was not so very different. Ivar Bårdsson mentions that countless reindeer gathered on Reinøy (Reindeer Island) outside Einarsfjord in autumn, and that they were regularly hunted there.

The usual hunting-weapon was the bow. In the great homestead of Sandnes in Vesterbygd a piece of carved juniper wood has been found which may well have been the middle section of a bow.[19] But we know nothing of how these bows were made. It is possible that the Norsemen, like the Eskimoes, used whalebone. Arrow-heads of both iron and bone have been found, of the same type as those in use in the Viking period. Another important weapon was the spear.

Hunting methods must have been introduced from Norway, for there were no reindeer in Iceland. As in Norway, stone-built hides may be found in Greenland where the hunter lay in wait for the deer. Especially important were the means used to bring down large numbers of animals. In Norway it was quite usual to catch deer in pitfalls, which in some places were laid out in a planned series, close together, so that great numbers were caught during the migration.[20] Such pitfalls often belonged to particular farms, and were accounted a valuable adjunct to the estate. I have looked in vain for reindeer pits in Greenland; there probably are some, but in many cases the föhn wind may have filled them with sand.

In some parts of Norway it was the custom to drive herds of deer over a precipice, and this would have been quite possible in Greenland. It is likely that yet another method was used – one that is very effective and was current among Eskimoes, Indians and other primitive races. The herd is driven into a lake, and when the deer start to swim, hunters who have lain in hiding put out in boats and attack the animals with spears. In this way great numbers can be killed.

There is little reason to suppose that the herds were much reduced during the time of the Norsemen. Their greatest danger was deep snow or the icing-over of the ground, which I believe to have been the reason for their extinction in north-east Greenland. Wolves too may have made havoc among them. In west Greenland reindeer would have found it easier to survive: the climate was milder and the vegetation richer than in the former region.

Reindeer were useful to the Norsemen in many ways. Their flesh was food, their skins were excellent for clothes and shoes, and the sinews of the back made good sewing-thread. The antlers were strong, and served to make spades, knife-handles and many other things. The skins, especially calf-skins, were valuable stock in trade; from Norway they were exported to England.[21]

Other useful game included hare and ptarmigan, which were caught with snares or by other means. Arctic foxes were caught in pitfalls, and these may still be found near the old Norse buildings. In Vesterbygd (Ujaragssuit)

Finns hunting on skis. From Olaus Magnus (1480–1557)

some larger pits have been discovered, which were no doubt for trapping wolves.

Lastly, there was falcon-catching. These birds were a valuable export: the Greenland falcon was known all over Europe and was much in demand by kings and princes for hunting. The King's Mirror tells us: 'In that country [Greenland] there are many great falcons which in other lands would be a treasure of great price. They are white, and there is greater abundance of them there than in any other country. But the people know not how to make use of them.'[22]

It is not known how these birds were caught, but probably, as elsewhere, the hunter lay in hiding, with a live ptarmigan as lure, and grasped the falcon by the leg as it stooped.

These handsome white birds from the Arctic were sent far and wide, to English and German kings, and even to the king of Egypt.

X VOYAGES TO NORDRSETUR

NORTH of the settlements the coast of Greenland stretched away into infinity, with its blue mountains, mighty glaciers and deep fjords where ice came drifting by. A cold land, but a land of promise. It had much to offer, but men sailed far to reach it. Here were the haunts of sea-creatures that were rarely seen near the settlements: those that preferred colder waters, such as walrus, narwhal, white whale, Greenland whale, bearded seal, ringed seal and others. The Greenland and hooded seal also moved north on their annual migration. For the Norse Greenlanders the hunting of these animals brought not only blubber, meat and skins for their own use, but also valuable wares for export; especially, as we have seen, the tusks of walrus and narwhal.

Bird-life too was more abundant in these regions of the high Arctic, and there was opportunity to collect both eggs and down. Reindeer were to be found right up as far as the Upernavik district. In many places there were great stretches of coast where ice and snow had melted and where these animals could wander far and wide and breed in peace. They were not timid, and hunting was easier here than among the settlements.

Next there was the driftwood: trees that once grew by the rivers of Siberia were carried far across the Arctic Ocean north of Svalbard, then southward along the east coast of Greenland, round Cape Farewell and up the west coast, until the force of the current ebbed out some way north of Disko Bay. The Norsemen kept constant watch for the ice-scoured timber that rode the waves or was tossed up on the beaches. In the settlements such flotsam had to be shared out among many, but along the northern coasts there was greater abundance.

The distant hunting-grounds north of the settlements were called Nordrsetur, or northern dwelling-places. Håkon Håkonsson's saga,[1] among other sources, shows us how frequent and how important were the voyages to that region. When the Norse Greenlanders gave their allegiance to the Norwegian Crown, it was decreed that the fine for manslaughter should be paid to the king, 'whether for Norsemen or Greenlanders, whether they were slain in the settlement or in Nordrsetur; yea, even in the extreme north under the Pole Star.'

Bjørn Jónsson (1574–1656), in his *Annals of Greenland*, which are based on older sources, writes:

> All the landowners in Greenland had great ships built for voyages to Nordrsetur ... furnished with all manner of hunting gear and hewn timber. Sometimes they themselves sailed aboard them ... Their greatest catch was seal-tar [oil], for seal-hunting there was better than in the settlements. Melted blubber was poured into leather sacks and hung up on racks to thicken; later it was prepared in the proper manner. The Nordrsetur men had their huts or houses in both Greipar and Kroks-fjardarheidr. There is driftwood but no standing timber. At this northerly end of Greenland trees and the like are washed ashore, and chiefly such as have drifted from the Markland bottoms ...[2]

Such expeditions had to start as soon as the sea was open in spring, and to allow of this, as was mentioned earlier, the owners whose homesteads lay far up the fjords beached their ships near the fjord mouth, for in some places the ice did not break up until May or June. If sailing was delayed in this way, valuable time was lost.

Both men and women were kept busy during the winter with preparations for the voyage to Nordrsetur. The ship must be overhauled, her timbers oiled, her sails and oars mended. Some worked at new shafts for harpoons, spears and arrows, others forged heads for them from bog-iron or carved them from bone, while the women stitched away at skin garments with their bone needles and sinew thread.

In spring or with the first breath of summer the vessels headed northward, now under sail, now pulled by the oarsmen, along a course strewn with drift-ice, among skerries, treacherous shallows and reefs. It was a hard life, fraught with perils, but the voyagers were tough, skilled men who knew all that was worth knowing about seafaring, ice and hunting with primitive gear. Most of them were no doubt professional hunters, and with them went young lads who were to be put through a stern school under a never-setting sun.

With the approach of autumn the time came for many of the Nordrsetur voyagers to return. The people in the settlements were all agog; some climbed to the look-out posts and gazed out towards the mouth of the fjord. At last the ships were sighted: a few vessels together, then perhaps singly, as under taut, square sails they headed into the fjord.

People thronged to the harbour and spirits were high as the ship came alongside. Rough jests rang out between ship and shore; then followed the great moment: the unloading. Here came leather sacks full of melted blubber, skins of walrus, polar bear, seal and reindeer, reindeer carcases, dried meat and great slabs of reindeer fat, sacks of down and masses of driftwood. At last, from the very bottom, came the most precious wares of all: walrus and narwhal tusks.

But some ships never returned. Storm or drift-ice had taken them.

It is certain that Nordrsetur lay somewhere on the west coast – but where? Bjørn Jónsson[3] in his *Annals of Greenland* gives a transcript of 'an ancient manuscript' in which appear the names of various points along the coast and the distances (i.e. 'days' rowing') between them. Of these Bjarney, an island in Nordrsetur, gives us a starting-point. It took twelve days to row round Bjarney, and if one reckons this as five sea-miles a day, this clearly indicates Disko, there being no other island of comparable size in those latitudes.

Working south, still reckoning a day's rowing as five nautical miles, we find that Karlsbudir lies at about 68° N., that is, the area in the neighbour-hood of north Strømfjord. An interesting discovery, for this is the centre of the walrus-grounds, which stretched northward from round Holsteinsborg to Egedesminde. These were also rich in seal, reindeer and driftwood.

The 'six days' rowing' southward from Karlsbudir brings us to the Norse Lysufjordr, at 66° N. Lysufjordr is difficult to pinpoint; it may correspond to south Strømfjord. From there it was said to be six days' rowing to Vesterbygd.

Eysunes (Fire Ness) is mentioned as lying north of Bjarney (Disko), and we may suppose it to have been near the north-west tip of the Nugssuaq peninsula (about 71° N.). Geological conditions make this very probable. In 1932 a landslide occurred on the north coast of the peninsula, followed by fire in the schist: the burning mountain of Niaqornat. According to Alfred Rosenkrantz[4] there are traces of similar burning on the south coast, though it is impossible to date them with any certainty. He adds that the Nugssuaq peninsula is the only place where the Norse Greenlanders could possibly have seen a burning mountain, so there seems little doubt about the location.

It was near the tip of this headland that the so-called 'bear-trap' was found, which according to an Eskimo tradition was built by the hero Kagssagssuk. In fact it is a ruined house which in all likelihood was erected by Norsemen. It is of stone and measures about 4·5 metres (15 ft.) square, was originally about 2 metres (7 ft. 6 in.) high, with an entry 3 ft. 6 in. long on the east side (see Plate 32, bottom).

Where do Greipar and Kroksfjardarheidr fit into the picture? According to our sources these were important hunting-grounds where there were huts; so the first question to ask is, where was game most plentiful? The answer must be between Holsteinsborg and Egedesminde, as well as in various parts of the great indentations marked by Disko Bay in the south and Vaigat in the north, including Disko Island. The best walrus-grounds in west Green-land are in this area, and there must also have been a wealth of other creatures such as seal, narwhal, Greenland whale and so on, besides reindeer. The

Vesterbygd and Nordrsetur. It was to the northerly hunting-grounds of Nordrsetur that Norse Greenlanders went every year to hunt walrus, seal, whale, etc., and to gather driftwood.

83

Dutch, for two hundred years, prized this as one of their richest hunting-grounds. In many places there are coves and bays where driftwood accumulates.

We are told that it was 'a long and great sea-voyage' to this place from the settlements, and mention of 'the northern land's end or point' takes our minds to the south shore of Disko Bay, where the coastline sweeps sharply to the east.

So far no traces of huts have been found, but this may be partly because in course of time the Eskimoes demolished them and used the stones to build their own houses. Therefore it is difficult to identify the places named. It seems likely that Greipar was the rich walrus area between Holsteinsborg and Egedesminde. Karlsbudir was probably here, as was said, and there would seem to be a natural connection between these huts and Greipar.

Kroksfjardarheidr* is thought by Nansen to have been Vaigat or Disko Bay, but there are indications that it is more likely to have been Disko Fjord on Disko Island, and that the southern arm of the fjord gave the place its name. This would have been an excellent starting-point for the Norse hunters, for the region was frequented by quantities of walrus and seal, driftwood was plentiful, and in the open sea off the south coast of Disko Island the Greenland whale passed by on their migrations. Moreover reindeer were numerous round Disko Bay. All this inclines one to think that Kroksfjardarheidr was what we now call Disko Fjord. Pastor Otto Rosing, who has spent many years in the north, tells me that the south-east arm of Disko Fjord is fairly large and rich in vegetation, and is reminiscent of the Faroese fjords. The mouth is about three miles wide, and there is no real harbour there; whereas the inner part may well be the 'crooked fjord', for it is shaped like a fish-hook. He adds that it is a convenient base for walrus-hunting or the gathering of driftwood.

Did all the hunters return south at the end of the season? It seems likely that a certain number were left to spend the winter in the north, for reasons which appear in the following extract from *Grønland* (1921):

> Walrus-hunting is carried on on a large scale in autumn on certain islands and headlands north of north Strømfjord, where from the beginning of September until well on in November the animals come ashore in such numbers that at last they lie as close-packed as herrings in a barrel, and a cloud of warm steam hangs over the landing-place.[5]

Many such opportunities could be exploited in autumn, winter and spring by hunters who stayed behind, so there is good reason to suppose that Karlsbudir and the so-called 'bear-trap' were winter huts.

* According to Nansen Kroksfjardarheidr means 'flat, barren moor by the crooked fjord'.

In accounts of these voyages we come now and again on some comment showing that the Norsemen were aware of strange people having arrived in the country. There is a certain tension; men were on the watch. Then in the fourteenth century the Eskimoes made a definite move towards the south, and the Nordrsetur hunters must often have encountered them on their yearly voyages. Those who stayed there over the winter most probably traded with them, as we shall see later.

Although the name Nordrsetur will have denoted the region between a point somewhat south of Holsteinsborg (about 66° N.), and a little to the north of the Nugssuaq peninsula (about 71° N.), in the course of centuries the hunters extended their field of operations, as always happens in a virgin land. There is evidence of many kinds to show how engrossed the Norsemen were with the vast country north of the settlements. Not only did the land-owners themselves take part in the expeditions, but churchmen too sailed far to the north. The question of just how far they went will be examined in the next chapter.

XI FARTHEST NORTH

IN 1267 a remarkable expedition was made to the far north. Bjørn Jónsson tells of it, quoting *Hauksbok* as his authority:

This account was written from Greenland by Haldor the priest to the Greenland priest Arnald, who had become chaplain to King Magnus Håkonsson aboard the merchantman that brought Bishop Olaf to Greenland ... That summer there came also men from Nordrsetur, who had been farther north than any knew of even by hearsay. They found no Skraeling dwelling-places but those in Kroksfjardarheidr; for which reason it is believed that they [the Skraelings] had the shortest way to travel, whencesoever they came ... After this the priests sent ships northward to learn how it might be north of the farthest regions to which they had yet attained, and they sailed out from Kroksfjardarheidr until the coast sank from sight. Then came a southerly wind and fog, and they had perforce to run northward before it; but when the storm abated and the weather cleared, they saw many islands and all manner of game: seal and whale and great numbers of bears. They came as far as Hafsbotten, and lost sight of all [ice-free] land, as well as the land to the south and the glaciers; yet [nearer] to the south of them lay glaciers as far as the eye could reach. There they beheld some Skraeling dwelling-places, but could not land because of the bears. Later they sailed back again for three days and nights, and upon going ashore on certain islands south of Snaefell they found Skraeling dwelling-places. They then headed south to Kroksfjardarheidr, one long day's rowing on the Feast of St James [July 25th] where there was a frost by night, albeit the sun shone both by night and by day, being no higher in the south than that a man lying across a six-oarer with his head against the side had the shadow of the gunwale nearest to the sun upon his face, though at midnight the sun stood as high as at home in the settlement when in the north-west. Then they returned to Gardar.[1]

This expedition, organized by the priests, seems to have been a voyage of discovery; but the abundance of game too must have been of vital interest.

The description of the sailing to Hafsbotten, whence they could see nothing but southern icefields, shows that the seafarers must have come some way north into Melville Bay. The emphasis on the great numbers of bears observed reminds us that according to Knud Rasmussen the bear is the one animal that is of prime importance to the Eskimoes in these parts. Mention of the islands and traces of Eskimoes there also fits in, for the Eskimoes passed across the expanse of Melville Bay on their southward route to the west coast.

The return journey to Kroksfjardarheidr is stated to have taken three days and one long day's rowing. Here arises the usual question of whether a day is reckoned as twelve or twenty-four hours, but it seems as if 'three days' means 'three days and nights'. It was light throughout the period and the midnight sun was unobscured by cloud, so that if wind and weather were favourable – and there is nothing to suggest the contrary – the voyagers would have no reason to lay to, least of all on their homeward voyage. Reckoning that at best they covered 120 sea-miles in twenty-four hours, and about 40 during the last 'long day's' rowing, we conclude the distance to have been about 400 miles or six degrees of latitude. Thus, if they started from Disko, on about 69° 30', they may have reached the area about 76° N.: that is to say near Cape York.

Then we have the notes concerning the height of the sun. The text implies that these observations related to Kroksfjardarheidr, and most students have accepted this without question. This would place the hunting-grounds very far to the north. C. C. Rafn[2] locates them at Lancaster Sound (about 74°), Alexander Bugge[3] at Inglefield Gulf (about 77°), and Gunnar Isachsen[4] at Jones Sound (about 76°).

This is hardly likely. As Fridtjof Nansen points out,[5] there would have been little object in pin-pointing so well known a hunting-ground as Kroksfjardarheidr. What mattered to these explorers, and what they evidently wanted to express as clearly as possible, was how far to the north they had been; just as it was essential for Leiv Eiriksson to take the height of the sun to determine how far south he had gone on his great Vinland voyage. Bjørn Jónsson's account of the expedition to north Greenland is misleadingly phrased, but it is after all a transcription, and a single word would be enough to distort the meaning.

The problem is first to calculate the latitude from the sentence: 'that a man lying across a six-oarer with his head against the side had the shadow of the gunwale nearest to the sun upon his face ... ' This gets us nowhere, unless we know the height of the rail above the man.

The second observation, namely that at midnight the sun stood as high as it did at home in the settlement when it was in the north-west, is also inconclusive. We lack certainty as to which part of the settlement is referred to (Gardar?) and on which day the height of the sun was taken. Almar Naess[6]

87

assumes that the height of the sun at midnight in the north was the same as that seen from Gardar at the summer solstice, when the sun was in the north-west. The height would then be 3° 42'. A similar view is put forward by Geelmuyden[7] and others, but such conclusions are drawn from uncertain data.

However, although information relating to the height of the sun allows of no accurate deductions, it does show us that the expedition travelled a considerable distance to the north: far enough at least for the sun to be visible at midnight. It supplements the record of the distances covered, by which it appears, as has been said, that the explorers reached about 76° N., the land of the Polar Eskimoes. This was far north of Kroksfjardarheidr, the old hunting-grounds of the Norse Greenlanders.

In the summer of 1824 the Eskimo Pelimut found a little rune-stone (about 10 cm. by 4 cm., or $3\frac{9}{10}$ in. by $1\frac{1}{2}$ in.) on the island of Kingigtorssuaq (i.e. the Great Peak), a dozen miles north of the colony of Upernavik (72° 57'–58' N.). The stone was lying on the ground beside an old cairn, most of which had collapsed, and had no doubt originally laid beside it. Close by were the remains of two other cairns. All three had stood on the bare top of the island which is something over 300 metres (984 ft.) high, and which commands an extensive view.

This is the most northerly rune-stone ever found, and it proves con-clusively that Norse Greenlanders penetrated something like 600 miles north of Vesterbygd. According to Magnus Olsen the inscription reads:

'Erling Sigvatsson, Bjarne Tordsson and Eindride Oddson erected these cairns on the Saturday before Rogation Day, and runed well.'[8]

Magnus Olsen deduces, from two of its own signs, that the inscription may date from 1333. The Saturday before Rogation Day was then April 24th, or, according to our Gregorian calendar, May 2nd. The inscription includes a number of mystical runes.

What men raised these cairns, and why? Magnus Olsen emphasizes that the inscription was cut by someone well practised in such work and that the spelling is surprisingly good. In this respect it may be ranked with a good medieval document. He regards the cairns and the inscription as a single unit: a memorial. The secret runes enjoin the cairns to stand fast upon the hill-top. Of the purpose of the cairns he says, among other things: 'In ancient literature we read of cairns that were set up in memory of some event, such as a slaying or a fight, or to mark the spot for a future visit, or in a special way to testify that someone through perils and difficulties had made his way to a certain point. It is no doubt in this third manner that we should interpret the three cairns on Kingigtorssuaq.'[9] Yet they stand equally as a memorial of the most northerly point to which the Norse Greenlanders, of that genera-tion at least, attained; and no doubt they also served to remind the Skraelings that at this point they were entering upon Norse territory, administered by the Lawman. 'Thus Kingigtorssuaq is the north-western equivalent of the north-eastern boundary of the realm: Ægistafr or Vegistafr on the Murmansk coast.'

The island lies near enough to the open sea to enable voyagers to land there – provided ice-conditions were favourable – as early as May 2nd. The essential factor, however, was the long and perilous voyage northward in April. The distance from Vesterbygd, as we have seen, is about 1,000 kilometres (600 miles), and the course lay along the fringe of the solid winter ice which, at its outermost edge, would have been readily broken up by winds and high seas. When drift-ice from the Davis Strait or Baffin Bay set in towards the land, seafarers had to seek shelter. Slushy ice was a danger, and there was no little risk of the open boats themselves being iced up at that early season of the year.

I believe that the men who built these cairns wintered there, and that they placed them to mark the entrance to their hunting-grounds and trading-post; for as I said before, it cannot have been unusual for the Norsemen to take advantage of a hunting-season which might bring them valuable supplies of blubber, skins, tusks, down and furs.

It is of particular interest that these cairns should have been raised on the eve of Rogation Day. As Magnus Olsen points out, this is the day before the great spring festival of the Church, when the people walk in procession over the fields, carrying the cross, to bless the land and cleanse it from all winter evil. If anywhere in the world spring moves men's hearts it is here, in the far north; and for those who have wintered here it is as if a curtain were drawn aside to reveal a new world, where the sun rises in a loftier arc every day and light floods land and ice, and where seal, walrus and narwhal sport in the open leads. No wonder three Norsemen might feel tempted to climb to a hill-top and mark the great spring festival by raising three cairns high against the sky.

It also provides a simpler explanation of the runes. It would have been important for those who braved the time of darkness and every kind of danger so far to the north to inscribe powerful runes in their fight against the forces of evil. Why three cairns were raised – one for each man – is unknown, but perhaps this too may have had something to do with magic. Later I shall be speaking of two other cases in which a number of cairns were raised on the same spot (see page 95).*

Just north of Upernavik is another little island that brings us a message from ancient times; this in Inugsuk, which lies under the lee of Kingigtorssuaq

* Three cairns are said to stand on a lofty summit near Tasermiut. *Grønl. Hist. Mindesm.*, III, page 805.

and other islands. I have already mentioned the Eskimo dwellings excavated by Therkel Mathiassen.[10] He identified a later phase of the Thule culture, and named it after Inugsuk. This presumably dated from the middle of the thirteenth century until the fifteenth. In time the Inugsuk Eskimoes made their way south along the west coast towards the Norse settlements.

A characteristic feature of this culture is the Norse influence it displays, of which the finds made in this Eskimo settlement at almost 73° N. give striking evidence. Firstly, objects were uncovered which *originated* with the Norsemen: fragments of a church bell, some woven fabric, pieces from some chequer-board game, parts of an iron harpoon blade, and other things. These may have been acquired by trade or by the plundering of abandoned homesteads.

Of particular interest are the articles made by Eskimoes after the Norse pattern: these include a saw of whalebone, and a round-bottomed wooden tub made of staves (see Plate 41, fig. 5), on the same principle as the milk-tubs of Norway. Barrel-staves have so often been found among Eskimo ruins, even as far north as Thule, that we must assume the Eskimoes to have learnt the cooper's art.

Yet the most important discovery was that of two dolls and a face carved in wood (see Plate 13, figs. 2, 3 and 4). The technique shows that the carvings were done by Eskimoes, although there is no doubt that they are intended to represent Norsemen. The face with its sharp nose, prominent chin and remarkable headdress or hair arrangement has an unmistakably Norse look. On the back of one there is a pattern which is presumably an imitation of something the Eskimoes had seen among the Norsemen (see Plate 14, fig. 2).

The dolls too are quite certainly intended to represent Norse Greenlanders. The carved dress is medieval, with jerkin and hood such as were found in the permanently frozen ground of Herjolfsnes churchyard, in the extreme south. Such garments were worn in fourteenth-century Europe.

These dolls and this face were carved, then, by Eskimoes, so that as Therkel Mathiassen points out, these Eskimoes must have seen Norsemen. Where?

Only a little way from Inugsuk lies the island of Kingigtorssuaq where, early in the fourteenth century, as we have seen, Norsemen inscribed runes and raised three cairns. This was presumably when Eskimoes were living on the neighbouring island.

It would be strange indeed if members of the two races had made no contact at this time; especially as the rune-carvers and their companions apparently spent the winter here. The Eskimoes would have had their models before them.

Another important point is that primitive peoples are strongly conservative in all that concerns their tool-culture. That they should have learnt to make implements on the Norse pattern indicates that the two peoples were in contact with one another for a considerable time.

Much has been said – on flimsy evidence – of the hostility between Eskimoes and Norse Greenlanders; far less of their friendly relations. As has been noted earlier, there was a cogent economic factor that was almost bound to bring the two races together: trade by barter.

We find a parallel to this in the Norway of the old days, and her commerce with Finnmark. History shows one persistent feature: white merchants or whalers have gone to extraordinary expense and trouble to seek out and do business with primitive Eskimoes. There was much profit to be gained: needles or coloured braid, to say nothing of iron knives, brought an incredible return. The Norsemen of Greenland had a similar opportunity, and it would be strange indeed if they failed to take advantage of it.

One of the most remarkable expeditions to north Greenland was undertaken in 1360 by an English monk and astronomer. He wrote a book about his voyages, and other matters, which was entitled *Inventio Fortunatae*, but which has since been lost. Hakluyt (1553–1616) identified him with the Oxford monk Nicholas of Lynne, a renowned mathematician and astronomer.

Information about this voyage is to be found in a note by the cartographer Gerardus Mercator (1512–94) on his map of the polar region extending from 70° N. northwards. Also, in a letter to John Dee the English mathematician, he gives the source used for his map. John Dee's transcription of this letter is in the British Museum.

Mercator based his work mainly on an account by Jacobus Cnoyen of the Netherlands, who had travelled the world and written a book about his experiences. This work has been lost, but in the above-mentioned letter to John Dee, Mercator includes what he affirms to be a copy made by himself – mostly word for word from the vernacular, the rest in an abbreviated Latin form – of all that the book contains concerning the northern regions.

Asgaut Steinnes[11] has had this letter photographed in its entirety, and commented upon it. This material has been hitherto unused in connection with medieval Norwegian history.

Mercator's extract from Cnoyen's book begins with a fantastic story of King Arthur's military expedition to Scotland, Iceland and 'Grocland', in about 530. This is all legend and fable, but in the middle of it we suddenly come upon this piece of straightforward information:

> But in the year 1364 eight of these men came to Norway, to the King [the following is given in Latin] and among them two priests, of whom one had an astrolabe, and one was kinsman in the fifth generation to a

91

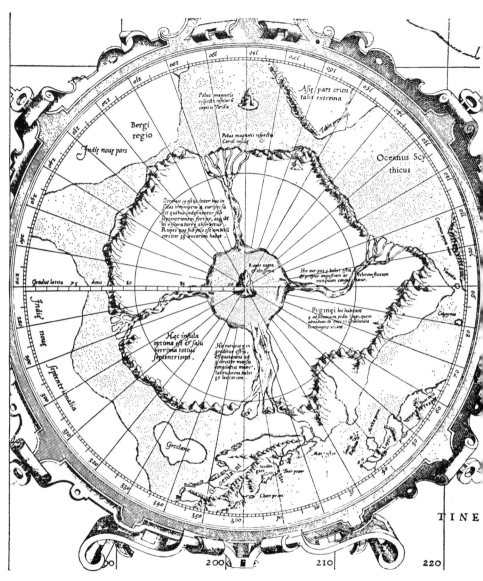

Mercator's map of North Pole area, dating from 1569. From Momard's Monuments de la
géographie. *Mercator based this work on what he had heard about a polar expedition made
in 1360 by an English astronomer-monk, who started from Austerbygd in Greenland.*

man from Brussels [here follow a few words, says Steinnes, which I will not attempt to translate, as some are missing] ... those who had penetrated to the region in the north with the first ships.

The priest who had the astrolabe told the King of Norway that in the year 1360 there had come to the islands a Minorite from Oxford, who was a good astronomer. He parted company with the others who had come to the islands, and voyaged farther, through the whole of the northern parts, and had written of all notable matters in a book which he called in Latin *Inventio Fortunatae*. This book begins with the last Climate, that is to say from 54°, and goes all the way to the pole.

There follows a somewhat curious description of the most northerly region: a ring of mountains encircles it like a wall; the sea penetrates this wall through nineteen channels which unite into four; there are thus four large islands between them, and on one of these dwell little people not above four feet in height (Eskimoes).

In the middle of the sea at the North Pole itself stands a solitary mountain of lodestone (magnetic rock). It is possible that the expedition went somewhat to the north of Smith Sound, as Steinnes suggests, and that on their return the travellers found themselves among the numerous islands south of Ellesmere Island, where there are many narrow straits and strong currents.

He thinks too that the priest with the astrolabe who returned to Norway with the seven other men and told of the English monk's voyage to the North Pole must have been Ivar Bårdsson, and adduces convincing evidence in support of this theory. Bårdsson came to Greenland in 1341, where for some years he was warden of Gardar, the episcopal seat. The indications are that he was there in 1360, but we know with certainty that in 1364 he was in Norway, where he held the post of canon at the Church of the Apostles in Bergen.

When the monk from Oxford arrived in Greenland he would have been more than likely to get in touch at once with the warden of Gardar. From Ivar he must have gained valuable information about the northern regions, for only a few years earlier Ivar himself had made an expedition to the north, primarily to expel the Skraelings from Vesterbygd.

It appears also that the English monk parted from his own men and took on a crew of Norse Greenlanders: presumably hunters who were familiar with those northerly regions. This carries conviction; for English seamen, however able, were not equipped to deal with polar ice.

Ivar Bårdsson designates the new crew as 'his' men. The monk made them a present of his astrolabe, which later came into Ivar's hands and which he took with him to Norway.

After his journey to the 'North Pole' the monk of Oxford returned to

93

Austerbygd, and then with his own crew sailed home to England. There he wrote his *Inventio Fortunatae*, and presented it to his king.

We know for a fact that the Norse Greenlanders went as far north as about 73° N., where the rune-stone was found. Is there any proof that they journeyed even farther?

Their course would lie across the expanse of Melville Bay, where the inland ice extends right down to the sea. North of that comes the land of the polar Eskimoes, much of which faces the relatively narrow waters of Smith Sound, Kane Basin and Kennedy Channel, which separate north Greenland from the Canadian Ellesmere Island. It was in this region that the Eskimoes migrating from North America made their crossing: a harsh country, but rich in game. Here were seal, whale, walrus, polar bear, reindeer and musk-ox, as well as rocks thronged with birds. The people were great hunters, and they throve.

It was in this area that in 1935–7 the Danish archaeologist Erik Holtved[12] made some noteworthy discoveries in the course of excavating a number of ancient Eskimo dwellings in Marshall Bay: that is to say near latitude 79° N., and about 900 miles north of Vesterbygd. Various objects were found there which originated with the Norse Greenlanders: a bone comb, a rusty lump of iron that turned out to be part of a chain-mail coat made of flat rings, an iron spear-head, a draughts-piece of turned whalebone,* a small piece of woollen fabric, a cauldron-leg of iron ore, part of an oaken barrel-head, and chessmen, including a whalebone* rook, turned and handsomely worked.

In Thule, somewhat farther to the south, another chessman was found, a pawn carved from walrus-tusk, and a wooden spoon-case of a type familiar from excavations in the settlements.

Part of a chain-mail coat: it brings a whiff of the Middle Ages. Only once do our sources mention such a coat in Greenland, and that was during the great dispute over inheritance at Gardar in 1132, between Norwegians and Norse Greenlanders. The latter offered an old coat of mail as part of the compensation they were willing to pay for the slaying of Einar Sokkesson. It was contemptuously tossed aside, and soon afterwards fighting broke out.

How are we to explain these finds? Some of the things may have been made by Eskimoes under the influence of Norse culture, others may have been plundered from abandoned Norse homesteads. There is also the possibility that they were acquired by barter with the Norsemen who visited those far northern regions. This is borne out, as we have seen, by the expedition of 1267 which presumably reached the 76th latitude, and by Nicholas of Lynne and his crew of Norse Greenlanders who may have sailed as far as Smith Sound, and even farther. The cairns and rune-stone show us that other

* True bone, not baleen.

Norsemen apparently wintered at about 73° N. and traded with the Eskimoes. And in this connection we may remember Ottar the Norwegian who as early as the ninth century undertook the long expedition round north Norway as far as Bjarmeland (Perm), to explore and to trade. His example was followed by many others; for Norsemen never feared to venture where there was profit to be made.

A few other touches remain to be added to this picture of the far north. During Otto Sverdrup's expedition (the second Fram voyage, 1898–1902) to the north Canadian archipelago, a number of stone-built nesting-places for eiderduck were found on two islands west of Jones Sound. Farther east on the same Sound two round cairns were also found, about five feet in height. This was at 73° 30′ N. or so.

Similar discoveries were made by Sir George Nares's expedition of 1875. At the summit of Washington Irving Island, in Kane Basin off the eastern side of Ellesmere Island, two moss-grown cairns were discovered, and on a neighbouring island some nesting-places for eiderduck. This was at about latitude 79° N.

Gunnar Isachsen, who took part in the second Fram expedition, and Fridtjov Isachsen[13] deduce that no earlier expeditions had visited Jones Sound. There were old Eskimo dwellings in the area, but it is unlikely that natives built the nesting-places; it would be at variance with the nature of this race of hunters to bother about such things. Kaj Birket-Smith, the Danish ethnographer and archaeologist, is of the same opinion. He had never heard of Eskimoes building them, and believes that the birds would have been of 'exceedingly little value' to the natives. In Norway and Iceland, on the other hand, it was a common practice, both in early and later times.

The cairns in Jones Sound differed in dimensions, material and shape from those which Otto Sverdrup's expedition had found elsewhere. G. and F. Isachsen point out as a curious feature the fact that in three different places in that northern region a number of cairns were found side by side.

1. Three cairns at Kingigtorssuaq, the site of the rune-stone (about 73° N.). These we know were erected by Norsemen.
2. Two cairns in Jones Sound, with eiderduck nesting-places in the neighbourhood (76° 30′ N.).
3. Two cairns on Washington Irving Island east of Ellesmere Island, with nesting-places near by (about 79° N.).

To this I can add another similar find in the same area, communicated to me by Henry Larsen, Norwegian-Born Superintendent of the Royal Canadian Mounted Police. He has had a long experience of the Arctic, and has made the north-west passage from the east and the west. He tells me that on the east side of Ellesmere Island he has come upon several stone-built nesting-

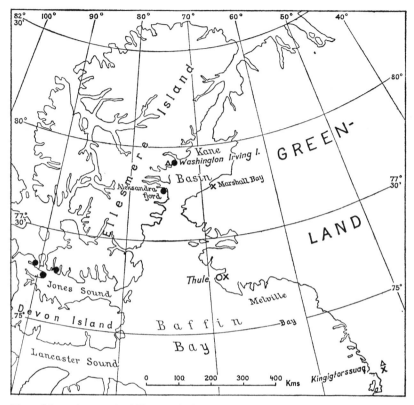

Map of the regions north of Upernavik. It is probable that the Norse Greenlanders visited these places.

places: e.g. in Buchanan Bay, Skraeling Island and at the mouth of Alexandra Fjord (about 79° N.). He saw about twelve nests, but made no closer investigation. He expressly makes the point that they could not be mistaken for hearths. I mention this because Erling Porsild[14] has maintained that such confusion is likely.

There is much to corroborate the Isachsens' belief that the eiderduck nesting-places must have been built by Norsemen. Never yet has it been demonstrated that Eskimoes did such a thing, and there can be no doubt that it would be quite foreign to their nature. They do occasionally raise cairns, but these are seldom as perfected as those now in question, and even more rarely would they raise more than one in a single place.

If Norse hunters built these nesting-places, we may assume that they wintered in those regions. For experienced Greenlanders a winter sojourn in

Eiderduck nesting-place, such as have been used in Norway and Iceland from ancient times. Unknown among Eskimoes, but found in Greenland as far north as approximately 79° N.

country so rich in game would not have been a matter of any great difficulty. In this connection it is worth noting that the two cairns and the nesting-places on the eastern side of Ellesmere Island lie as it were opposite the places in Greenland where the Norse objects were found. The relatively narrow channel may be crossed in small craft or with dog-teams.

When we consider the known facts in relation to the voyages to Nordrsetur and beyond – the rune-stone at about 73° N., the probable wintering in those regions, barter with the Eskimoes, the cairns, the eiderduck nesting-places and the remarkable discoveries of Norse objects in Eskimo dwellings far to the north – it appears very likely that Norse hunters and traders journeyed as far as the land of the polar Eskimoes.

A chessman in the frozen ground where once Eskimoes lived – a rook made of whalebone: the most northerly piece ever found. It tells us that the ever-young game of chess was dear to the Norse Greenlanders. But what it might tell us of its long and remarkable journey to a place over nine hundred miles north of the settlements, and of what happened to it afterwards, we shall never know.

XII THE WASTE PLACES OF EAST GREENLAND

I c y winds off the sea blow in over the coasts of east Greenland, where huge masses of ice are swept southward by the current. The sea captains who sailed to the Greenland settlements were no doubt familiar with the wild, strange coast behind the pack-ice: steep, blue-black mountains, mighty glaciers and here and there a glint of the white shield of the inland ice.

They believed that the country was part of northern Europe: a continuation of Bjarmeland (Perm) on the White Sea. From there the coast was thought to curve northward and then south again to Greenland. Indeed, it was thought possible to travel on foot from Greenland to Norway. There was a saga in medieval Iceland about a man called Hall, who crossed mountains and icefields, through deserts and past the heads of fjords, until he came to Norway. He led a nanny-goat and lived on her milk.[1]

The Norse Greenlanders called the coasts of east Greenland *ubygder* – the unbuilt (uninhabited or waste) places. There were no homesteads east of Cape Farewell; the land was barren. The ruin discovered on the Lindenow fjord was probably originally a hunter's hut, as has been suggested.

Our sources give a few scattered pieces of information about the east coast, and make frequent mention of shipwreck and men's desperate struggle for life, though they speak also of new country, of hunting and of fishing.

Gunnbjørn Skerries,[2] which most probably lie off the Angmagssalik district, were as we noted discovered by the Norwegian Gunnbjørn Ulvsson in about the year 900. It was this discovery that gave the impulse to Eirik the Red's expedition.

In the year 1000 or so Torgils Orrabeinfostre[3] was wrecked on the east coast of Greenland and took four years to reach the settlements. The saga gives a dramatic account of all that happened to him, much of it based on popular imagination, though certain things are described so accurately that the story must have a factual basis. It also mentions witches, no doubt to be interpreted as Eskimoes. It is quite possible that Eskimoes were living on the east coast at that time.

Bjørn Jónsson has reported a remarkable story about Lik-Lodin,[4] which dates from the first half of the eleventh century. Part of it runs thus:

In this ice from the northernmost bays most ships in olden times were

98

wrecked, and much is told of this in the story of Toste, for Lik-Lodin*
was so nicknamed because in summer he would often search the
wastes to the north and bring back to the church the bodies he found in
caves and on rock-ledges. They had come there from the drift-ice or
wrecked ships, but always near them runes were carved, describing all
events and sufferings.

One summer Lik-Lodin sailed to Norway and met with Harald Hårdråde's
fleet, which was bound for the west. He went aboard and met the king, who
asked for news. Lik-Lodin then told how he had sailed so close to a volcanic
eruption that part of his sail was burnt. He spoke also of omens which boded
ill for the king's campaign. It was then secretly agreed that he should accompany the fleet, to bury such of the king's men as fell in battle. This was
shortly before Harald Hårdråde lost his life at the battle of Stamford Bridge,
in 1066.

Another medieval extract narrates:

> Men say that when the king [Harald Hårdråde] lay off the Sule Islands
> [outside Sognefjord in west Norway] a Greenland ship sailed in from
> sea. The skipper was a man who went by the name of Lik-Lodin because
> he had carried the bodies of Finn Fegin and his ship's company from
> Finnsbu, which lies east of the icefields in Greenland. This he had been
> ordered to do by St Olav, because this Finn was the son of Ketil Kalv
> from Ringnes in Hedmark, and Gunhild, King Olav's sister ... [5]

This sheds light on contemporary conditions, and shows among other
things that members of Norway's most distinguished families sailed to
Greenland, presumably to trade. I shall return to Finn Fegin later. Magnus
Olsen believes that it is his death that is referred to in the runes on the Hønen
stone of Ringerike. That a man of such high birth lost his life in the 'unbuilt
places' must have made a deep impression, for three hundred years later
Ivar Bårdsson says of the disaster:

> Item eastward nearer the icebergs lies a harbour named Fimbuder, so
> called because in St Olav's time a ship was wrecked there ... and in this
> ship was St Olav's page, and he drowned there with others; and they
> who lived thereafter buried the dead in that place and raised great stone
> crosses on the graves of the dead, and they stand there to this day. [6]

In *Groenlendinga þáttr* we hear of Arnbjørn the Norwegian,[7] who in about
1125 set course for Greenland, but was wrecked on the east coast. There
were two vessels, and all lives were lost. A year or so later the bodies were

* 'Lik' means corpse.

99

found by the Greenland fisherman Sigurd. He brought one ship and her cargo back to the bishop's seat of Gardar, which had just been built, and a bitter quarrel later ensued between Norse Greenlanders and Norwegians, who came over to claim their inheritance.

Another tragedy occurred in 1189, when the ship *Stangarfoli* was cast up with Ingemund Torgeirsson the priest,[8] and others, on the east coast of Greenland. The disaster remained undiscovered for fourteen years, when the ship was found, and seven of the bodies in a cave.

> Among them was the priest Ingemund; his corpse was intact and un-rotted, as were his clothes, but the skeletons of six men lay beside him. There were also waxes [wax tablets] by him, and runes telling how they perished. But folk held that this was a great sign that God had been so well pleased with priest Ingemund's conduct that He permitted him to lie there thus long with his body whole and unharmed.

In Gudmund Arason's saga we hear of Ingemund Torgeirsson's brother Einar,[9] who was wrecked on the coast of east Greenland in the last half of the twelfth century. The crew fell out over their rations, split into two parties and finally came to blows. Einar and two others tried to cross the inland ice to the settlement, but perished. Their bodies were found the following year and buried at Herjolfsnes.

The Icelandic Annals[10] relate that in 1189 Asmund Kastanraste reached Iceland from the Greenland settlements after touching at the Kors Islands and Finnsbu. The ship was held together with wooden pegs and sinews.

In 1285, say the same Annals, two Icelandic priests, Adalbrand and Torvald, discovered new land to the west: Nyland and Dunøyene.[11] From a number of circumstances we deduce that these places must have been off east Greenland; for one thing, as Gustav Storm points out, the priests returned that same autumn. It is hard to say with certainty which part of east Greenland this was, though presumably it was a region rich in game, such as the walrus-grounds in Scoresby Sound. A few years later, we hear, the Norwegian king, Eirik, sent a man to Iceland to organize an expedition to the new land. This man was given the name of Landa-Rolf.

In about 1385 that remarkable adventurer Bjørn Jorsalfare[12] was cast up on the coast of Greenland, where he stayed for two years as district judge and revenue officer. Bjørn Jónsson's account of him states that he touched at Gunnbjørn's Isles off the east coast and found them inhabited – presumably by Eskimoes.

Olaus Magnus,[13] in his well-known work on the North (1555), states that European ships touched at the south-east coast and that there were Eskimoes there. Of the famous seafarer Didrik Pining and his companion Hans Pothorst he reports that in about 1494 they stayed on Kvitserk mountain, said to stand in the middle of the sea between Iceland and Greenland; and he accompanies the chapter with an illustration showing a fight between a European and a 'pygmy' (Eskimo).

This story must have a core of truth. In a letter dated March 3rd, 1551, from burgomaster Carsten Grip of Kiel to King Christian III, we read of a great seamark erected on the rock Kvitserk 'on account of the Greenland pirates, who with a number of small keel-less vessels attack other ships'.[14] I shall be returning to this later, as well as to an indication that Pining also traded with Greenland.

The sources mention several places on the east coast which formed landmarks for those at sea. Eirik the Red 'came in from sea towards Midtjøkul which is called Blåserk'.[15] We don't know where this may have been, nor are we more certain of the location of the other spots mentioned, such as Berufjord, Finnsbu, Kross Islands and Gunnbjørn Skerries.

Knowledge of the coasts of east Greenland was gained chiefly through fishing-trips from homesteads in the southern part of Austerbygd. The great manor of Herjolfsnes was certainly involved in these, and although people from that southerly region undertook expeditions to Nordrsetur, far up the west coast, it is reasonable to suppose that they were attracted primarily to the wealth of game on the east coast, which was so much nearer. There they would find Greenland seal, hooded seal, polar bear and whale quite far to the south, and if the hunters reached more northerly regions such as Scoresby Sound they would have come upon walrus, narwhal, musk-ox, reindeer, etc. In some places, too, there were quantities of driftwood.

Texts tell us little of these hunting-trips: they were everyday affairs; yet a few scattered notes give a strong impression that such journeys were frequent. To a great extent the hunters must have rowed or sailed along the leads within the pack-ice.

Ivar Bårdsson[16] speaks of great whale-hunts in Berufjord. This fjord belonged to the cathedral, and no one could hunt there without leave from the bishop. The same was true of the Kross Islands 'farther east of the glaciers [jøkler]', though there it was the hunting of polar bear that was under ecclesiastical control.

How far north along the east coast did the Norse Greenlanders go? Probably as far as the Angmagssalik area, at least. This is an excellent hunting-ground, where there are many kinds of game: ringed seal, Greenland seal, hooded seal, whale, polar bear, sea birds, and salmon in the rivers. In earlier days there were also reindeer.* It may be wondered whether the Norsemen went even farther north, past the difficult Blosseville coast and on to the rich game-country round Scoresby Sound. In north-east Greenland,

* A small breed of deer, about the size of a St Bernard dog. Cf. Magnus Degerbøl in *Grønland*, I (1957), p. 11 et seq.

among many other animals, walrus and narwhal were to be found, of which the tusks were valuable, as well as musk-ox.

Hauk's *Landnámabók*[17] states in some navigational instructions: ' ... from Kolbeinsøy northward it is a day and a night's sailing to the *ubygder* [uninhabited places] of Greenland.'[17] (Kolbeinsøy is a small island north of Iceland.) Assuming that the compass-reading was given as roughly as it would be in ordinary conversation among Arctic sea-captains of today, the course may well have lain slightly towards the west: that is to say that the waste places here referred to may have been those round Scoresby Sound or Franz Josef fjord. True, the time required is underestimated, but this often happens even in the case of far better-known routes.

Amdrup's expedition to east Greenland in 1898–90 made a remarkable discovery at an old Eskimo habitation on Dunholm, slightly south of the entry to Scoresby Sound.[18] This was a comb of walrus-tusk in the shape of a stylized human figure, with banded decoration and two crosses engraved on the front and back of the handle (see lower half of Plate 21). This object is competently, even artistically, made. The shape and decoration of the comb are Eskimo in character, but the cross is not: it is a Maltese cross, which originated in the Middle Ages. W. Thalbitzer, who described the find, says of it: 'A cross of this type in Eskimo decoration is something unique and baffling.'

Also on Dunholm a winged needle-case of walrus tusk was found, a small cross being carved on each of the wings or lugs.

The Maltese crosses bear a close resemblance to some of the crosses known to us from the settlements of west Greenland. They are remarkable finds and appear to have had some more deeply significant background, but it is difficult to pronounce upon them with certainty. Norse influence certainly played its part in them, in one way or another.

It would not have been impossible for Norse hunters to get so far north by way of the land trails, as has been done by Eskimoes and by G. Amdrup. Yet it must be admitted that from the settlements the journey would have been long and arduous. An important factor is that the drift-ice off the coasts of east Greenland is very variable. At times it may extend up to two hundred sea-miles offshore, though there are also favourable years when navigation is easy. In 1936 and 1940, for instance, the fairway off Scoresby Sound and northward was practically free of ice throughout the summer.

Lastly I may mention two remarkable pieces of information to which so far little attention has been paid. The first is from the old manuscript *Gripla*, which is incorporated with Bjørn Jónsson's *Grønlands Annaler*.[19] This self-taught yeoman seems to have made use of various ancient writings which have since been lost, including *Gripla*. Occasionally he interpolated his own comments. We read in his *Grønlands Annaler*:

THE WASTE PLACES OF EAST GREENLAND

From Bjarmeland (Perm) the *ubygder* [uninhabited places] lie to the northward as far as the country called Greenland. But bays run in there, and the land stretches towards the south-west. There are glaciers [*jøkler*] and fjords; off the glaciers lie islands. One glacier cannot be explored. To the second is half a month's sailing, to the third a week's sailing. This one lies nearest the settlement and is called Kvitserk. From there on the land swings north ...

This description shows firstly that something was known of east Greenland, and quite northerly regions of it at that. Into the above text Bjørn Jónsson has woven the following, to explain that the land is not entirely desolate and empty of life:

But the Greenlanders do not confirm this, and hold that conditions are otherwise, both because of the driftwood that has been wrought by men, and reindeer bearing ear-marks or bands about the antlers; also because of the sheep that appear there, whereof we have evidence in Norway, where one head hangs in Trondhjem and another in Bergen; and there are many more.

A similar statement is made by Arngrimur Jónsson.[20] The essential difference is that Arngrimur declares the 'sheep' to have been found on the grazing-grounds of the Norse Greenlanders. He further states that the Greenlanders themselves brought that sort of sheep's head to Norway, and gives the added particular that they were hung up in churches there and in other public buildings, as in Nidaros and Bergen. He tells also of reindeer with unknown marks in their ears and antlers.

These are curious statements. Firstly it is important to bear in mind that Bjørn Jónsson takes the old geographers' view of a continuous territory running from Bjarmeland to Greenland. Thus Svalbard (formerly Spitzbergen) may well be included in the picture; and this is interesting in connection with the reindeer stated to have ear- or antler-marks. The origin of the Svalbard reindeer was for a long time problematical, for five hundred miles of drift-ice separate these islands from Novaya Zemlya. In 1912 a bull reindeer was shot in West Spitzbergen, and part of a bird's leg was found lashed with cotton thread to one of its antlers. This gave proof that the domesticated reindeer of the Samoyed could make their way to the Svalbard group across the ice. The bird's leg was connected with a primitive cult. Could it be that the account of the marked reindeer refers to Svalbard?

Mention of the 'sheep' raises a number of interesting questions. It is obvious that 'sheep' in this connection cannot denote the creature commonly known by this name, for the head of so common a domestic animal would never have been hung up in a church. Here the term must be applied to the musk-ox: that odd prehistoric beast that may well have put men in mind of a sheep, being equally shaggy-coated, tame and foolish.

The further statement that the Norse Greenlanders took many heads to Norway, and hung them in churches and public buildings – even in Nidaros Cathedral itself – has all the ring of truth. It was an old Norwegian custom to present gifts to the Church, and many objects were hung up or preserved there. In Borgund church hung a large reindeer antler. In Nidaros Cathedral, as has been said, a polar bear's skin lay before the altar; and here too a magnificent walrus tusk was kept for about three hundred years.[21] Claudius Clavus, the Danish geographer (*c.* 1426),[22] relates that in Nidaros Cathedral there was one large and one small skin-boat, presumably a kayak and an umiak (women's boat). Olaus Magnus[23] says that in 1505 he saw an Eskimo boat (kayak) hanging above the west door of St Hallvard's church in Oslo. A stuffed musk-ox head would have been something rare and very well worth seeing: certainly a precious gift to the Church.

It has also a wider significance, for the musk-ox region has a well-defined boundary to the south: that is to say, we can establish how far north the Norse Greenlanders must have travelled in order to obtain these animals, which came from the Canadian islands and crossed to Greenland by way of Smith Sound or Kane Basin, in the north-west. Southward along the west coast the great glacier region round Melville Bay formed a barrier, so that the animals never came farther than Cape York on about the 76th latitude N. Another stream of them flowed round the north of Greenland and southward along the east coast, where today there are about 15,000 head of them. The southern limit to this stream was Scoresby Sound, at about 70° N., after which glaciers and steep mountains prevented further migration.

It might be supposed, therefore, that the musk-ox heads mentioned in the records originated on the north-west coast. This would fit in with what I said earlier of probable hunting-expeditions as far as the land of the Arctic Eskimoes. But Bjørn Jónsson speaks of these heads in connection with the waste lands between Bjarmeland and east Greenland, so it seems probable that it was in these parts that the animals were killed.

In that case the Norse Greenlanders must have gone at least as far north as Scoresby Sound. Might there be a connection between their musk-ox and other hunting and the mysterious cross carved on the comb discovered on Dunholm, near the mouth of that fjord? Scoresby Sound leads in to one of the richest musk-ox areas in Greenland.

⊠⊠⊠⊠⊠⊠⊠⊠⊠⊠⊠⊠⊠⊠⊠⊠⊠⊠⊠⊠⊠⊠⊠⊠⊠⊠⊠⊠⊠⊠⊠⊠⊠

XIII   THE SAGA TELLS OF THE EARLIEST TIMES

Torgils Orrabeinfostre

ORGILS Orrabeinfostre was a noted Icelander who lived at the beginning of the eleventh century, that is to say at the same time as Eirik the Red. We have our account of him in the *Flóamanna saga*,[1] which may have been written down at the end of the fourteenth century. It tells among other things of Torgils's shipwreck on the east coast of Greenland and of his arduous journey to the settlements, which was said to have taken him four years. The saga is not among the most reliable, and contains a fair amount of superstition and fable, yet it has interesting features which may be genuine. It presupposes knowledge of the east Greenland coasts.

Torgils came from a Norwegian chief's family which ruled over a large tract of country on the west coast of Norway. His immediate forbears were banished under Harald Hårfagre's monarchy, moved to Iceland and took possession of land there, where they ranked among the most respected men of the island. The saga gives Torgils an exceptionally good character: he was, it says, not only a doughty and widely-travelled Viking, but also astute and magnanimous in his ways.

In his youth Torgils set off to Norway to claim his family inheritance – large estates in Sogn – and visited Håkon Jarl, who at that time was regent. Here he met Eirik the Red, then in the prime of life and owner of a homestead in Iceland. We learn that Eirik was a man of courteous demeanour and that he and Torgils were friends.

On Håkon Jarl's recommendation Torgils went to press his claim in the Hebrides: a difficult task which he carried out so competently that he was rewarded by receipt of the Sogn lands. Later he went on warring and trading expeditions to Ireland and elsewhere, and after a long and turbulent period he at last returned to his homestead in Iceland, where he remained for thirteen years.

Then word came to him from Eirik the Red, who by now had discovered and colonized Greenland and was living in the chief's manor house of Brattalid. He urged Torgils to join him in the new country, promising him the best possible living conditions. Torgils agreed, and decided to emigrate.

One summer's day in 1001 a medium-sized ship sailed from Iceland on a south-westerly course with about thirty people on board, besides livestock and gear. There seem to have been two parties: Torgils with his wife, closest relations, bailiff and ten thralls; and Jostein of Kalfholt with wife, son and eleven men.

A storm blew up; for a long time the ship was buffeted about the seas and the prospect looked black. A week before the onset of winter the vessel was wrecked somewhere on the east coast of Greenland. The voyagers escaped with their lives; the ship's boat and most of the equipment were saved, but the cattle were lost.

They were cast up on a sandy beach, flanked by mighty ice-fields. Here they built a hut and set about seal-hunting and fishing, for they had scant provisions for so many people. Sickness – probably scurvy, that old scourge of the Arctic – attacked them, and many died. But Torgils's wife Torøy bore him a son there in the hut, on the ice-packed coast of east Greenland.

It was impossible to head south in the ship's boat, for pack-ice lay like a wall along the coast throughout the year. For two winters they were im-prisoned there, and in that frozen, desolate land their situation was desperate.

In the account of the voyage we hear of the god Thor, who appears as an evil omen when things are at their worst. It was a time of transition: at the meeting of the great Parliament (the *Althing*) Christianity was introduced into Iceland – Torgils himself was a Christian – but the ancient gods Thor and Odin still wielded their power. Thus as one after another succumbed to sickness, the survivors were faced with a further frightful peril: ghosts.

Spring again. One clear day Torgils, his son Torleif, with Koll and Starkad, climbed up to the nearest icefield to get a view of the pack-ice. Might there not be some leads of open water out there? Back at the camp were his wife and child and the bailiff Torarin. The thralls had been ordered to go fishing.

When Torgils and his companions returned they were met by a most sorrowful sight: Torøy lay murdered on the sleeping-bench, 'the baby was suckling its mother's corpse.' Torarin and all the thralls had disappeared, and with them the ship's boat and the stores.

The situation was as desperate as it could be, but Torgils did not give up. He and his companions set vigorously to work at hunting and fishing, and at building a boat of skins stretched over a framework of driftwood. And the baby? Torgils cut into his own nipple: first came blood, then serum and lastly milk: he suckled his child.

One day, we learn, Torgils came upon two 'troll-women' or 'witches' cutting flesh from a large animal in a stretch of open water. 'Troll' is an expression often used in old writings to describe Eskimoes, in the sense of real, though heathenish and mysterious, people. Later on their journey they sighted two other 'trolls'. According to recent archaeological research there may well have been Eskimoes on the east coast in the eleventh century.

At last the ice broke up, and Torgils and his companions groped their way southward in the skin boat, through drift-ice and past glaciers. They journeyed under great difficulties; when their need was greatest Torgils slew with his sword a polar bear that was swimming about in a lead with a broken foot. The third year they wintered at Seleyr.

The following year they were away again through the ice-filled fairway; and after long rowing they caught sight of a tent which proved to be that of Torarin the bailiff, who had deserted with the thralls and stolen the ship's boat. He attempted to defend himself, pleading that the thralls forced him to join them, but was put to death.

The travellers were now near the southernmost point of Greenland, where the going was easier. In one of the fjords they spied a boat-house: 'walking up from the beach they came to a homestead before which a man stood and greeted them.' His name was Rolf: he had been outlawed from the settlements and made a home for himself alone in this out-of-the-way corner. They stayed with him that winter. In the spring Torgils borrowed his ship and with a promise to do what he could to get Rolf's outlawry rescinded, he set sail northward along the west coast towards Austerbygd.

They reached Brattalid in Eiriksfjord. Eirik the Red had invited Torgils to live there with him, yet he received him coldly. Could this be because Torgils had lost everything and might prove a burden? Relations were in no way improved when Torgils slew a polar bear among the very buildings: a cattle-killer that had wrought great havoc among the livestock. For this he was highly honoured, and rivalry arose between the two chiefs.

Once, when the housefolk were all in Brattalid bath-house, they talked of Torgils's many exploits and compared them with the achievements of Eirik the Red. Quarrelling broke out, in the course of which one of the Brattalid servants was killed. Eirik and Torgils effected a reconciliation, but the atmosphere remained so tense that the latter felt it prudent to leave.

Torgils went northward to Vesterbygd to collect the 'bear-toll' for the creature he had killed. Eirik had asked him also to do away with a gang of outlaws – thirty in all – who had made great depredations among the people. Torgils consented to take arms against them on condition that Eirik joined him with his own men at short notice, and this was agreed upon.

In Vesterbygd Torgils and his men lodged with a man named Bjalfe. He sent word to Eirik the Red, but Eirik did not join him as had been arranged. By guile and a surprise attack Torgils succeeded in eliminating most of the outlaws and took much booty, including the vessels *Stakanhøvde* and *Vennegøyt*.

He then tracked down the thralls who had deserted from him on the east coast. They had married and achieved some measure of prosperity. Torgils seized all their property and sold the men again as thralls. Just at this time his fosterfather Torstein Kvite arrived in Greenland; Torgils boarded his ship and headed west. The saga says: 'Then Torgils sailed away with much honour and renown. They kept out to sea and the wind carried them to the western coasts of Ireland.'

Skald-Helge

The story of Skald-Helge, the lawman of Greenland, is told in a long commemorative poem[2] which dates apparently from the fifteenth century. The poem is based on an old saga which has been lost, and which in turn was probably taken from an older lay composed by Helge's contemporary, Hallar-Stein. This man lived in the early eleventh century, largely abroad and especially in Norway, where he was a celebrated skald or bard at the court of both Harald Hårdråde and Olav Kyrre.

It is a love-poem, but more besides: it portrays the Icelandic skald and the wandering life of a warrior in many lands. In about 1017 he comes to Greenland, where he remains until his death. The part of the poem that deals with the latter country has many interesting features which were certainly based on actual conditions, and include information as to Norse hunting-grounds in the North.

It begins in Iceland. Haldor, a man of distinguished family, had two beautiful daughters, Tordis and Torkatla. Helge, a poet and a bold fighter, fell in love with the second daughter, and she with him. They met in secret – an unseemly thing to do until after betrothal – and gossips told Haldor that Helge was seducing his daughter. He was incensed; and when Helge asked for Torkatla's hand in marriage he met with a flat refusal, and Torkatla was sent away.

Curiously enough Haldor offered Helge his elder daughter Tordis. Helge's kinsmen urged him to accept, and the wedding took place. The marriage lasted two years, after which Helge sent wife and dowry back to her father, and went to Norway, where he joined the bodyguard of Jarl Eirik Håkonsson.

But his longing for Torkatla had not left him and he returned to Iceland. Now the two lovers met often, and this gave rise to malicious talk. Helge was not one to put up with this: he came to blows with the tell-tales and slew a number of them. But his enemies were powerful: at the *Thing* or local parliament he was outlawed and had no choice but to flee the country. Once more he went to Norway where St Olav was now king, and thereafter he set off on pilgrimage to Rome.

On his return to Norway in about 1017 he bought a third share in a trading vessel. Sailing out of Trondhjem for Iceland he met with frightful storms which drove the ship westward, and conditions on board were as bad as they could be. Then at last a chain of ice-covered mountains rose above the horizon: Greenland.

Helge was received hospitably by a rich farmer named Forne, who lived at Solarfjøll homestead in Eiriksfjord. Yet he was still sad, and never ceased thinking of his beloved Torkatla. Forne urged him to propose marriage to the rich widow Torunn of Herjolfsnes, the great estate in the southern part of the country. There was something peculiar about her: three of her betrothed had lost their lives.

They set off, and the betrothal took place after the widow's demands were met: she received a betrothal-gift (Forne made over Hørnes farm to her) and a promise that Helge should avenge the slaying of her husband Skjegge and her brother Ørnulf. His slayers were men skilled in witchcraft: the sons of Hreim, who had been banished from the settlement and who lived far to the north in Greipar.

Helge was then struck down by a long illness which clouded his mind. Torunn nursed him and, with the help of her arts, restored him to health. A great wedding was held at Herjolfsnes, but Helge's love for Torkatla remained unchanged.

The wily Torunn distracted his mind from brooding by urging him to battle, to wreak vengeance on Hreim's sons as he had promised. Helge built a ship, and with thirty well-armed men sailed north to Greipar in the waste places, where the outlawed family lived. Vengeance was achieved after a keen struggle, and Helge returned to Herjolfsnes with honour.

He held a strong position in the settlements; he was rich in lands and famous as an eminent warrior. Added to this were his gifts as a skald and his wide and varied knowledge: he had valuable experience of Iceland, of the Norwegian court and of other countries. Now he received official recognition of his status in Greenland and was made lawman.

In distant Iceland Torkatla too held fast to her old love. When after some time she learned that her beloved was in Greenland she took ship to Norway, arranged a passage to Greenland and one day sailed in towards the settlements. The merchants erected their booths on the shore, and at last Helge arrived and found his love. Theirs was an ardent but despairing meeting.

Then Torunn the wife took action. She arranged for Torkatla to stay at their homestead, so that she might keep a continual eye on the lovers. When spring came and the ice broke up she told Torkatla to sail with the Norwegian merchant-ship, since there was no place for her in Greenland. There was little that Helge could do about this, but he begged that he and Torkatla might be left alone for as long as three torches took to burn. Torunn agreed, and the lovers withdrew.

Then Torkatla left Greenland and returned to Iceland, where she bore a daughter, Helge's child. She herself died in childbirth, but the daughter, who was also named Torkatla, was sent to Greenland. Helge took charge of her and gave her a splendid wedding. He then moved to Brattalid, where he died at a ripe old age.

Tormod Kolbrunarskald

The Fosterbrothers' Saga[3] narrates among other things the events in Greenland round about the period 1024–7. Certain portions are fanciful, but others are well-founded and illustrate conditions in that country in olden days. It is interesting to note, incidentally, that the story is known to us not only from thirteenth-century Icelandic manuscripts, but also from Faroese folksongs.

The two Icelanders Tormod Kolbrunarskald and Torgeir Håvardsson were fosterbrothers, and each had pledged the other ceremonially to avenge whichever of them was slain first. While still youths they travelled about Iceland, arrogant and eager for a fight, killing people whenever the mood took them. Torgeir was the worse; he was a thoroughly unpleasant fellow. Tormod, who was fond of women and something of a skald, leaves a better impression.

Then the fosterbrothers parted. Torgeir continued his slaying. Once when he was aboard his ship at Raunhavn in Iceland a larger vessel headed inshore. She belonged to Torgrim Einarsson who went by the name of Trolle; he was one of the most powerful men in Greenland. He was now returning from a trading-voyage with forty men aboard and a valuable cargo.

Torgrim learned that Torgeir had killed one of his friends, and this demanded revenge. Taking Torgeir by surprise he killed him, together with most of his men. Torgrim then sailed to Greenland.

'Tormod Kolbrunarskald was ill at ease after the slaying of Torgeir,' says the saga. 'He put to sea and came to Norway, where he joined the household of the Norwegian king St Olav, as member of the bodyguard and as skald.'

His next task was to avenge his fosterbrother and put Torgrim Trolle to death. The king gave permission for the Greenland voyage, presented him with a sword and a gold ring, and wished him good fortune. A ship belonging to a man named Skuf had come in from Greenland and was due to make the return journey. Tormod sailed in her.

After a long and stormy passage Greenland was sighted, and the vessel sailed up Eiriksfjord to Brattalid. At that time the chief there was Torkel, Leiv Eiriksson's son: a powerful and well-liked man and a good friend of St Olav. When the ship dropped anchor before the homestead he came down, greeted the voyagers and traded with skipper and crew. He also invited Tormod to stay at Brattalid. The master of the ship crossed the fjord to Stokkanes, which he owned jointly with a man called Bjarne, a skilled blacksmith.

A woman named Sigrid was engaged to serve Tormod. She lived with Lodin, a good and able workman on the Brattalid estate. Torkel and his guests dwelt in a small cabin separate from the other buildings, and lights burned there every night. It seemed to Lodin that Sigrid stayed too late in that cabin of an evening, and that she paid him less attention than before. This grieved him, and he recalled an ancient scrap of ballad from Håvamål about loose women.

The amorous Tormod was indeed the culprit. Lodin took Sigrid to task, but she did not care. One evening when she again sought to visit the house a fierce quarrel broke out between the two men.

Christmas came. Torkel brewed good ale: 'he desired to hold the yuletide feast and win renown thereby, drinking-parties being rare in Greenland. Torkel invited his friends, and many came.'

Carousal went on throughout the days of Christmas, with much jesting and mirth. Then came the day of departure. Lodin brought out the clothes, swords and gloves that had been in his care, and shoved Skuf's and Bjarne's boat into the water. He was wearing sealskin jacket and breeches.

Then with three other men he went up to the cabin. Only Tormod and Bjarne were there. Tormod was lying on the sleeping-bench nearest the bedpost. When the four men entered the cabin Lodin grabbed Tormod's legs and hauled him off and across the floor. Bjarne sprang up, seized Lodin round the waist and hurled him headlong, then cursed those who were dragging Tormod and ordered them to let go. This they did, whereupon Tormod stood up saying: 'We Icelanders reck little of such pranks: we are used to it from the skin-game [tug-of-war].'

He then went out as if nothing had happened.

When Skuf and his followers had made ready to leave, Torkel and his housefolk accompanied them to the boat. She was a large craft and a gangplank had been run out to her. Bjarne stood waiting for Skuf, who was talking to Torkel. Lodin had given the departing guests their clothes and stood at a little distance. Tormod was close by.

Suddenly Tormod drew out an axe that he had held hidden under his cloak and delivered so violent a blow at Lodin's head that the man fell down dead. Torkel heard the sound of the blow, turned and beheld Lodin lying on the ground. He called to his men to attack Tormod, but they were so thunderstruck that they did not stir.

Then Skuf stepped in as mediator and others joined in; reconciliation followed and the payment of a fine was promised. But Tormod could stay at Brattalid no longer. He boarded Skuf's and Bjarne's boat and sailed across the fjord with them to Stokkanes.

It was no light task that Tormod had undertaken in planning revenge on Torgrim Trolle for the slaying of his fosterbrother. The saga describes Torgrim thus: 'He was a good, a mighty chief with many followers, proud by nature. He lived in Einarsfjord at Løngunes homestead with his widowed sister Tordis and her four lusty sons. Another sister was named Torunn, and she dwelt at Langanes in Einarsfjord with her grown son Ljot.'

At Stokkanes Tormod bided his time. Skuf gave him a henchman – the great, strong, foolish 'Tomse-Egil' – and Bjarne forged him an axe.

The following summer the people of the settlement went to attend the *Thing* at Gardar in Einarsfjord. The Eiriksfjord folk erected their tents some little distance away from the place where the men of Einarsfjord had raised theirs, and most of the booths were ready by the time Torgrim Trolle arrived. He sailed in aboard a splendid ship, attended by a numerous and well-armed following. So great a man was Torgrim that people scarcely dared speak to him.

When the vessel touched the shore all swarmed down to meet her, and Tormod was among them. A number of things were thrown ashore, including a seal-harpoon. Tormod picked it up and examined it; whereupon one of Torgrim's men snatched it and told him to leave it be, adding that Tormod did not know how to handle such a weapon. Tormod was prompt with a retort.

One day during the session of the *Thing* Tormod lay asleep in Skuf's booth; the rest had gone over to the meeting-place or to the other booths. Tomse-Egil came hurrying, woke him and told him he was missing a lot of fun, for Torgrim was even then relating an exciting saga. He was sitting in front of his booth, and the greater number of people attending the parliament were standing there listening.

'Whom does that saga tell of?' asked Tormod.

'Torgeir [Tormod's fosterbrother] is the name of a great champion in this saga. Torgrim himself played his part in it, and boldly. Go over and hear.'

'And so I may,' Tormod replied, and he rose. He turned his fur cloak black side out and put it on, grasped his axe and went over to Torgrim's booth. There he and Egil stood behind the wall to listen to what was being narrated.

Until then the weather had been clear and sunny, but now heavy clouds gathered overhead and there was a sudden violent downpour. People fled to their booths, many of them into Torgrim's. Tormod remained sitting outside alone, waiting until the doorway should be less thronged.

Then Tormod went forward to the front of the booth where Torgrim was seated, and said:

'What saga was that that you were telling?'

Torgrim replied:

'The notable deeds in that saga are not told in a few words. But who are you?'

'Utrygg is my name.'

'And whose son are you?'

'I am the son of Tortrygg.'

Torgrim tried to rise from his seat, but Tormod struck him such a blow with his axe that his head was cloven to the shoulders. Then, hiding the axe beneath his fur jacket, Tormod sat down, supported Torgrim's back and shouted, 'Hither, all! Torgrim is wounded!'

Many ran up. They asked who the assailant was, and Tormod answered that he knew not which way he had gone; he had thought only of speeding to Torgrim's support. Others now took away the body. People searched for the slayer, and some seized Tormod down by the shore. By now he had turned his fur cloak the other way out, so the white side showed, and when they accosted him he replied that his name was Vigfus and that he too was searching for the killer. Thus he saved himself.

Then came Skuf and Bjarne with a boat. When Tormod had told them what had happened they said that he must now be content with his revenge, for he had killed the second greatest chief in all Greenland.

Then they took Tormod to a cave somewhere in Eiriksfjord which was later given the name of Tormod's cave. The saga tells us that it 'went into some crags by the sea on the other side of the fjord from Stokkanes'.

Soon everyone knew who had done the killing, and thenceforth Tormod was an outlaw in the settlements. His most dangerous enemies were Torgrim's sister Tordis and her four bold sons Bodvar, Falgeir, Torkel and Tord. Also the other sister Torunn and her son Ljot.

We hear of a cunning and successful attack on Tord's life and another's, and of a fierce fight with Falgeir ending in the sea. Tormod won, though he was seriously wounded. Friends carried him to Vik homestead at the inner end of Eiriksfjord. There below the glaciers lived Gamle the fisherman and his wife Grima, who was skilled in the magic arts and had the image of Thor carved on a chair.

His enemies came to the place, but Grima saved Tormod by means of her witchcraft. At last he slew Ljot, and with that had taken the lives of four of Torgrim Trolle's nearest kinsmen, besides others: a thoroughgoing vengeance.

Then, together with Skuf and a couple of other Norsemen, he returned to Norway. Once more he joined Olav the Holy and won great honour by his exploits in the Arctic land. Tormod attended the king to the last, and fell mortally wounded at the battle of Stiklestad.

Audun of the Western Fjords

The tale of the Icelander Audun of the Western Fjords[4] brings us an amusing glimpse of Greenland's earliest history. It was written down in the fourteenth century. Oral tradition has embellished it – the striking, popular theme lent itself to such treatment – but the simple core of it seems genuine. There is nothing unreasonable about a man buying a polar bear and later giving it to a king: we know of other similar incidents.

The presence of a polar bear in more southerly latitudes must have attracted a good deal of attention in the old days, and certainly captured popular imagination. Indeed the story of the White Bear spread to many parts of Europe.

Audun was a man who lived in Iceland in modest circumstances about the middle of the eleventh century. He once did the Norwegian merchant Torer of Møre a good turn, which led to his sailing with Torer to Norway. He spent a winter at Torer's homestead, and when his host set off on a trading voyage to Greenland in the summer of 1061, Audun went with him.

They arrived in Eiriksfjord. All men of means took up residence in Austerbygd, while the rest continued northward to Vesterbygd. Among the latter went Audun.

He then met a hunter by name of Eirik, who had captured an unusually fine polar bear. Audun bought the animal with all he possessed and took it aboard with him the following summer when he returned to Norway in Torer's ship. His plan was to sail to Denmark and present the bear to King Svein Estridsson.

But he touched at Norway first. At Møre he parted from Torer and continued southward along the coast in another vessel. On the way the ship put in somewhere on the coast of Hordaland, where as it happened King Harald Hårdråde was holding a banquet. When the king heard that there was a polar bear in the neighbourhood he sent for its owner, desiring to buy the animal, which was regarded as an object of great value.

Audun replied that he was unwilling to sell the bear, as it was intended as a gift to the Danish king Svein Estridsson. At this time there was enmity between Harald and Svein, so Audun's conduct was either bold or foolish. Harald allowed him to sail on condition that on his return to Norway he would visit him and report the outcome of his encounter with the Danish king.

When Audun arrived in Denmark with his bear he found the greatest difficulty in obtaining food either for himself or for the animal, being so poor. He met a Dane by the name of Åge who was the king's steward, told him of his journey and asked if he might have some food for the animal. Åge, being a shrewd man, offered to feed it in return for a half-share in it, and the penniless Audun was forced to agree.

Together they went to King Svein with the beast, and when the king heard how his steward had taken advantage of the stranger he was enraged, and banished him from the country. Audun received grateful thanks for his gift and the offer of a place in the household.

For a time Audun remained in Denmark, and then went south on pilgrimage. He suffered great privations, fell sick and nearly starved to death, and when at length he returned to Denmark he was in a most wretched state.

King Svein continued to bestow his favour upon him, and when Audun desired to return to Iceland he gave him a laden merchant ship, a leather stocking filled with silver pieces and a valuable gold ring. The fact that he knew Audun would be meeting the Norwegian king and giving an account of his journey no doubt stimulated his liberality: it was well that the enemy should know of the Danish king's wealth and power.

When Audun arrived in Norway he visited King Harald as he had promised, told him of his journey and of King Svein's great generosity. He then presented the king with the gold ring he had been given, and sailed for Iceland, where he remained until his death, the progenitor of a respected line.

XIV NEW LAND IN THE WEST

A<small>N</small> air of freshness blew about the settler community during the period immediately following colonization. The people had come to a virgin country of untouched resources, where there were fish in the fjords, seal, walrus and whale among the pack-ice, stacks of driftwood along the shores, reindeer in the hills, good pasture, and land stretching into the blue distance as far as the eye could see.

The Norse Greenlanders could not have been unaware that beyond their regular hunting-grounds lay a world of unknown territories, for whenever they set a northerly or westerly course they almost always sighted some dim strip of coastline along the horizon.

Long trips in search of game and driftwood were undertaken from the earliest days. I have spoken of the yearly voyages to Nordrsetur, those rich grounds that extended to Disko Bay and beyond. Near Holsteinborg the Davis Strait is at its narrowest, no more than 200 sea-miles across, and a crew would not need to sail far out to sea before sighting the lofty mountains of Baffin Land. In spring the walrus have their haunts well out on the drift-ice in these parts, and are hunted by the Greenlanders of today, as they were also, no doubt, by the Norsemen. From the higher mountains near Holsteinborg one may also glimpse the loom of the Cumberland Peninsula. In short, it is more than probable that at quite an early period the Norsemen had knowledge of the coasts of Baffin Land, and these pointed the way to other parts of North America.

How easily, too, a ship bound for Greenland from Iceland or Norway in gales or fog might be swept too far to the south and then drift westward. This happened to Bjarne Herjolfsson, the voyager to Vinland, and it would be strange if others through the centuries did not have the same experience.

It is also significant that the distance from Bergen to Herjolfsnes, near the southernmost tip of Greenland, is about 1,520 sea-miles, and that this long route was the one regularly followed by ships bound for Greenland. From Herjolfsnes to Newfoundland is only 600 miles, that is, less than half as far.

The ships of the Viking age were marvellously seaworthy. The slender lines of the Gokstad ship* tell their own tale. The fact was clearly demon-

---

* The Gokstad ship is believed to date from 850 or 900.

strated in 1893, when the Norwegian Magnus Andersen[1] crossed the Atlantic in *Viking*, a replica of the Gokstad ship. This vessel has a maximum width of 5·25 metres (17 ft. 7 in.) and is 23·33 metres (88 ft.) in length. The measurement from the bottom of the keel to the level of the rail amidships is 1·95 metres (6 ft. 3½ in.), and she has a draught of 0·85 metres (2 ft. 9½ in.). The weight of the hull and complete equipment has been estimated at 20·2 tons. The replica had a burden of 31·78 registered tons and, like the original, was equipped with a square sail and steering oar.

The ship proved surprisingly swift, maintaining a steady 5 to 6 knots, sometimes attaining up to 11 knots. She once averaged 9·3 knots in 24 hours. Of this Magnus Andersen writes:

'It was a splendid voyage. Through the twilit night the Aurora Borealis cast its pale, fantastic glimmer across the sea, as the *Viking* glided over the crests of the waves like a gull. We observed with wonder the graceful motion of the ship and with pride her speed, which from time to time attained 11 knots.'

Thus it was that many a time the Norse Greenlanders set sail. But it was a different story when gales tossed the vessel and seas foamed in over the gunwale, while exhausted men baled and baled. The Viking ships could survive a storm but were ill suited to head into it; they had to run before the wind, and could thus be driven far off course.

At the time of colonization the compass had not reached the North; it was first known there in the thirteenth century, by the name of lodestone. We may well marvel at the way the Norse seamen made their long sea-voyages so surely without this aid, whether to the White Sea, Iceland, the British Isles, France, the Mediterranean, Greenland or North America. This seamanship was rooted in ancient tradition: a skill in navigation of which we have only scanty particulars. Men took bearings from sun and stars to 'discern the quarters of heaven', as the saga terms it. Probably the *leidsagnarmadr* (meaning 'guide' or 'pilot', i.e. navigator) used a bearing-dial of the kind found by C. L. Vebaek at the old nunnery of Siglufjord in Greenland.[2]

A distinctive seafaring community must have developed within Greenland society at a quite early date. Skippers, navigators, ordinary seamen, yeoman farmers and the like would gather to discuss the experiences of many voyages. They sat round the open hearth in their stone-and-turf houses, comparing notes on winds, currents and ice, on distant waters and shores. Knowledge was added to knowledge until whole areas took shape, and a tradition was born. The information given in the sagas is meagre indeed compared with the knowledge possessed by these widely travelled and experienced men.

It was in this setting that the Vinland expeditions were born. Eirik the Red and his family, and with them the chief's manor of Brattalid, form the focus of the period; and conditions in Greenland made it almost inevitable that the Greenlanders should have discovered America hundreds of years before Columbus.

We have no Greenland records of the Vinland voyages, although some may have existed at Gardar or in the two monasteries. Our knowledge of the expeditions is derived from scattered sources of a more random kind, some of which are of especial value in that they aim at more than supplying information about Vinland. We have also Icelandic sagas which were written down a couple of centuries after the event, and were intended primarily to describe the voyages to the new land in the west.

In what follows I will mention the more important of the incidental sources, and in the next chapter summarize the sagas.

The earliest notes on Vinland date from 1070, and appear in Adam of Bremen's description in his *Nordens Geografi*[3] (*Descriptio insularum aquilonis*). He obtained his information during his stay in Denmark, most probably at the court of Svein Estridsson, and from it we learn of the existence of Vinland and one or two of its peculiarities, though nothing further of its discovery.

He spoke also of another island, which many have found in this great ocean, and which is named Vinland because grapes grow wild there, and yield the best wine. There is also abundance of unsown corn, as we know not from hearsay only, but from the sure report of the Danes ... Beyond this isle, he says, there is no habitable land in the ocean; all that lies beyond is full of formidable ice and impenetrable fog ...

Finally he tells of a perilous Arctic journey undertaken by the Norwegian Harald Hårdråde 'when he desired to survey the breadth of the Northern Ocean with ships'.

In Icelandic literature Vinland is first mentioned in the *Íslendingabók*, written by the celebrated Are Frode. He lived close to these events, having been born in 1067 and in a milieu that was to give him surer knowledge of the lands in the west than most men possessed. His uncle, Torkel Gellison, as we have seen, had first-hand information, having been to Greenland himself. The *Íslendingabók* says:

The country called Greenland was discovered and settled from Iceland. Eirik the Red was a man from Breidafjord who sailed thither from Iceland and there took possession of land which was later called Eiriksfjord. He named the country Greenland, believing that people would feel a greater desire to go thither if it had a good name. And there, both in the east and in the west of the country, they found dwellings, fragments of boats and stone tools, from which it could be seen that the people who had formerly lived there were like those of Vinland, whom the Norse Greenlanders called Skraelings. He began to settle the land some fourteen or fifteen years before Christianity came to Iceland, as was told to Torkel Gellison in Greenland by one who had sailed thither with Eirik the Red.[4]

Are Frode believes that Eirik the Red and his people encountered no natives in Greenland, and to explain what kind of people had left the remains of boats, etc., he has to compare them with the natives of Vinland, of whom he had some knowledge. Of its kind this source of information is of prime importance.

In 1121, say the Icelandic Annals,[5] Eirik of Upsi, bishop of Greenland, set off to visit Vinland. There is something mysterious about this man and his life. We hear that he was consecrated bishop, and the *Landnámabók*[6] states that Eirik Gnúpsson was bishop of Greenland from 1112: that is to say that he was the first prelate of that country. There are many indications that he resided in Vesterbygd and most probably at Sandnes: a point to which I shall return later. We know nothing of either of his life in Greenland or his voyage to Vinland: he fades from history. Not until 1126 did the first of Greenland's permanent bishops cross the sea, and that was Arnald. From that time onward the episcopal seat was Gardar in Vesterbygd.

In the *Landnámabók* there is a brief note about 'Tord Hestehode, father of Karlsevne, who discovered Vinland the Good'. We hear too of Are Mársson's fantastic journey to Hvitramannaland, which 'lies in the western part of the sea near Vinland the Good. It is said that one may sail thither in six days and nights.' This source may be regarded as a myth, but is significant in that it mentions Vinland as a familiar country.

In the thirteenth-century *Kristni saga* and *Snorre* it is stated that Leiv the Lucky discovered Vinland. The *Eyrbyggja saga* (written in about 1250) relates the following:

> The summer after the reconciliation between the men of Eyr and of Alptafjord, Snorre and Torleiv Kimbe, the sons of Torbrand, sailed to Greenland. It is after the latter that Kimbevåg in Greenland is named. It lies among icefields. Torleiv dwelt in Greenland and lived to be a very old man, but Snorre sailed with Karlsevne to Vinland. There they fought with the Skraelings, and Snorre's son Torbrand, who was one of the boldest, fell in that battle.[7]

In Gretti's saga (*circa* 1300), Torhall Gamlesson is called a Vinlander (*Vindlendingr* and *Vinlendingr*).

The Icelandic Annals of 1347 make it clear that parts of North America were well known:

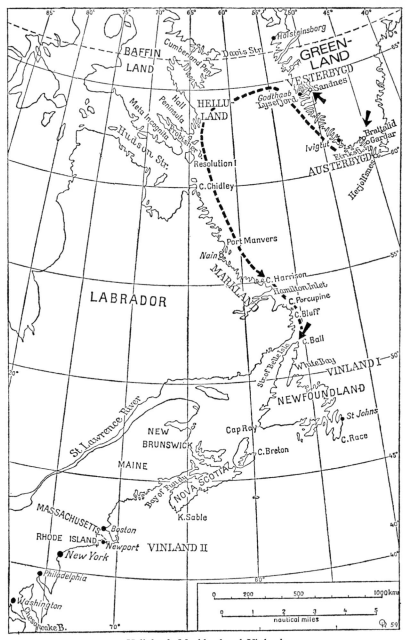

Helluland, Markland and Vinland.
Dotted line shows Vikings' route to Newfoundland.
(National Geographical Society, Norway)

There came also a ship from Greenland that was smaller than the small Icelandic vessels. She put in at Ytre Straumsfjord. She had no anchor. There were seventeen (some say eighteen) men aboard; they had sailed to Markland, but were afterwards driven hither by storms.[8]

There are interesting geographical descriptions in some of the fifteenth-century manuscripts. In one of them, which according to Gustav Storm originates partly with the much-travelled abbot Nikolaus of Thingeyre (d. 1159), we read:

From Bjarmeland [Perm] there is uninhabited country running northward to where Greenland begins. South of Greenland lies Helluland, and next to that Markland, whence it is not far to Vinland the Good which some hold to be continuous with Africa. If this be so, the Outer Ocean must run in between Vinland and Markland.[9]

From this we see how Vinland has been incorporated with the cosmography already described. First we have continuous land running from Bjarmeland (White Sea) to Greenland. In these northern regions lay Svalbard, also Risaland and Jotunheimar, where troll-like beings had their dwelling. The whole world was surrounded by the Outer Ocean, but between Greenland and Helluland the Ocean flowed in, and this glimpse of Mare Oceanum is called, in the old manuscript *Gripla*,[10] Ginnungagap.

A remarkable document which, according to Sophus Bugge,[11] relates to Vinland, is a rune-stone: the so-called Hønen stone. It was found between 1814 and 1824 at Vestre Hønen farm, in Norderhov, Ringerike, eastern Norway. The inscription was copied down in 1823; the stone itself afterwards disappeared and was never found again. The original transcription too has been lost, but we have another made by no less a man than W. F. K. Christie, president of the Storting and founder of the Bergen Museum.

It was a sizeable rune-stone, over four foot high, and was most probably intended to stand as a memorial. It was found in the central part of an area which in olden days was historic ground. The Norwegian royal line had its roots here, and Magnus Olsen mentions the Hønen stone as having stood near the place which we think of as Sigurd Syr's homestead. It is significant that at Hønen and the neighbouring property Tandberg no fewer than five rune-stones have been found. According to Sophus Bugge the inscription runs as follows:

Ut ok vítt ok þurfa
þerru ok áts
Vínlandi á ísa
í óbygð at kómu;
auð má illt vega
(at) deyi ár.

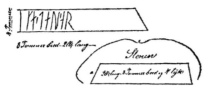

The runes on the Hønen Stone, in Christie's transcription

His translation is:

> They came out (to sea) and over great distances, in need of clothes to dry themselves upon, and of food, up towards Vinland and upon the ice of the uninhabited places. Evil can take away good fortune so that one dies early.

Sophus Bugge assumes that the journey here described started from Norway, that the goal was Greenland and that the ship drifted westward in the direction in which Vinland was thought to lie. Some of the crew may have escaped, but at least one young man of Ringerike perished, and it was to his memory that his family erected a memorial stone in his home district. Bugge believes the stone to date from not later than 1050, and adds:

> If this is correct, the great interest of the Ringerike inscription is clear. In it we have the earliest evidence of Norwegian-speaking men's acquaintance with part of America, and of the discovery of Vinland; a testimony probably older than Adam of Bremen's account, which dates from 1070, and independent both of this and of the Icelandic writings in which we read of Vinland.
>
> This testimony is of value in itself, for it shows that the name Vinland, which Leiv the Greenlander gave to the newly-discovered country, was soon afterwards known and adopted in Norway as well.

Magnus Olsen[12] has put a slightly different interpretation on the Hønen inscription. The essential difference is that instead of 'Vinlandi á ísa' he writes 'Vindkalda á ísa'. His translation runs as follows:

> Out (towards the west) and far (across the sea), in need of towels and food, they came in (to land), up on to wind-cold ice and (forward) to the uninhabited places (i.e., the *ubygder* of east Greenland). Evil – (the workings of cruel destiny) that one should die early – can take away happiness.

The inscription according to his interpretation refers to the drift-ice off the coasts of east Greenland and to the uninhabited regions there. Magnus Olsen believes too that it alludes to a particular event: Finn Fegin's death. He assumes that Finn lost his life on a trading-trip to the Greenland settlements.

I have already mentioned (see pages 98–9) the documentary information about Lik-Lodin who found Finn Fegin's body at Finnsbudir on the east coast of Greenland and took it to Norway by command of St Olav, because Finn was the son of Ketil Kalv of Ringnes and the king's nephew. Magnus Olsen sees this incident in a wider perspective, and deduces that from the beginning the Greenland trade was in the hands of a few rich and eminent families in Norway, one of which was probably the Ketil Kalv family of Ringnes (Hedmark).

Other circumstances indicate that there was co-operation between the Ringnes line and the royal line of Ringerike. We know that the kings engaged in commerce. The fitting-out of a merchant ship was so costly that it would have been only practical for a number of men to club together; and in this case the kinship between the two families would have played its part. Finn Fegin was descended on his mother's side from Harald Hårfagre, and was nephew to two kings: St Olav and Harald Hårdråde.

The interpretation of the rune-stone is thus uncertain. Sophus Bugge takes it to refer to Vinland, Magnus Olsen to the east coast of Greenland; and until the rune-stone itself is found[13] we are unlikely to come to a final conclusion.

At about the time when the Hønen stone was erected another man from Ringerike is supposed to have undertaken or caused to be undertaken a voyage to the Arctic regions: King Harald Hårdråde. Adam of Bremen speaks of it, as we saw: he says that the celebrated Harald 'wished to survey the breadth of the sea', that he came to the abyss of the world's end and barely escaped with his life. We do not know where his journey took him.

Harald Hårdråde was not only a warrior and explorer, but also a notable poet. One of his *gamanviser* or humorous verses[14] runs:

> Born was I where inlanders
> drew their bows.
> Now my vessels
> disliked by yeomen
> rock off the skerries.
> Far and wide then my prow
> plunged through the seas.

This gives us a glimpse of the spirit of the times among Norwegian leaders shortly after the settling of Greenland. The poem is rooted in the Ringerike environment from which sprang the Norwegian royal line, and where eyes were turned not only towards Europe but to more remote places: Greenland and it may be Vinland.

🞕🞕🞕🞕🞕🞕🞕🞕🞕🞕🞕🞕🞕🞕🞕🞕🞕🞕🞕🞕🞕🞕🞕🞕🞕🞕🞕🞕🞕🞕🞕🞕

XV THE SAGAS TELL OF THE VINLAND EXPEDITIONS

IN the last chapter I mentioned various scattered sources in which Vinland is mentioned. In this one I will cite the most important of those narratives that give a direct account of the Vinland voyages. They are preserved in two sagas: Eirik the Red's Saga and the Greenland Saga.

Eirik the Red's Saga exists in two manuscripts, Hauk's Book and the Skálholt Book. The first is believed to date from the beginning of the fourteenth century, the second from about the fifteenth, and both are based on older writings. The author of Hauk's Book was Hauk Erlendsson, who was born in Iceland in about 1265. He later became lawman of Bergen and a member of the Norwegian *riksråd*, or Council of the Realm. He died in Norway at about the age of seventy. It is of special interest to note that Hauk was a descendant of the great Vinland voyager, Torfinn Karlsevne.

The Greenland Saga is preserved in the Flateyar Book. It was written down by Jón Tordarsson the priest in the 1380s and completed by another priest, Magnus Torhallsson.

Eirik the Red's Saga includes: (1) Leiv Eiriksson's voyage to the west where he discovers a new country (Vinland), (2) Torstein's abortive journey, and (3) Torfinn Karlsevne's three-year expedition to Vinland.

The Greenland Saga includes: (1) Bjarne Herjolfsson's voyage, when he was blown off course and so discovered the North American coasts; (2) Leiv Eiriksson's expedition to the new territories which he calls Helluland, Markland and Vinland; (3) Torvald Eiriksson's Vinland voyage; (4) Torstein Eiriksson's ill-fated journey; (5) Torfinn Karlsevne's Vinland expedition; and (6) that of Freydis.

The two sagas have much in common, though they differ in certain respects. Gustav Storm and others were sternly critical of the Greenland Saga, and were of the opinion that Eirik the Red's Saga alone preserved the genuine tradition. This view is no longer generally held, and we must recognize that both sagas enshrine valuable records. This has been demonstrated by A. W. Brøgger in his admirable book *Vinlandsferdene*, and Sigurdur Nordal* makes this pronouncement:

> Lastly, as regards the two sagas about the Vinland voyages (Eirik's

* *Nordisk Kultur*, VIIIB (1953), pp. 244, 248 et seq.

124

and the Greenland Saga), we should note that there seems little reason to regard the latter as much more recent (or more unreliable) than the former. On the contrary, these two sagas which deal in part with the same subject, are so independent of one another that the most natural explanation would appear to be that they were written at about the same time, but in different parts of the country ...

In what follows, the most important sagas, somewhat abridged, will be rendered in Gathorne-Hardy's translation.*

BJARNE HERJOLFSSON SIGHTS A NEW LAND
(From the Greenland Saga)

Herjulf was a son of Bard the son of Herjulf, who was related to Ingolf the founder of the Iceland colony. Ingolf gave land between Vóg and Reykjaness to Herjulf (the elder) and his people. Herjulf (the younger) lived first at Drepstok. He had a wife named Thorgerd, and their son was Bjarni, a very promising man. He had taken to foreign voyages from his youth. This brought him both wealth and credit, and he used to spend his winters alternately abroad and with his parents.

Bjarni soon had a trading-ship of his own, and the last winter that he was in Norway was when Herjulf undertook the voyage to Greenland with Eric, and removed his home there. Herjulf had on board his ship a Christian from the Hebrides, who composed the Song of the Tidal Wave, which contains this verse:

> Almighty God, to whom alone
> The hearts of all thy saints are known,
> Sinless and just, to thee I pray
> To guide me on my dangerous way:
> Lord of the heavens that roof the land,
> Hold o'er me thy protecting hand.

Herjulf settled at Herjulfsness; he was held in the greatest respect. Eric the Red lived at Brattahlid; he was the most distinguished person there, and was obeyed by all. Eric's children were Leif, Thorvald and Thorstein, and a daughter named Freydis, who was married to a man named Thorvard: they lived at Garda, where the cathedral is now: she was a very haughty woman, but Thorvard was a man of no account; she was married to him mainly for his money. People were heathen in Greenland at that time.

* G. M. Gathorne-Hardy, F.R.G.S., *The Norse Discoverers of America* (Clarendon Press, Oxford, 1921). In the passages quoted, the forms of the proper names used by Gathorne-Hardy have been retained.

Bjarni arrived in his ship at Eyrar [in Iceland] in the summer of the same year in the spring of which his father had sailed away. Bjarni was much concerned at the news, and would not discharge his cargo. His crew thereupon asked him what he meant to do; he replied that he meant to keep to his custom of passing the winter with his parents, 'and I will', said he, 'take my ship on to Greenland, if you will accompany me'. They all said that they would abide by his decision; upon which Bjarni remarked, 'Our voyage will be considered rash, since none of us have been in Greenland waters.'

Notwithstanding this they put to sea as soon as they had got ready, and they sailed for three days before the land was laid; but then the fair wind ceased, and north winds and fogs came on, and they did not know where they were going, and this went on for many days. After this they saw the sun, and so were able to get their bearings, whereupon they hoisted sail, and after sailing that day they saw land, and they discussed among themselves what land this could be, but Bjarni said he fancied it could not be Greenland. They asked him whether he would sail to this land or not. 'I am for sailing in close to the land,' he said, and on doing so they soon saw that the land was not mountainous, and was covered with wood, and that there were small knolls on it, whereupon they left the land on the port side, and let the sheet turn towards it.

Then after sailing two days they saw another land. They asked Bjarni if he thought this was Greenland; he said that he did not think this was Greenland any more than the first place, 'for it is said that there are very large glaciers in Greenland.' They soon neared this land, and saw that it was a flat country and covered with wood. At this point the fair wind dropped, whereupon the crew suggested that they should land there: but Bjarni would not. They considered that they were short both of wood and water. 'You are in no want of either,' said Bjarni, but he got some abuse for this from his crew.

He ordered them to hoist sail, which was done, and they turned the bows from the land, and sailed out to sea for three days before a south-westerly breeze, when they saw the third land: now this land was high and mountainous, with ice upon it. So they asked if Bjarni would put in there, but he said that he would not, since – as he put it – this land appeared to him to be good for nothing. Then without lowering sail they kept on their course along the coast, and saw that it was an island: once more they turned the bows away from the land, and held out to sea with the same breeze; but the wind increased, so that Bjarni told them to reef, and not crowd more sail than their ship and rigging could stand.

They now sailed for four days, when they saw the fourth land. Then they asked Bjarni if he thought this was Greenland, or not. Bjarni replied, 'This is most like what was told me of Greenland, and here we will keep our course towards the land.' So they did, and that evening they came to land under a cape, which had a boat on it, and there on that cape lived Herjulf, Bjarni's father, and it is from him that the cape received its name, and has since been called Herjulfsness.

Bjarni now went to his father, and gave up voyaging, and he was with his parents as long as Herjulf was alive and afterwards he succeeded his parents, and lived there.

LEIV EIRIKSSON DISCOVERS VINLAND
(From Eirik the Red's Saga)

In the sources mentioned there is a brief account of Leiv Eiriksson's discovery of Vinland. Having visited the Norwegian king Olav Trygvason in Nidaros he turns his face once more towards Greenland, and the saga tells us:

Then Lief set sail, but he was at sea for a long time and found land that no one had ever known of before. Fields of self-sown wheat grew there, and vines. There were trees of the kind known as 'masur' and of all these things he took samples. Some of the trees were so large that they were used as building-timbers. Leif found some people adrift on a ship's raft and he took them home with him. In this as in many other things he showed magnanimity and helpfulness, and he brought Christianity to the country. He was known ever afterwards as Leif the Lucky ...

In the Greenland Saga the story is presented differently: here Leiv Eiriksson's voyage is carefully planned and he sets off to find the country that Bjarne Herjolfsson has beheld from the sea:

LEIF DISCOVERS WINELAND
(From the Greenland Saga)

Now the next event to be recorded (after the death of Olaf Tryggvason, September 1000) is that Bjarni Herjulfson came over from Greenland to Earl Eric (who became the ruler of a large part of Norway after Olaf's death), and the earl gave him a good reception. Bjarni told the story of his voyage when he saw the (strange) lands, but people thought he had been lacking in curiosity, since he had nothing to report about those countries, and some fault was found with him on this account. Bjarni was made an officer of the earl's court, but the following summer he went out to Greenland.

There was now much talk of exploration. Leif, Eric the Red's son from Brattahlid, went to Bjarni Herjulfson and bought a ship of him, and engaged a crew of thirty-five men. Leif asked his father Eric still to be leader of the expedition. Eric excused himself, saying that he was now an old man, and less fitted to bear all the hardships than formerly. Leif said that he was still the member of the family who would bring the best luck; Eric thereupon gave way to Leif, and as soon as they were ready for it he rode from home, and came to within a short distance of the ship. The horse which Eric was riding stumbled, and he fell off and hurt his foot. Then Eric said, 'I am not fated to discover more countries than this in which we are now settled, and we ought not to bear one another company any longer.' So Eric went home to Brattahlid, but Leif went on board with his companions, thirty-five men. There was a southerner (German) on the expedition called Tyrker.

Now they prepared their ship, and when they were ready they put to sea, and they found first the country which Bjarni found last. There they sailed up to the land, and having cast anchor and lowered a boat went ashore, and saw no grass there. The background was all great glaciers, and all the intermediate land from the sea to the glaciers was like one flat rock, and the country seemed to them destitute of value. Then Leif said, 'We have not failed to land, like Bjarni; now I will give this country a name and call it Helluland (the land of flat stone).'

Thereupon they returned on board, after which they sailed to sea and discovered the second land. Again they sailed up to the land and cast anchor, then lowered the boat and went ashore. This land was low-lying and wooded, and wherever they went there were wide stretches of white sand, and the slope from the sea was not abrupt. Then Leif said, 'This land shall be given a name from its resources, and shall be called Markland (woodland),' after which they returned to the ship as quickly as possible.

And they sailed after that in the open sea with a north-east wind, and were out two days before they saw land, towards which they sailed, and having come to an island which lay to the north of the mainland they landed on it, the weather being fine, and looked round; and they perceived that there was a dew on the grass, and it came about that they put their hands in the dew, and carried it to their mouths, and thought that they had never known anything so sweet as that was.

Then they went back to the ship, and sailing into the sound which lay between the island and the cape which ran north from the mainland they steered a westerly course past the cape. It was very shallow there at low tide, so that their ship ran aground, and soon it was a long way from the ship to the sea. But they were so very eager to get to land that they would not wait for the tide to rise under their ship, but hurried ashore where a river came out of a lake; but when the sea had risen

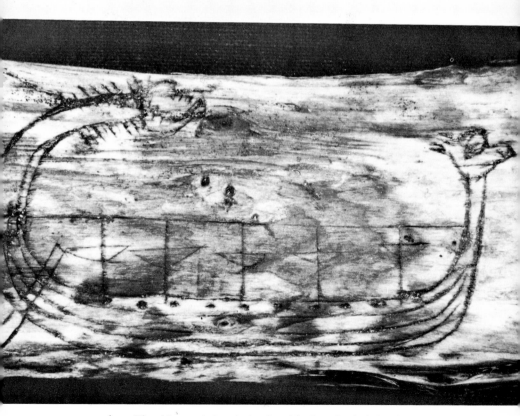

above: The oldest runic inscription found in Greenland, dating from about Eirik the Red's time. It was in the ruins of a homestead at Narssaq at the mouth of Eiriksfjord (see p. 52). (Photograph: National Museum of Copenhagen.) *below:* This vessel and the inscription 'Her ferr Hafdjarf' (Here sails the Sea-bold) were carved on a stick found at the German Quay in Bergen. (Photograph: Universitetets Oldsaksamling, Oslo.)

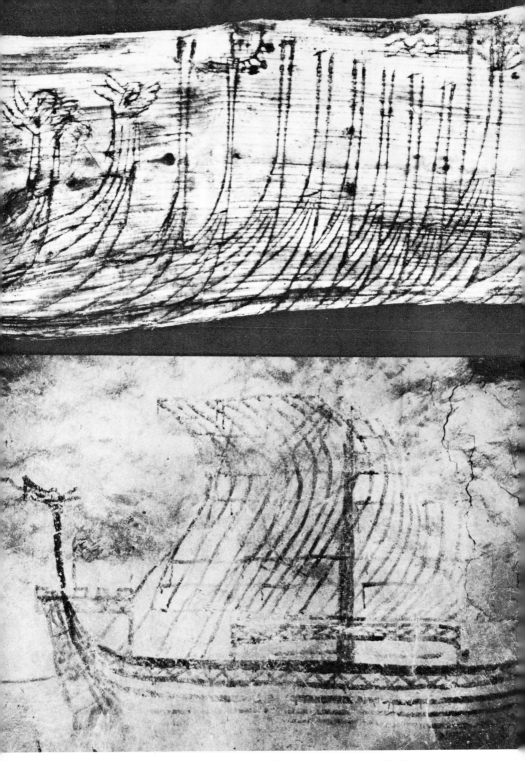

above: A fleet of Viking ships carved on the Bergen rune-staff (see Pl. 8). In the Middle Ages Bergen was the staple town for the tributary countries and port for the Greenland trade. *below:* Viking ship painted on the wall of Siljan church in Telemark, Norway. (Photograph: Universitetets Oldsaksamling, Oslo.)

above: In Holsteinborg we met the huskies – massive beasts that roamed about in gangs. *below:* From the head of Amerdloq fjord we went up this narrow river. It is said that a Norse house once stood near the place where our boat is moored (see pp. 339–40).

Preserved in the frozen ground of Herjolfsnes churchyard, in the southernmost part of Austerbygd, were these woollen garments. *above, left to right:* Burgundian cap, chaperon and flat cap. *below:* Children's clothes. (Photographs: National Museum of Copenhagen.)

Woman's woollen dress found in Herjolfsnes churchyard. The skirt is very full and has twelve gores in it. (Photograph: National Museum of Copenhagen.)

above, left: Polar bears. *right:* A loom of this type was probably used in Greenland. *below:* The so-called 'bear-trap' at about 71° N – probably a hunting-hut. (Photographs: Knud Lauritzen, Folk Museum, Oslo; and Jørgen Meldgaard.)

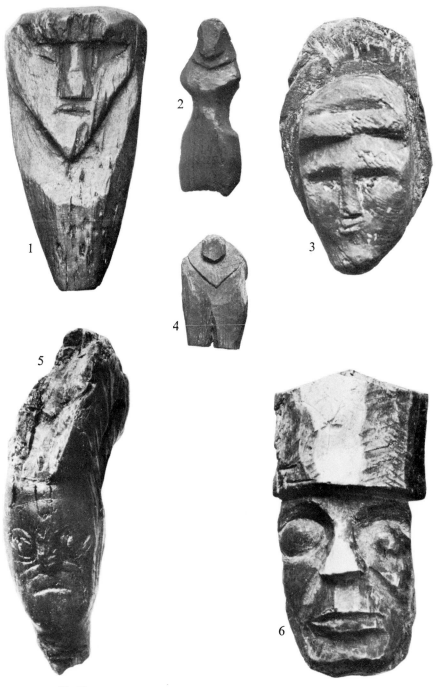

(2), (3) and (4) were found at the Eskimo site of Inugsuk at about 73° N. They were carved by Eskimoes and represent Norsemen (see p. 90). (1) is from Umiviarssuk, (5) from Austmannadal and (6) from Sandnes in Vesterbygd. (Photographs: National Museum of Copenhagen.)

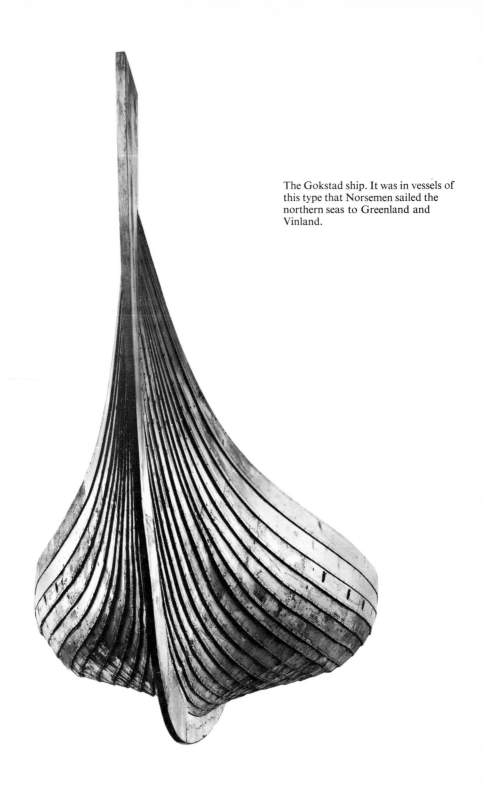

The Gokstad ship. It was in vessels of
this type that Norsemen sailed the
northern seas to Greenland and
Vinland.

under their ship they took the boat and rowed to the ship, and took her up the river and afterwards into the lake, where they cast anchor, and carrying their leather kitbags ashore they put up shelters, but later, on deciding to pass the winter there, they made large houses.

There was no want of salmon, either in the river or the lake, and bigger salmon than they had seen before; the amenities of the country were such, as it seemed to them, that no cattle would need fodder there in the winter; there came no frost in the winter, and the grass did not wither there so much. Day and night were more equally divided there than in Greenland or Iceland: on the shortest day the sun was up over the (Icelandic) marks for both nones and breakfast time.*

Now when they had finished building their houses, Leif said to his men, 'Now I will divide our party into two, and have the country explored: and one half shall stay at home in camp while the other explores the country, going no further than they can return by the evening, and not separating.' And so for a time they did this, Leif sometimes going with the explorers and at others staying at home in camp. Leif was a big, strong man, the handsomest of men in appearance, and clever; in fact, he was in all respects an excellent commander.

It happened one evening that a man of their party was missing, and this was Tyrker the southerner. Leif was much distressed at this, for Tyrker had been long with his father and him, and had been very fond of Leif as a child: so now Leif, after finding great fault with his men, prepared to look for him, taking a dozen men with him. But when they had got a little way from camp Tyrker came towards them, and was received with joy. Leif saw at once that his foster-father was in good spirits.

Tyrker had a projecting forehead and a very small face with roving eyes; he was a small and insignificant man, but handy at every kind of job.

Then Leif said to him, 'Why are you so late, my foster-father, and why did you separate from your companions?' Tyrker at this spoke for a long time in German, rolling his eyes and grimacing, but the others did not distinguish what he was saying. But a little later he said in Norse, 'I did not go much further than you, (but) I have found something fresh to report. I found vines and grapes.'

'Is that true, foster-father?' said Leif.

'Certainly it is true,' he replied, 'for I was born where there was no lack of vines or grapes.'

Now they slept that night, but in the morning Leif said to his crew, 'We will now do two things, keeping separate days for each; we will

* Lit: 'the sun had there *eyktarstaðr* and *dagmálastaðr* on the shortest day.'

gather grapes and cut down vines, and fell wood, to make a cargo for my ship,' and this suggestion was adopted. The story goes that their pinnace was full of grapes. So a cargo was cut for the ship, and in spring they made ready and sailed away, and Leif gave the country a name according to its resources, and called it Wineland.

So after this they put to sea, and the breeze was fair till they sighted Greenland, and the mountains under its glaciers. Then a man spoke up and said to Leif, 'Why are you steering the ship so much into the wind?'

'I am paying attention to my steering,' replied Leif, 'but to something else as well: what do you see that is strange?'

They said they could see nothing remarkable.

'I do not know', said Leif, 'whether it is a ship or a reef that I see.'

Then they saw it and said that it was a reef. But Leif was longer sighted than they, so that he saw men on the reef.

'Now,' said Leif, 'I wish that we should beat up wind, so as to reach them if they need our help and it is necessary to assist them, and if they are not peaceably disposed we are masters of the situation and they are not.'

So they came up to the reef, and lowered their sail and cast anchor: and they launched a second dinghy that they had with them. Then Tyrker asked who was the captain (of the shipwrecked party).

'His name is Thori,' was the reply, 'and he is a Norseman, but what is your name?' Leif told his name.

'Are you a son of Eric the Red of Brattahlid?' said Thori. Leif assented.

'Now,' said Leif, 'I will take you all on board my ship, and as much of your stuff as the ship can hold.'

They agreed to these terms, and afterwards they sailed to Ericsfjord with this freight, until they came to Brattahlid where they unloaded the ship. After that Leif invited Thori and Gudrid his wife, and three other men to stay with him, and procured lodgings for the rest of the crews, both Thori's men and his own. Leif took fifteen men from the reef; he was subsequently called Leif the lucky. So Leif gained both wealth and honour. That winter Thori's folk were much attacked by sickness, and Thori and a great part of his crew died. Eric the Red died also that winter.

TORVALD EIRIKSSON'S VOYAGE TO VINLAND
(From the Greenland Saga)

Now there was much discussion of Leif's expedition to Wineland, and Thorvald, his brother, thought that the exploration of the country

A page from Eirik the Red's saga in the Hauksbok manuscript (late 1320s). Leiv Eiriksson sailed from Greenland to Nidaros, Norway, and became one of Olav Trygvason's bodyguard. On his way home he was blown off course to an unknown land in the west, where he found 'fields of self-sown wheat, and wine-trees': Vinland.

had been confined to too narrow an area. So Leif said to Thorvald, 'If you wish, brother, you shall go to Wineland in my ship: but I wish the ship to go first for the wood which Thori had on the reef.' And this was done.

Thereupon Thorvald prepared for this expedition, taking thirty men, by the advice of Leif, his brother. Afterwards they made their ship ready and held out to sea, and there is no report of their voyage before they came to Wineland to Leif's camp. There they laid up their ship, and remained quiet that winter, catching fish for their food.

But in the spring Thorvald told them to make ready their ship, and ordered the ship's pinnace with some of the crew to go to the west of the country and explore there during the summer. It seemed to them a fine wooded country, the trees coming close down to the sea, and there were white sands. There were many islands, and many shoals. They found no traces either of men or beasts, except that on an island to the west they found a wooden barn.* Finding no further human handiwork they returned, and came to Leif's camp in the autumn. But the next summer Thorvald sailed to the east with his trading ship, and along the more northerly part of the country: then a sharp storm arose off a cape, so that they ran ashore, breaking the keel under the ship; so they made a long stay there to repair their vessel. Then Thorvald said to his companions, 'Now I wish that we should raise up the keel here on the cape, and call it Keelness,' and so they did.

Afterwards they sailed away thence and eastward along the coast and into the nearest fjord mouths, and to a headland which ran out there: it was all covered with wood. Then they moored their ship, and put out the gangway to land, and there Thorvald went ashore with all his crew. Then he remarked, 'This is a beautiful spot, where I should like to make my home.'

After this they returned to the ship, and saw on the sands inside the headland three lumps, and on approaching they saw three canoes of skin, with three men beneath each. Thereupon they divided their party, and laid hands on all of them, except one who escaped with his canoe. They killed the eight, and afterwards went back to the headland, when they saw inside in the fjord some mounds, which they took to be dwelling-places.

After this there came over them so great a heaviness that they could not keep awake, and they all fell asleep.

Then came a cry above them, so that they all woke up, and the cry was, 'Awake, Thorvald, and all your company, if you value your life:

* *Kornhjálm af tre* ... What was actually seen may well have been a deserted wigwam of poles and bark.

and return to your ship with all your men, and leave the land with all speed.'

At that there came from within the fjord countless skin canoes, which made towards them. So Thorvald said, 'We must set the war-shields over the side and defend ourselves as well as we can, while assuming the offensive but little.'

So they did, but the savages,* after shooting at them for a while, afterwards fled away, each as quickly as he could.

Then Thorvald asked his men if they were wounded at all; they said there were no casualties.

'I have got a wound under the arm,' said he; 'an arrow flew between the gunwale and the shield under my arm and here it is, and it will be my death. Now my advice is that you prepare to go away as quickly as possible, after carrying me to that headland which I thought the best place to dwell in: maybe it was the truth that came into my mouth that I should stay there awhile. Bury me there with a cross at my head and at my feet, and call it Crossness hereafter for ever.' Greenland was then converted, though Eric the Red died before conversion.

Now Thorvald died, but they carried out all his instructions, after which they went and met their companions, and told each other such tidings as they knew, and they stayed there that winter, gathering grapes and vines for their ship. Then in the spring they prepared to go back to Greenland, and arrived with their ship in Ericsfjord, with great news to tell Leif.

TORSTEIN EIRIKSSON'S UNSUCCESSFUL VOYAGE
(From the Greenland Saga)

Now Thorstein Ericson wished to go to Wineland for the body of Thorvald his brother, so he made ready the same ship, choosing his crew for their strength and size; and with twenty-five men and Gudrid his wife they put to sea when they were ready, and lost sight of land. All the summer they tossed about in the open and did not know where they went, and in the first week of winter they made the land at Lyse-fjord in Greenland in the Western Settlement.

TORFINN KARLSEVNE'S VOYAGE TO VINLAND
(From Eirik the Red's Saga. The text is taken both from the Skálholt Book and Hauk's Book, quotations from the latter being italicized.)

... *Thord Horsehead had a son called* Thorfin Karlsefni, who lived in the north at Reynisness in Skagafjord, as it is now called. Besides

* Skrælingar.

being of good stock Karlsefni was a wealthy man. His mother's name was Thorunn. He was in the cruising trade, and had a good reputation as a sailor.

One summer Karlsefni made ready his ship for a voyage to Greenland. Snorri Thorbrandson from Alptafjord joined him, and they had forty men with them. A man named Bjarni Grimolfson from Breidafjord and another called Thorhall Gamlison* from Eastfjord both made ready their ship the same summer as Karlsefni to go to Greenland; they had forty men on board. They put to sea with these two ships, when they were ready.

We are not told how long they were at sea; suffice it to say that both these ships arrived at Ericsfjord in the autumn. Eric and other settlers rode to the ships, where they began to trade freely: the skippers told Gudrid† to help herself from their wares, but Eric was not behindhand in generosity, for he invited the crews of both ships to his home at Brattahlid for the winter. The traders accepted this offer and went with Eric. Thereupon their stuff was removed to the house at Brattahlid, where there was no lack of good large out-buildings in which to store their goods, and the merchants had a good time with Eric during the winter.

But as it drew towards Christmas Eric began to be less cheerful than usual. One day Karlsefni came to speak to Eric, and said: 'Is anything the matter, Eric? It seems to me that you are rather more silent than you used to be; you are treating us with the greatest generosity, and we owe it to you to repay you so far as lies in our power, so tell us what is troubling you.'

'You have been good and courteous guests,' replied Eric, 'my mind is not troubled by any lack of response on your part, *it is rather that I am afraid it will be said when you go elsewhere that you never passed a worse Christmas than when you stayed with Eric the Red at Brattahlid in Greenland.*'‡

'That shall not be so,' replied Karlsefni, 'we have on our ships malt and meal and corn, and you are welcome to take of it what you will, and make as fine a feast as your ideas of hospitality suggest.' Eric accepted this offer, and a Christmas feast was prepared, which was so splendid that people thought they had hardly ever seen so magnificent a feast *in a poor country*.

And after Christmas Karlsefni asked Eric for Gudrid's hand, since it

* This is corroborated by Grett's Saga, Chapters 14 and 30, where one 'Thorhall Gamlison the Winelander' is mentioned.
† Hauk's Book: 'Eric'.
‡ Following the text of Hauk's Book, as the clearer sense.

appeared to him to be a matter under Eric's control, and moreover he thought her a beautiful and accomplished woman. Eric answered, saying that he would certainly entertain his suit, but that she was a good match; that it was likely that she would be fulfilling her destiny if she was married to him, and that he had heard good of Karlsefni.

So then the proposal was conveyed to her, and she left it to Eric to decide for her. And now it was not long before this proposal was accepted, and the festivities began again, and their wedding was celebrated. There was a very merry time at Brattahlid in the winter with much playing at draughts and story-telling, and a great deal to make their stay pleasant.

At this time there was much discussion at Brattahlid during the winter *about a search for Wineland the Good, and it was said that it would be a profitable country to visit*; Karlsefni and Snorri resolved to search for Wineland, and the project was much talked about, so it came about that Karlsefni and Snorri made ready their ship to go and look for the country in the summer.

The man named Bjarni, and Thorhall, *who have already been mentioned*, joined the expedition with their ship, and the crew which had accompanied them. There was a man named Thorvald (evidently Thorvard) who was connected by marriage with Eric the Red. *He also went with them, and* Thorhall *who was called the Hunter*, he had been long engaged with Eric as hunter in the summer, and had many things in his charge. Thorhall was big *and strong* and dark, and like a giant: he was rather old, of a temper hard to manage, taciturn and of few words as a rule, cunning but abusive, and he was always urging *Eric to* the worse course. He had had little dealings with the faith since it came to Greenland. Thorhall was rather unpopular, yet for a long time Eric had been in the habit of consulting him. He was on the ship with Thorvald's men, for he had a wide experience of wild countries.

They had the ship which Thorbjörn had brought out there, and they joined themselves to Karlsefni's party for the expedition, and the majority of the men were Greenlanders. The total force on board their ships was 160 men.

After this they sailed away to the Western Settlement [Vesterbygd] and the Bear Isles. They sailed away from the Bear Isles with a northerly wind. They were at sea two days. Then they found land, and rowing ashore in boats they examined the country, and found there a quantity of flat stones, which were so large that two men could easily have lain sole to sole on them: there were many arctic foxes there. They gave the place a name, calling it Helluland.

Then they sailed for two days with north wind, *and changed their course from south to south-east*, and then there was a land before them on which was much wood and many beasts. An island lay there off shore to the south-east, on which they found a bear, and they called it Bjarney (Bear Island), but the land where the wood was they called Markland (woodland).

[Then when two days were passed they sighted land, up to which they sailed. There was a cape where they arrived.* They beat along the coast, and left the land to starboard: it was a desolate place, and there were long beaches and sands there. They rowed ashore, and found *there on the cape* the keel of a ship, so they called the place Keelness: they gave the beaches also a name, calling them Furdustrands (the Wonder Beaches) because the sail past them was long. Next the country became indented with bays, into *one of* which they steered the ships.

Now when Leif was with king Olaf Tryggvason and he commissioned him to preach Christianity in Greenland, the king gave him two Scots, a man called Hake and a woman Hekja. The king told Leif to make use of these people if he had need of speed, for they were swifter than deer: these people Leif and Eric provided to accompany Karlsefni. Now when they had coasted past Furdustrands they set the Scots ashore, telling them to run southward along the land to explore the resources of the country and come back before three days were past. They were dressed in what they called a '*kjafal*'† which was made with a hood above, and open at the sides without sleeves: it was fastened between the legs, where a button and a loop held it together: otherwise they were naked.

They cast anchor and lay there in the meanwhile. And when three days were past they came running down from the land, and one of them had in his hand a grape-*cluster* while the other had a wild (lit: 'self-sown‡) ear of wheat. They told Karlsefni that they thought that they had found that the resources of the country were good.

They received them into their ship, and went their ways, till the country was indented by a fjord. There was an island outside, about which there were strong currents, so they called it Straumsey (Tide or Current Island). There were so many birds§ on the island that a man's feet could hardly come down between the eggs. They held along the fjord, and called the place Straumsfjord, and there they carried up their

---

* From [Hauk's Book has: 'Thence they coasted south for a long while, and came to a cape', &c.

† Presumably Gaelic.

‡ Hauk's Book has 'newly-sown'. § Hauk's Book: 'eiders'.

goods from the ships and prepared to stay*: they had with them all sorts of cattle, and they explored the resources of the country there. There were mountains there, and the view was beautiful. They did nothing but explore the country. There was plenty of grass there.

They were there for the winter, and the winter was severe, but they had done nothing to provide for it, and victuals grew scarce, and hunting and fishing deteriorated.

Then they went out to the island, in the hope that this place might yield something in the way of fishing or jetsam. But there was little food to be obtained on it, though their cattle throve there well.

After this they cried to God to send them something to eat, and their prayer was not answered as soon as they desired. Thorhall disappeared and men went in search of him: that lasted three successive days. On the fourth day Karlsefni and Bjarni found Thorhall on a crag; he was gazing into the air with staring eyes, open mouth, and dilated nostrils, and scratching and pinching himself and reciting something. They asked him why he had come there. He said it was no business of theirs, told them not to be surprised at it, and said that he had lived long enough to make it unnecessary for them to trouble about him.

They told him to come home with him, and he did so. Soon afterwards there came a whale, and they went to it and cut it up, but no one knew what sort of whale it was. Karlsefni had a great knowledge of whales, but still he did not recognize this one.

The cooks boiled this whale, and they ate it, but were all ill from it: then Thorhall came up and said: 'Was not the Red-Beard (Thor) more useful than your Christ? This is my reward for chanting of Thor my patron; seldom has he failed me.' But when they heard this none of them would avail themselves of the food, and they threw it down off the rocks and committed their cause to God's mercy: *the state of the weather then improved and* permitted them to row out, and from that time there was no lack of provision during the spring. They went into Straumsfjord, and got supplies from both places, hunting on the mainland, and eggs and fishing from the sea.

Now they consulted about their expedition, and were divided. Thorhall the Hunter wished to go north by Furdustrands and past Keelness, and so look for Wineland, but Karlsefni wished to coast south [and off the east coast, considering that the region which lay more to the south was the larger, and it seemed to him the best plan to explore both ways.† So then Thorhall made ready out by the islands, and there

---

* The Greenland Saga states that Karlsevne's expedition took up their quarters in Leiv Eiriksson's house. – Helge Ingstad.
† From [omitted in Hauk's Book.

were no more than nine men for his venture, the rest of the party going with Karlsefni. And one day as Thorhall was carrying water to his ship he drank it, and recited this verse:

> *They flattered my confiding ear*
> *With tales of drink abounding here:*
> *My curse upon the thirsty land!*
> *A warrior, trained to bear a brand,*
> *A pail instead I have to bring,*
> *And bow my back beside the spring:*
> *For ne'er a single draught of wine*
> *Has passed these parching lips of mine.**

After this they set out, and Karlsefni accompanied them by the islands. Before they hoisted their sail Thorhall recited a verse:

> *Now let the vessel plough the main*
> *To Greenland and our friends again:*
> *Away, and leave the strenuous host*
> *Who praise this God-forsaken coast*
> *To linger in a desert land,*
> *And boil their whales in Furdustrand.**

Afterwards they parted, and they sailed north past Furdustrands and Keelness, and wished to bear westward; but they were met by a storm and cast ashore in Ireland, where they were much ill-treated and enslaved. There Thorhall died, *according to the reports of traders.*

Karlsefni coasted south with Snorri and Bjarni and the rest of their party. They sailed a long time, till they came to a river which flowed down from the land and through a lake into the sea: there were great shoals of gravel there in front of the estuary and they could not enter the river except at high tide. Karlsefni and his party sailed into the estuary, and called the place Hóp.

They found there wild (lit: self-sown) fields of wheat wherever the ground was low, but vines wherever they explored the hills. Every brook was full of fish. They made pits where the land met high-water mark, and when the tide ebbed there were halibut in the pits. There was a great quantity of animals of all sorts in the woods. They were there a fortnight, enjoying themselves, without noticing anything further: they had their cattle with them.

And one morning early, as they looked about them, they saw nine

---

* These verses follow the Hauk's Book text, which is here less corrupt than the other according to Gathorne-Hardy.

skin canoes, on which staves were waved with a noise just like threshing, and they were waved with the sun. Then Karlsefni said, 'What is the meaning of this?'

Snorri answered him, 'Perhaps this is a sign of peace, so let us take a white shield and lift it in answer,' and they did so.

Then these men rowed to meet them, and, astonished at what they saw, they landed. They were *swarthy* men and ugly, with unkempt hair on their heads. They had large eyes and broad cheeks. They stayed there some time, showing surprise. Then they rowed away south past the cape.

Karlsefni and his men had made their camp above the lake, and some of the huts were near the mainland while others were near the lake. So they remained there that winter; no snow fell, and their cattle remained in the open, finding their own pasture.

But at the beginning of spring they saw one morning early a fleet of skin canoes rowing from the south past the cape, [as many as if the sea had been sowed with coal,] and on each boat there were staves waved. Karlsefni and his men raised their shields, and they began to trade: the (strange) people wanted particularly to buy red cloth, *in exchange for which they offered skins and grey furs.* They wished also to buy swords and spears, but Karlsefni and Snorri forbade this. *The savages got for a dark skin a span's length of red cloth, which they bound round their heads.* Thus things continued for awhile, but when the cloth began to give out they cut it into pieces so small that they were not much more than a finger's breadth. The savages gave as much for it as before, or more.

It happened that a bull belonging to Karlsefni's party ran out of the wood, and bellowed loudly: this terrified the savages and they ran out to their canoes, and rowed south along the coast, and there was nothing more seen of them for three consecutive weeks.

But when that time had elapsed they saw a great number of the boats of the savages coming from the south like a rushing torrent, and this time all the staves were waved widdershins, and all the savages yelled loudly.

Upon this Karlsefni's men took a red shield and raised it in answer. *The savages ran from their boats and* thereupon they met and fought; there was a heavy rain of missiles; the savages had war-slings too. Karlsefni and Snorri observed that the savages raised up on a pole a *very* large globe, *closely resembling a sheep's paunch,* and dark in colour, and it flew *from the pole* up on land over the party, and made a terrible noise where it came down.

Upon this a great fear came on Karlsefni and his party, so that they wished for nothing but to get away up stream, *for they thought that the savages were setting upon them from all sides, nor did they halt till they came* to some rocks where they made a determined resistance.

Freydis came out, and seeing Karlsefni's men retreating she cried out, 'Why are such fine fellows as you running away from these unworthy men, whom I thought you could have butchered like cattle? Now if I had a weapon it seems to me that I should fight better than any of you.'

They paid no attention to what she said. Freydis wished to follow them, but was rather slow because she was not well; yet she went after them into the wood, pursued by the savages. She found before her a dead man, Thorbrand Snorreson, with a flat stone standing in his head: his sword lay beside him. This she took up, and prepared to defend herself with it. Then the savages set upon her, but she drew out her breast from beneath her clothes and beat the sword upon it: with that the savages were afraid, and running back to their ships they withdrew. Karlsefni's men came up to her and praised her courage.

Two men of Karlsefni's force fell, but four* of the savages, although the former were outnumbered. So then they went back to their huts, *and bound their wounds*, and considered what that force could have been which set upon them from the land side: it now appeared to them that the attacking party consisted solely of those who came from the ships, and that the others must have been a delusion.

Moreover the savages found a dead man with an axe lying beside him. *One of them took up the axe and cut at a tree, and then each of the others did so, and they thought it a treasure and that it cut well. Afterwards* one of them cut at a stone, and the axe broke, whereupon he thought that it was useless, since it did not stand against the stone, and threw it down.

It now appeared to Karlsefni's party that though this country had good resources yet they would live in a perpetual state of warfare and alarm on account of the aborigines. So they prepared to depart, intending to return to their own country. They coasted northward, and found five savages in skins sleeping *by the sea*; these had with them receptacles in which was beast's marrow mixed with blood. They concluded that these men must have been sent from the country: they killed them.

Later on they discovered a promontory and a quantity of beasts: the promontory had the appearance of a cake of dung, because the beasts lay there in winter.† Now they came to Straumsfjord, where there was plenty of every kind.

Some men say that Bjarni and Freydis‡ stayed there with a hundred

---

* Hauk's Book has 'several'.
† Hauk's Book: 'at night'. ‡ Hauk's Book: 'Gudrid'.

men and went no further, while Karlsefni and Snorri went south with forty men, staying no longer at Hóp than a scant two months, and returning the same summer.

THORVALD'S VOYAGE*

Karlsefni went with one ship to look for Thorhall the Hunter, while the main body remained behind, and they travelled north past Keelness, and then bore along to the west of it, having the land on their port side. There there was nothing but desolate woods, with hardly any open places. And when they had sailed a long time, a river came down from the land from the east to the west: they entered the mouth of the river, and lay by its southern flank. It happened one morning that Karlsefni and his men saw before them on an open place a speck, which glittered before them and they shouted at it; it moved, and it was a uniped, which darted down to the bank of the river by which they lay. Thorvald, son of Eric the Red, was sitting by the rudder, and the uniped shot an arrow into his entrails. Thorvald drew out the arrow, crying, 'There is fat about my belly, we have reached a good country, though we are hardly allowed to enjoy it.'† Thorvald died of this wound soon afterwards. Then the uniped rushed away, and back northward. Karlsefni and his men pursued him, and saw him from time to time. The last they saw of him was that he ran towards a certain creek. Then Karlsefni and his men turned back. Thereupon a man sang this little ditty:

> Hear, Karlsefni, while I sing
> Of a true but wondrous thing,
> How thy crew all vainly sped,
> Following a uniped:
> Strange it was to see him bound
> Swiftly o'er the broken ground.

They considered that those mountains which were at Hóp and those which they now found were all one, and were therefore close opposite one another, and that the distance from Straumsfjord was the same in both directions.‡ They were at Straumsfjord the third winter.

* This text is from Hauk's Book. According to Gathorne-Hardy the companion text is badly confused.

† The dying speech ascribed here to Thorvald is evidently borrowed from that of Thormod Kolbrunarskald after the battle of Stiklestad, where the point is much more easy to grasp. Thorvald means that he has come to a land providing plenty of nourishment, otherwise he would not be fat.

‡ Following Hauk's text. Eric's Saga reads: 'They intended to explore all those mountains which were at Hóp, and those which they found.' It continues: 'they went back, and the third winter', &c.

At this time the men were much divided into parties, *which happened because of the women*, the unmarried men claiming the wives of those who were married, which gave rise to the greatest disorder. There Karlsefni's son, Snorri, was born the first autumn, *and he was three months old when they left.*

On sailing from Wineland they got a south wind, and came to Markland, where they found five savages, one of whom was bearded. There were two women and two children: Karlsefni's men caught the boys, but the others escaped, disappearing into the ground. But they kept the two boys with them, and taught them speech, and they were christened. They called their mother Vaetilldi and *their father* Uvaegi. They said that the savages' country was governed by kings, one of whom was called Avalldamon and the other Valldidida. They said that there were no houses there: people lived in dens or caves. They reported that another country lay on the other side, opposite to their own, where people lived who wore white clothes, and uttered loud cries, and carried poles, and went with flags. It is thought that this was Hvítramannaland, *or Ireland the Great.*

So then they came to Greenland, and stayed with Eric the Red for the winter.

It is further related that Bjarne Grimolfsson was swept into the Irish Sea, where his ship foundered; apparently there were no survivors. Karlsevne went to Norway, where he sold his Vinland wares at a good profit. The wood called 'masur' was bought by a German merchant for a high price. Torfinn Karlsevne and his wife won great honour, and settled in Iceland. After Karlsevne's death Gudrid went on pilgrimage to the south, and later entered a convent. Their son Snorre, who was born in Vinland, was the progenitor of a line of eminent Icelanders.

FREYDIS

(From the Greenland Saga)

Lastly, a few words about Freydis Eiriksdatter's voyage to Vinland, which is thought to have taken place shortly after Torfinn Karlsevne's return. The two Icelanders Helge and Finnboge had sailed from Norway to Greenland, and she persuaded them to join the expedition. She herself sailed in her own ship. We hear that the party arrived in Vinland and that she moved into Leiv Eiriksson's house there.

This account contains little of factual interest, though we hear something of how Freydis slew men and women from the Icelandic ship. A real Valkyrie.

*   *   *

We are thus dealing with four main accounts, each of which has something to tell us.

First there is Bjarne Herjolfsson's voyage, which pioneered the rest. His drifting ship came in sight of a new coastline. Bjarne did not land; he was no explorer but a strayed seaman who desired only to bring his vessel safely home to Greenland. This saga remains in a class by itself as the simplest and most factual, being, as Brøgger puts it, a ship's log.

Leiv Eiriksson's saga is mainly concerned with Vinland itself, but also gives interesting information about the voyage. We hear that his ship was manned by a crew of thirty-five, and that he aimed at reaching the place sighted by Bjarne. He arrived in Vinland and remained there for a year. The Greenland Saga's account of his voyage seems more reliable than the scrappy one in Eirik the Red's Saga, and it also includes the important astronomical data about *eyktarstaðr* (see pp. 160–63). Leiv Eiriksson remains the true discoverer of North America.

Torvald Eiriksson's voyage too seems genuine in its main features. He continued his brother Leiv's work and benefited by his experiences. Having arrived with a crew of thirty at Leivsbúdir in Vinland, he continued eastward, intending to settle, but encountered some of the natives – he was the first European to set eyes on them – and fell in battle against them. His expedition remained in Vinland for two years.

Torfinn Karlsevne's saga tells of a magnificent voyage that reminds us of Eirik the Red's settlement of Greenland. With three ships, one hundred and sixty people, livestock and gear, he crossed the sea and settled in Vinland. This was the name he gave to both a northerly region of harsh winters where he established his headquarters, and to areas farther south. Living conditions were good, but the native inhabitants numerous and fierce. After three years the enterprise was abandoned and the expedition returned to Greenland. Torfinn Karlsevne's detailed saga offers a wealth of interesting information. It is written in a strikingly matter-of-fact style and in all essentials bears the stamp of truth.

The sagas of the Vinland voyages were written down some two hundred years after the event, and are in fact popular tales that took on their traditional form in the course of repetition through the ages. It is easy enough to point out their shortcomings. These were only to be expected, for the subject was one that appealed strongly to the imagination.

The remarkable thing is that so much of these folk-tales tallies with the facts. The fabulous elements and exaggerations are surprisingly few, the style is sober – quite seamanlike at times – and a number of factual observations establish beyond a doubt that these people visited North America.

It was Gustav Storm[1] who pioneered the more recent research on Vinland. He made a reasoned assessment of the sundry items of factual information given in the sagas. They are of many kinds and relate to seafaring conditions, geography, astronomy, ethnography, botany, etc.

There is one aspect to which I feel too little attention has been paid, and that is the psychology of the characters. In evaluating the content of the Vinland sagas it is of particular importance to bear in mind that they originated with a race whose way of thinking was formed in bleak northern lands. How would people of this mentality react to a journey southward along the coast of North America? What kind of country would be preferred as a home by these men and women whose life and culture were fully adapted to Arctic or sub-Arctic regions?

REGIONS SIGHTED BY BJARNE

To which part of North America did these various expeditions go? First let us try to establish the regions sighted by Bjarne from the sea. Bjarne Herjolfsson's pioneer voyage gives us a clue, both because later seafarers seem to have followed his route in the reverse direction and because his story differs from the rest in its practical notes as to seas, winds, spread of sail, distances, etc. These observations enable us to identify, in broad outline, the regions he sighted. On the basis of this identification it should be possible to work out the approximate positions of Helluland and Markland. These names appear only in sagas relating to subsequent voyages.

Bjarne sailed from Iceland, and was bound for Herjolfsnes at the southern tip of Greenland, where his father lived. He encountered a northerly wind and fog, and was astray for several days. Then the sun came out and after a day's sailing he sighted a coast which 'had no mountains, but was wooded, with low ridges'. This corresponds perfectly with the north coast of Newfoundland, where in earlier times the forest must have extended to within a short distance of the sea.

Unwilling to land, Bjarne sailed on 'with his sheet to the coast'. This must mean that he went north, roughly parallel to the coast of Labrador. After two days and nights – against the current – they sighted 'a level, wooded land'. This must still have been Labrador, where incidentally the tree-line extends to about 57° N.

Bjarne still would not go ashore and they stood out to sea again, this time with a sou'westerly wind. They sailed for three days and nights, and sighted a new land. 'It was mountainous and lofty, and there were icefields.' Here, as Brøgger points out, we have no choice: we must go north to the southern part of Baffin Land to find country fitting this description. On the Cumberland Peninsula and in the Frobisher Bay region there are high mountains and great icefields which here and there come right down to the sea. Bjarne says that this land was unprofitable; and this too is consistent with the region.

They kept on their course and, after four days and nights of hard sailing, reached Herjolfsnes in south Greenland.

The periods of sailing noted here fit in well with the distances involved. A ship of those days could presumably travel 120 sea-miles in 24 hours (2 degrees of latitude): that is to say at an average speed of 5 knots. From Hamilton Inlet in south Labrador to the most southerly point of Hall Peninsula in Baffin Land is about 560 sea-miles: a distance that Bjarne might have covered in about five days and nights.*

How then do the relative nature and position of the lands that Bjarne sighted from sea (of which the positions are here approximately given) correspond to those regions of North America which were later known to Leiv Eiriksson, Torvald Eiriksson and Torfinn Karlsevne?

Helluland

It is important to remember that Bjarne's was the pioneer voyage that gave impetus to the rest. His successors in the field made use of his experiences and may have taken some of his men with them. Indeed, in Leiv Eiriksson's saga it is expressly stated that he began with the land that Bjarne Herjolfsson had seen last, which is to say south Baffin Land; and of this it is said that 'they saw no grass there, but great icefields, and all that lay between the sea and the icefields looked like one great slab.' The country seemed to offer no advantages. He called it Helluland (land of flat stones or slabs).

Torfinn Karlsevne first sailed from Eiriksfjord to Vesterbygd. Why did he sail so far north along the Greenland coast before crossing the Davis Strait? He may have had a number of reasons for this, the chief one being that the route by way of southern Baffin Land and thence southward along the coast of Labrador had become customary through earlier voyages. It was practical to take advantage of the current that ran northward along the Greenland coast, then to cross the Davis Strait at its narrowest and so catch the southward-running current off Labrador. Karlsevne may also have wanted to visit his wife Gudrid's farm at the inner end of Lysefjord, and perhaps engage men in Vesterbygd; for according to the saga many Norse Greenlanders sailed on that voyage.

From Vesterbygd Karlsevne sailed to Bjørnøy,† which we cannot locate, and then went south for two days, when he reached a land of *great rock slabs and many white foxes*. He called it Helluland. Karlsevne says nothing of the high mountains and the icefields, but circumstances indicate that he followed Leiv Eiriksson's route and reached the same part of Baffin Land.

* The word *døgr* is here, as hereafter, interpreted as meaning a day and a night: 24 hours. This has been disputed, and by some the word has been taken to mean 12 hours.

† We know from other sources that Disko Island was called Bjarney, but it is unlikely that he sailed so far north.

Markland

In Leiv Eiriksson's saga few details are given of the voyage southward from Helluland. We are told simply that he put to sea and found the other land (already sighted by Bjarne). *This land was flat and wooded, with stretches of white sand wherever they looked and no steep shores.* Leiv called this country Markland, i.e. forest land.

Torfinn Karlsevne's expedition sailed for two days after leaving Helluland, with a northerly wind, and reached a land of *great forests and many animals* which they named Markland. Of special interest in this saga are the notes about the Furdur Strands – those long beaches that took so long to pass – and about Keel Ness (Kjølnesset). The indications are that these landmarks may be identified respectively as the stretch of coast a little to the south of Hamilton Inlet, and Porcupine Point, Labrador. We will consider this in more detail later.

Whether the landfall of Leiv Eiriksson and Torfinn Karlsevne were identical, and whether their expeditions arrived exactly at those places sighted by Bjarne Herjolfsson, is uncertain; in any case it seems likely that both accounts allude to the wooded country on the east coast of Labrador.

The land was named after its nature, says the saga, and it is significant that its name tells of forest and not of pasture. This is consistent with the Labrador coast, which is ill suited to stock-raising. Cold winds blow in off the drift-ice, and the fjords are not open until the middle of June.

In Torfinn Karlsevne's saga we hear of an encounter with Skraelings (Eskimoes?), and two boys are taken back to Greenland.

There were many animals in Markland, says the saga, and that too is true of Labrador. The explorers may have been particularly impressed by the herds of reindeer, which at that time must have been numerous. In addition there were salmon in the rivers and cod in the sea, as well as seal, whale and many fur-bearing animals.

This wealth of game in Markland must have meant a great deal to the Norse Greenlanders, for through subsequent ages they might have sailed there many times. People in Greenland needed timber too, especially for shipbuilding – the driftwood from Siberia was insufficient and of inferior quality – and their own woodland consisted merely of scattered patches of dwarf birch. In many parts of Labrador there are tall spruce firs, Scotch firs, larches, birches, etc., and it must have been a revelation for the Norse Greenlanders to come upon such a wealth of standing timber.

It appears that Markland was known for a long time after the Vinland voyages, which indicates that these were factual. Their tradition endured. Here I will merely mention that the name Markland appears in connection with the storm-driven Greenland ship of 1347, which arrived at Iceland and Norway. Again, Bjørn Jónsson speaks of 'the Markland bottoms' (i.e., the inner ends of the fjords). We shall go into this in more detail when we discuss the Norsemen's later voyages to North America.

The conclusions we draw from the foregoing are therefore these: Helluland corresponds to the glacier-covered mountain region of south Baffin Land. Markland is Labrador, and where forest is mentioned, the reference must be to the areas south of 57° N.

XVI WHY VINLAND?

BEFORE attempting to locate Vinland we must be clear as to the meaning of its name. The commonest notion is that it refers to grapes and wine, and this restricts us to those places in North America where there are vines.

The northern boundary for wild grapes lies near the coast at about 44° N. Inland we find them growing farther north. If the commonly accepted meaning of the name is the right one, neither Newfoundland, Nova Scotia nor other northerly regions can be identified with Vinland, unless the climate there was very different from what it is today. But should the name bear a different significance the field is greatly extended, and certain statements in the saga present themselves in a new light. In other words we are faced with an important question of interpretation: What is meant by Vinland the Good?

The Norse Greenlanders and Icelanders were above all practical men, and they came from bleak lands where they had to toil hard for their food. Their main livelihood derived from stock-raising, hunting and fishing. The products of their livestock – meat, milk and wool – were basic. When therefore they arrived in new territory where they thought of settling, it was no more than natural that they should give it a name embodying some essential information as to the possibilities of existing there.

As V. Tanner[1] points out, this would be consistent with other names given by the same race to new lands: Greenland, for example – the green land that gave promise of good pasture; Helluland – a place with stone *heller*, or rock slabs, denoting a barren place; Markland – the land of forests. Leiv Eiriksson's saga expresses this principle in saying: 'We will give this land a name that accords with its condition [nature], and call it Markland.'

Yet these names, besides being enlightening, are also sonorous: in the name Greenland there is poetry. They were a strange race, these Norsemen: tough fighters and toilers, but deeply imbued with a sense of the value of words and their imaginative evocation. Even some of their laws are lyrical.

If we study the text of the Vinland sagas, we find a few small but important indications to which Tanner draws our attention. They show how concerned people were to seek out the possibilities for grazing in the new land. Of

WHY VINLAND?

Helluland Leiv Eiriksson's saga says: '*But they saw no grass there.*' Torfinn Karlsevne's saga says of Vinland: '*There was much grass.*' I would like to add the beautiful words about Leiv Eiriksson's Vinland which illustrates the profound pleasure felt by these men of the North at the sight of this fertile ground:

'Here they went up and looked about them in good weather. They found dew upon the grass, and now and again they plunged their hands in the dew and put them to their mouths, and it seemed to them that they had never known such sweetness.'

Their joy was understandable. Anyone who has roamed Greenland in search of Norse ruins knows that he must begin by looking for scattered patches of grass among stones and barren ridges.

The question then arises as to whether Leiv Eiriksson and those who followed him actually found grapes, and whether they knew anything about such things. And was this discovery striking enough for them to name the new country accordingly, and so break with the tradition of using a practical name corresponding to the resources available?

The sagas declare that many of the Vinland voyagers found grapes, but the accounts of such discoveries are often of a fable-like nature. We should bear in mind that the wild grapes of North America are small and sometimes sour, and that there are quantities of other berries which are at least as delicious and of which wine can be made. Certain kinds would have been strange to the Vinland voyagers, such as for instance squash-berries (*Viburnum Pauciflorum*), red gooseberries and currants, which among others are plentiful in northern Newfoundland.

It is difficult to say whether the Norsemen who sailed to North America, and of whom a large number were Greenlanders, had ever seen grapes. The most we can assume is that they had heard of them.

Thus we cannot altogether ignore the possibility that the 'wine berries' of the sagas may denote fruit other than grapes. Nevertheless the core of the matter seems clear: the voyagers to Vinland found berries of which wine was made. This is made plain by Torhall Veidemann's ballad: he was expecting to drink wine – no doubt because during earlier Vinland expeditions wine had been made.

If, on the other hand, Leiv Eiriksson's and the other expeditions did find grapes, it can only have been on long journeys south of headquarters. Evaluation of the statements in the various sagas leads to this conclusion, and it is significant that many of the sixteenth-century expeditions, which re-discovered regions likely to have been visited by the Vinland-voyagers, record the discovery of wild grapes.

From the travellers' point of view, then, the discovery of wild grapes was interesting: something to tell of when they returned home. Yet it is not easy to understand how such a discovery could have overshadowed the vital fact that in this new country they found richer pasture than almost any of them had ever seen before. It was a place to live in. It seems, therefore, that they intended the name to convey the entirely new potentialities offered here for stock-raising – one of their chief means of livelihood; to make it clear to everyone, in other words, that in this country there were excellent prospects for any who wanted to emigrate and take their animals with them.

In considering the connotation of the name Vinland we are struck by reference in the saga to a *northern Vinland* where grapes did not grow, but where the grazing may have been good. In the account of Torfinn Karlsevne's journey for instance, we hear of the headquarters at Straumfjord, where winters were harsh, and of other circumstances also, indicating that the people had settled in a northerly region. Torhall Veidemann complains bitterly in his song that not a drop of wine touched his tongue, although it had been promised him. At last he sails away. Yet in Torfinn Karlsevne's saga this same place where no grapes grew is called Vinland. When he left Straumfjord for Greenland he is described as having 'sailed from Vinland'. Note also that the account of Leiv Eiriksson does not suggest that the discovery of grapes had anything to do with the name: 'Leiv named the country after its qualities (*eptir landkostum*), and called it Vinland.'

Concerning the etymology of the name Vinland, the late Swedish philologist Sven Söderberg[2] has put forward the opinion that *vin* in this connection has nothing to do with wine, but is the ancient Norse word for pasture.

Vin,[3] plural *Vinjar*, goes back to prehistoric times and was in common use in the North. In many cases *vin* stands alone, as in Vinja, and that is probably the oldest form. Elsewhere it appears in combination with other names, sometimes as a prefix, e.g. Vinas, but most often as a suffix as in Bjørgvin. Originally the word most likely denoted the name of a place: a region of natural grazing-land, a good place to settle in with one's livestock. In time *vin* became part of a farm-name.

It was objected that the name *vin* had become obsolete before the days of the Vikings, but Söderberg, studying it against its etymological background, believed that *vin* in the sense of pastureland must have been known to the Greenlanders and Icelanders in about the year 1000: that is, at the time of the Vinland voyages.

This is consistent with the conclusions reached by Magnus Olsen[4] in his research into names in the Shetland Islands, which were peopled by Norwegians in the ninth century. Olsen points out a number of place-names formed with *vin*, where this is most often a prefix. To him this indicates that *vin*-names continued to be used in the formation of Norwegian place-names, and that there is no reason to set a time-limit for the latest use of this word.

WHY VINLAND?

Vin-names are not found in the Faroes or Iceland. Söderberg thought that Iceland was lacking in areas corresponding to the geographical concept expressed by this word, but that this was not to say that the word itself was obsolete.

Only one source suggests that the name Vinland refers to grapes and wine, and that is Adam of Bremen's *Descriptio*,[5] dating from the 1070s. Here, in Latin, it is stated:

> He spoke also of another island which many have found in this great ocean and which is called Vinland because grapes grow wild there and yield the best wine. There is also abundance of unsown corn, as we know not from hearsay only but from the sure report of the Danes ... Beyond this isle, he says, there is no habitable land in this ocean; all that lies beyond is full of formidable ice and impenetrable fog ...

Söderberg believes that Adam of Bremen heard the name Vinland in Denmark, at the court of Svein Estridsson, but was unaware that it might also denote pasture. He therefore invented what was to him the most probable explanation, though it was incorrect. Söderberg points out other similar errors in the text, such as that Greenland was so named because its inhabitants had bluish-green faces. Indeed he goes further, and concludes that the Icelandic saga-writers derived their knowledge of the grapes and self-sown wheat exclusively from Adam of Bremen; consequently their statements concerning these things bear no relation to the facts. This view is held also by Fridtjof Nansen and V. Tanner.

Söderberg is probably right in saying that Adam of Bremen misunderstood the meaning of Vinland, but this does not necessarily imply that everything he says about grapes is pure imagination. On the contrary, it is natural to suppose that it was just because he *had* heard of the discovery of grapes or the making of wine in the new country, that Adam misinterpreted the name. And although the discovery may not have been important enough to earn the country its name, there was yet something about these wild grapes that fired the imagination and, together with Skraelings and so forth, made up a vivid picture of the voyage. No doubt many marvels connected with the great expedition to the unknown land were recounted at Svein Estridsson's court. The events were still fresh in men's memories, for they had taken place no more than a generation earlier.

The story of the grapes or wine must have made an impression on Adam of Bremen, a South German who came from a wine-growing country, and it was natural that he should have associated it with the Norse name Vinland. Being a foreigner, he could not be expected to know that it bore any other meaning. Nevertheless it is startling to hear him declare that beyond this island there was only fog and ice, and no place for men to live in; it may indicate that the voyagers arrived at some northerly island and that the berries of which they made wine were something other than grapes.

Lastly it should be mentioned that there is not a single passage in any of the other texts – including all the Icelandic ones – indicating that the name Vinland has reference to grapes or wine. The saga says, as we saw, merely that the land was named after its possibilities; and this interpretation seems to have been a permanent tradition that survived in Iceland for quite a long time. Legend B of the Skálholt map, dating from 1590,[6] states: 'Here lies Vinland which by reason of the fertility of the soil and other useful things has been called Vinland the Good.' The fertility of the soil: good pasture where Norsemen could settle with their livestock. That was the first essential.

XVII WHERE WAS VINLAND?

North Vinland

WE come now to the most important and most difficult question of all: where was Vinland? Opinions have been divided on this point, and the location of Vinland has been identified with widely varying places over an area extending from Florida to Hudson's Bay, yet up to now no trace of the Norse discoverers has been found.

They sailed as we have seen, from Greenland across the Davis Strait first to Helluland (Land of Flat Stones), probably Baffin Land, then south to Markland (Woodland), probably Labrador. The last stage was the voyage to the third land: Vinland.

The Leiv Eiriksson account describes the country he came to in Markland as flat and wooded, and says that for as far as the eye could see there were long beaches of white sand and no cliffs. From there he sailed with a north-easterly wind, and after two days and nights sighted land. He went ashore on an island, then sailed on between the island and a northward-pointing promontory, and into a bay where a river ran out. Here the sea-bed was so shoal that their vessel grounded. At high water they took the ship upstream and into a lake, and found good country with plentiful grass and, in the rivers, bigger salmon than those of Greenland. Leiv called this land Vinland, and here he and his thirty-five companions built 'big houses'.

Torfinn Karlsevne too sailed from a place in Markland where there were long beaches, which he named Furdurstrandir because it took so long to sail past them. There was also a cape which he called Kjølness (Keel Ness). Continuing his way south he came to Straumøy and Straumfjord, where he dug in for the winter with a following of about a hundred and sixty men and women, besides livestock. It was good country, with abundant pasture and other vegetation, and the saga gives it the name of Vinland. The following year Karlsevne left this base and sailed far south to another region (Hóp) where he remained for some time.

How much importance should we attach to the alleged sailing-time of two days and nights from Markland to Vinland?

It is reasonable to suppose that seafaring folk would in the main hand down an accurate tradition in all that concerned ships and the sea; and the time taken to reach a new and remarkable country which many Norsemen had visited was a matter of great importance. It would be strange if later generations of Greenlanders and Icelanders, who preserved so much factual information about the Vinland voyages, had no clear notion of this most vital point: the number of days – weeks? – needed to sail from Greenland to Vinland. Did it take longer than from Greenland to Iceland or to any other known place? From the very beginning the answer must have been on the tip of the tongue of everyone concerned in these notable voyages to an entirely new land. Errors or obscure passages may occur in the manuscripts, but it is worth noting that sailing-times are given in figures; so we have reason to believe that the times given for the run from Greenland to Markland, and from Markland to Vinland (two days and nights), are in the main correct.

But Markland – Labrador – has a long coastline, and it would be a great help in locating Vinland if we could determine the area in Labrador which formed the voyagers' starting-point for the two days and nights of sailing mentioned in the saga. As we saw, the account of both Leiv's and Karlsevne's journey describes that area as having unusually long, white beaches, and in the Karlsevne narrative we also hear of Keel Ness. It is more than probable that the Canadian W. A. Munn and the eminent Finnish researcher, V. Tanner, are right in identifying these features with the long beaches and Cape Porcupine, south of Hamilton Inlet. No other such beaches exist in Labrador; there are practically no offshore islands, so seafarers would have been bound to notice those white sands. They form one of the few really good landmarks along the indented coast of Labrador. And the remarkable Cape Porcupine has the shape of a keel.

Here, then, is one starting-point, and the question now is where Vinland could be if it took forty-eight hours to get there from the long beaches. There are only two possibilities: the southern part of Labrador or the north coast of Newfoundland. For a number of reasons the latter is the more likely location.

The distance from Cape Porcupine to this coast is about 200 nautical miles. A Viking ship could average something like 5 miles an hour, or 120 in 24 hours; that is to say, she would take approximately two days and nights to cover the whole distance. On this point saga and fact are in striking agreement.

A vessel heading south along the coasts of Labrador would naturally make for the north coast of Newfoundland which, with the well-defined seamark of Belle Isle, would be visible from a great distance, and dead ahead. It projects like an arm into the sea, so that the seafarers could hardly fail to find it.

It is also interesting to note that the saga is geographically correct in alluding to a 'third land', meaning surely a land separate from the others. This is consistent with the position of Newfoundland in relation to Baffin Land and Labrador.

An important factor is that on the north coast of Newfoundland there is good pasture, whereas in south Labrador grass is scanty. It is also worth noting that Bjarne's description of the first land he came to – afterwards Leiv's third (he was sailing in the reverse direction) – mentions a striking characteristic of the north coast of Newfoundland: 'the country was without mountains, wooded, and with low hills'.

In connection with Torfinn Karlsevne the saga does not mention the sailing-time from the long beaches in Markland to Straumfjord, where he wintered, but it seems clear that he cannot have sailed so very far, and Karlsevne's Vinland may be identical with Leiv's. Moreover the Greenland saga states that Karlsevne moved into Leiv's house.

The question is, then, whether other descriptions in the sagas or other sources point to a northerly location of Vinland. The narrative about Leiv Eiriksson is little more than a brief outline. In it we hear of the discovery of grapes, but the description smacks so much of a fable as to suggest that popular imagination went to work on it in later times. It is said, for example, that men cut vines and loaded them on the ships and that a man became drunk by eating grapes. It is true that Leiv made exploring expeditions from his headquarters, and if he really did find grapes it may have been when he went south in his swift ship, which could probably reach a speed of ten knots. The solar observations mentioned in the account may also have been made on such expeditions. The description is so difficult to interpret and, as will be seen, has been interpreted in so many different ways, that little can be deduced from it with certainty.

The further statement that there was no frost in winter, that the grass never withered and that the stock might not need any winter forage is certainly an exaggeration; one would have to go a quite disproportionate distance south to find such conditions. Yet the story may be founded on fact, and should perhaps be considered in relation to the great hardiness of the Greenland livestock. There was nothing new about certain animals doing without winter forage, but this applied solely to sheep and horses, which in Greenland remained in the open all the year round. The remarkable thing about the new country must have been that here cattle could do the same. These tough little beasts were probably able to survive out of doors in a milder climate, even if there were some frost and snow, and this so much impressed the Vinland voyagers that in course of time the plain facts were embroidered into travellers' tales. We may note that the coastal areas in question lie considerably to the north of the wild-grape region, and that from time to time very mild and almost snowless winters occur here, when cattle could be left out for much of the season. Thus on this point the saga may well refer to a northerly region.

The story of Torfinn Karlsevne is not only longer but is also more detailed.

It is true that we find in it a fanciful account of grapes brought back from the wilderness by those remarkable runners Hake and Hekja; yet on the other hand in Torhall Veidemann's *kvad* or lay there is a more convincing statement to the effect that he never tasted a single drop of wine. It is, however, of importance that this *kvad* does not state that the wine was made of grapes. In northern countries like Newfoundland there are different kinds of berries such as squash-berries, currants, gooseberries, etc., of which excellent wine could be made. The description of Karlsevne's headquarters at Straumfjord also gives us a strong impression that it was located in a northerly area where winter conditions were very hard. It is interesting that it should have been named Vinland (Wineland) despite the fact that no grapes can have grown there. This is consistent with what I said before about the name Vinland referring not to grapes but to grass (good grazing grounds for cattle).

In addition we have another entirely independent historical source which suggests that the distance from Markland to Vinland was short, and that the latter must have been in northern parts. It is, as mentioned (page 121), a cosmography of ancient origin, and in it we read: '... South of Greenland lies Helluland, and next to that Markland, whence it is not far to Vinland the Good.' Later I shall speak of Sigurður Stefánson's remarkable map which also indicates that an Icelandic tradition of a northerly Vinland persisted through the ages.

In estimating how far south the Vinland voyagers sailed on their first journey, we have to take certain practical considerations into account. By reason of the ice in the Labrador current they could not have sailed before the end of July or beginning of August, assuming the climatic conditions to have approximated to those of today. Next, they would have been compelled to seek winter quarters in the new land in time to allow important preparations to be made before the cold weather set in: house-building, hunting, fishing, the storing of winter provisions and the exploration of the country.

It follows that they would not have delayed in making camp once they had found a favourable winter-site.

Another important aspect is that northerners would choose surroundings suited to their own particular culture-pattern: that of stock-raising, hunting, fishing and so on. They were 'north-minded'; why then should they not end their voyage and build their base-camp in a place like north Newfoundland, where local conditions were not only similar to those they were accustomed to, but in many ways far more favourable? We find a parallel to this in our own day: Scandinavians who emigrated to North America went for choice to northerly states such as Minnesota, Dakota, Washington and Alaska, and to Canada.

What must have made the strongest impression on the newcomers was the pasture and forest land. By modern standards Newfoundland is not particularly good farming country, but its impact on people from Arctic regions a thousand years ago would have been very different. In 1956 it had over 2,000 farms, about 13,500 head of cattle and something like 80,000 sheep. The grazing was far richer than that of Greenland. The people of the Codroy Valley to the south-west live mainly by agriculture, and that beautiful countryside of woods and mountains is very reminiscent of Norway.

For the Norse Greenlanders, coming from an Arctic country, these forests must have represented great riches. Today about 64,750 square kilometres of the country are forest land, and there are two paper-mills. Even a man of the south like Cortereal was impressed by these forests when in 1501 he sailed along the east coast of Newfoundland. He describes them as huge and endless, and mentions magnificent Scotch pines, suited to masts for the largest ships. His name for the country is also significant: Terra Verde, the green land.

Newfoundland was also rich in fish and game, and what is perhaps the world's largest concentration of cod is to be found here, while salmon run up the rivers – a larger variety than that of Greenland, as is noted in the saga. Along the coasts were whale and an abundance of seal, and some way north of the country the Greenland seal has one of its great breeding-grounds. In earlier times walrus came right into the Gulf of St Lawrence, and polar bears were found farther south than today. Of the land animals the reindeer must have been of the greatest importance; thousands of them migrated southward in winter and northward to the coast in the mild seasons. There were also furred animals and great quantities of birds.

Thus a number of circumstances suggest that the Vinland voyagers settled in Newfoundland, probably along the north coast, and that they called the place Vinland.*

The identification of Vinland with the north coast of Newfoundland also provides an answer to the question that arises when one reads the sagas: how was it possible for the different Vinland expeditions to find a particular little spot on the far-flung coasts of North America, where there are such vast numbers of fjords and such an infinity of islands that even today local people have been known to lose their way? We learn that at least three expeditions reached Leiv's houses in Vinland, and that Leiv was unwilling to sell the buildings to Karlsevne but was willing to lend them to him. It is clear that he regarded them as part of his estate and knew that others could find their way to them without any great difficulty; it is also a striking fact that Leiv set his course correctly for the countries that Bjarne had seen from the sea.

* A few researchers, including W. A. Munn and V. Tanner, have formed the same opinion.

One would think that the sailing-instructions and geographical descriptions in the sagas were too meagre to be of practical use in locating one particular place on that mighty, broken coastline. But here, as so often, the saga is justified. Having crossed the Davis Strait and reached Baffin Land, the Vinland voyagers would have no difficulty in making Vinland, so long as they observed a few simple directions. First the lofty mountains of north Labrador provided a clear sea-mark, after which the travellers had only to follow the Labrador coast southward until they raised the north coast of Newfoundland dead ahead. This coast has only a limited number of fjords, and it would not have been too difficult to locate a particular landmark or grazing area along it.

Leiv Eiriksson might sit in his hall in Greenland and, in about as few words as the saga, give sailing-directions precluding any error.

Lastly we may mention that Cortereal, during his voyage along the east coasts of Newfoundland in 1500, was presented by the natives with a broken sword inlaid with gold; he also noted that one of the native children wore two pieces of silver in its ears. The provenance of these things is unknown.

Now for Sigurður Stefánson's ancient map. Sigurður Stefánson was rector at the Latin School of Skálholt in Iceland and drew the map in about 1590. The original is lost, but we have a copy drawn by Bishop Tord Torlaksson in 1670 (see map). According to this, Vinland may be identified with northern Newfoundland. It is true that the Strait of Belle Isle is described as a fjord, but we need attach little importance to this, knowing as we do that it was some time after Cabot's re-discovery of the country that this so-called fjord was found to be a strait.

Most researchers have been unwilling to accept this map as a source of any value, believing it to have been based on statements in the sagas and so on. The well-known authority on Vinland, G. M. Gathorne-Hardy, maintains on the contrary that no other known map of that day gives so realistic a picture of the North American lands. Carl Sølver,[1] who is of the same opinion, has redrawn the map so as to preserve the correct relation between longitude and latitude according to Mercator's system. In doing so he made the distance from Herjolfsnes (one of the most southerly of the old Norse farmsteads in Greenland) to Promontorium Winlandiae (Cape Bauld) 640 nautical miles on a course of S. 50° W. Modern charts give distance and course for the same stretch as 622 nautical miles and S. 40° W: a strikingly consistent result.

Another map, drawn by Hans Poulson Resen in 1605, has much in common with the Skálholt map. It has been thought that Resen's was a copy of the latter, but this is unlikely. The text on Resen's map expressly states that the work is based on a map some hundreds of years old (*ex antiqua quadam*

Sigurður Stefánson's map, 1590

mappa, rudi modo delineata ante aliquot centenos annos ...). It would be strange if the cartographer had so expressed himself if he had copied a contemporary map drawn only fifteen years before. Probably both maps are based on a single old source. But they also share a characteristic emphasizing their reliability, which is that the two Greenland settlements have been correctly located on the west coast. It was known that Vesterbygd lay there, but for a long time Austerbygd was thought to be on the east coast. Expeditions were even sent there to find it. The map therefore was true to the original source.

These maps raise fascinating problems, but they show that in any case there was a tradition among the people of Iceland that Vinland lay considerably farther north than is commonly assumed: probably in the most northerly part of Newfoundland.

This tallies with what is stated in the sagas and old geographies, and with other known facts.

I will not attempt to pinpoint the position of North Vinland in northern Newfoundland. The sagas give a certain amount of geographical information

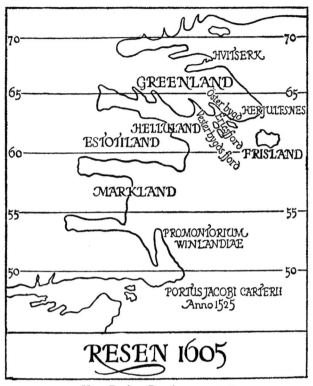

Hans Poulson Resen's map, 1605

which up to a point may be of help, but it would be a mistake to be altogether bound by it. Only by a systematic examination of the ground may one hope to locate the exact situation of North Vinland where Norsemen built their homes.

South Vinland

It is likely, as has been shown, that the headquarters of both Leiv Eiriksson and Torfinn Karlsevne were situated in some northerly region, probably north Newfoundland. On the other hand we have strong reason to believe that both they and Torvald went on voyages of exploration to the south, to a warmer land: south Vinland.

In the account of Leiv Eiriksson's journey (the Greenland saga) we find a remarkable astronomical observation in connection with Vinland: There were more equinoctial days than in Greenland or Iceland, and the sun had *eyktarstaðr* and *dagmálastaðr* on the shortest day. That is to say, in Gathorne-Hardy's translation: 'on the shortest day the sun was up over the (Icelandic) marks for both nones and breakfast time.'

160

Few experts doubt the reliability of this statement, which must be based on observations made during the Vinland voyage. It has been interpreted in varying ways through the years. Gustav Storm and H. Gelmeyden declared that *eyktarstaðr* was a point on the horizon from which a bearing could be taken. But where was this point? If that were known, an astronomical calculation would establish the latitude.

For this, help was to be found in the customs of Norwegian farmers, and especially in two documentary sources. In *Grágás*, the Icelandic law-book, we read: 'It is *eykt* when the *utsudrs aett* [south-west quarter of the heavens] is divided into three parts and the sun has passed through two of them.' Snorre's *Edda* states: 'Autumn lasts from the autumn equinox until the sun sets at *eyktarstaðr*.'

Storm and Gelmeyden concluded that *utsudrs aett* was the term denoting *eyktarstaðr* 52° 30' west of south. From this an astronomical calculation placed Vinland at 59° 55', which is to say on a level with Newfoundland (St Paul–White Bay).

Other researchers came to the following conclusions:

M. Wormskiold: 49° N.	L. M. Turner: 48° 57' N.
C. Rafn and Finn Magnussen: 41° 24' 10" N.	E. Tengstrøm: about 31° N.
T. Bugge: 41° 22'	H. R. Holand: about 42° N.

The late M. M. Mjelde of Norway tackled the problem in a new way, and the results he arrived at are set forth in an excellent work by Almar Næss.* Here *utsudrs aett* is interpreted as covering the whole of the south-west quadrant, two-thirds of which was 60°, the point of *eyktarstaðr*. Astronomical calculation on this basis placed Vinland at about 36° 54' N., which is to say in the area of Chesapeake Bay, Virginia.

This reckoning may be based on a true appreciation of the problem, but we have to bear in mind that Leiv's methods of navigation were primitive, so there was always a likelihood of inaccuracy. A moderate unevenness of the horizon-line is enough to bring about a variation of several degrees in the calculation of latitude: an error which could take us from the coast of Virginia to Massachusetts.

The conclusions arrived at by various authorities, then, differ widely, and comprise locations from Labrador to Virginia. At the same time we should remember that Leiv aboard his swift-sailing ship may have gone quite far south during his expeditions from his base in north Newfoundland. Moreover it is natural to assume that the leader of such expeditions would be sure to stress the most distant point reached in unknown country. We find a parallel in the account of the priests in Greenland, who journeyed northward from Austerbygd, far into the unknown. Here too we are given a solar

* *Hvor lå Vinland?* (Oslo, 1954).

observation which was apparently taken at the farthest point reached by the expedition.

Of Torfinn Karlsevne it is expressly stated that in the second year he headed south from the Straumfjord base, and 'sailed far'. His party came to a place (Hóp) where a river ran out, first into a lake and thence into the sea, where there were long shallows. At high water they sailed their ship up into the lake, and built their houses there.

We find a similar description in Leiv Eiriksson's saga in connection with the place where he set up his headquarters and which was presumably in north Newfoundland. There is much to suggest that one saga borrowed this passage from the other, and one is tempted to believe that the original text is the one in the narrative of Karlsevne's voyage to the south.

The description of the landing and the lake seems convincing: this was the kind of thing that seamen would remember. On the basis of this and of our knowledge of Viking ships, including the Gokstad ship, Henry Berg[2] has calculated that the difference between high and low tide must have been at least 7 ft. 6 in., to correspond with the account given in the saga. A chart of the tides along the outer coast between Newfoundland and Florida shows that the only area where such tides occur lies between Cape Cod and the Bay of Fundy to the north, where the difference between high and low water is the greatest in the world: up to 45 ft.

On their southward expedition, Karlsevne and his men are said to have found wild grapes. This should mean that they went south of Portland, for on the coast the northern limit for vines is about latitude 44° N.

We also hear of wild wheat. Could this be sandwort (*Elymus arenarius*)? It grows, as we have seen, in Greenland, Iceland and Norway, and was used for food in olden days. Another theory is that it was maize (or Indian corn), which grows as far north as 44° N. It is worth noting that later explorers such as Cartier mention having seen stretches of 'wild wheat'. Identification of this 'wheat' is not easy.

Can the voyagers' encounter with the natives – the Skraelings – help us to locate south Vinland? The Leiv Eiriksson account says nothing of any native inhabitants. Torvald was the first man to meet them, on his way from base. Fighting broke out and he was killed. In the Greenland saga we hear that Torfinn Karlsevne met the natives at Leivsbuder, where he first traded with them and then fought them. In Eirik's Saga it is told that this happened at 'Hóp' during his long voyage south of his headquarters at Straumfjord. He met a few on the return journey to Straumfjord, and also on the way back to Greenland; this last occasion must have been in Markland (Labrador).

Indians or Eskimoes? We know nothing definite about the distribution of Eskimoes in the eleventh century, but they are unlikely to have gone farther south than the seal, which means that their southern limit probably lay along the north coast of the Gulf of St Lawrence and the coast of Newfoundland.

In some areas, then as now, Eskimoes and Indians were neighbours. Beotuc Indians and Dorset Eskimoes were probably contemporaries in Newfoundland, and conditions were similar in Labrador. There were occasional clashes between them, but there must surely have been periods of peace, when they traded and feasted together, and intermarried.

In such border areas it would have been hard for anyone without good knowledge to distinguish between the two races; and the Norsemen, who had as yet met no Eskimoes in Greenland, probably failed to do so.

In connection with the Skraelings whom Karlsevne met on his northward voyage, the saga tells us that they had vessels containing animal marrow and blood. This does not help to identify their race, but is interesting in that it bears the stamp of truth. I myself have seen such food both among Canadian Indians and the Eskimoes of north Alaska, and it was probably eaten elsewhere by natives in North America.

There are indications that Karlsevne's natives in south Vinland were Indians. The saga relates that in the battle they used a catapult: a big black ball on a staff. It was hurled against the enemy and made a dreadful noise on landing. H. R. Schoolcraft tells us the interesting fact that a similar weapon is known by tradition to the Algonquin Indians.

In general we may say that the saga-passages relating to the natives furnish important evidence of Norse landings on the coasts of North America. The Vinland voyagers must have met with both Eskimoes and Indians, the latter being encountered quite a long way south during Karlsevne's journey; but where Norsemen and natives made contact is unknown.

All these clues taken together suggest a North American location for south Vinland, though they do not help us to pinpoint it more exactly. I shall now deal with material of a different kind which seems to provide us with fresh data.

At Vesterbygd in Greenland there was a large farmstead at the head of Ameralikfjord (Lysefjord), which must have been the Sandnes of the saga (see map on page 120). Beside the homestead stood a church. It was apparently here that Eirik the Red's son Torstein lived, with his wife Gudrid. As has been noted, she afterwards married Torfinn Karlsevne, the great Vinland voyager, and he then became joint owner of Sandnes.

In 1930 the homestead was excavated by Poul Nørlund in co-operation with Aage Roussell, and the latter has produced some interesting material. In one of the living-rooms of the dwelling, at a low level under the floor, an extraordinary find was made: a lump of coal. Roussell adds that on the Sandnes hearth only wood-ash was found, and that coal-ash has never been

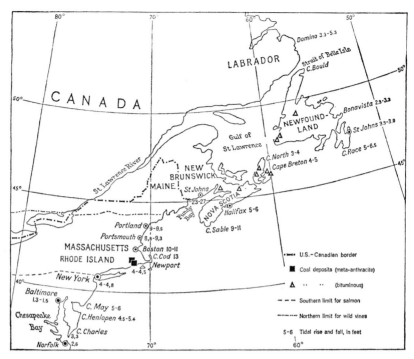

Map showing approximate limits of wild vine country (northerly) and of salmon (southerly);
also coal-deposits

discovered in any Norse ruins in Greenland. He abstained from offering any explanation,[3] and took no further steps in the matter.

It is strange enough that this lump of coal should have been found in a Norse house in Greenland, and at a low level, but the oddest thing about it is that it is anthracite. Roussell states: 'And from a deep layer in this room we found a lump of coal (No. S. 657) which according to Professor Bøggild's kind communication is anthracite, and therefore could not have been mined in North Greenland's coal-seams, which are nothing but lignite ... '

Where did this lump of coal come from? In Europe there are scattered concentrations of anthracite, but it is unlikely that this piece originated there. In the countries that were in communication with Greenland (Iceland and Norway) there is no anthracite. Moreover the coal was found in a deep layer of the house-site, and is probably contemporary with the early period of colonization. The most reasonable explanation must be that this coal – found in the house belonging to Torfinn Karlsevne, the explorer of America – was brought to Sandnes from North America.

A pronouncement by such an authority as the late Professor Bøggild

164

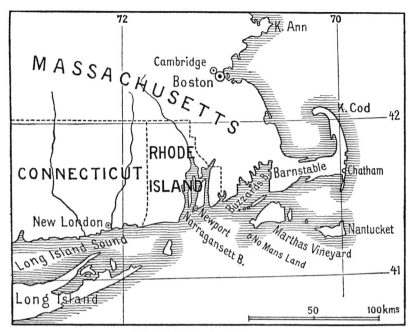

Rhode Island and adjoining areas

would suffice in itself, but in view of the comprehensive geological research that has been going on in Greenland in recent years I submitted the matter to another Danish geologist, Professor Alfred Rosenkrantz at Copenhagen University. He kindly informed me that he knew nothing of any anthracite having been found in any part of Greenland. Having touched on the possibility that when in contact with veins of basalt normal coal-strata may be transformed into anthracite, he concluded: 'For the present, however, I think it more probable that the northerners brought it back from their voyages to America.'

Nevertheless, despite the existence of anthracite in North America, the decisive question remains: does it occur near enough to the coast and in such places as to be readily come upon by the Vinland travellers?

I referred the matter to John F. Caley, director of the Fuels and Stratigraphic Geology Division of Canada, and he has been kind enough to give me the necessary information. He indicates the coal deposits along the east coast of North America, describing the nature of the coal in each case (see map on page 164). From this it appears that anthracite occurs in only two places, both on Rhode Island. Caley states that the deposit is meta-anthracite. It is very hard, but because of 'its high ash and moisture content it breaks down easily during handling and exposure to weather'. The deposit lies very near the sea and is the only one on the east coast of the United States. No anthracite has been found on the east coast of Canada; the coal there is of bituminous or similar character.

Hitherto I have confined myself to strictly geological considerations. If we now think of Rhode Island in connection with what the sagas say of wild grapes, Indians, etc., it strikes us as a place which might well correspond to south Vinland. Here grapes grow wild quite near the sea, as well as in Martha's Vineyard and elsewhere in the region.

There is much to suggest that it was Torfinn Karlsevne's ship that anchored off Rhode Island. Firstly the lump of coal was found at his homestead in Vesterbygd, where he probably went on his return from the Vinland voyage. It is also important to bear in mind that most of those who took part in his expedition were Norse Greenlanders; thus not only he or his wife Gudrid but other settlers might have brought back souvenirs from Vinland.

Rhode Island is the site of the well-known Newport Tower, whose origin has been so much discussed. Certainly it is a curious coincidence that it should stand in the area in which Torfinn Karlsevne is presumed to have been, but hardly grounds for concluding that the tower was built by his people. We shall consider this in more detail later.

Another find made at Sandnes must have originated in North America, and as it bears out what I have said of the lump of coal we can have little doubt that the Vinland voyagers must at one time have cast anchor before the Sandnes homestead.

The object was an arrow-head of quartzite (see Plate 40, fig. 10), discovered in the north-west corner of the churchyard. It is not of the Norse type, and is of a shape unknown among the abundant material orginating from the Eskimoes of Greenland. In all probability it is Indian.

The arrow-head and the lump of coal from Vinland (Rhode Island) and presumably from Torfinn Karlsevne's camp in North America, turn our thoughts to the events in that country. The throng of boats was described by means of an image drawn from the coal, but what of the arrow-head? Is it a souvenir from the battle with the Indians at the same place? The saga relates:

'Then Karlsevne and his men took the red shields and went forward. The Skraelings ran from their boats, whereupon they ran upon one another and fought.'

XVIII LATER VOYAGES TO NORTH AMERICA. WHAT CLUES?

F ROM scattered sources we learn, as we might expect, that more expeditions to North America were made than those of the eleventh century. A number of them will be discussed in detail in connection with the fate of Vesterbygd, but, for the sake of a general survey, I include them here in briefer form.

The year 1121 brings us the remarkable reference to Bishop Eirik Gnúpsson, who sailed from Greenland to visit Vinland.[1]

In 1350, or thereabouts, Ivar Bårdsson[2] went to Vesterbygd to drive out the Skraelings and found it deserted, although horses and other stock were running wild. Later I shall show how this may point to the inhabitants having emigrated to North America. A passage in Gisle Oddsson's annals[3] for 1342 lends colour to this theory: 'The settlers of Greenland voluntarily abandoned the true faith and turned to the American people.'

The Icelandic annals for 1347 mention the ship from Markland[4] which was storm-driven to Iceland and which in the following year sailed for Norway. This weather-beaten ocean-goer must have attracted widespread attention, both by her cargo and by the tales her crew had to tell. This was only fifty years before the sagas concerning Markland and Vinland (in the Flatey Book) were written down in Iceland, and no more than twenty years after Hauk Erlendsson wrote the saga of Torfinn Karlsevne. He was then living in Bergen, Norway.

Shortly afterwards, in 1349, the Black Death reached Norway and struck a paralysing blow at the population. In 1355, however, we hear of a singular kind of enterprise sponsored by King Magnus Eriksson: he authorized Pål Knutsson of Onarheim to fit out an expedition to Greenland.[5] The royal letter emphasized that the king desired to support Christianity in that country; what his forbears had introduced he would not permit to decay. But there can be little doubt that the main purpose of the expedition was economic. It may have been prompted by the ship from Markland which brought valuable wares to Bergen, and was perhaps influenced by the return, in 1346, of the richly laden Greenland vessel. We know no more than this of Pål Knutsson's expedition, and can only guess that he too had plans to visit North America.

At the beginning of the seventeenth century, as we saw, Bjørn Jónsson[6] spoke of driftwood from the 'Markland bottoms': i.e. the inner ends of the fjords. Here is further evidence that his contemporaries were familiar with Markland, so that no explanation was needed.

In 1567, Absalon Pederssøn Beyer, who lived in Bergen, wrote in his work on the Norwegian Realm:[7] 'Greenland is a country rich in wild game, white bears, sable and marten; there are marble, crystal, fish, wadmal, butter, mighty forests, deer and reindeer; there are many kinds of whale and strange beasts.'

Much of this – e.g. sable, marten, deer and mighty forests – had nothing to do with Greenland, and it seems remarkable that it should have been so categorized in a town that was the staple for the Greenland trade. The mistake may have arisen because some Greenland ships carried cargoes originating partly in North America.

The Danish zoologist Herluf Winge[8] accepted this as a possibility in connection with a number of animals mentioned in Archbishop Erik Valkendorf's records. This prelate planned to fit out an expedition to forgotten Greenland, and in about 1516 he collected relevant information. Being one of the greatest merchants in the country he was much interested in economic matters, and his notes include the statement that the following animals were native to Greenland: black bear, beaver, otter, stoat, sable, wolverine and lynx. They were not; nor were black bear or sable to be found in Norway.

Here, then, are two sources which tell similar stories. Absalon Pederssøn can hardly have read Valkendorf's notes, or he would have mentioned him in his record, and it is probable that both men based their work on a single source which has since been lost. The archbishop seems to have been in the habit of visiting the archiepiscopal seat in Bergen in late summer, to hold a court of justice there. Absalon Pederssøn lived in Bergen. Both would thus have had access to whatever ancient writings the town possessed.

In any event it is quite understandable that confusion should have arisen between the wares from Greenland and those from North America. When Greenlanders sailed to North America, the furs, skins and so on that they collected were shipped first to Greenland. When the merchantman from Bergen arrived goods from both America and Greenland were stowed in her. On discharge at Bergen, 'sack-geld' or Crown tax had to be paid upon them, which indicates that the king's bailiff drew up a list of the items. He would hardly have troubled himself about their place of origin, and in any case such particulars would have been unlikely to appear in the public registers; on these the whole cargo would be listed as an import from Greenland. The archiepiscopal seat must have had its own records relating to Greenland, but they may well have included the same schedule of imported goods, which would have given rise to the same misunderstanding.

In order to obtain furs and hides from Labrador, Newfoundland, etc., some Greenlanders must have wintered there, or traded with the natives during the summer half-year when they sailed there to fetch timber. This bears out the saga's account of Torfinn Karlsevne during his sojourn in Vinland,[9] from which we learn that he acquired from the natives 'squirrel-skin, sables, and all kinds of furs'.

Did the Norse tradition of new lands in the west precipitate the re-discovery of North America? It appears that Columbus visited Iceland in about 1477,[10] and it is only reasonable to suppose that he then learned of the northerly route to America. This may have inspired him, but we should not attach too much importance to it, for Columbus was aiming at a more southerly route which should bring him to the wealth of Asia.

The case of the Norwegian-Portuguese expedition of about 1476[11] may be different. It followed a northerly route and presumably touched at places formerly visited by the Vinland voyagers – Labrador and possibly also more southerly regions – and the navigator Jon Skolp was a Norwegian. Thus it seems likely that the enterprise was based on the tradition of earlier days.

The same may be true of the Cabot expedition which in 1498 reached Newfoundland. It started from Bristol, where so many Norwegians had settled and which at that time traded extensively in fish with Iceland. We know, among other things, that John Cabot's son[12] sought leave of the Danish-Norwegian king to trade there.

Thus the Vinland voyages – those epic adventures – had far-reaching consequences. A line runs from Leiv Eiriksson to the Greenlanders' subsequent voyages to North America and perhaps farther: to the re-discovery of the northern part of the continent before the time of Columbus.

Are any traces of the earliest Vinland voyagers or of later expeditions to be found in North America?

It has been claimed that the well-known Kensington Stone[13] is evidence of these journeys. It was found in Minnesota at the end of the nineteenth century, and the inscription upon it records that of eight Swedes and twenty-two Norwegians exploring westward from Vinland, ten lost their lives, while ten others remained to guard the ships, which were fourteen days' journey away.

For a whole generation Hjalmar R. Holand has devoted himself to proving the authenticity of the Kensington Stone, and in the course of this attempt he has cast valuable light on early Norwegian–Icelandic history. But in a matter such as this, the views of those who specialize in runic research cannot be ignored. Such authorities – including Magnus Olsen – maintain that the Kensington Stone is not genuine.

In Newport, Rhode Island, there is a cylindrical stone-built tower eight metres (26 ft.) high. It has eight vaulted passages and windows. The masonry is solid, somewhat primitively constructed, and mortared with lime. The town of Newport was founded in 1639, and the tower is first mentioned in 1677.

There are many theories as to who built this tower. Some believe it was erected by Norse Vinland voyagers before the days of Columbus,[14] others maintain that it was built by Englishmen, Spaniards, Portuguese or Dutchmen in the seventeenth century. Its purpose? The answers vary: watchtower, windmill, church ...

In 1948-9 William S. Godfrey[15] started a dig beside the tower. The only finds he made were of the colonial period, and he took this as proof that it could date no earlier than the seventeenth century. Yet according to Hjalmar Holand[16] there had been earlier excavations, and he draws attention to circumstances which cast doubts on the discoveries that have been made there. We must admit that the riddle of the Newport Tower has not yet been solved.

The Beardmore find is the name given to the following objects said to have been discovered in 1930 in the course of a dig in Ontario, not far from Lake Nipigon: (1) a fragment of an iron sword, (2) a flat strip of iron measuring 19 cm. ($7\frac{1}{2}$ in.) by 2·7 cm. (1 in. approx.), which may have been a rattle of the Viking period, (3) an iron axe, and (4) three small pieces of iron.

There is little doubt that these objects are genuine and that they date from the Viking age. Yet an element of uncertainty has been introduced by the fact that a Norwegian, Lieutenant John Bloch, is said to have brought similar objects with him from Norway. This raises the question whether the man who is thought to have discovered these things in Canada was guilty of fraud. We lack conclusive proof either way.

In recent times there has also been much discussion of the so-called mooring-stones: holes made in the rock for ring-bolts to which the Vinland voyagers are alleged to have moored their ships. It is unlikely that they would have troubled about such things; moreover it is hardly possible to pronounce any valid judgment on the many holes in rocks and crags which have the appearance of having once received ring-bolts, which indeed had such a purpose, but date from post-Columbian days.

We must acknowledge, therefore, that no certain traces of the Vinland voyagers have yet been discovered in North America; but then no systematic attempts have been made to find them. It is now high time that such attempts were begun.

Among the discoveries that may present themselves for investigation, traces of the smelting of bog-ore – such as slag-heaps, furnace-hollows, etc. – would provide some of the soundest evidence of the Vinland voyagers. Smelting was general in Norway, Iceland and Greenland; and we may assume that Norsemen continued the practice in Vinland. The known expeditions to that country remained there from one to three years, and during that time much renewal of tools, weapons and nails must have been necessary.

I myself have recently undertaken such investigations both by sea and air; and although I have adduced a series of reasons for seeking north Vinland in the most northerly region of Newfoundland, I was unwilling to be unduly tied by my own theory, and therefore investigated extensive stretches of the North American coast.

In 1960 I explored the coasts from Rhode Island to the northern areas of Labrador, and came upon a group of unknown house-sites on the northern tip of Newfoundland at a place called L'Anse au Meadow, which looked most promising. By 1961 the expedition had its own boat. Starting from Montreal we went down the St Lawrence River, and explored the north coast of St Lawrence Bay, large tracts of Newfoundland and the coast of Labrador as far as the northern tip. On the way, archaeologists landed at the sites discovered the previous year, and the dig began. I made further archaeological expeditions in 1962, 1963 and 1964 in which scientists from five different countries took part, the leader of the work throughout being my wife Anne Stine Ingstad.

The results of these digs are most interesting. Eight sites were excavated, of which one measured 20 metres by 16 (about 66 ft. by 53) and comprised five rooms, including a large hall, with a long hearth in the middle. A primitive smithy with a stone anvil has also been uncovered, in which several hundred pieces of slag, iron and bog-ore were found. All this points to the manufacture of iron from bog-ore: a process unknown to the natives, but familiar to the Vikings. In view of what the sagas say of the Vinland voyagers' encounter with the natives, it is of special interest to note that traces of natives were also found in the neighbourhood.

Some interesting artefacts were also found, particularly a Norse-type spindle-whorl of soapstone.

Thus the archaeological finds make it clear that the sites are Norse and pre-Columban. A number of tests have dated the finds of carbon at about the year 1000 – the time when Leiv Eiriksson and other Norsemen made their voyages to Vinland, or the New World.

XIX TO HVALSØY CHURCH

L EAVING Eiriksfjord we set our course south towards Einarsfjord, another important part of the central area of the settlements. Whereas Eiriksfjord was dominated by the chief's manor house of Brattalid, it was the cathedral and the great episcopal homestead that lent splendour to the neighbouring fjord.

Sunny weather was still with us, a kindly sea plashed merrily along the hull, and the drift-ice gave us little trouble. Once again Eirik's Island lay ahead, and we took a turn ashore. Here were no signs of Norse habitation, though in the old days Eskimoes had quite a large colony on the northern side. Ruins of some twenty stone huts are to be found at Igdlutalik (i.e. the dwelling-place), as the Eskimoes called this spot.

Many remains of stone huts, graves and other things belonging to various Eskimo tribes may be seen along the coasts of Greenland, but this dwelling-place is of especial interest. The inhabitants were apparently contemporaries of the Norsemen. The island lies directly opposite Narssaq, where the Norse Greenlanders had both homesteads and a church; and only a mile or so of sea separated the two races.

Something similar occurs elsewhere in Austerbygd, as for example on the north side of the large neighbouring island of Tugtutôq (meaning 'where there are many reindeer'). There, within a narrow area, lie ruins of about twenty Eskimo huts. It was the Inugsuk Eskimoes who lived in these places, which were usually halfway down the fjords or near the mouth. As we mentioned before, from the fourteenth century onwards these people migrated southward along the west coast.

There is something appealing about these little round stone huts, half underground, with a long, sunken passage to the door to keep out the cold air: they present a complete contrast to the neighbouring big Norse farmsteads with their byres and outhouses. Nevertheless, they survived, these tough and hardy nomads, whose forbears lived in Asia, Alaska and Canada. So highly skilled were they in hunting that with stone and bone as tools and weapons they took up the struggle for existence in the cold lands where death was never far away. Bone-finds tell us of seal-, whale- and reindeer-hunting. They had dogs as well, though the use of these so far south was limited.

Many of these Eskimo houses have been excavated by Therkel Mathiassen and Erik Holtved,[1] the Danish archaeologists, and in the main the tools found were of the type discovered in the Inugsuk dwellings, at nearly 73° N. Here in the south, Norse objects have been found in their dwellings, such as a knife, pieces of iron, part of a church bell which must have measured three feet in diameter, spindle-whorls – one bearing a runic inscription – a piece of woven cloth, etc. Such things may have been acquired by barter, or taken from farms and churches as these were deserted.

On what terms did the two races meet, when hunting among the islands? Did they meet at other times – to trade, for instance, or at sports and contests? Did a Norse boy ever steal off to an assignation with a black-haired Eskimo girl?

As I stood in that ruined hamlet with its simple stone masonry – the remains of homes – surveying mountains and green hillsides, bare islands and blue-green sea with its drifting ice, the past came alive: laughing youngsters played on the sands, skin-clad men crawled from their huts and shoved off into the blue in their kayaks, watched by the women.

As evening drew on, the women scanned the waters. Then in came the men, one after the other, far out there among the ice-floes, their slender craft riding the seas like birds. Seal? Laughing and joking folk ran down to the shore … Then, perhaps, they stopped to listen as a silvery, insistent sound rang out over land and sea: from the Norse church across the straits the bell was ringing to vespers. People there made their way to the house of God, cattle grazed on the slopes and the evening sun slanted across the turf-roofed homes.

Away once more through the archipelago. To the west lay the islands called by Ivar Bårdsson Lambøyene and Langøy, the latter being presumably identical with Tugtutôq. He says[2] that there are eight large farmsteads, and this tallies with the number of ruins to be seen there today. The people of the islands seem to have lived well. Besides fish and reindeer they had the Greenland seal and the hooded seal, which they could hunt from their very doors during the regular northward and southward migrations.

Once again there was drift-ice to contend with, and the motor-boat had to be manoeuvred forward with care. The mighty icebergs were a magnificent sight as they rode northward in line, glittering in the sun, some of them streaked with blue or green thaw-water. They came from the huge Greenland glaciers. At times powerful forces were at work within them, for suddenly they would split, great fragments plunged with a crash into the water and vanished in seething green seas. Then was the time to look alive and keep bow-on to the waves. There were also belts of pack-ice from the Arctic Ocean or Siberia.

But the ice we liked least was fresh-water ice: hard blue lumps of it that barely broke surface, and lay in wait on purpose to hole our hull.

It was a fresh day, with a breeze playing over the dark sea. Steadily the motor-boat chugged southward, now and again shipping salt spray across the deck. Suddenly a small whale shot up vertically to its full height above the surface; for the fraction of a second it hung there quivering in the sunny blue air, then splashed below. This happened again and again: a grampus.

Fascinated by the sight, I peered across the water, my cine-camera at the ready. I was so engrossed by the spectacle that I only dimly registered Anne Stine's efforts to attract my attention. Finally she screamed into my ear with all her might:

'Look! Don't you see? A *bear!*'

Then I came to. And indeed there he was, standing on the huge flat iceberg to the left. Softly, clumsily he loped away – out of sight.

'He was there for ages,' said Anne Stine in despair. Then, sternly: 'Well, that shows you. Why can't you ever *listen?*'

It would have been easy enough to take up the chase through the drift-ice, which offered many wide leads. But what had we to do with a bear – above all a summer bear with a poor coat? Besides, chasing a polar bear with a motor-boat is more butchery than hunting. Let him go.

Nowadays polar bears are seldom met with here along the south-west coasts, and few are shot. How it may have been in the days of the Norse Greenlanders is hard to say; but at that time these animals had far more extensive sanctuary off the coasts of east Greenland and on the drift-ice in general, so it is likely that a large number of them reached the west coast.

Apart from this, animal life was strangely sparse where we were; hardly a seal was to be seen. My thoughts turned to Svalbard, where we continually glimpsed the round head of the hooded seal alongside or in our wake. The warmer climate of recent years has to a large extent driven the seal northward to cooler regions; and of course considerable depredations are made among them.

We paid a short visit to Julianehåb, the largest Danish colony in the south. It was founded in 1775 by the Norwegian Anders Olsen,[3] or Anders Nord-laender, as he signed himself. He was the son of a farmer of Senja, born in 1718; he came to Greenland in 1742, at the instigation of Hans Egede, who at that time brought over five Norwegians. Their intention was to raise livestock.

For forty years he played a great part in the life of the country, especially at the various trading-posts; he also founded the colony of Sukkertoppen, and went on research expeditions. He married the Eskimo woman Tuperna, and in their old age they moved to the head of Einarsfjord, to the green plains where once the old Norse bishops had their residence, and began the breeding

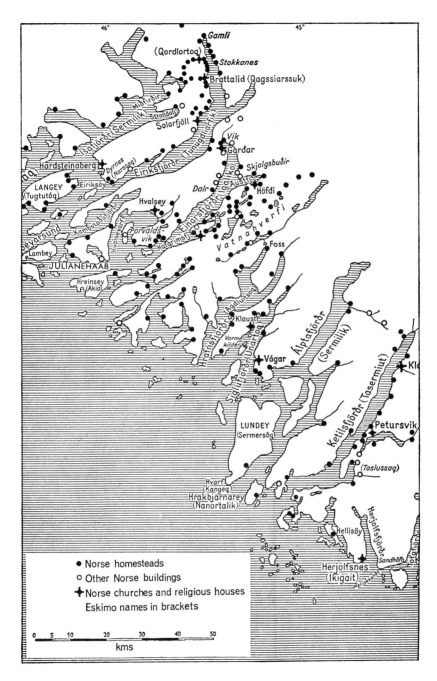

Map of the principal part of Austerbygd

of livestock. This pioneer work was carried on by his successors, whom we shall shortly be meeting. It is not for nothing that Anders Olsen's name is engraved in the square in Julianehåb, beside those of Knud Rasmussen and Henry Rink.

Julianehåb consists of a scattering of houses among bare rocky outcrops, a pretty little square, a quay and a harbour. We cast anchor, whereupon a crowd of smiling youngsters swarmed down to the shore to stare. The Norwegian flag at the masthead was the attraction. Greenland has long been a closed land, and the sudden arrival of a foreign craft was an event.

In Julianehåb, as elsewhere along the west coast, there are few true Eskimoes; these are only to be found in any numbers farther north or on the east coast. The blending of races began with the whalers of the seventeenth century, and has continued throughout the Danish colonial period.

Four kayaks lay at the landing-stage: a meagre remnant from a vanished era. Once upon a time these slender craft were essential to the Eskimoes of the west coast. Kayak life meant a continual battle with ice and sea on the everlasting hunt for seal, an existence demanding a trained body, keen sight and a skilled hand to speed the harpoon or handle the boat in storm-whipped seas. It meant a breath of salt air and adventure in the little stone huts, where folk sat by the light of blubber lamps, listening to the ancient tales of their race.

And now? In the southerly regions there are not enough seal: the traditional staple livelihood is failing, and the people of the west coast have become fishermen; civilization has gained a hold over them and the humdrum, uninspired atmosphere of our own day prevails.

These people are living through a difficult period of transition. Their ancient culture is crumbling, and much of the new is alien to them. They have no sheet anchor. A few years ago Greenland became part of the Danish realm, and Greenlanders acquired a certain amount of political freedom. But to use this freedom rightly is no easy matter. Then there is sickness, especially TB, which has ravaged the Greenlanders of today.

We were welcomed in Julianehåb and given valuable information, especially by Director A. Jensen. He has the difficult task of teaching modern Greenlanders how to breed sheep. As I mentioned earlier, there are now no fewer than 20,000 head in the district, and a vital industry is being born.

As we were on the point of leaving Julianehåb, the pastor's wife – whom we didn't know at all – arrived with a bag of Greenland potatoes: a most friendly gesture to foreign travellers. The potatoes were small, but firm and with an unusually good flavour.

We continued eastward towards the mouth of Einarsfjord. To the south appeared the great island of Akia which must be identical with Ivar Bårdsson's Renøy (Reindeer Island), where great numbers of reindeer were said to congregate, and where, with the bishop's permission, they were hunted in autumn. Bårdsson tells us also of abundant deposits of soapstone, of which people made great cooking-pots and vessels, and which 'fire cannot consume'.

Then we swung into Hvalsøyfjord, to look at the ancient church there: the best-preserved Norse ruin in Greenland. We passed the island of Arapatsvik, and ahead of us the peak of Qaqortoq soared like a pyramid into the sky. Green slopes at its foot ran down to the water. The day was glorious. Rivers flashed and drift-ice glittered in its whiteness as it rocked on the blueblack waters.

We peered inland – and there, below the hill a little way in from the sea, we saw it – the old church of Hvalsøy.[4] We pulled ashore, to be met by a vision: buttercups spread a golden cloth before the ancient house of God.

The building, which is rectangular, has an external measurement of 8 by 16 metres (26 ft. 8 in. by 53 ft. 4 in.) and lies east–west, its long side to the sea. In this wall were two doors, one for the congregation, the other for the priest. The main door was at the west end and had a lintel-stone measuring over 13 feet in length. The wall facing the sea had four square windows in it, while the long wall opposite, facing the hillside, had one. At the east end was one large arched window. All windows were narrow on the outside, and widened inwards.

The church was built of stone; but doors and roof must have been wooden. The mortar was clay, though the pointing was done with lime which was no doubt obtained by burning mussel-shells. Hvalsøy church and a small building at Gardar are the only structures where lime was used; and this is no doubt why their walls have been so well preserved.

The foundations, however, have subsided somewhat, and for many years the south wall has leaned considerably out of true. Let us hope that the building may be preserved from utter ruin by the necessary shoring-up of the foundations, draining, etc. It would indeed be a tragedy if this unique monument to the Norse age were allowed to disintegrate and disappear.

The structure, both in its proportions and its plan, is strongly reminiscent of many late thirteenth-century Norwegian stone churches.

We entered it through the laymen's door, passing a niche for the holy water stoup used by the congregation before they set foot in the holy house. There we stood on the earth floor, with heaven above us ... and it was all emptiness.

It was not always so. Once there was surely a soapstone font, an altarpicture with carvings, an altar-cloth, candlesticks and the rest. Near the place where the priest stood were two niches (in the south and north walls) in which the treasures of the church were kept. Beneath the floor where we were standing remains were found of a coffin and of human bones that crumbled at a touch.

There was a chilly solemnity about the old church, and a sour smell rose from the earth floor. Bright sun and dark shadows fell upon the walls, and the arched window at the east end rose mildly against the blue sky. A snow-bunting perched there, twittering. There was something touching about this primitive masonry, and one felt the builders had worked hard at it, determined to achieve their arch. Through the priest's door one caught a colourful glimpse of buttercups, sea and drift-ice.

I thought of the young couple who were married here on a day in September 1408, or, as it is worded in the old records, the first Sunday after Holy Cross Day. Their names were Torstein Olavsson and Sigrid Bjørnsdatter, the former being an Icelander of excellent family, and the latter perhaps a girl from the Greenland settlements. On this occasion there were many in the church, both local people and others from a ship which had come in, and they stood closely thronged on the earth floor. Near the arched window, where little blubber-lamps flickered on the altar, knelt the young people.

Sira (priest) Pål Halvardsson officiated, and the Roman ritual rang out in the little church. He blessed the young people and pronounced them man and wife. Afterwards all the people went out on to the grassland, where the buttercups had long since faded, for chilly autumn had set in and already snow lay white on the highest peaks.

As it happens we have unusually detailed records of this marriage.[5] In 1406 a ship bound from Norway to Iceland was blown off course and arrived at Austerbygd in Greenland, where she remained for four years. Her crew probably took advantage of their time there to amass a valuable cargo of walrus tusks, hides, blubber and other goods. In Iceland the vessel was presumed lost, and the leader's wife there was given leave to marry again.

Then came the wedding in Hvalsøy church between Torstein and Sigrid. They sailed in their ship back to Iceland, where they settled, and many of the best families in that country can trace their descent from these two. It was important to attest the legality of this marriage, which had taken place abroad, and we have no fewer than three quite detailed documents concerning it. Two were made out by persons present at the wedding, and the third by the bishop's deputies in Greenland, *Sira* Eindride Andresson and *Sira* Pål Halvardsson. We hear among other things that the banns had been called on three Sundays and that many people were present in church. At the same time a dozen Icelandic men then staying in Greenland are mentioned by name.

Many things happened in the four years during which the ship had remained at the settlement, including (in 1407) the following drama. One of the Icelanders was called Torgrim Sølvesson, and with him was his wife, Steinunn Rafnsdatter, who came of a distinguished family. We will let the Icelandic Annals[6] tell the story:

A man in Greenland named Kollgrim was burned for lying with another man's wife who was called Steinunn and was a daughter of the lawman Rafn who perished in the landslide at Langelid. She married Torgrim Sølvesson. Kollgrim enticed her with the black arts, and was later burned in accordance with the law. The wife was never afterwards in her right mind and died within a short time.

Another event, characteristic of the age, is also narrated in the Icelandic Annals.[7] One of the Icelanders belonging to the same ship was Snorre Torfasson. His wife Gudrun, who had remained in Iceland, believed the vessel to have been lost at sea, and married again. Then Snorre returned, which must have given her some anxious moments. But all went well: the Annals relate that she rode to meet Snorre and that he received her very affectionately and took her to a new home as his wife. Shortly afterwards he died, and Gudrun returned to husband number two.

These sources cast a sudden fleeting light upon conditions in the Greenland settlements; but from this point the Icelandic Annals cease to tell us anything of that country. The ship that left there in 1410 was the last vessel that is known with certainty to have touched at the settlements while the Norse Greenlanders were living there.

We came out of the church and at the west corner sat down on a ledge projecting from the wall, which seems to have been intended as a bench. From here we had a view over the fjord and far away across ranges and hills. So must churchgoers have sat many a time through the ages, watching for others to arrive.

Sooner or later the ships would come into sight, first one, then another, moving under taut sails between the ice-floes, or with oars flashing in the sun. And the hillside came alive with riders followed by their pack-animals: the men of Einarsfjord.

Keels ground on the shore; men, women and children flocked down to meet the newcomers; horses neighed, children and dogs dashed hither and thither. There was life on the green slopes and a tingling in the air. Church-meetings were great events, not only because of holy things to do with the Virgin Mary and salvation, but also because they gave one the chance of meeting other people.

But from some of the ships long, heavy boxes were brought ashore; they were made of roughly-hewn driftwood and held together with wooden nails or strips of whalebone. These were the coffins. For the present they were carried into a stone building near the water. It had been a hard task to bring them, but nothing was more important for salvation than to be buried within the churchyard wall.

*

In the old days the church was merely one of many buildings on the green slope running down towards the water, at the foot of the pyramid-crag. A number of ruins make this clear.[8] First came the main homestead fifty yards or so west of the church, consisting of ten or twelve buildings grouped together in a massive complex. Here, as we have seen, were dwelling-house, byres, and a large banqueting-hall. Next a little forge in the background, a boat-house on the shore, a big round sheepfold and other structures forming part of a farm. Farther east was another holding with its buildings, lying on fertile ground that sloped up to two beautiful lakes. To the east the fjord became a narrow gut leading to an excellent harbour where the churchgoers moored their boats.

The chief homestead must have loomed large in the landscape. Here, somewhat apart, the banqueting-hall may still be seen, with walls the height of a man and a wide door facing the church. It is about 33 feet by 18 in area and was once some eight feet high. Traces remain in the floor of the holes made to take the posts, some of which must have supported the roof; and traces also of the long hearth.

Here the churchgoers assembled; for, as in Norway, it would have been the custom for travellers from afar to stay at the church-place for many days. There might be weddings and funerals, and the grassy plain became the scene of games and contests. The wayfarers brought dried meat and fish with them, and cheese and butter. They sat in the hall about the blazing fire and had a great time together.

Nor was there any lack of conversational topics among people who met so seldom and led so active a life. They told of all the notable things that had happened since their last meeting – of reindeer- and seal-hunting, of farming and fishing; of the Skraelings, those strange folk who at first were fabled beings in the far north, and who later became a near reality: people of another kind, who had to be watched. And always there was the never-ending subject: the ship from Norway. No doubt it was in this hall, too, that Torstein Olavsson and Sigrid Bjørnsdatter celebrated their wedding on the Sunday after Holy Cross Day, 1408.

Fifty years earlier, Ivar Bårdsson had been warden of Gardar, the bishop's seat, and he must have visited Hvalsøy many a time. In his description of the country he mentions that Hvalsøy church owned the whole fjord as well as the neighbouring fjord to the north: Kambstadafjord.[9] He says also that in this latter place there was a large homestead called Tjodhildstad, which belonged to the Norwegian king. This must have been the dwelling of the king's commissioner, who would doubtless have occupied a place of honour in the great hall of Hvalsøy.

If we go back to about the year 1000, when the first settlers were building their homes, we find even in those heathen times some interesting notes about Hvalsøy. In the *Landnámabók* it is stated that Torkel Farserk,[10] a cousin of Eirik the Red's, took possession of the area comprising Hvalsøy and the greater part of the land between Eiriksfjord and Einarsfjord. He settled on Hvalsøyfjord, and the people there were his descendants.

Torkel is said to have been incredibly strong. Once when Eirik the Red came to visit him he prepared a feast, and for this he needed a ram that grazed on one of the islands. There was no boat at hand, so Torkel swam over, took the animal by the back and swam back with it. His story ends:

'Torkel was buried under a mound in the home-fields by Hvalsøyfjord, and since then he has often walked again among the buildings there.' This barrow has never been found.

XX GARDAR

IGHTY Einarsfjord stretched before us into the blue distance. Not
far from the mouth we turned into a little bay called by Ivar
Bårdsson Torvaldsvik, and looked at the ruins of some Norse
farms that once existed there. The most interesting memorial to the old days
was a well-preserved storehouse built on a huge, steep-sided boulder, well
out of reach of dog or fox (see Plate 21, top).

We took a walk up among the hills, and found the land quite fertile.
Here and there stone walls had been built round clefts and hollows in the
rocks, as shelters for sheep. Anne Stine came upon a *bogastille*, a stone-built
hide where the hunter lay in wait with bow and arrow for reindeer. Later
we were to see more of them, built at places where the deer would be sure
to pass on their migrations.

Then we went farther up the fjord. To the south, near the mouth, we
glimpsed a fjord named after the chief Hafgrim who came over with Eirik
the Red. He took possession of land there and beyond, in Vatnahverfi, a
beautiful and rich area where there are many lakes. The chief's homestead
must certainly have been at the head of Hafgrimsfjord, where the Danish
archaeologist C. L. Vebaek recently found the ruins of a church. This may
have been the church at Langanes which is mentioned in the story of Einar
Sokkesson.[1]

Einarsfjord is less wild in character than Eiriksfjord, and the glaciers do
not reach the sea. Here the ice melts earlier, usually in April and May.
There were farmsteads on each side of the fjord, and on the western side
Ivar Bårdsson mentions a point called Klining, the bay of Gravavik and the
homestead Dal which belonged to the church.

At sunrise we headed in towards the head of the fjord, and before us a
mountain ridge soared up under blazing clouds. We peered ahead and there,
at the foot of the range, we beheld Gardar: a kindly plain on which the
houses of latter-day Greenlanders were scattered.

We cast anchor in a little harbour, rowed ashore and walked up to the
houses. Behind us followed a trail of Greenland children twittering away in
Eskimo. An impressive plain spread before us, unmatched anywhere in the
country. The narrow spit running out between Einarsfjord and Eiriksfjord,

Eid, was only a short distance away, and offered an easy approach from the northern hamlets. In short, the episcopal seat and the meeting-place of the *Althing* were ideally situated at the heart of Austerbygd.

There were now about thirty Greenlanders' houses, built chiefly of stones taken from the ruins. Gardar, or Igaliko (the abandoned cooking-place) as the Eskimoes called it, has today a population of about one hundred and fifty. As was mentioned earlier, these people are descended from the Norwegian Anders Olsen who married Tuperna, an Eskimo woman, and settled here in 1780. His grave lies in the middle of the hamlet.

It is a strange coincidence that in the place where Norwegian bishops once raised stock, a Norwegian should have settled a few hundred years later and carried on the same occupation. His successors now have about 4,000 head of sheep, 12 cows, 25 horses and a number of pigs. Hay, potatoes and green vegetables are grown, and fodder is brought by boat from other Norse fields. Cod-fishing in the fjords and salmon-fishing in the rivers are also important for the people, who prosper well enough without having to work too hard.

Anders Olsen's successors are sturdy folk, and famed for being among the most advanced in Greenland; but they are known also to be headstrong. They hold fast by their race; they are a clan to themselves and regard the head of Einarsfjord as their own land by virtue of the tradition of more than a hundred and fifty years. They even had a 'king'; his name was Amos. He was a stocky little fellow of about eighty, with shrewd eyes and a grey beard. We called upon him and were warmly received; indeed we met with quite extraordinary hospitality at this place, partly perhaps because we were from the same country as their Norse ancestor.

The people of Gardar have often taken wives from other places, so the Greenland element is very marked among them. Yet it was striking how often Nordic characteristics survived: we met several children who had fair hair and blue eyes.

We called on Peder Motzfeldt, one of the leaders of the community: a dark-skinned, sturdy man of about forty. He invited us in, and his lovely daughter set milk, butter and cakes on the table. Indoors the house was home-like and orderly. It turned out that this man was related to my wife, though distantly. There was a good deal of merriment over this, and the two of them sat there feeling the blood-tie with all their might. To such a pitch, indeed, was Peder affected that he proposed an exchange of wives.

We looked over the wide plain, where flowers tossed in the breeze by the old ruins.

Many things have happened at Gardar through the centuries. Here Einar, the first settler, went ashore; he wandered inland rejoicing at the sight of the

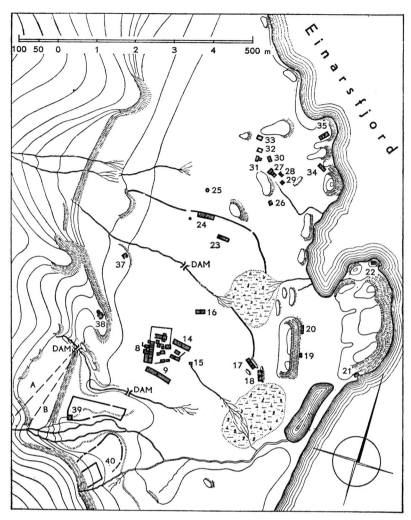

Map of Gardar and its Norse ruins. 8. bishop's homestead, with cathedral immediately to the north. 9 and 14. byre and barn. 15. well. 30–3. Thing-*booths. The rest are dwellings, byres, sheds, warehouses, forge, fishing-huts, sheep-folds, etc. A and B have been inserted by author and denote ditches leading from the river to the 'crag-pool', which was the reservoir for the irrigation system (see page 190). (Based on map in National Museum, Copenhagen)*

green countryside, and wondering where he might best build his homestead. His son Torvald, accounted a simpleton in the saga, married the formidable Freydis, Eirik the Red's daughter; she who halted the onslaught of the Indians in Vinland by baring her breasts and making as if to cut them off with her sword. It was on the parliament-plain of Gardar that Tormod Kolbrunarskald wrought blood-vengeance and slew the mighty Torgrim Trolle.

This happened in the early years of the eleventh century, and we hear no more of Greenland's largest manor until 1124, when it became the home of the bishop. It was first under the authority of Lund, and then from 1152–3 under the archbishopric of Nidaros. In the next chapter I shall describe in greater detail how Christianity came to Greenland and how, during the course of some two hundred and fifty years, a series of Norwegian bishops made their way there. What ruins we saw about us date from them.

The first description of Gardar was written by Aaron Arctander, who visited the place in 1779.[2] Since then a number of eminent researchers have examined the ruins, which for a long time were not known to be those of the bishop's house; it was H. Schirmer,[3] the architect, who in 1886 came to the correct conclusion. In 1926 the cathedral, bishop's house and other buildings were excavated by Poul Nørlund,[4] who in this performed a basic work. Some of his findings will be discussed in what follows.

The episcopal seat of Gardar must have been an impressive structure. There are more than forty different ruins of church, dwelling-house and other buildings connected with stock-raising, fishing and hunting, all scattered over a wide area on the plain and by the water.

How many people lived here in its heyday is hard to say, but there cannot have been fewer than there are today. The bishop would have had assistant priests to help him in his spiritual work; there was also the farm, the live-stock, fishing and other pursuits requiring a large labour-force to keep all running smoothly.

In the course of time the modern Greenlanders have carried away quantities of stones from the ruins, so that these have been greatly diminished; nevertheless we were able to gain some fascinating impressions. The largest buildings – church, dwelling-house and two long byres – lay more or less in a group round a large open space or *tun*. In this were a well, a forge and a few other things.

Close beside the bishop's house was another large building whose walls still rise in places to a height of five feet. This was probably the bishop's tithe barn, which would have contained tribute consisting of walrus-tusks, hides, furs, butter, wadmal cloth, etc.

We were impressed by the size of the stones used in these central buildings; several of them weighed from five to ten tons. They had to be brought from a considerable distance, and transport must have been arduous, even if carried out in winter by horse and sledge. These massive blocks show how concerned the bishop was to make the important buildings not only impressive but lasting.

The cathedral was dedicated to St Nicholas, the patron saint of seafarers. It was cruciform, with chancel and two side chapels in the east, and was unusually large, measuring 90 feet long by 53 at the widest part. Three walls were of stone, the west end-wall apparently of wood. Pieces of green glass have been found, so the windows must have been glazed: great magnificence in a country like Greenland, where windows were mostly made of the membrane of calves' stomachs and similar material.

Fragments of carved soapstone show that the church was finely decorated in the Catholic manner. In this connection we have an interesting piece of historical information: in a will dated 1347, Magnus Eriksson, king of Norway and Sweden, and his wife Blanca presented 100 marks for ornaments for the cathedral of Greenland.[5]

In both the nave and the south chapel there were holes for open fires – no doubt most needful on a cold winter's day. Many a time the bishop must have stood shivering and rubbing his hands in front of the blaze before stepping forth to his congregation.

Beneath the transept traces have been found of an earlier church which had no side chapels, only a narrow chancel. This church may have been built in the twelfth century by the first bishop.

Round the churchyard there was as usual a wall, near which were some small buildings. Where the church bell hung is not known. An old Eskimo tale affirms that this bell was so big that it could be heard as far as the mouth of Einarsfjord.

In 1926, in the north-east chapel, a find was made which is unique of its kind. This was the skeleton of a man wearing a gold episcopal ring on the fourth finger of his right hand. In this hand he held a crosier, of which the lower part was of ash, with an iron ferrule, and the upper of walrus-tusk, skilfully carved and with a crook ending in a leaf-pattern.

He was a strongly built, middle-aged man. He wore shoes, but strangely enough part of his right foot was missing. Which bishop was this? Nørlund has good grounds for thinking he may have been Jon Smyrill (sparrowhawk), King Sverre's fosterfather, who died in 1209.

Another remarkable find was made partly in the church itself and partly in the churchyard: about twenty-five walrus skulls. The majority of these were at the east end, where they were buried in rows, and in 1832 five narwhal skulls were found at the east end of the chancel. In every case the tusks were missing.

As was mentioned earlier, walrus and narwhal were of great importance, not least for church economy. The hunting of these animals was carried on chiefly during the long voyages to Nordrsetur. It seems as if ancient superstition had survived, and that this practice had its origins in heathendom. So far as the narwhal is concerned, it is possible that the medieval concept of the unicorn persisted. In any case the people may well have wanted to ensure success in hunting by keeping the heads of these valuable animals in the holy place.

An interesting point is that a walrus skull with carvings on it was found at the Sandnes homestead in Vesterbygd. Walrus skulls dating from the Middle Ages have also come to light in Bergen, Oslo, Trondhjem and Uppsala, some of them carved.[6]

The bodies in the churchyard lay closely side by side, some in coffins, others shrouded in their own garments; but much has crumbled away. Examination of the skeletons has shown that the people were healthy and strong, with no sign of degeneration.

At the east end of the church a large tombstone was discovered (see Plate 24, bottom left). It lay close up against the wall, under the eaves, where only people of high birth were buried. It probably dates from the thirteenth century, and it bears the following inscription: 'Vigdis M.D. [Magnus's daughter] lies here. God rejoice her soul.'

The bishop's house lay close beside the cathedral, at right angles to it. It must have been a massive building. In front of the main entrance lay a huge, flat stone which was brought from a great distance, although it weighs a good ten tons. From it a flagged path crossed the churchyard to the cathedral, and along this path the bishop passed in his vestments to celebrate Mass.

Originally the building was a simple long-house, but through the centuries it was built on to and altered in various ways. There were ten or twelve rooms, including three apartments for the bishop and his family, a kitchen (fire-house), store-rooms, bath-house, etc. An interesting feature of the kitchen is that the fireplaces were sunk in the earth.

But the most important room was the great hall. It measured 16·75 metres by 7·8 (55 ft. by 24) and could accommodate two or three hundred people. It was, in fact, larger than the banqueting-halls of the great manors of Brattalid, Hvalsøy and Herjolfsnes. Nørlund mentions that it was twice the size of Flugumyr hall in Iceland, where there was space for two hundred and forty people; indeed, many an English nobleman had less room for the reception of guests than the bishop of Greenland.

It was above all at the great Church festivals that the people met together in the great hall, though they certainly did so at other times, as for example when the Norway ship came in with wares and news. Then the message token went from farm to farm and the people flocked together here.

Pieces of the church bell have been found in various places, and from an especially large fragment it is estimated to have weighed about 500 kilos (1,100 lb.). It may have come from England or have been cast by an Englishman in Bergen, like so many Norwegian and Icelandic bells in the Middle Ages.*

In connection with the fragments of this bell Poul Nørlund has pointed out an interesting fact:[7] many of them have been at least partially melted. He believes that the bronze was used to cast other objects: a process unknown to the Eskimoes. It is true that many groups in north Canada and in Greenland had long made use of natural copper, also meteoric and tellurian iron, but the metal was always hammered out cold.

That the people of Gardar practised casting appears from a number of moulds cut from soapstone. Delicately carved moulds for an arrow-head of Viking type, for crosses, spindle-whorls and even runic inscriptions have been found, including one engraved in mirror-writing with the words: 'Haldor owns me.'

Such moulds were found not only at the bishop's residence, but at Brattalid and Vatnahverfi as well. They were primarily intended for the casting of bog-ore, and if the church-bell fragments show signs of having been exposed to great heat the reason is probably that the church was destroyed by fire.

Other items found at Gardar include various objects or fragments of soapstone, such as bowls, jars, spindle-whorls, ornaments, etc. Many of them are engraved with personal marks or a cross. A piece of a small hand-quern has also been discovered, and a bronze candlestick. Iron objects are relatively few and consist of knives, rivets and so on; but then Gardar is a place where an exceptional amount of plundering by Eskimoes and others has been carried on through the ages. A kayak-scraper of Eskimo origin has also come to light here, and it is unusual to find such a thing on a Norse culture-site.

There were chessmen, too. No doubt through the long winter evenings the bishop sat pondering over the board. But the most ancient find made at Gardar consists of two rings, dug up near the church. One is made of twisted gold thread, the other of bronze. These rings are of the Viking age, and may date from the settlement period.

It was a beautiful day when we strolled among the ruins of the bishop's

---

* Bell-founding seems to have been a craft practised to a great extent by Englishmen. Ravn Sveinbjørnsson's saga speaks of an Icelander in about 1195 who bought bells in England. Håkon V bequeathed to St Olav's at Avaldsnes 'a great bell which was cast in England'. In 1343 the Archbishop of Nidaros and the bishop of Bergen entered into a contract with some English merchants, requiring them to send skilled bell-founders to Bergen to cast one large bell and two small ones.

homestead. Mighty stones from the church wall rose like russet islands from the green grass, and some chattering Eskimo children were clambering about the walls of the tithe barn. Beyond, Einarsfjord stretched away to the hills that soared in sharp silhouette on the farther side.

I kicked something that tinkled; it was a little piece of metal from the church bell. It lay heavy in the hand, and seemed to bring a message of destiny from a vanished age: in what circumstances was the bell shattered – that most sacred treasure of the cathedral?

The bishop of Greenland was more than just a churchman. Like his colleagues in Norway he seems to have engaged in a number of economic activities and employed many people. He leased church property and drew rent; he apparently ran hunting- and fishing-boats and had commercial interests. Last but not least, he directed the greatest farming enterprise in Greenland.

Carvings in soapstone, Gardar

The numerous ruins near the homestead and far away from it are evidence of thriving activity. There were dwellings, cook-houses and store-rooms of various kinds; there were byres, barns, dairies, large and small paddocks for sheep and horses, smithies where iron extracted from bog-ore was forged; there were boat-houses and warehouses by the water, fishing huts and structures for drying fish out on the two islands, and much else.

Clearly defined depressions in the ground still show the course of the old highway leading across the fields to the bishop's residence. It passed through the long stone wall which is still visible, through a gap where there must once have been a gate. Through this came cows from the outer pastures, sleds laden with manure, and riders on a variety of errands.

Near the dwelling-house are the ruins of two great byres. In length they measured 63·5 and 41 metres respectively (210 ft. and 133 ft.), and were 4·2 metres wide (over 13 ft.). As usual they were designed to take two rows of cows, and had room for about 100 head. Sheep-folds and other structures show that a considerable number of these animals were kept too, as well as goats and pigs.

The home-fields that extended round the homestead to a considerable distance amount to about 20 hectares (50 acres), and were even larger before the ground subsided. The remains of about 1,300 metres (1,500 yards) of well-built boundary walls of stone and turf may still be seen; these were probably quite high. Today part of the enclosed area is rather dry and in places the grass is scanty.

Here, as elsewhere, this fact has been ascribed to climatic change, but there is much to indicate that other causes were the decisive ones. The soil in many places has degenerated for lack of manuring and other care. Moreover the cutting down of trees and bushes and the collapse of the high walls has allowed the föhn wind from the south-east to ravage unchecked, blowing much of the soil away and bringing in sand. There is a further important factor which has already been mentioned: in the old days the bishop's lands were irrigated by a system similar to that used in Norway.

It is evident that at least three dams were linked to this system. Two of them were built within the home-field area each on its own river, north and south of the buildings respectively. The latter one lies on the same water-course as the third dam, which I will call the crag-dam. It is built some way up the slope at a height of about 160 feet above the meadowland and the pool contained there must have held a considerable quantity of water.

Poul Nørlund mentions[8] that the pools indicate a damper climate in Norse times than prevails today, but he suggests no satisfactory explanation for them. The two situated within the home-field area he describes as super-fluous. He had not taken irrigation into account, and it is significant that in his day it was hard to find any reason for these artificial pools.

In connection with the crag-pool, the Greenlander Abel points out an interesting fact which makes it clear that irrigation was here involved. It was found that most of the water had been led there: there were obvious traces of two ditches running from the main river to the south down across the slope to the pool, and measuring something like a hundred yards in length. In other words the bishop was not content with the natural supply from the stream, but made sure of a constant and abundant flow from the river itself.

This crag-pool was situated in the most favourable place, behind and high above the central area of the gently sloping home-fields, and from it water could be carried in wooden gutters resting on cross-set posts. For the irriga-tion of the land farthest to the east – that is to say nearest the sea – the pool lying south of the homestead was used. As was mentioned earlier, it lies on the same watercourse, so that to feed it the crag-pool sluice was opened. The two pools must have been used alternately. The pool north of the home-stead provided water also for other areas (see map on page 184).

We are considering therefore an irrigation system so constructed as to water the greater part of the episcopal lands; and it follows that these lands must have been far more fertile in those days than they are now.

The episcopal seat had its out-fields too, and no doubt obtained winter cattle-feed from house-men or tenants. There were also great numbers of people out with boats, or with pack-horses up in the hills to collect moss, heather, sandwort and the like.

Livestock grazed on both sides of the fjord. Ivar Bårdsson's description reads: ' ... upon the right hand as one sails into the fjord towards the cathedral, which stands at the head of the fjord, is a great wood, and in that wood the cathedral has all its cattle, both large and small.' Today there is no wood in the Greenland sense on the opposite side of the fjord to Gardar, or beyond. But such a wood may have existed.

As in Eiriksfjord, fishing must have been of prime importance to the episcopal household. Einarsfjord too must have had its spawning-beds: and there were char in the rivers. Most probably dried fish was produced on a large scale, for the ruins of several buildings along the shore and on the islands furnish evidence of this. The fish of Eiriksfjord could be exploited too, for the distance to the fjord across the intervening promontory was quite short. The midden has revealed the bones of reindeer, Greenland seal, hooded seal, walrus, whale, etc.; so the bishop must have had men out hunting far and wide. Nor was there any lack of small game such as ptarmigan and hare.

The texts tell us that the *Althing* was held at Gardar. In the Foster-brothers' Saga we read:[9] 'The following summer people went to attend the *Thing* at Gardar. Those of Eiriksfjord tented their booths there, and there was some distance between them and the place where the Einar-folk tented theirs [i.e. stretched covers of hide above the permanent stone walls].' It is difficult to pinpoint the exact site of the assembly. Mogens Clemmensen[10] believes it to have been on the sloping land north of the harbour, and identifies certain ruins there as the remains of booths.

In the course of centuries the bishops' residence and all that pertained to it expanded across the plain of Gardar. What happened at last to this most wealthy centre? The earliest investigations[11] suggest that the cathedral was ravaged by fire. It contained inflammable material enough, such as, for example, the roof, the west wall, pews, and perhaps also inner panelling.

Once upon a time, then, a mighty blaze soared above the Gardar plain: the cathedral of St Nicholas, the ancient sanctuary, went up in flames. Never again would the note of the great bell ring out across Einarsfjord.

XXI FROM THOR TO WHITE CHRIST

IN the autumn of 999 a weather-beaten vessel headed into Trondhjems-fjord in Norway. Her master was Leiv Eiriksson, son of Eirik the Red. He had sailed all the way across the North Atlantic from Greenland and was now making for the market town of Nidaros. There he waited upon the king – Olav Trygvason – and, says the saga, was received with great honour,[1] for he behaved like a man of breeding. He spent the winter in the king's household, and received baptism.

Olav Trygvason was a singular blend of Viking and zealous missionary. Sternly he went forth to convert not only Norway but also the Isles of the Western Ocean, where Norwegians had settled. He bade Leiv Eiriksson promote Christianity in Greenland, and to this Leiv consented, taking with him 'priests and teachers' when he set sail for the west.

The saga of Olav Trygvason tells us that he had converted five countries, 'but it was not to be expected that the people should be obedient in decency of conduct or in perfect faith in God, for time was short and the people stubborn and stiff-necked in their unbelief'. Christianity was indeed introduced into Iceland in the year 1000, by a resolution passed at the *Althing*, but it was to be long ere it was truly adopted. It is significant that even the Norwegian kingdom of Dublin, which lay so near to Christian lands, remained heathen until about 1000. Irish writings[2] of the day tell of 'Thor's chiefs', 'Thor's ring' and 'Thor's forest in Dublin'.

In a remote country such as Greenland, heathendom must have maintained an even firmer grasp on the people; yet the Christian faith was not unknown. In Are Frode's *Landnámabók* we read that Iceland was founded chiefly by people from Norway and from the Norwegian Islands of the Western Ocean; and many of these must have been widely travelled men with varied knowledge – including knowledge of the new God. Nor was this God unknown to the Icelanders who later emigrated to Greenland. We hear that Herjolf, who took possession of land at the southern tip of that country, brought with him a Christian man from the Hebrides, who composed a *kvad* or lay – *hafgerðingadrápa* – in thankfulness to the Lord for bringing him safely through the storms.

What Leiv Eiriksson's missionary work in Greenland achieved we hardly

above: In foreground ruins of Sandnes homestead, Vesterbygd. This belonged to Torfinn Karlsevne and his wife Gudrid, and it was here that the Indian arrowhead and the lump of coal from North America were found (see pp. 163–6). *below:* Humber River, Newfoundland. (Photographs: National Film Board, Ottawa.)

The old church stood at the head of Hvalsøyfjord, at the foot of mighty Qaqortoq.

above: The plain of Gardar at the head of Einarsfjord. Here stood the cathedral and the bishop's house. The Greenlanders of today raise stock here. *below:* There are still traces of the old highway leading to the cathedral and bishop's house. Here we see part of the boundary wall enclosing the home-fields, and the gap in it where there was probably a gate. (Photographs: National Museum of Copenhagen.)

Deep Bight, Trinity North, Newfoundland. The Vinland voyagers could hardly have avoided touching at Newfoundland. Would they have failed to profit by such a country as this? (Photograph: National Film Board, Ottawa.)

1. Crucifix from Sandnes, Vesterbygd. 2. Wooden spoon-case found on an Eskimo site at Jakobshavn, Disko Bay. 3. Wooden platter from Vesterbygd. (Photographs: National Museum of Copenhagen.)

Crucifix carved in wood, found at the highest farm of Austmannadal, Vesterbygd, at the edge of the inland ice. (Photograph: National Museum of Copenhagen.)

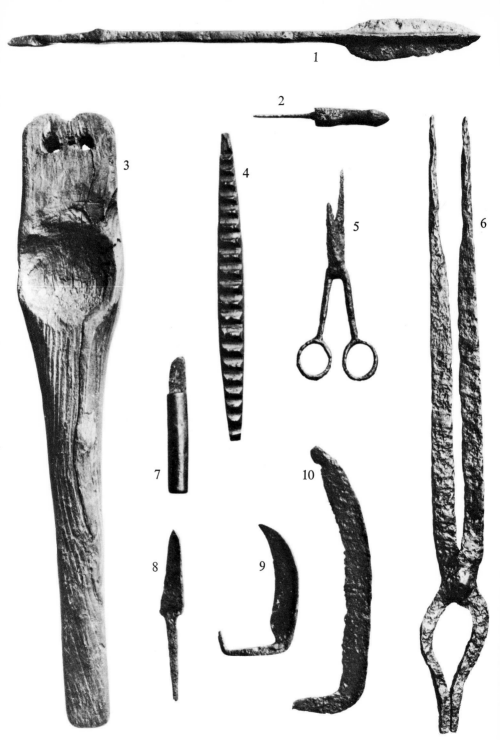

1. Spear. 2. Awl. 3. Press for horn spoons. 4. Tally-stick. 5. Scissors. 6. Smith's tongs 7–10. Knives, sickle and scythe. All were found in Austmannadal, Vesterbygd. (Photographs: National Museum of Copenhagen.)

know. Luck may have been against him, for his father, mighty Eirik the Red, was an obstinate man and held to heathen beliefs. When Leiv, on his way back from Norway, rescued an entire ship's crew from a reef and gained renown thereby, Eirik remarked sarcastically: 'The rescue of a whole ship's company is offset by the bringing of a hypocrite [priest] to Greenland.' His wife Tjodhild, on the other hand, received baptism, as was stated earlier, and built a church at Brattalid.

It is likely that some of the fjord chieftains of Greenland built their *hov* or temples and worshipped the ancient gods. Here as in other islands of the Western Ocean Thor seems to have been the deity to whom they chiefly paid allegiance and, as has been mentioned, pieces of soapstone with Thor's emblem upon it were found both at Brattalid and Herjolfsnes. In the Foster-brothers' saga we hear that an old woman living at Vik at the head of Eiriksfjord had the mark of Thor carved on her chair.[3] Torgils Orrabein-fostre, who was a Christian, though deeply rooted in the old faith, 'fought' against Thor during a perilous voyage to Greenland which ended in ship-wreck on the east coast.

Another echo from heathen times: when Torgils killed a bear near Brattalid, Eirik the Red was displeased. 'Some said that he followed the old customs and practised a sort of cult of this animal.' It is interesting to note that a number of primitive peoples have taboos connected with the bear.

In general we are struck by the space given to superstition in old stories of Greenland – more than in Iceland and Norway. It was a wild, stern country where dangers abounded and where there was much to stimulate the imagination: endless inland ice, black mountains, blue-green glaciers with bottomless crevasses; Eskimoes, strange beasts, drift-ice that swept the coasts and, in the west, unknown shores beyond the horizon. Mighty and mysterious forces were at work and, as among the Eskimoes, thoughts took wing into a world of superstition.

We hear much of dreams and omens, and particularly of ghosts, which people feared to an extent that we can scarcely imagine. In Eirik the Red's saga there is an account unique of its kind, dating from the early eleventh century, about a witch named Torbjørg.[4]

She lived in the most southerly part of Austerbygd, where in winter she would wander from homestead to homestead telling people's fortunes or prophesying about the crops of the coming season. Then a year of great famine struck Greenland: little fish or game was caught, and some hunters did not return from their expeditions. The chief of Herjolfsnes summoned the soothsayer. A high seat was prepared for her, and she was given cushions stuffed with chicken-feathers to sit on.

She wore a dark-blue cloak fastened about the neck with a cord; it was adorned from top to bottom with stones. Round her neck she wore glass beads, on her head a cap of black lambskin lined with white cat-skin; she carried a staff that had a brass knob, round which stones were inlaid. Her waist was girded with a tinder-belt, from which hung a big pouch to contain the magic materials she needed for her soothsaying. On her feet were furry calfskin shoes with long laces ending in large pewter buttons. Her gloves were of cat-skin, white and furry within.

She was greeted with veneration and led to the table by Torkel.

Porridge was made with cow's milk and there was a dish of the hearts of every kind of animal on the farm. She had a brass spoon and a tusk-handled knife with a double mounting of copper; the point was broken off.

The witch asked for help to prepare her magic; she needed someone who knew the words of a *kvad* called 'Vardlokur', for this was part of the spell. It was found that the beautiful Gudrid knew the verse, and although a Christian she consented to recite it. The witch now gained the power to see hidden things; she foretold that the famine would be over when spring came and that the epidemic that had attacked the settlement would pass off more quickly than was expected.

In heathen days it was the bold and reckless way of life that was thought most excellent in Norse countries; the important things were personal courage, achievement and reputation after death.

> Beasts die,
> Kinsmen die,
> Thou diest likewise.
> One thing I know
> That never dies –
> Judgment on a man who is dead.

Ancestry was all-important: it was the source of a stream that flowed to each individual member of the clan. Blood-vengeance was a duty. And there was strength in their fatalism: the threads of destiny spun by the Norns at every birth could not be severed even by the gods. Death was not to be feared, for it led to joyous Valhalla where Odin ruled.

Then, in sharp contrast, came Christianity with its message of sin, atonement and the punishments of hell. How it gained ground in Greenland is unknown. In Norway it was forced through by kings who used threats, torture and murder in the good cause. We hear of nothing like this in Greenland, but then our sources of information are scanty.

One by one tiny churches sprang up in the settlements. They were usually built beside the homestead of the fjord chief, perhaps on the site of the old heathen *hov* or temple, as in Norway. Most of these early churches were no doubt small and primitive, to be replaced later by larger ones. Beneath ruins now uncovered, traces of older foundations have come to light.

Distances were great, and for a long time churches were few and far between, so that the carrying of bodies to consecrated ground was a toilsome business. Of Torstein Eiriksson's death in Vesterbygd in about the year 1000 the saga relates:[5]

> It had been the custom in Greenland, after the coming of Christianity, to bury the bodies at the homestead where death had occurred, in unconsecrated ground, and to plant a stake upon the breast of the deceased. When next a priest came to the place, the stake was pulled up and holy water poured into the hole, and there was chanting over the bodies – even though a long time might pass before this could be done.

In the early days the great problem must have been to ensure an adequate priesthood, for there was nothing alluring in the prospect of setting forth across the ocean to convert hard-headed heathen in a remote Arctic country. Economic conditions for churchmen in Norway were miserable enough, and in Greenland they were certainly even worse. It seems too that men of God were held in low regard. Adam of Bremen rebuked them for their covetousness, and there is an illuminating entry in the Gulating Law: ' ... we have ceased to beat the priests to make them behave ... '

The Norwegian kings appear to have been greatly concerned to promote Christianity in Greenland and other islands of the Western Ocean; that this may have been a stage in their plans for temporal supremacy is another matter. In a variant of the Faereying Saga it is said:[6] 'King Olav (the holy, or St Olav) had already made the Orkneys subject to himself and sent word to Iceland, Greenland and the Faroes, where he had won many friends.' We know that his Christian legislation gained ground in Iceland, and it is reasonable to suppose that it found its way to Greenland as well.

In time the Church of Greenland became linked more officially with the parent Church. A document dating from 1055[7] tells us that from that year Greenland came under the archiepiscopal See of Hamburg. Adam of Bremen relates that delegates from the ends of the earth – such as 'the remotest Icelanders and Greenlanders' – waited upon Archbishop Adalbert, to entreat him to send priests to them or to appoint bishops. In 1056 Adalbert consecrated Isleiv bishop of Iceland, and by him sent letters to the people of Iceland and Greenland.

The Norse Greenlanders' connection with the See of Hamburg must have been of a tenuous nature, one reason being that vessels sailing from Greenland were normally bound for Norway or Iceland. And indeed, the learned Adam of Bremen seems not to have known much about the Greenlanders, for in the 1070s he writes:[8]

The people there are turned bluish-green by the salt sea from which this country takes its name. They live in the same manner as the Icelanders, except that they are more cruel, and torment seafarers by attacking and plundering them. It is said also that Christianity is widespread among them.

In 1104, in Lund (Sweden), an archbishopric was founded for the three Nordic countries, and it was natural that a number of the islands of the Western Ocean should come under the same authority.

Next we have the mysterious story of Eirik Gnúpsson, first bishop of Greenland, already referred to on page 119, who sailed (from Iceland?) in 1120, and in 1121 set off to visit Vinland, after which we hear no more of him. During his stay in Greenland he probably lived in Vesterbygd. Ivar Bårdsson speaks of a large church there which for a time was a cathedral and episcopal seat, and a number of finds suggests that this was Sandnes church, at the head of Lysefjord.

At this time the chief Sokke Toresson and his son Einar were living at Brattalid. It is said[9] that they were the foremost chiefs in Greenland and wielded great power. In 1123 Sokke summoned all homesteaders to a *Thing*, where he made it clear that the people could no longer do without a bishop, but must all contribute towards the setting up of a diocese. It was decided that Einar should sail to Norway to submit their case to the king, Sigurd Jorsalfare.

It was not ecclesiastical considerations alone that impelled the Greenlanders to support this cause so wholeheartedly. They were thinking that if Greenland were given a bishop, the Church would be bound to maintain sea-communications with Greenland, and this link with the outside world was always vital.

Einar set sail with a cargo of valuable goods which included walrus-tusks, hides, etc., and a live polar bear. These were to be gifts to the king and the chiefs to win their favour.

He arrived safely in Norway and presented his case to Sigurd Jorsalfare. This king was a widely travelled, tough fellow, yet deeply interested in ecclesiastical affairs; it was he who founded the bishopric of Stavanger. He agreed that the Greenlanders could well do with a bishop, and picked on the cleric Arnald for the post. Arnald fought shy of the honour, pleading that the Greenlanders were difficult people, but he had to comply and was later consecrated by the bishop of Lund.

Once negotiations were well under way, Einar produced his live polar bear. He seems to have kept it craftily in reserve until all was settled, and it may be that so rare a gift had its effect with the king. A polar bear in exchange for a bishop!

Einar and the new prelate set sail for Greenland, but were blown off course to Iceland, where they wintered. They reached Einarsfjord the following autumn, and Arnald settled at Gardar, which was to be the episcopal seat of the country for centuries to come.

At about the same time another Norwegian put to sea, bound for Greenland. His name was Arnbjørn Austmann. He owned two ships laden with valuable cargo, and apparently meant to trade with the Greenlanders. But time passed, and no word came from Arnbjørn or his men.

There was a man in Austerbygd whose name was Sigurd Njálsson: a fine seaman and hunter. His custom was to set sail on fishing- and hunting-expeditions, with a crew of fifteen, to the *ubygder* or waste places: that is, the ice-filled waters along the coasts of east Greenland.

One summer he and his men came upon some hearths close by the icefield called Kvitserk. At the head of a large fjord they spied two ships, a tent, a big hut, many corpses and a great quantity of goods. It was here, then, that Arnbjørn Austmann and his party had lost their lives.

Njálsson and his men boiled the corpses in cauldrons, and only the bones were later brought to church. One of the ships was a near wreck, and from her they salvaged all the iron nails. The larger ship was not only seaworthy, but was an exceptionally fine ocean-goer 'with a carved and painted figure-head: a great treasure'. They carried all the goods aboard and sailed the vessel back to Austerbygd.

Here the finders waited upon Bishop Arnald at Gardar, and it was agreed that the diocese should receive the costly vessel in return for Masses for the dead. The remaining valuables were shared out among the finders 'according to the laws of Greenland'.

When news of this reached Norway, the heirs took action. Arnbjørn's nephew Ossur and others who had lost kinsmen in the disaster off east Greenland equipped a trading-vessel, sailed to Greenland and entered Eiriksfjord. At that time there were two other trading-vessels at the settlements. One was Norwegian, and was commanded by Kolbein Torljotsson from Hadeland and Ketil Kalvsson, the latter being a descendant of the celebrated Ketil Kalv of Ringnes, in Hedmark, married to Gunhild the sister of Harald Hårdråde and of St Olav. The other was an Icelander, and the leaders aboard her were Hermand Kodransson and his brother Torgils.

Ossur took up residence with the bishop, and towards winter he pressed his claim as heir, demanding for himself and his men both ship and goods that had belonged to Arnbjørn Austmann. Arnald the bishop returned a flat refusal, whereupon Ossur left the bishop's house. The following spring he preferred his claim at the *Thing* of Gardar, but both bishop and Einar Sokkesson attended the meeting with a numerous following, and Ossur lost his case.

Resentful and humiliated, he made for the place where the disputed vessel lay and smashed two of her planks nearest the keel. He then sailed to Vesterbygd, where the other Norwegian ship was trading. He told Kolbein Torljotsson and Ketil Kalvsson what had happened, and they agreed to unite with him against the bishop and the chief of Brattalid. The situation was now critical.

On discovering the damage done to that splendid ship Bishop Arnald was enraged. He sent for Einar Sokkesson and reminded him of the oath he had sworn in Norway to support the rights of the Church in the face of all comers. He ended by saying: 'If this matter goes by default, I shall deem you a perjurer.' This was an arrogant way to treat the son of the chief of Brattalid, and it well illustrates the power wielded by the bishop of Greenland.

One day the people assembled to hear Mass and to attend a banquet at Langanes. Here, we learn, there was no resident priest, and the bishop himself was the celebrant. Many people attended, among them Einar and Ossur.

When divine service was over, the bishop made his way towards the place where the banquet was to be held. Einar was in attendance, but when they reached the door he turned abruptly, went back to the church door, snatched an axe from the hand of a bystander and struck the unsuspecting Ossur a mortal blow. He then entered the great hall where the tables were decked for the banquet, and reported the slaying; whereupon the bishop remarked: 'Such deeds are not good, yet this one may be excused.'

When these things became known, Ketil Kalvsson told the men of the Norwegian ships that he was familiar with the laws of Greenland and would undertake to bring an action for the killing. After a vain attempt to present his case it was agreed that the parties to it should seek reconciliation at the midsummer *Thing* at Gardar. And here they met, attended by many well-armed men.

Austmann's men arrived first, and concealed themselves in a cove. From here they spied Einar Sokkesson and his following heading towards Gardar. It so happened that just at this moment the bell rang for High Mass in the cathedral. The Norwegians thought the ringing was in honour of Einar and were angered, for at that time only kings and the highest ranking churchmen were so greeted. But Ketil said coolly: 'Heed it not. That bell may toll a knell ere evening.'

The two parties met on the parliament-plain. They included Bishop Arnald, old Sokke Toresson and his son Einar; Ketil Kalvsson, the leader of the Norwegians; Simon, the next of kin of the slain Ossur; and others. Sokke, as arbitrator, offered various objects in compensation for the killing, including an old coat of mail. Simon tossed it aside, saying that it was an insult to offer such rubbish for a Ossur like man.

This set the spark to the tinder. Kolbein struck Einar a mortal blow, and the two forces flew at each other in furious combat. Many were wounded and some killed. Austmann's people then headed across Einarsfjord to Skjalgs-budir and made their ships ready for sea.

Sokke was deeply stricken by the death of his good son Einar, the heir to the manor of Brattalid, and he spurred his people on to fight. Hall, from Solarfjøll in Eiriksfjord, now made his appearance: a man who seems to have been held in great respect. He doubted whether the Greenlanders could do much with their little boats against the great ships of the Austmann family, and he also doubted whether Sokke's men would fight hard enough. He offered to negotiate, and the offer was accepted.

Hall was given safe conduct aboard the Austmanns' vessel, and was nominated as arbitrator. His decision was that most of the slayings should cancel each other out without fines, but that because of the difference in standing between Einar and Ossur the Austmann claimants should be out-lawed in Greenland.

The Norwegians were short of provisions, but during a nocturnal foray ashore Ketil Kalvsson chanced upon a secret food-store in a pit, where he found 60 slaughtered cattle, about 500 kilos of butter and a quantity of dried fish. Having carried this aboard, he and his men hoisted sail and returned to Norway.

Kolbein had a live polar bear which he presented to the king, Harald Gille. Later he joined Sigurd Slembe's followers and was their accomplice in murdering the king. Ketil Kalvsson settled in Bergen, where he was held in high esteem.

Thus quite soon after his arrival in the country, the first Bishop of Greenland had a somewhat stormy time of it; yet he mastered the situation. Arnald gives us the impression of forcefulness and guile, which he used to consolidate ecclesiastical power. He did not even shrink from speaking his mind to the household of the chief of Brattalid.

Arnald held office in Greenland for over twenty years, and then, in 1152, was appointed bishop of the newly restored diocese of Hamar, in Norway. Among the ruins of the bishop's house there an ornamented piece of whale-bone was found, which may have been among the Arctic objects brought by Arnald to his new home.

XXII THE CHURCH
FLOURISHES — AND FAILS

SOMETHING new and significant happened in Greenland when the mighty Catholic Church struck firm root among the people. The King's Mirror says: 'If [the country] had lain nearer to other lands it might have been called the third part of a diocese. Yet they have now got their own bishop, as nothing else would serve, the distance between them and other people being so great.'

In 1152–3 the Norwegian Church was organized by the English cardinal Nicholas Breakspear (later Pope Adrian IV) in council with the Norwegian kings, Harald Gille's sons, at a great assembly in Nidaros. Thenceforth Norway had its own archbishop, who was to reside in St Olav's town. Not only the episcopal Sees of Norway came under his authority, but also those founded in the Islands of the Western Ocean where Norwegians had settled. He therefore ruled over the churches of Norway, Iceland, the Faroes, Orkneys and Hebrides, the Isle of Man and Greenland. The Church of Norway retained its independence down to the time of the Reformation.

In the course of centuries a series of bishops were appointed to Greenland.[1] The last one whom we know with certainty to have lived there was Alf, who took up residence in 1368 and died there in 1377; though it is probable that Bishop Anders came to Greenland about 1406. According to Oluf Kolsrud[2] there is mention of this in Lyskander's *The Greenland Chronicle* and of so factual a character that it may well be based on original documents. The rest of the bishops, Alf's successors, never visited the country, and *Episcopus Grenlandiensis* or *Gardensis* became an empty title.

During the period of resident bishops there were many gaps in continuity. There may have been various reasons for this. Certainly it cannot have been easy to find able men who were willing to make the perilous voyage to that cold and distant land. Some who were appointed allowed years to elapse before taking up residence there. Nor could it always have been a simple matter for the Archbishop of Nidaros to keep himself informed of ecclesiastical affairs in Greenland, so uncertain were sea-communications.

Two examples illustrate this. In a letter dated June 22nd, 1308, Bishop Arne[3] writes from Bergen to Bishop Tord in Greenland of events that had taken place nine years before. Arne was appointed to Greenland in 1315, and at the beginning of the 1340s a new bishop was nominated to replace him, as he was thought to be dead. It turned out that he was both alive and active. After Arne's death in 1348 Greenland was without a bishop for nineteen years or so; the reason this time being probably the Black Death, which struck so paralysing a blow at the Norwegian Church. The death of Alf was not known in Norway until six years after it occurred.

At times there were deputies to take the bishop's place, the best-known of these being Ivar Bårdsson. He administered the See from Arne's death in 1348 until his own departure from the country in about 1363.

Seal of Jakob Treppe, bishop of Greenland, consecrated 1411. He never went to Greenland. Inscription: 'The seal of Jacob by the grace of God bishop of Gardar.'

Olaf[4] seems to have been one of the most energetic prelates of Greenland, as well as a man of daring. He went to Greenland in 1247, charged by the Norwegian king Håkon Håkonsson to bring the Greenlanders under the Norwegian Crown. During his period of office he made the voyage to Norway via Iceland (where he was shipwrecked). On Maundy Thursday, 1276, he was in Nidaros, where he attended the consecration of Archbishop Håkon together with other bishops and in the presence of King Magnus (Lagabøter) and Queen Ingeborg. Four years later he returned to Greenland, where he remained until his death in 1280.

The establishment of the diocese led to increased activity in the life of the Church. The number of priests increased and more churches were built. As we have already seen, the numbers for Austerbygd are given in the records as twelve churches and two monasteries, and for Vesterbygd five churches. Most of these have been found, as well as three chapels-of-ease (see page 24).

The churches of Greenland were built of stone, though to what extent this was supplemented by turf and timber we cannot tell, as only the foundations survive. Hvalsøy church is an exception: its walls are still something like twenty feet high.

The cathedral of Gardar is in a class by itself, on account of both its size and its plan. As was mentioned, it measured 90 feet in length and had a chapel on each side of a large chancel. The other churches were of two types, the older having a chancel at the east and an open west wall which was presumably of wood (Gardar in its older form, Herjolfsnes, Sandnes and others). The newer ones were rectangular (Hvalsøy, Brattalid, etc.).

It is evident that the stone churches of Greenland are unrelated to those of Iceland, where wooden churches were common well into the Middle Ages. Later the material was turf. For many reasons it was natural that the Greenland churches should have been influenced by the Norwegian style of church-building. Norway was the mother-country with which trade was carried on and from which emigrants came, among them the bishop and other clergy. The bishop of Gardar was suffragan to the Archbishop of Nidaros.

The Sees of Iceland and the Faroes were in a similar position; thus many of Iceland's old stave-churches were built on the pattern of the Norwegian ones. The sagas tell us that St Olav presented timber for a church in the Westman Islands, and that Torkel of Helgafjell copied King Olav's church in Nidaros. At the episcopal seats of Skálholt and Holar in Iceland, in the fourteenth century, there were greater timber churches based on the type common in the archdiocese of Nidaros at that time.

One would expect the mother-country to exert an even greater influence on church-building in Greenland, which was more isolated from other cultures; and this was indeed the case. It is true that in Greenland (Hvalsøy excepted) lime mortar was not used as in Norwegian stone churches, but that was from lack of materials. Apart from this the two styles have much in common.

In Norway we may see old stone churches with a narrow chancel like those of Herjolfsnes, Gardar I, Sandnes, etc. There are also a considerable number of rectangular stone churches resembling Hvalsøy in ground-plan and style. Aage Roussell draws a parallel with Eidfjord and one or two other such churches, but one might mention at least a score of similar type. He has also pointed out that these, like Hvalsøy, are twice as long as they are broad, taking the outside measurement. This indicates that the Greenland churches inherited the style of those of west Norway; in the eastern part of that country they were shorter and wider in plan.

As regards the cathedral of Gardar, excavation has shown that originally

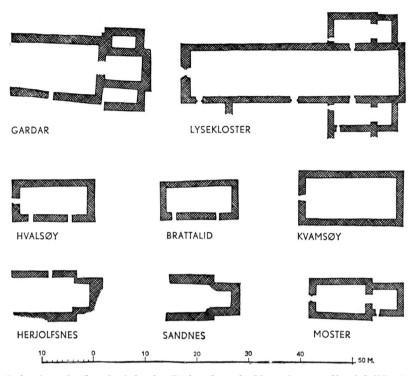

GARDAR   LYSEKLOSTER

HVALSØY   BRATTALID   KVAMSØY

HERJOLFSNES   SANDNES   MOSTER

10   0   10   20   30   40   50 M.

Left: *plans of 3 Greenland churches*. Right: *those of 5 Norwegian ones*. *Church-building in Greenland seems to have been strongly influenced by that of Norway*.

it had no chapels, only a somewhat narrow chancel. After its enlargement (Gardar II), it had a plan comparable only to that of Lysekloster near Bergen and to an early stage in the development of Nidaros Cathedral (1070–1100). The similarity is striking.

How old are the Greenland churches? It is important to bear in mind that most churches in Norway were built between 1150 and 1250. In the medieval period succeeding 1350, very few were erected. Moreover, it would have taken some time for a new building-style to reach the Arctic.

Of the earliest Greenland churches, traces of which can be seen beneath the later ones, we know little. Some of them may well have been small wooden stave-churches, for during the first hundred years the Norse Greenlanders had big ships and like the Icelanders were able to bring timber from Norway. At first, too, there must have been vast quantities of driftwood along the coasts.

The earliest stone churches in Norway had a narrow chancel, but by the end of the thirteenth century rectangular churches were commoner, and it

203

is natural to presume a parallel development in Greenland. There too the churches with the narrow chancel must be the oldest, though in individual cases a more precise dating is difficult, as we have no finds to give us a sure clue. Gardar I, of which a number of walls are to be found beneath the newer church, appears to have been the first cathedral of the new diocese, begun by Bishop Arnald. He arrived in Greenland in 1127, but as the organization of both diocese and church-building took time, the structure could hardly have been finished until later in that century.

The situation in Norway further indicates that the rectangular churches of Greenland, such as Hvalsøy, Brattalid, etc., were built about 1300.

The Norse Greenlanders did not copy their models slavishly, but worked out their own solution to particular building-problems. An example of this is the west end-wall which in a number of churches appears to have been of timber. Such a wall would have been an enlivening feature; it may be that the planks were erected as in a Norwegian stave-church and embellished with carvings. The people had also evolved an efficient method of building in the local stone, clay being often used as mortar.

The widespread influence gained by the Catholic Church in so remote and sparsely populated country is surprising. In relation to the environment, the bishop's 'palace' and the cathedral were impressive; and in addition to churches the Greenlanders could boast of a nunnery and a monastery.*

The prelate seems to have maintained full prestige and to have abated nothing of ecclesiastical dignity. Clothes, too, had to conform to a pattern befitting princes of the Church. In 1308 Bishop Arne of Bergen writes to Bishop Tord of Greenland to say that he is sending a cask of currants as a gift to the monasteries, also 'a consignment of cloaks and surcoats, and chaperons [hoods] of a pale-blue colour, all lined with minever, and there-with a coat of the same stuff'.[5]

But it was not always easy to obey the rules of the Church in such a land. What did the clergy do about bread and wine for Holy Communion? Corn did not grow in that country, and sometimes years might pass between the arrivals of ships from Norway. The difficulties that might arise are reflected in a pronouncement addressed by Pope Gregory in 1237[6] to Archbishop Sigurd. From this it appears that he permitted some substitute for wine, but insisted that bread must be used for the Holy Eucharist. How did the Green-landers solve this problem?

That the Church attained such supremacy in Greenland is partly owing to the fact that in the twelfth and thirteenth centuries the country had certain economic resources. Tusks, hides, etc., fetched good prices in the European markets. The Church exploited this potential wealth to an extent that must

* The former dedicated to St Benedicta, and the latter to SS Olav and Augustine.

have imposed burdensome taxation on the Greenlanders. It was the laity who paid for the building of churches, the running of the episcopal estate, the maintenance of bishop and clergy, and the like.

The dues payable to the Church increased as its position in Norway strengthened, and payment was enforced by such effective means as penalties, fines, confiscation of property, excommunication and so on. Besides the customary tithes the people of Greenland had to contribute Peter's Pence, and the clergy were liable for the crusade-tax. In 1327 these last two exactions alone brought in between four and five tons of walrus-tusks. Bertrand de Ortolis, the papal legate, sold them to a merchant from Flanders for a huge price: an incident to which I shall refer in more detail later.[7]

The crusade-tax from Greenland is mentioned in no fewer than three papal letters. At a council in Lyons in 1274 it was decided that archbishops themselves should travel about their dioceses and collect this tax. The Archbishop of Nidaros begs to be spared the long voyage to Greenland and to be allowed to send a representative. In a letter dated December 4th, 1276, Pope John XXI includes the comment:[8] 'You say that it would be a matter of great difficulty to undertake a personal visitation, since the diocese of Gardar which is subject to your province and government lies so far from the See of Nidaros, that because of the wildness of the ocean and the like, five years would hardly suffice ... '

In a letter dated January 31st, 1279,[9] from Pope Nicholas III, the archbishop received permission to send a deputy with full powers to collect the crusade-tax, and also to remit any penalties incurred by the Greenland clergy through contravention of ecclesiastical laws.

The emissary must have made a fairly rapid voyage, for by 1282 he was back in Norway. The archbishop wrote to the Pope[10] setting forth the various difficulties involved in levying taxes in Greenland. He mentions among other things that the people have no money, and can pay only in hides, seal, walrus-tusks and walrus-rope: commodities that fetched no very high price. He then asks what action he is to take with regard to this distant and impecunious diocese, from which the tax collected is of little monetary value.

The Pope did not yield, and in a letter dated March 4th, 1282,[11] he replies that the crusade-tax shall be paid in kind and the produce sold in Norway. This is an interesting illustration of how by its fishing and hunting the little Arctic community had to contribute towards the cost of the crusade that was launched to win back Palestine from the Saracens.

The amount collected must have been considerable. Payment was made in kind: walrus-tusks, butter, wadmal, dried fish, skins, wool and other wares. In Iceland butter and wadmal were customary tribute, and in the eighteenth century we hear that each of the two episcopal seats received about 15,000 kilograms of butter.[12] This was 'sour' (unsalted), and it kept for many years, says the Icelander Eggert Olafsen.[13] The bishop had spacious warehouses to contain all this, as well as the goods he imported from Norway. From the mighty stones that formed the foundations of a large building facing the bishop's house at Gardar, we may deduce that the prelate had ample storage-space for his many valuable goods.

It appears, too, that in time the Church became the greatest landowner in the country and held a dominant position. This was very largely made possible by Cardinal Nicholas's decree of 1152, whereby each man might bequeath up to a quarter of the property (land and goods) that he had himself acquired, and a tenth of his inheritance, without reference to his heirs. And no doubt in Greenland – as elsewhere – there were sick and dying who sought to ensure salvation by making gifts to the Church.

From Ivar Bårdsson's description it seems that in the first half of the fourteenth century, the bishop's seat, the churches and the monasteries owned nearly all the land round the fjords where they were situated. Indeed, the bishop had a monopoly of reindeer-hunting on a large island outside Einarsfjord, and of whaling and bear-hunting at profitable points as far as the east coast. He probably fitted out his own boats and hired men to exploit these rights.

This too is illuminating, for it suggests that a large number of Greenlanders were leaseholders of the Church. If so, it was in line with developments in Norway, where from the twelfth century onward the Church was expanding vigorously and gradually increasing in power and wealth, to become in course of time a greater property-owner than either the Crown or the nobility. It possessed about a quarter of all cultivated land in the country, whereas a sixth belonged to the Crown, a sixth to the nobles and the remainder – two-fifths – to freeholders (udallers). Landed estates were concentrated in so few hands that three-quarters of the farmers in the country had become tenants.[14]

The Norwegian clergy had special privileges and, after the Tønsberg agreement of 1277, wide judicial powers. The Archbishop of Nidaros was a dominating figure, and other prelates ruled their dioceses like petty kings. The Church added to its prosperity by many means, not least through commerce. The Archbishop of Nidaros was one of the greatest merchants in the land; he owned fishing-stations, eggeries and seal-rookeries, he was a wholesale buyer and ship-owner, with his own vessels in north Norway, Iceland and England. The same was true, to a lesser degree, of other Norwegian prelates, besides a number of churches and monasteries.

These conditions were reflected in Greenland, as was only to be expected, since the Archbishop of Nidaros was the primate of all the Islands of the Western Ocean. It is also significant that the Norwegian Church's great period of expansion occurred in the twelfth and thirteenth centuries, and thus coincides with the period of church-building in Greenland. After the Black Death in 1349, the Norwegian Church declined steeply and the shortage of priests became acute. This blow seems to have had even stronger repercussions in Greenland, and it was not long before bishops ceased to be sent there.

The Church exerted its authority in many departments of everyday life, and its demands were often especially burdensome for people leading a hard and isolated existence in an Arctic country. There were many holy days to be observed, much time was spent in travelling to and from church, church buildings had to be kept in repair and there were duties to be performed in the service of priest or bishop. A bare existence demanded such unremitting labour that any loss of working time bore hard on the family. When the reindeer migrated, or whales headed into the fjord, or seal flocked in among the offshore islands, little meat and few skins were to be won if the hunter was working for the bishop. Then on long hunting-expeditions when meat was the daily fare, fast-days were another problem. It is true that the Catholic Church could give dispensation from certain rules, but we may well wonder whether this was done to an extent adequate to so vast and outlandish a country.

The Pope's prohibition of marriage within seven degrees of consanguinity must have been another hardship, the more so as the ban extended to 'spiritual kinsfolk' – that is to say godparents, for example, whose role brought them into 'spiritual kinship' with each other and with the child's parents.

In this connection an interesting letter has recently come to light, written by Pope Alexander III between 1164 and 1181. As Knut Robberstad[15] has shown, it must refer to Greenland. Envoys from the Archbishop of Nidaros had petitioned the Pope on behalf of people living on an island twelve days' sailing away – too far for them to find wives elsewhere – requesting permission for them to marry among themselves even when within four degrees of consanguinity. The Pope could not consent to this, but said that the archbishop might give dispensation on advice from his subordinates to allow marriage between persons related in the fifth, sixth or seventh degrees.

Superstition was never uprooted – the roots went too deep – and magic went hand in hand with Christianity, or was interwoven with it.

From time to time the Church may have met with contrary winds, for the Norse Greenlanders were tough folk, and no doubt when spiritual leaders were exorbitant in their demands some priest or other came to a sudden and untimely end. Such things happened in Norway all through the ages, especially in remote areas.

Relations with the Eskimoes may have been another consideration. According to the laws of the Church it was forbidden to associate closely with heathen, heretics and excommunicated persons. This did not mean that the Norse Greenlanders kept away from the Eskimoes, but that the Church set limits as to how far the two races might mix. Co-habitation with an Eskimo was certainly unlawful. Yet from time to time the barrier would be crossed, and then as now, no doubt, a white man set up house with an Eskimo girl.

Such breaches must have been exceptional, however, and there is much evidence to show that the Norse Greenlanders were steadfast in the faith. In the course of centuries it gained firm hold on these people, who fought for their livelihood amid harsh and perilous surroundings. Their way of life made for simplicity of mind, and the Catholic Church with its splendour and ritual must have wrought upon them with powerful effect.

Both texts and archaeological finds show how particular the people were in obeying the injunction to bury the dead in consecrated ground. The rule of the Church was that clergy should be buried in the church itself, other eminent persons outside under the eaves, and the rest elsewhere in the grave-yard. But sometimes it was necessary to bury the body where it was, and to hope that sooner or later a priest might come to make the sign of the cross over it. Thus on an island off Ivigtut, far from any church, a tombstone has been found on which is carved in runes: Ossur Asbjørnsson.

During long sea-voyages it was the custom to drop the dead overboard: to sail with such a cargo was not auspicious. In the churchyard at Herjolfs-nes, inside a coffin, a rune-staff was found on which was plainly engraved: 'This woman whose name was Gudveig was lowered overboard in the Greenland Sea.' In Christian soil she must lie, even if only symbolically, with empty grave and a rune-staff, just as in Norway burial mounds were raised for Vikings who perished on the high seas.

It appears that the Norse Greenlanders held fast to Christianity to the last – even after the link with Norway was broken. Archaeological finds all point to this; not one suggests that the people reverted to heathendom. Bodies from as late as about 1500 or so have been uncovered in Herjolfsnes churchyard, clad in their strange woollen garments, with hands folded and often a little wooden cross at their breast.

It is hard to estimate just how much the Church meant to the Green-landers; for that our sources are too sparse. On the practical level, it brought about an improvement in sea-communications with Norway, yet on the other hand it deprived the people of much of their land and their freedom.

Then in 1377, or it may be 1406, the Church ceased to send any more bishops to the country, and shortly afterwards it completely abandoned the little community in the distant west. The union of Norway and Denmark had been accomplished, and new ecclesiastical problems were more im-portant. One can understand that the German Danish–Norwegian kings in

Copenhagen should have left the Norse Greenlanders in the lurch; for the Danes, Greenland was something quite alien and outside their traditions. But for the Catholic Church it was another matter: throughout several hundred years it had assumed obligations towards the people in that far country. And now it failed them.[16] This is a dark page in the history of the Church.

XXIII GLIMPSES OF AN ARCTIC COMMUNITY

I N what follows I shall mention a few of the circumstances that helped to shape the community and give it its character. Yet how little we know of this world which for five hundred years was the scene of so many strange events and destinies!

In Norway and Iceland the great families were an essential part of society: they were like a community within the community. The family was linked to the land, and its members had the obligation to protect and avenge their own. A number of the leading Greenland houses are mentioned in the texts, and although few details are given, there are strong indications that the Norse concept of the importance of the family was preserved.

Were there feuds in Greenland, such as we hear of in Norway and particularly in Iceland, where vengeance was a perpetual nightmare? The sources are silent. We do indeed hear of Tormod Kolbrunarskald's revenge, but that was a 'star turn' by a stranger to the country. It seems likely that the Arctic soil was less productive of family feuds. The struggle for existence demanded such intensive effort that the people had their hands full. It was more important to hunt reindeer and seal than to pick quarrels. Also most of the chiefs owned their own separate fjords, so there would have been less occasion for rivalry in the matter of land, forest and pasture. (Among the hunting-grounds it may have been otherwise.) A contributing factor to peace and good order was no doubt the scarcity of alcohol.

We saw that when in 1120 or so Sigurd Jorsalfare chose Arnald as bishop of Greenland, Arnald begged to be excused, partly on the grounds that 'the Greenlanders were headstrong folk, difficult to deal with'. That was no doubt true: they had been trained in a hard school, and now and again through the years there may have been wrangles and fights, though neither sagas nor archaeological finds tell us much about this. In the Fosterbrothers' Saga a coat of mail is mentioned, and from Austmannadal a primitive carving on a weaver's batten shows two men fighting with swords. From Gardar comes a drawing of a man carrying a sword or cudgel, and in the Narssaq ruins, a little north-west of Julianehåb, part of a wooden sword was found: a child's toy, no doubt, but modelled on some grown-up original. Finally, in an Eskimo ruin in Marshall Bay, at about 79° N., a fragment of a coat of mail came to light.[1]

In general, however, conditions in the Arctic must have tended to make the Norse Greenlanders first and foremost a hard-working people.

We find in the records a note or two about men who fell foul of the community. The *Flóamanna saga* from the eleventh century tells of an outlaw named Rolv who lived alone a little to the east of the southern tip of Greenland. It was Torgils Orrabeinfostre who came upon him on the way to the settlements after being wrecked on the east coast. When Torgils arrived at Brattalid he interceded for Rolv and had him proclaimed *fredhellig* – in sanctuary – which meant that he might rejoin his fellows in the settlements.

Outlawry was somewhat different in character from that of Norway and Iceland. There the condemned man had to leave the country, but it was a difficult matter to get away from Greenland which was so far from anywhere. The solution was to banish the outlaw to a remote corner of the country, and some of the loneliest of the ruins may have been the homes of such men. Their lot must have been hard indeed, not only because they had to maintain life in the poorest and least fertile parts, but also because they were alone in a land where co-operation with others was almost a necessity. It is possible that some outlaws joined the Eskimoes.

The sagas give us an occasional glimpse of the women of Greenland, who seem to have held as influential a position in the community as they did in Norway and Iceland. There was Sigrid, wife of the steward Lodin of Brattalid, who no doubt had her romantic adventure with that tempestuous guest Tormod Kolbrunarskald while her husband morosely recalled the old Håvamål song about the faithlessness of women. Then there was Freydis, illegitimate daughter of Eirik the Red: a headstrong, ruthless woman.

Gudrid Torbjørnsdatter was of a different type. She was a radiant figure: not only was she exceptionally beautiful, but she seems also to have had a remarkable personality. Gudrid came to Greenland about the year 1000, and as has been mentioned was married first to Eirik the Red's son Torstein, with whom she lived in Vesterbygd. Next she married Torfinn Karlsevne and sailed with him to Vinland, where she stayed for three years and bore a son, Snorre. She then returned to Iceland via Norway. After Torfinn's death she journeyed to Rome, took the veil on her return and thereafter lived as a hermit.

The demands made upon the women of Greenland were harsh and exacting, and women's contribution towards the life and fortunes of the community is impressive. They sailed with their menfolk on perilous ocean-voyages, and tackled a life as stern as it could well be. A heavy burden of toil lay upon their shoulders, for besides the work of house, byre and meadow, there was the never-ending weaving. Weaving had to go on, not only for clothes, bedding, tents, sails, etc., but also for barter with Norway. They must have had great stamina, of mind as well as body.

During the first hundred years, thralls were a singular feature of the Greenland community. As in Iceland, they were often of Irish origin and sometimes of distinguished birth. I have already mentioned the importance of this labour-force in a country like Greenland (see page 59). The close of the Viking era cut off the supply of thralls, and to rear such a class at home proved very difficult; so we may suppose that as in Norway the system came to an end during the eleventh century. Instead, the big landowners attached free-born men to themselves by giving them smallholdings, and claiming a certain amount of labour from them in return. In Greenland this must have been a sound arrangement, for it meant that the chiefs need not maintain a large labour-force all the year round, but could demand help at busy times, whether on the farm, or in the fishing and hunting seasons.

There were also the Eskimoes. There had been a time when to the Norse Greenlanders they seemed unreal: imaginary creatures dwelling far to the north. They had been seen by an occasional hunter, whose kinsfolk and neighbours would flock to listen in amazement to tales of these Skraelings – these beings who were not like ordinary folk.

Then slowly the Skraelings moved south, right down to the mouth of the settlement fjords, and remained there. They had become neighbours; and this set its own mark on the Norse community. We have seen how the two races had made contact with each other already, no doubt largely through trade, and later I hope to demonstrate how little foundation there is for the belief that their relations were mainly hostile.

The description of Bjørn Jorsalfare's stay in Greenland (1385–7) includes a moving little anecdote about two 'trolls' – Eskimoes.[2] Bjørn rescued a young brother and sister from a rocky islet; they attached themselves to him in deep devotion and were of most valuable help in all kinds of fishing and sea-hunting. What the girl most enjoyed was looking after her mistress Solveig's new-born baby boy. Desiring the same kind of headdress as Solveig's, she made her own out of whale-entrails. When Bjørn Jorsalfare and his family sailed from Greenland and would not take the Eskimoes with them, the youngsters threw themselves from a cliff into the sea and were drowned.

Nevertheless the Greenlanders' life did not consist entirely of toil, and as in the mother-countries they must certainly have gone in for many kinds of sports and games, dancing, singing and saga-telling. When folk from far and near had tented their booths on the parliament-place there was merriment enough, as there was at the banquets and parties in the various homesteads at the great festivals.

Among the house-ruins many chequer-board pieces have been found, showing that draughts and chess were a favourite diversion. Dice too have been discovered, but no boards. The pieces were made of walrus-tusk or occasionally wood, and some were lathe-turned.

The simpler draughts game arrived in Norway from the Romans via the south Germans, and excavation shows that it was known there a few years after the birth of Christ. There was more than one sort of chequer game, some involving the use of dice; and this tallies with the finds made in Vesterbygd. Both draughts and dice-games are often mentioned in old Norse literature.

The Norse Greenlanders were keen chess-players, and not only the chiefs and clergy. Pieces have been found on a farm right up at the edge of the ice-cap (Austmannadal in Vesterbygd). This remarkable game found its way to the Arctic from India. It reached the North probably in the twelfth century and became widespread there, not least in Norway and Iceland. In the Middle Ages the rules of the game differed somewhat from those observed today; for one thing the king could move more freely, and the queen's function was not the same.

Among the most ancient of the Norwegian chessmen are the fifty-eight pieces,* finely carved from walrus-tusk, which were discovered in the Hebrides: these date from the thirteenth century. A certain number of medieval pieces have also been found in Oslo, Bergen, Borgund and Trondhjem.

The Greenland chessmen are simple, and are not shaped as human figures. A number of them greatly resemble those found in Bergen and Trondhjem. The ones from Vesterbygd [3] are distinctive by their primitive and in some instances unique pattern. The knight looks like the pointed head of an Arctic fox on a little round stump (see Plate 26, fig. 1).

It is understandable that the Norse Greenlanders should have been attracted by this game. When winter gales whipped the homesteads it must have been a delight to sit by the blubber-lamp and lose oneself in the strange world of chess; and it adds a telling stroke to our image of these Arctic people to learn that they loved a game which demands so high a degree of concentration and imagination.

Hard though life in Greenland may have been, and isolated though the inhabitants were, there was fertile soil for poetry. When, in about the year 1000, famine ravaged the country, Gudrid reluctantly chanted the old *kvad* called Vardlokur, while the soothsayer Torbjørg worked her magic (see pages 193–4). The saga relates that Gudrid sang it more beautifully than anyone had ever been known to sing it before. Probably there was such music to Vardlokur as was sung in the magic songs of the Edda.

I spoke earlier of the Icelander Skald-Helge, who in the eleventh century

* At the British Museum.

settled in Greenland. We know nothing of his *kvad* except for the long fourteenth-century cycle which relates to him. This derives from older sources: there was a saga about Skald-Helge, and an Icelandic contemporary – a skald named Hallar-Stein – sang of him; but the poem has been lost. Hallar-Stein was well known: he served the Norwegian kings Harald Hårdråde and Olav Kyrre. Helge's son too was a poet.

Bjørn Jónsson's Annals of Greenland[4] tell of the northerly hunting-grounds of Nordrsetur, and say that these regions were much spoken of 'both in Skald-Helge's saga, and in this story of Tordis'. The latter document, which probably was lying on his desk as he wrote, has disappeared. No line of it survives.

Torhall Veidemann's two poems about Vinland, 'Hafgerdingardråpa', the song of the Hebridean priest, and 'Nordrseturdråpa', of which we have only a few fragments, have already been mentioned.

It is especially interesting that the Edda manuscript *Codex Regius* contains a long heroic *kvad* of about a hundred verses, called 'Atlamål det grønlandske', which must have been composed in Greenland, probably in the eleventh century. The theme is the story of King Atle and his relations with Gudrun and her brothers – a story of blood and revenge. It is remarkable in that it presents us with a Greenland version of a Germanic theme based on events occurring at the time of the great migration, especially those connected with Attila the Hun.

The poem testifies to its own origin. The natural setting is that of Greenland. The heroine *rows* across a fjord to King Atle's kingdom; king and queen are depicted on a reduced scale. King Atle prefers charges at the *Thing* like any yeoman chief; he has a bodyguard of thirty men, and regards this as more than adequate. And in the dream the polar bear appears:

> In came a bear and
> Smashed down our posts;
> Lifting his paw he
> Lamed us with terror;
> Gaping towards us he
> Drained us of strength.
> Frightened we ran into
> All the house-corners.
>
> Tempests await us, and
> Perilous storms. Of
> Easterly blizzards the
> Bear was an omen.

The 'Atlamål' of Greenland is not borne on the wing-beats of great poetry: too many details are dragged in, and they hamper the flight. Nevertheless it contains powerful and vivid – indeed haunting – features. It was conceived in an isolated community, amid a wild and savage landscape: we feel this as we feel an undertow. It may well be that the Norse Green-landers were singing chiefly of their own life – as do the Eskimoes – whereas the fortunes of kings and heroes in foreign lands soon receded into some-thing hazy and remote, with which a poet of Greenland would not naturally identify himself.

With the Edda, however, the Greenlanders were familiar, and they treated the story of Atle in their own manner. In addition to the Greenland *kvad* and one or two sagas already mentioned, I may add Snorre Sturlason's 'Háttatal', which speaks of a 'Greenlandish verse-speech', from which we may deduce an independent form of poetry.*

The Sturlunga saga names a certain Greenlander called Styrkar Sigmunds-son who moved to Iceland, and there spoke of conditions in Greenland.[5] Of him it is said that he 'was a great and truly able saga-teller'. This gives us a glimpse into a world which is now a mystery. No Norse race can have lived for nearly five hundred years in a country like Greenland without handing down a verbal tradition deeply rooted in the past. We recall now not only sagas and *kvad*, but also myths and folk-songs.

This world vanished with its people. Never shall we know what stories the weatherbeaten old fellow told beside the long-fire to the wide-eyed boys sitting round him on the earthen floor. Never shall we learn the song sung by the young girl of Greenland, when sunshine flooded the blue heights and her heart was full.

We do know something of Greenland's artists. On two coffin-boards from Herjolfsnes are carved a bold animal-head and a number of twisting bands (the loop pattern), indicating the Urnes style. Similar bands have been found on the Sandnes farm in Vesterbygd, also a chair-arm carved with heads of animals, and a wooden crucifix shaped by a sure hand and with a great sense of effect.[6] Then there are the pastoral staff from Gardar and some ornaments of soapstone and wood. On the whole it is a modest art that has been preserved. Lastly may be mentioned a small crucifix from the highest homestead in Austmannadal, one of the remotest in Vesterbygd (see Plate 37). It is easy enough to criticize this Christ-figure, but the very crudeness of the execution – its very deficiencies – are what move one in this carving made in the shadow of the inland ice.

The eleventh-century Fosterbrothers' Saga tells us that Torgrim Trolle's 'Thing-booth' at Gardar was adorned with splendid tapestries.[7] It seems

* The word 'poetry' here should be taken in its widest sense. There is no exact equivalent in English for the original Norwegian word *diktning*, which denotes any creative and imaginative literary form, whether or not it is ever written down. [Trans-lator's note.]

likely that some of these were picture-weavings like those of Iceland, where the hangings in such booths sometimes had figures and inscriptions in colour. In Norway picture-weaving had been known since the beginning of the Viking period (the Oseberg ship), and it is often mentioned in sagas and *kvad*. The plants from which dye was extracted grew also in Greenland, and among all the weaving that the women did there, it would be strange if they did not sometimes produce examples of this work.

The arrival in Greenland of bishop and clergy, and their sojourn there for years on end, must have caused repercussions far beyond the ecclesiastical sphere. The senior clergy of Norway came from the best families in the country, and from the middle of the twelfth century most of them had probably studied abroad, especially in England and France. They learned Latin and widened their horizons, and it did not take long for currents from the Continent to reach Norway.

It must have seemed very strange to a bishop bred to a studious collegiate life in seething Paris to arrive in Greenland, where people lived in houses of stone and turf and hunted polar bears on the drift-ice.

Even if many of the priests who came were imperfectly trained, still the sons of the Church were bearers of culture and exerted their influence in many ways on this isolated and primitive community. This influence should not be overestimated, however, for the country was vast and the people scattered.

We might imagine that through the ages the Church of Greenland would have preserved a considerable quantity of pictorial art and documents of various kinds. Much of the weaving, carved objects of wood and soapstone for the adornment of churches and so on, and perhaps also paintings, must have disappeared; even though, compared with other countries, the collection was a modest one. The episcopal seat surely had some sort of muniment-room for church books and documents, in the Catholic manner; and now and then – as in Iceland – some learned bishop or monk may have written of other than churchly matters.

Of pictorial art little remains, of writings none. Yet perhaps one day we may stumble upon some yellowed parchment in the frozen soil of Greenland.

A little rune-staff; nothing to look at – just a piece of flotsam polished in its drift across the Arctic Ocean from Siberia. But the stiff characters engraved upon it many hundred years ago evoke an image of the past, and people who were living then seem suddenly quite close to us. A Norse Greenlander once held this stick in his hand, and bending over it with great solemnity carved rune after rune in the firm belief that it would win the aid of higher powers. At the beginning of time, so men said, runes were hidden and bound here and there about the world – on the paw of a bear, the claw of a wolf, the beak of an eagle, the nail of a Norn. But the god Odin released them, and from the mountain he fetched down also the drink of the skalds.

The runes had magic force which could guard men's lives; they were the key to Nature's secret workshop where destiny was forged. Rightly used they were a defence against sickness, distress at sea, arrows, swords, hatred, revenge and other evils, and they could bring the most fervent wishes to fulfilment. Under the floor of Urnes stave-church in Sogn (Norway)[8] was found a little rune-staff bearing the following inscription:

Arne the priest wants Inga.

In the old Norwegian-speaking area – Norway and the Islands of the Western Ocean – about 1,100 inscriptions in the later runic writing have been found, of which something like 750 were in Norway itself. The rest were scattered among the new Norwegian settlements in the west: the Faroes, Greenland, the Shetlands, Orkneys and Hebrides, the rest of Scotland, the Isle of Man and Ireland. As regards Iceland in particular, runic writings of the Viking era and later, until the thirteenth century, are entirely lacking.[9]

Among the most fascinating inscriptions from the Isles of the Western Ocean are those of the large group of runic crosses – thirty in all – found on Man. Of no less interest are the thirty or so runic inscriptions of Maeshowe in the Orkneys: a strange, dome-shaped barrow dating from a prehistoric era. A long, covered-in stone corridor leads into a great vault, also of stone. Here in this chilly chamber, where some time in the eleventh century Norsemen carved their runes, there lingers a peculiar atmosphere of past ages. One of the inscriptions reads: 'These runes were carved by the man most cunning in [i.e., with the best knowledge of] runes west of the ocean.'

The importance of runes, as has been said, lay in their magic powers, which were especially potent in the secret runes. They were used far into the Christian era; indeed, in Telemark and Dovre (Norway), as late as the nineteenth century.[10] To some extent, it seems, runes were used also for practical purposes, like the ones discovered in recent excavations of the German Quay of Bergen, which seem to have been connected with buying and selling.

'Atlamål', the heroic *kvad* composed in Greenland, makes frequent mention of runes. They are important: they intervene in men's lives. We read, for example:

> Wise was Kostbera,
> Cunning in runes;
> Rune-staff she read
> By the light of the fire ...

End of The Greenland Atlamål (*so named in the manuscript itself*). *From the Elder Edda,
MS. dating from about 1270. The entire* kvad *or lay was probably composed in Greenland.*

Here then is vivid evidence from the Arctic that the Norse Greenlanders
were versed in runic mysteries at a very early date.

There are a couple of other records of runes in Greenland. In Bjørn
Jónsson's account of Lik-Lodin,[11] who lived about the middle of the eleventh
century, we read that he was in the habit of sailing to the northern *ubygder*
or waste places in the summer, and bringing back the bodies of those who
had been wrecked in the drift-ice. He found them in caves and crevices, and
with them runes telling of the disasters they had met with. Again, the Sturlunga saga,[12] speaking of Ingemund the priest who perished in a cave in
east Greenland, tells us that wax tablets and runes were found, recording the
circumstances in which he met his death.*

As a background to these inscriptions we note that the sagas relating to
Greenland are much concerned with magic and the supernatural. We hear of
the witch who cast spells when famine set in; of Torhall Veidemann who
by means of sorcery caused a whale to run aground when the need was
greatest, and of Torgils Orrabeinfostre who threw an ox overboard for the
god Thor, to ensure success to his voyage. Visions, omens and ghosts
('walkers-again') make frequent appearance.

Life in the Arctic, beset with danger, bred superstition. The Eskimoes

---

* Magnus Olsen has been kind enough to tell me that the wax tablets consisted of
pieces of wood covered on the inner side with wax. Writing was done with a stylus, of
which the other end served as an eraser.

had their own: they protected themselves with conjurers and amulets; and in a corresponding manner the Norse Greenlanders sought to secure their existence by invoking the aid of the supernatural, often by means of runes. In Greenland sixty runic inscriptions have been found, of which thirty-five were in Austerbygd and the rest in Vesterbygd, except for one, which was discovered on the island of Kingigtorssuaq, far to the north of inhabited areas.[13]

The oldest and one of the most remarkable inscriptions was found at Narssaq, somewhat north-east of Julianehåb. It was mentioned earlier (page 52), but for the sake of this general survey I repeat the main points. On three sides of the rune-staff are carved, respectively, a complete 16-character runic alphabet, secret runes, and a text. Here the older alphabet of the later runes is used (the Norwegian–Swedish runes), which in Norway became obsolete about the year 1000. The inscription apparently dates from the early eleventh century – that is to say, from the time of the first settlers. As for the text: Erik Moltke, as we saw, renders it provisionally as: 'Bibrau is the name of the maiden who sits in the blue.'

The remaining inscriptions date presumably from about 1300, except for the one on the grave at Brattalid, 'Ingibjørg's grave', which is thirteenth century.

Especially interesting is the inscription on the little stone found in connection with the three cairns on the island of Kingigtorssuaq, away to the north on latitude 72° 57'. This, as we noted earlier (pages 88–9), is inscribed with a clear text and with some secret runes skilfully carved. Magnus Olsen calls this inscription an historic document, and perceives in the runes an affinity with those discovered at Maeshowe in the Orkneys, and in Urnes church in Sogn.

The inscriptions of Austerbygd include those on four gravestones: two from Gardar, one from Brattalid and one from an island off Ivigtut, in what is known as Mellombygd or Middle Settlement. This last one carries the inscription: 'Ossur Asbjarnarson'. Finnur Jónsson[14] suggests an interesting possibility regarding this man's family. Among the emigrants who in the tenth century sailed from Norway to settle in Iceland was one Asbjørn from Sogn. One of his sons who went with him was named Ossur. In view of the rigid tradition by which names were handed down from generation to generation in Norse families, it is quite possible that Ossur (Asbjarnarson) from Sogn was an ancestor of Ossur (Asbjarnarson) of Greenland, who died on an offshore island and whose grave was marked by a rune-stone.

Then we have the rune-staff of Gudveig, she who died at sea but nevertheless was given a grave in Herjolfsnes churchyard (see page 258). There are also inscriptions on seven small wooden crosses, probably made by priests. On some of them the Virgin Mary's name is written *maria* or *maia*.

On one is written 'God Almighty protect Gudleiv [woman's name] well.' On another: 'Torleiv made this cross in praise and adoration of God Almighty.' On a third: 'Jesus Christ help', and then, strangely enough, in Latin: 'Christ was born for us.' One of the crosses bears a long rigmarole of sacred words, much abbreviated and partially incomprehensible. This is clearly a magic formula of the kind known in Norway, as for instance in Borgund stave-church. Two grave-inscriptions are in Latin characters and on one of the stones is carved part of a name: apparently Roar Kolgrimsson.

But runes were not only for the protection of the dead. More than a dozen small implements from Gardar and Undir Höfdi have inscriptions on them, most often meaningless. Soapstone spindle-whorls have their runes here as in Vesterbygd and the Shetlands. But then in a country like Greenland it was most important that weaving should prosper.

The twenty or so runic inscriptions from Vesterbygd came from Sandnes homestead and from the farm at Umiviarssuk; there was also another at the highest farm in Austmannadal. They contain few Norse words and are most often carved on implements and objects in practical use, such as barrel-staves, wooden platters, handles, spindle-whorls, etc. On one of the oldest finds, a carved chair-arm (?) from Sandnes, the name Helge (hael[k]i) is written. There are also runes on a fish made of wood, no doubt to ensure good fishing-luck. In Vesterbygd as at Herjolfsnes magic formulas have been found composed of sacred and sometimes incomprehensible words; one at Sandnes and another in Austmannadal[15] cut into a board.

Thus, wherever they lived in Greenland, the Norsemen sought to make their existence secure by means of the magic powers of runes, and it is evident from this that such things were part of daily life.

Runic writings cast a light on the Greenland community and are a pointer to the deeper levels of the mind. They also tell us much about the evolution of the Norse language under exceptional conditions. For several hundred years it developed in a community so strictly isolated as to make us think of a laboratory where cultures are grown. Studies undertaken primarily by Magnus Olsen, Finnur Jónsson and Erik Moltke have produced striking results.

In their speech the Greenlanders were strongly conservative and on the whole they held fast by the old forms. Yet at the same time there was independent growth. To illustrate this I will cite a few essential observations from Magnus Olsen's work.[16]

A number of new runic forms were devised – those for example denoting ð, b, p and r – while older characters, obsolete in other countries, were preserved.

The Greenland idiom inherited characteristics from the settlement period, which at the time the runes were written (about 1300) were obsolete in Iceland and the other Norse countries. This applies to the vowel-sounds, to give one example. Features peculiar to Greenland survived, and to some extent the west Norwegian influence is evident.

From the earliest settlement period there was a tendency for the language to split up into dialects. The settlers came from different places: from Iceland and Norway, and some no doubt from the Faroes and the Scottish islands. The new population was scattered over a wide and mountainous country, as in Norway, where so many local dialects developed.

These facts appear from the runic inscriptions of Greenland. Their many individual characteristics, seen as a whole, lead to the conclusion expressed by Magnus Olsen in this way:

'By 1300 one cannot speak of an Icelandic language as including that of Greenland; we should think rather of a series of Norse dialects: Greenlandish, Icelandic, Faroese and other variants from the Western Ocean, as well as the different dialects of west Norway and other parts of that country.'

Place-names too have something to tell us about people and conditions. In the course of the long life of the Greenland community countless places along the east coast and among the hunting-grounds far to the north on the west coast must have been given names. The most northerly one we know of is Ivar Bårdsson's *Hammelradzfeld* – 'farther may no man sail who would preserve his life ... ' In all we know about a hundred names.[17]

A characteristic of this naming was the general use of terms descriptive of the landscape, as well as compounds embodying personal names. The first settlers sometimes called fjords and places after themselves: Herjolfsfjord, Herjolfsnes, Ketilsfjord, Einarsfjord, Eiriksfjord, etc. This is understandable: throughout the ages it has always been a human impulse for the first-comers to a new country to commemorate their discoveries and achievements in this way, and the Norsemen set great store by renown.

Among names descriptive of the country or based on some event we may mention [in English translation]: Whale Island Fjord, Seal Islands, Bear Island, Beast Point, Cove, Unfound Fjord, etc.

It is especially interesting to note that the Norse Greenlanders and the Eskimoes gave certain places names meaning the same thing in their respective languages: for example Isafjord (Ice-fjord) = Sermelik. It is hard to say whether the Eskimoes borrowed it from the Norsemen or whether it was chosen independently by both races.

One island is called Hrakbjarnarey, that is: 'the island where the bear was chased.' This had a primitive ring, and reminds one of the descriptive and often vivid names given by Indians and Eskimoes. It brings an event to life: at some time Norsemen sighted a bear; he lumbered off in his soft, clumsy way, and briskly the chase began with bow and arrow and spear – a tense, perilous pursuit ending, perhaps, with a spear-thrust through his chest.

We shall never know the outcome, but afterwards when the hunters gathered about the long-fire to talk, something special about that hunt gave birth to a new name: 'The island where the bear was chased.'

⌧⌧⌧⌧⌧⌧⌧⌧⌧⌧⌧⌧⌧⌧⌧⌧⌧⌧⌧⌧⌧⌧⌧⌧⌧⌧⌧⌧⌧⌧⌧

XXIV   THE LAW OF THE LAND

THOUSANDS of people were wresting a livelihood from the Arctic. How did they order their society?

'By law shall the land be built,' says the old Norse constitution – the Frostating Law. A firmly based judiciary was something essential to Norway, and it followed Vikings and emigrants across the seas. It became the backbone of the new states that were founded in the Islands of the Western Ocean: Iceland, the Faroes, the Shetlands and Orkneys, the Hebrides, etc. Among the many Norse names to be found on foreign shores some variant or other of the word *Tingvollen* occurs. It denoted the place of assembly, the place where right and justice ruled. Indeed, in the Isle of Man the Norse legal tradition is so strong that ancient ordinances still prevail in connection with Tynwald Hill – *Tingvoll-haugen*.

Norse law reached Greenland too. But let us first consider a little of the background – the state of justice in the lands from which most emigrants came: Iceland and Norway.

By the end of the ninth century Norway had been gathered into one realm by Harald Hårfagre – this was about a hundred years before the settlement of Greenland. During the first period the royal power was somewhat restricted: it took time to weld the many petty kingdoms into one.

From ancient times local *Things* had been held in rural districts and *Althings* for large areas – the juridical circuits. All independent yeomen had to attend the *Althing*, but this was difficult for those who lived a long way off. In about 950 therefore, a delegates' *Thing* was instituted under the name of *Lagting* or law-meeting. Here the principle of representation took effect: those who attended were homesteaders nominated in the various districts of the law-circuit, officers of the Crown and later also priests and bishops. Final decisions rested with the homesteaders. The *Lagting* had both legislative and judicial authority, and its leader was the law-man who recited the laws and settled legal points.

The old Norwegian legal system was chiefly one of precedent: it was based on usage and on resolutions passed by the courts and formulated in the law-man's speech. Not until the eleventh century were the laws first written down, as for example the Gulating Law which was valid for the whole province of Vestlandet, from Sunnmøre to Agder; and it was from this long stretch of indented coastline that so many vessels put out on Viking raids or carried emigrants to Iceland and Greenland.

Iceland was settled in the period 870–930 and mostly, as we saw, by Norwegians from west Norway or the Isles of the Western Ocean. Chiefs and landowners sailed across the sea with their following, took possession of large domains and shared out land among kinsmen and friends. With the new homestead a temple or *hov* was usually built, and often it was the chief himself who became the *gode* – that is the leader in the worship of the gods. Those who wished to attend the *hov* paid him a fee. Local *Things* were also formed, the chiefs having jurisdiction each over his own estate. In 930 Iceland instituted its *Althing* – one central meeting-place for the whole country. It met at midsummer, and all the *goder* (or *hov*-chiefs) had the duty of attending. The *Althing* had a court of law where the *goder* sat and of which the function was to make laws, dispense from laws and answer legal questions. The president was the 'law-saying-man' who had to recite the laws in a manner similar to that of the Norwegian law-man. The *goder* set up four courts of justice, one for each quarter of the country.

In 930 the Ulvljot Law was brought into force; this was modelled on the Gulating Law. In 1117 the Icelandic laws were written down, and the lawbook was called Havlidaskrå. No copy of this exists, but an essential part of its contents may be found in later transcriptions of the old Icelandic law *Grágás*.[1]

Iceland became a free state, and a peculiar feature of its constitution was that all power lay in the hands of the chiefs. Norway was a kingdom, yet at the *Thing* power lay with the commoners, and resolutions had to be passed by them all. Another point was that in Iceland there was no official machinery for the enforcement of law: this was a matter for the individual. In Norway it was the king who upheld and maintained the law, and had the right to claim compensation for any breach of it.

What was the situation in Greenland? Our sources furnish only scanty information, but occasional glimpses help us to build up some idea of what was done.

From the beginning it appears to have been an aristocratic society, in which every fjord-chief had dominion over his possessions. It is reasonable to suppose that some of them founded both *hov* and local *Thing*-place, like the Norwegian settlers of Iceland. The question remains whether these little communities along the Arctic coasts were linked together and whether Greenland was organized as an independent free state.

The Fosterbrothers' Saga[2] tells of a *Thing* at Gardar in Einarsfjord round about 1020, where Tormod Kolbrunarskald took revenge and slew the mighty Torgrim Trolle. The same meeting-place is mentioned also in the saga of Einar Sokkesson, in which is narrated the setting up of the bishopric, and the quarrel between Norwegian merchants and Greenlanders in the 1120s.[3] Both accounts show that the assembly concerned was an *Althing*: it is called the 'Greenlanders' *Thing*'.

From this and other evidence it is clear that the Greenlanders founded their *Althing* at a very early period – long before the country became subject to the Norwegian Crown. Gardar was a favourable site, lying as it did in the middle of the richest estates, and being easy of access.

The *Althing* of Greenland always had judicial powers, and although it is not expressly mentioned, we may safely assume that it had a corresponding legislature, as in other Norse countries. Mention in the texts of a law-man indicates this. In the fifteenth-century poem about Skald-Helge,[4] based on an old saga, the hero is elected law-man. Ivar Bårdsson,[5] writing in the middle of the fourteenth century, states that the law-man usually lived at Brattalid in Eiriksfjord.

It is also clear that Greenland had its own laws. The saga of Einar Sokkesson[6] mentions 'the Greenland laws' no fewer than four times in connection with a dispute over inheritance (see pages 197–9). Especially illuminating is the note that after Ossur the heir had been killed, Ketil Kalvsson undertook to present the Norwegian case, although not closely connected with it, because he knew the laws of Greenland.

Other facts go to show that the Greenland community stood on its own feet, and there is no hint that it was subject in any way to the authorities of Iceland or Norway until the middle of the thirteenth century, when it voluntarily gave its allegiance to the Norwegian Crown. Greenland was a free state.[7]

As in other Isles of the Western Ocean, the legal code was based on that brought over by the old Norse settlers, yet through the centuries the population developed their own special laws based on usage and precedent, largely as a result of the geographical and social conditions in which they lived.

Study of the individual customs (e.g. the 'bear-toll' and the burying of the dead in unconsecrated ground with a stake driven in above the breast, later to be removed so that holy water might be poured into the hole – both customs unknown in Iceland) shows that Norwegian laws obtained to some extent. This is what one might expect. It may well be that Icelandic law prevailed at first, inasmuch as most of the earliest settlers came from Iceland; although Eirik the Red himself was Norwegian by birth, and his family in Jaeren came under the Gulating Law. Later, many factors may have contributed to the strengthening of Norwegian influence. Not only was there trade between the two countries, but bishop and priests originated in Norway: people who at that time were better informed than most, and who gained a strong position in the Greenland community.

We have already seen how from the time of Eirik the Red the kings of Norway took an interest in Greenland, as for example Olav Trygvason, who in the eleventh century propagated Christianity in that country with the help of Leiv Eiriksson, and in the early twelfth century Sigurd Jorsalfare,* who gave the Greenlanders a bishop.

Many eminent Greenlanders made the voyage to Norway and were guests at court. Lastly, it seems that certain eminent Norwegians, closely related to the royal house, engaged in trade with Greenland during the first two hundred years (see page 237). We may therefore take it that the Norwegian kings were well informed as to that country and its economic potentialities, and that there were sound political reasons for their interest in the free state.

In 1247 Håkon Håkonsson set about bringing both Iceland and Greenland under the Norwegian Crown, strongly supported by Cardinal William of Sabina, who that summer was staying in Bergen.[8] At the same time Olaf was consecrated bishop of Greenland, and sailed from Norway, charged with the task of bringing about the subjection. But the Greenlanders do not seem to have been easy to persuade, for another fourteen years elapsed before the king had his way. He had kept three representatives there for four years, and they returned with this message:

> ... the Greenlanders laid upon themselves the duty of paying tax, and promised to pay fines to the king for manslaughter, whether it were Norwegians or Greenlanders who were slain, and whether it happened in the settlement or in Nordrsetur [the northern hunting-grounds]; yea, though the slaying should occur under the Lodestar [the North Star], the king should have his blood-fine.

Sturla sang:

> Northward ye would extend
> Your sway, o'er realms of cold;
> Pleasing this is to all good men,
> King beneath the lodestar!

> No chief before hath ruled
> Over such a kingdom,
> Ye shed the glory of your reign
> Farther than the sun can shine.

In 1262 Iceland too became subject to Håkon Håkonsson, and Norway's dominion was at its height. Besides Greenland and Iceland it embraced Finmark, the Kola Peninsula, the Shetlands, Orkneys and Faroes, and was a power in northern Europe.

We know nothing more of the agreement between the Greenlanders and

* Jorsalfare: 'the traveller to Jorsal' – i.e. Jerusalem.

the king, but we may suppose that for them as for the Icelanders the most important consideration was the maintenance of regular sea-communications with Norway.[9] By this time the Greenlanders no longer had any big ships at their disposal.

The king consolidated his power over the tributary countries by introducing his own laws. Magnus Lagabøter's land-law was chosen as the basis for the Icelandic law-book known as the *Jonsbok*, adopted at the *Althing* of 1281. But what of Greenland? Certain unreliable sources[10] have been accepted as evidence that the *Jonsbok* was introduced there also. It is possible that the Norwegian king was anxious to found a legislature that should be common to both countries, and that he made proposals to this end; but a resolution passed at the Icelandic *Althing* would have been meaningless in Greenland, which was in no way dependent on Iceland. The laws of Greenland had developed separately, and it would be strange if any proposal of a new law-book had not been submitted for the consideration of the *Althing* of Greenland.

That newer Norwegian laws gained ground in Greenland appears in the account of Bjørn Einarsson Jorsalfare.[11] He was a widely travelled, zestful and well-informed man. Together with his wife he not only sailed to the Holy Land, but twice visited Rome, and journeyed also to Spain, France, England and elsewhere. A skald (Einar Fostre) accompanied him everywhere, and he also kept a diary of all that happened; but this record has been lost. The fragments that survive of his travel-records are not all equally convincing, but those relating to Greenland bear in the main the stamp of truth.

In 1385, Bjørn Jorsalfare's ship and three others bound for Iceland were storm-swept to Austerbygd, where the crews wintered for two years. The Greenlanders made Bjørn district judge and revenue-officer, for which he received the emolument of 130 legs of mutton, plus other wares.

We find then that the Norwegian system of administrative districts and local government had been adopted in Greenland. Since the time of King Sverre the Norwegian district judges had held a special status and were in fact the executors of royal authority. They had police and punitive powers; they collected taxes, organized *Things*, defended the population against attack, and maintained men-at-arms for the preservation of order and the king's service.

A diploma of 1387[12] mentions a royal *ombudsman* who seems to have been the king's commissioner in Greenland. As Ivar Bårdsson's fourteenth-century description tells us that the king owned two 'court farms' in Austerbygd, named Foss and Tjodhildstad, it seems likely that this officer lived there.

How much the Greenlanders had to pay the Norwegian king in tax and duty is unknown.

What were the relations between the old ruling houses in Greenland, the Church and the Crown? We find that Church and king co-operated in bringing the country under the dominion of the Norwegian Crown. If later there was any struggle for power, we know nothing of it. But we do know that in the fourteenth century the Church's position was very strong and that it owned the most valuable lands about the fjords of Austerbygd.

Of the ruling families we hear a fair amount during the first hundred years or so, above all of the people at the manors of Brattalid, Gardar and Herjolfsnes. They must have been highly respected and powerful, and it is clear that the chief of Brattalid held a unique position among them. It is said of Eirik the Red that 'all were guided by him'; we find too that his successors, Leiv Eiriksson, Torkel Leivsson and Sokke Toresson wielded wide authority. But in 1126 the bishopric was founded, and immediately the Church made its power felt. From now on the records are silent about the

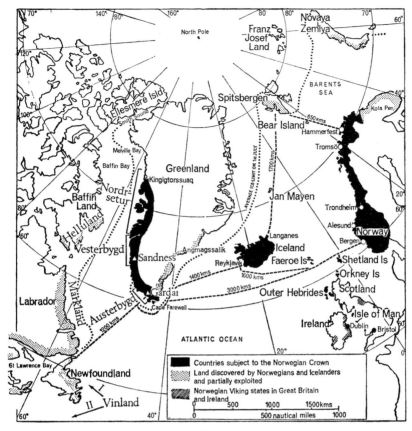

Map of the Norwegian realm

chiefs; the ancient families that colonized Greenland and discovered North America recede into obscurity. Yet Ivar Bårdsson tells us that the law-man lived at Brattalid.

It is difficult to say with certainty whether the Norse Greenlanders benefited by acknowledging Norwegian sovereignty. This is a complex question which is bound up with Norway's period of decline as a whole, but we do know that such a move must have had a marked effect on the Greenland community.

The point has been made that the Norwegian king acquired a trade-monopoly, yet it is doubtful whether there was any monopoly in the true sense of the word. I shall be returning to this question in greater detail later, and for the moment will mention only that a letter from Håkon IV dated June 18th, 1361, plainly states that merchants of Bjørgvin should have leave to carry wares to the tributary countries and there trade freely.

XXV PERILOUS SEAS AND RICH CARGOES

THEN they set sail, and when they were come out to sea the fair wind failed; they were swept off course and were forced to battle with many hardships that summer. Sickness also struck down upon the vessel. Orm died, also his wife Tordis and half the crew. Gales whipped up the seas and there was toil and suffering for those aboard; but at last they reached Herjolfsnes, and this was the beginning of winter.[1]

This description of Torbjørn Vivilsson's voyage in about 1000 gives a convincing picture of what the Greenland run might mean to the deckless ships of the Viking age. Streamlined and seaworthy the vessels might be, and handled by expert crews; yet when the Northern Ocean rose against them, men were puny indeed.

Worst of all, as a rule, was the drift-ice, 'the rigid sea', ramming its way south along the east coast of Greenland and then northward along the western shores. On a calm, sunny day this ice is like a smiling plain, with glittering bergs and black channels; but the picture can swiftly change. The ice crowds together, huge floes are smashed and pack-ice heaves to the sky. God help the craft thus imprisoned. The King's Mirror[2] gives a superb picture of the scene:

> ... As soon one crosses the first deeps, there is such a vast quantity of ice in the ocean that I know not its match ... Some of these floes are as flat as if frozen upon the sea itself, four or five ells thick, and they lie so far off shore that it may be four or five days' journey for men to reach land across them. But such ice lies north-east or north of the country rather than to the south, south-west or west; wherefore any man seeking land must sail south-west and west until he has circumvented all this ice, and thence put in to shore. Yet ever have men attempted to land too early, and came thereby into the midst of this ice. Some sank, others saved themselves; we have met a number of these and heard their accounts. All who were caught in the ice sought escape by taking the ship's boats and dragging them across the floes, and so they reached land. But the

ship and all her cargo remained and went down. Some men lived four or five days upon the ice, and some even longer, ere they made the land.

From the days of the Vikings onward there were in the main two types of ship: warships (long-ships) and trading ships. The former vessel was comparatively narrow, with little freeboard, and the mast could be lowered. She was designed primarily for speed, both in sailing and rowing. The commonest model was perhaps the 'twenty-thwarter' that accommodated forty oarsmen, though the largest could hold sixty oarsmen and might have a length of up to 166 feet. The merchantman was basically the same, but broader in proportion to her length; she had a deeper draught and higher freeboard, and the mast could not be unstepped. She could be rowed from the fixed fore- and after-decks, but the whole of the waist was reserved for the cargo. The main aim here was a capacious hold.

The largest type of cargo-vessel was the *knarr*, and this was the ship most commonly used in the Greenland trade. In the thirteenth century the German 'cog' first came to Norway: a model which by its great hold-capacity superseded Norwegian vessels on European routes. Whether this type was ever used on the Greenland run is unknown.

The ships from Norway occasionally touched at Iceland, but very soon it was customary to take the direct route. Leiv Eiriksson was the first to cross the great ocean: he sailed from Brattalid to Nidaros and back. Sailing-directions were simple: in Hauk's Book we read:[3]

> Men who know say that from Stadt in Norway to Horn on the east coast of Iceland is 7 days' sailing, but from Snefellsnes to Hvarf in Greenland is 4 days. From Hernar in Norway* one must head due west to Hvarf in Greenland, passing north of the Shetlands so that in clear weather they may scarce be discerned, but south of the Faroes so that one sees the mountains there to but half their height, and so far south of Iceland that the seabirds and whales of the island come in sight ...

This was a scanty guide for those crossing the Atlantic without a compass and making for a particular coast. But those seafarers of old must have had certain simple principles of navigation to supplement their extensive experience. Carl V. Sølver[4] believes they used a bearing-dial, which presumably is what is called in the texts a 'solar stone'. When the pole star was visible the dial was set accordingly, and it was then relatively easy to maintain any given course. Probably they also took the height of the sun at noon. When the angle of the sun is known the bearing-dial can be set by it, and from this all horizontal directions can be found. The course from Bergen to

* Hernar is the old Norse name of an island group just north-west of Bergen.

Greenland ran due west; it was a latitude-sailing, and this was important. If by reason of gales, fogs or overcast skies the vessel went off course, the *leidsagnarmðr* or navigator took the height of the sun at the first opportunity, calculated the approximate degree of drift and set a course along which the solar bearing would be maintained throughout the voyage to the coast of Greenland. But if the cloudy period was prolonged it was another matter.

Herjolfsnes, by its position, was naturally the first port of call, and was the only large estate on the sea-coast. Ivar Bårdsson describes it as the common harbour for Norwegians and merchants. Here the ships would lay to for a time for trade with the local inhabitants before continuing northward to Gardar and Brattalid.

The King's Mirror mentions the following wares that were bartered for the goods brought by the merchants from Norway: 'buckskin, cow-hide, seal-skin and such rope as we spoke of earlier which men cut from the fish they call rostung [walrus] and which is known as *svardreip*.' White falcons are also mentioned as being greatly prized. In the papal letter of 1282,[5] based upon information given by the Archbishop of Nidaros, we hear that the Greenland tithe was paid only in cow-hide, sealskin, walrus tusks and walrus rope.

As we have seen, many other wares must have had a considerable export-value, such as blubber, whale- and seal-oil, polar bear-skins, live bears, down, dried fish, narwhal horn, reindeer-skin, the pelts of white and blue fox, whalebone (baleen), wadmal cloth, wool and butter.

Walrus tusks were greatly prized and seem to have competed with African ivory. A number of such tusks were brought back by the Norwegian expeditions to Bjarmeland (Perm, on the White Sea) and perhaps from Svalbard (formerly Spitzbergen), which was discovered in 1194.[6] But for a long time the majority came from Greenland. Most of the objects made from walrus tusk that are scattered throughout Europe date from the period following Eirik the Red. For the Greenlanders, walrus-hunting must have been one of the richest sources of income.

The tusks were wrought into a variety of precious objects, such as cruci-fixes, caskets, chessmen, crosiers, hunting-horns, etc. Evidence of their value comes to us from 1327,[7] when between four and five tons of them arrived in Bergen, of which all but 53 lb. was the clergy's six-year tithe (the crusade-tax), the remainder being Peter's Pence. The tusks were sold to a merchant from Flanders for a sum amounting to about 28 lb. of pure silver: a mighty sum in those days.*

* According to the rates of exchange in the same tithe-accounts, it equalled in value £39 sterling, or 195 head of cattle, or about 20,000 lb. of butter.

Hunting-hawks carved on a monolith with runes dating from about A.D. *1000.*
(Found at Alstad, Toten, Norway)

Narwhal horn was no less valuable; and with this was bound up the super-stition of the unicorn. Crushed narwhal horn had healing powers.

Walrus skin was in great demand for ships' hawsers and was sold – among other places – in the market of Cologne.

Greenland's white falcons were famous. Falconry was a very ancient sport both in Europe and the Orient, and throughout the Middle Ages it was the recreation of kings and nobles. Birds fetched high prices, and an Arabian writer, Abul-Hasan Ali Ibn Said, who lived in the thirteenth century, relates that the Sultan of Egypt paid 1,000 dinars for a single white falcon. Falconry was practised with singular passion; an Arabic proverb runs:

'A good dog, a swift horse, and above all a noble falcon, are worth more than twenty women.'

The kings of Norway held the monopoly for the purchase of hawks and falcons both in their own country and in the tributary states, but an

233

exception was made for the Archbishop of Nidaros. In the fourteenth century falcons were taken to the royal residence in Bergen and trained there; they formed a substantial contribution to the exchequer. From time to time the Norwegian kings sent birds to the kings of England,[8] and such gifts were the most highly prized of all.

We may presume that the skins of polar bears rose in value on the European markets, being rarities at that time. Querini the Venetian mentions that during his visit to Norway in 1432 he beheld a perfectly white bearskin at the foot of the metropolitan throne in the church of St Olav in Trondhjem.

Blubber, whale- and seal-oil were important exports, for they were the usual means of providing artificial light all over Europe.[9] The skins of reindeer and of foxes (white and blue) are mentioned in the Norwegian scale of fines[10] and were exported to England, among other places, as were also whetstones from Telemark (in Norway). Good whetstone is to be found also in Greenland, as for instance at Sitdlisit in Eiriksfjord.

Wadmal (woollen fabric) was a common article of trade, and was also used as a unit of measurement. We get the impression that wadmal from Greenland was well esteemed in the early days, and in the eleventh century we hear that Leiv Eiriksson gave his Hebridean mistress 'a finger-ring and a cloak of wadmal'.[11] It may be doubted, however, whether it commanded the same price throughout the Middle Ages as cloth-production increased and with it the demand for higher quality.

The records show that dried fish was prepared in Greenland.[12] Even to this day there are great quantities of cod and other fish in the fjords and on the banks of Greenland, and there are many indications that conditions were no worse when the Norse Greenlanders inhabited the country. With the advance of the Middle Ages dried fish became of increasing importance in Europe, and we learn from Iceland that in the fifteenth century it was fetching high prices.[13] Long though the supply lines were, it is an open question whether dried fish did not in time prove one of Greenland's most important exports.

No doubt there was a market too for the products of home handicrafts, produced during the long Arctic winter, such as woven fabrics and carvings from walrus-tusk of chessmen and other things. On the 'German Quay' of Bergen a beautiful little walrus, carved from walrus-tusk and dating from before 1400, has been discovered.

Whatever the cargo shipped across the ocean, it was a mixed one, and we may suppose that the *knarr* (freighter) from Greenland caused something of a sensation when she put in at Bergen. Her bulky load amidships, lashed down under sewn hides with walrus rope, comprised cages of white falcons and crates wherein polar bears roared across the harbour, to the delight of the longshoremen on the wharf. When they were followed by furs, hides, sealskin and bearskin, casks and leather sacks of blubber and oil and much else, ending with the precious walrus-tusks, we may be sure that countryfolk as well as townsmen found plenty to talk about.

What goods did the foreign merchants leave in exchange? Few relics of these have been found among the Greenland ruins. The King's Mirror mentions iron and timber. We do know that the Norse Greenlanders made use of bog-ore, but fuel for smelting was so hard to come by that imported iron was very welcome. Of the people of Hardanger Absalon Pederssøn Beyer[14] says: 'In olden days these Hardanger folk were so rich, so manly, so able, that they sailed to Greenland, Iceland and Bjarmeland, carrying thither salt, iron and other good wares ... '

Salt is a useful means of preserving food, but fish and meat could be dried and smoked or laid down in tubs with sour milk. Food could be kept for a long time in that cold climate, and a pit dug in the frozen ground made a good ice-box.

Ships from Norway brought various supplies such as corn and malt, honey – the sugar of the period – linen, flax, tape, simple iron tools, barrel-staves,[15] pots, etc. There might also be goods of less practical use, such as ornaments for the women or some delicacy. At Eirik the Red's homestead nutshells were found.

The Church too had its own needs, and some cargoes may have included church-bells, incense, wax candles and much else.

The King's Mirror states that everything brought to Greenland from abroad was expensive, as is always the case with remote Arctic outposts. We do not know whether the Norse Greenlanders regulated their commerce in any way, such as for instance by fixing prices, but it seems likely. We know of a resolution passed at the *Althing*[16] whereby anyone purchasing food in Greenland was obliged to buy other goods as well. Trade was chiefly by barter; no coinage has been found. At Sukkertoppen (Sugarloaf) far north of the settlements a weight was discovered; it is in the shape of a little brass horse, and dates from about 1300, the time of Håkon V.

Merchant ships carried passengers as well as goods, and made their profit by them. From the colonization period onward great numbers of people must have been brought to or from Greenland; and when we hear that in 1265 a Greenland-bound vessel was lost with forty aboard it is clear that not a few of these must have been passengers. Often the travellers were church-men, but there were others too, and in greater numbers. As time went on some, no doubt, wearying of the toilsome life of the Arctic, sold up and left, to settle in Norway. The saga mentions one such case, and in the King's Mirror we read: ' ... I have often met men who had been long in Greenland.' Then there were the young people who crossed the ocean to seek their

Two brass weights for weighing coins or silver, found in Greenland. Left: *horse from Sukkertoppen, weighing 46·97 grammes. The other weighs 25·25 grammes.*

fortune in the new land of which so many wonders were told. It was adventure that enticed them: voyages into the unknown, where a lucky man might meet with great herds of walrus and acquire wealth by tusks and skins; thrilling bear-hunts – all the promise of the Arctic. They set sail, like the youth of today, with high hopes and expectations. Yet it may be that as the emigrants stood beneath the square sail looking aft at the vanishing coast of Norway they were moved by some such feeling as inspired the words of an unknown skald:

> Away from the land ... we are carried,
> Eastward along our wake I behold
> Peaks all a-sparkle in sunlight.

What sort of men were they who traded with Greenland? The ancient Norwegian–Icelandic laws decreed that commoners too might share in commercial enterprises abroad. The skipper was usually the owner – though there might be a partnership, so that shareholders each owned a part of the cargo. These men travelled aboard and paid their freight-charges in labour. In questions of importance they sat in council with the captain: they were no servants, but freemen and equals.

Where long and exacting voyages were involved, necessitating a costly ship and a particularly valuable cargo, chiefs, kings and clergy played their essential part. The Archbishop of Nidaros became the greatest merchant and shipowner in Norway; other bishops, churches and monasteries owned vessels overseas. Their estates were large enough to be productive; also they had men enough at their disposal to build ships from timber grown in their own forests.

Where trade with Greenland was concerned, so much capital was required that business lay mainly in the hands of the great men. Shortly after the settlement we hear of two Icelandic merchant-ships, one of which belonged to the Vinland voyager Torfinn Karlsevne. In 1061 there was Tore of Møre,[17] who came from a part of Norway that played an important role during the

Viking age. Excavations now being carried out by Asbjørn Herteig at Borgund in Møre indicate that this market town was in existence in the eleventh century.

Records from the same period tell us, as we have seen, that the Norwegian royal house engaged in the Greenland trade. Lik-Lodin's voyage to Norway with the bodies of Finn Fegin and his crew (see pages 98–9) was undertaken at the behest of St Olav; and it is probable that the object of Finn Fegin's journey was trade with Greenland.

In the early twelfth century we meet Ketil Kalvsson[18] as captain of a Norse ship berthed at the Greenland settlements. We have reason to believe that he was descended from Ketil Kalv of Ringnes, Finn Fegin's father. In other words, members of the same Norwegian chiefs' line were Greenland voyagers for about a hundred years.[19] It is of interest too that this family came from Hedmark, and had intermarried with the Norwegian royal house whose seat was in the neighbouring country of Ringerike (Sigurd Syr's homestead). This shows that leading men from the inland communities of south Norway also took part in the Greenland trade.

In connection with the disputes between Greenlanders and Norwegian merchants in the early twelfth century, we learn that the latter sailed across Einarsfjord to Skjalgsbúðir.[20] We may take this to have been Foxhavn at the head of the fjord, opposite to Gardar, where there must have been a permanent trading-post. Finnur Jónsson[21] assumes the name to derive from Skjalgr, the second son of Erling Skjalgsson of Sole, the powerful chief of Jaeren who lived about the year 1000. Skjalgr too was closely related to the Norwegian kings, being Olav Trygvason's nephew; and we may remember that Eirik the Red was born in Jaeren, and was descended from an eminent Norwegian line.

Such are the scattered, almost random pieces of information we have about the period immediately following colonization. In 1125, as was mentioned earlier (page 197), Arnbjørn the Norwegian sailed for Greenland with two large merchant ships, which were wrecked on the east coast. In 1131 no fewer than three such vessels were berthed at the settlements: two Norwegian and one Icelandic.[22]

As time went on, Bergen became the natural trading-port and many Greenland-bound vessels must have hailed from there or from neighbouring districts such as Hardanger and Møre. But Nidaros too, in the province of Trøndelag, was a traditional starting point, for it not only became an important centre of commerce but was the seat of the archbishop, the head of the Church of Greenland. As he was a merchant and a shipowner, he is likely to have had interests in the Greenland trade.

An interesting document of 1325 [23] casts a sidelight on the activity of the men of Trøndelag in Greenland. Some of these merchants – Olav of Lexå,

237

Eindride Arnesson and their partners – had arrived in Bergen aboard the Greenland *knarr*. They refused to pay the tithe on their wares there, to the annoyance of Bishop Audfin. The bishop wrote to Archbishop Eilif of Nidaros, pointing out that he and his parish priest had a traditional right to this tithe. The archbishop replied in pious but unequivocal terms that it was the custom for the clergy of Trøndelag to collect the tithe from the Greenland vessels that belonged there. In proof of this he referred his correspondent to 'all the oldest Greenland voyagers and all old people, both here and elsewhere in the country'. We sense here a very longstanding Greenland tradition in Trøndelag.

In this connection it is interesting to note that one of the texts giving the most plentiful and reliable information about Greenland, the King's Mirror, was most probably written in Trøndelag. Fredrik Paasche believes the author to have been Einar Gunnarsson, Archbishop of Nidaros from 1255.

Throughout the centuries great numbers of ships found their way to the colony in Greenland. Icelandic texts mention some, but of many that sailed direct from Norway we know nothing. When such a vessel is mentioned, there often seems to have been something special about the voyage: something that caused a stir and became widely known. From the Icelandic Annals[24] we may take a few random examples. 1346: the *knarr* from Greenland made port in good order with a great abundance of wares. 1347: the Greenland vessel arrived at Iceland from Markland. 1368: Bishop Alf arrived in Greenland. (No bishop had been seen there for 19 years.) 1369: the Greenland *knarr* foundered off Norway, but all aboard her came safely to land.

Changing conditions in Norway, both economic and political, naturally exerted a great influence on the Norse Greenlanders throughout their history. Not the least fateful was Norway's foreign trade, by means of which goods from Greenland found their market.

Greenland was colonized at the end of the Viking era, when conditions in Europe were simple. Generally speaking a natural economy prevailed. In Norway there were a few scattered trading centres along the coast: Vågan, Nidaros, Borgund, Bergen, Skiringssal, Tønsberg and one or two others. In England stock-raising was still the most important industry.

During the eleventh century, however, something new began: industries and towns began to spring up in Belgium, the Rhineland and northern France. There was an increased production of cloth, metal wares, etc. Slowly England followed suit. With the crusades, fresh winds from the Mediterranean countries and the Orient blew into Europe. Producer-regions needed a larger market and the growing populations more imports.

At this time Norway ranked high as an export country, having an abundance of the kind of goods in general demand: dried fish, blubber, furs, hides, skins, down, timber, etc. Norwegian foreign trade was pioneered in the Viking age, its most important export area being then north Norway. Here among many others lived Ottar, the explorer, merchant and hunter, who visited King Alfred of England with walrus-tusks and other wares. Many regions in south Norway too were favourably situated for the export of raw materials. Egil's saga gives us a contemporary glimpse: the chief Brynjulf of Sogn refuses his son a long-ship for a Viking expedition, and says, 'I will give thee a merchant ship and goods to trade with. Go south to Dublin, for that voyage is now the most rewarding.'

Between the eleventh and thirteenth centuries overseas trade branched out into the Baltic and North Sea countries, the Channel and the Irish Sea, the Islands of the Western Ocean, Bjarmeland (the White Sea region), Iceland and Greenland. The North Sea trade was the most important. Norwegian ships sailed to Holland, Flanders and Normandy, and cities such as Utrecht, Bruges and Rouen were vital centres.

Even in the Viking period an extensive Norwegian trade had been built up in the British Isles. In 991 Olav Trygvason signed a trade agreement with King Ethelred, and under Canute's rule Norse activity increased. Many Norwegians and Danes had settled in London, York and other towns near the east coast. The Norwegian colonization of the Shetlands, Orkneys, Hebrides, Man and the Dublin area made St George's Channel like a Norwegian inland sea. Twelfth-century English writers indicate that the population of Bristol was predominantly Norwegian or Norse, while Chester was so much under the influence of Norwegian colonization that in the early eleventh century currency was reckoned in *mark* and *øre* rather than in the contemporary English units.[25]

These conditions offered great advantages to Norwegian merchants, and enabled them to deal with their own kinsmen. Trade on the east coast of England increased in importance, and in the thirteenth century a considerable amount of Norwegian shipping plied from Grimsby, Lynn, Kingston-upon-Hull and Ravensworth, as we may see from the excise accounts. There was also close contact between the kings of Norway and England.

Imports included corn, cloth, honey, wine, ale, weapons, ornaments, etc. A French description dating from the thirteenth century gives an illuminating picture of the wares exported at that time. Some of them probably came from Greenland.

One day a great ocean-goer came to the country [France] and cast anchor below the castle. The men had come thither from the far north: Norse merchants with many kinds of wares such as miniver, hawks, white pelts, beaver, sables, tusks [walrus], bearskins, grey falcons and

Municipal seal of Bergen, 1299

many white falcons, hides, buckskin, dried fish, pitch, fish-oil, sulphur and all manner of Norse goods.

Norwegian towns sprang up to keep pace with increasing trade. The English author Odericus Vitalis, writing in the twelfth century, mentions six: Bergen, Konghelle, Kaupang, Borg, Oslo and Tønsberg.

For a long time Nidaros was the most important commercial centre, but by the end of the twelfth century Bergen was in the lead. In a contemporary document dealing with the Danes' expedition to Jerusalem,[26] we find a vivid picture of this busy town, which was the largest in northern Europe and vital to Greenland trade:

> This is a town which is very excellent and mighty in that land, with a magnificent royal fortress ... The town is most populous and immeasurably rich in all kinds of wares, and of dried fish which is called skrei there is such abundance that it is beyond count or measure. Ships and people from every part flock thither in their multitudes: Icelanders, Greenlanders, Englishmen, Germans, Danes, Swedes, Gothlanders and many other races can be found there ...

This has the ring of prosperity, and in general we may say that from the

Viking period to the mid-thirteenth century Norwegian foreign trade throve, and economic conditions within the country were good. Under Håkon Håkonsson (1217–63) Norway reached the height of its power.

Yet the seeds of decline were there. Slowly but surely the Hanseatic towns, led by Lübeck, had been catching up, and by the middle of the fourteenth century their commercial empire in Norway had gained a firm footing. They also forced the Norwegians out of the English market, and became middlemen for the pelt and fur trade of mighty Novgorod, to the detriment of exports from Greenland and Norway. Contributory factors, such as the Black Death, the Church, the attitude of the nobility, stagnation in shipbuilding and not least the union with Denmark, all played their part. Norwegian supremacy toppled and fell.

The events outlined above naturally had repercussions on the trade of Greenland and on conditions within the country. There too, for the first two and a half centuries, there was prosperity; and it was during that period that most of the churches were built. Later came decline.

When in 1261 Greenland became subject to Norway, it is probable, as we saw, that the Norwegian king undertook to maintain sea-communications with the dominion; and this guarantee set commerce on a different basis altogether. We hear now of the 'Greenland *knarr*': no doubt the regular ship that plied between the two countries and provided their main link. Foreigners were forbidden to trade with Greenland or with the other tributary countries, and all goods were to go through Bergen, which became the staple town.

In the 1350s[27] when King Magnus Eiriksson made over the rule of Norway to his son Håkon VI, he reserved to himself part of the realm, including the tributary countries. Probably by some means or other he secured the income from the Greenland trade, though how we do not know. What we do know is that by the royal edict of June 18th, 1361,[28] it was expressly confirmed that the merchants of Bjørgvin had leave to carry their wares to the tributary countries and trade freely there.

A court judgment of May 20th, 1389,[29] gives us an interesting glimpse of trade conditions. It concerns the crews of four Icelandic ships which had sailed to Greenland without the king's permission and spent two winters there. They were charged in Bergen with having carried on illegal trade, but were acquitted on the following grounds: (1) They had put into Greenland in distress. (2) The *Althing* of Greenland had decreed that no 'Eastman' might buy food without also buying export goods. (3) They had bought nothing belonging to the king, but had offered to carry his wares home with them: an offer which the king's commissioner refused because they could show no authority for so doing. (4) In Bergen they had paid the proper 'sack-dues' – customs duty – on both Greenland and Icelandic goods.

It appears from this that in the time of Queen Margaret the Icelanders had no right to undertake trading-voyages to Greenland without royal permission. That they should have paid duty was not surprising, for they had to do this on Icelandic goods brought to Bergen. The amount was probably about five per cent of the value of the cargo, and can hardly have been burdensome enough to cause the decline in commerce.

So far as the export trade from Norway to Greenland is concerned, we may take it that the king derived some profit from it, but there is nothing to show that he was so extortionate as to discourage the shipment of goods; and indeed this would have been very foolish. Nor are there grounds for speaking of a monopoly: in 1325 we hear of vessels making the Greenland run from Trøndelag, and in 1361 we find the Bergen merchants trading freely with the dominions, so it hardly looks as if commerce lay in the hands of any particular group or was engaged in by the king himself. On the other hand it was natural that the king should try to keep foreign merchants away from his overseas territories and secure that trade for his own country. He failed to do this in Iceland, where the English carried on extensive illegal commerce, and the same thing probably happened in Greenland.

In 1383 [30] we hear for the last time of a Norwegian merchant ship visiting Greenland. The Icelandic Annals say: 'From Greenland a ship arrived in Norway; she had wintered there for two years, and aboard her were some men who had escaped from Torlaksuden. They told of Bishop Alf's death, which had occurred six years before.'

In 1406 [31] an Iceland-bound ship from Norway was driven by gales to Greenland, where the crew spent four winters. This is the last certain record we have of any vessel arriving there while the Norse community endured.

☒☒☒☒☒☒☒☒☒☒☒☒☒☒☒☒☒☒☒☒☒☒☒☒☒☒☒☒☒☒☒☒

XXVI TO VATNAHVERFI AND KONGSGÅRDEN

LEAVING Gardar we headed south-east to a branch of Einarsfjord known to the Norse Greenlanders as Austfjördr. A fresh wind was blowing, and our little craft *Benedicte* ploughed heavily along as the fine sea-spray flew over us with a rainbow glint in the sun. After a while we glimpsed a natural harbour on the western shore. This is most probably the site of Skjalgsbúðir, which may have been named after the second son of mighty Erling Skjalgsson of Sole, in Norway. It is thought to have been a trading post, with warehouses; and here, as early as the year 1000 or so, Norwegian chiefs were bringing their merchant ships to port.

We drew near to the eastern part of the great peninsula dividing Einars-fjord from Hravnsfjord, and beheld a rich landscape of lakes and rivers teeming with fish, of smiling valleys, gentle slopes and wild mountains: a countryside lush in many places, rich in grass, with some birch and even a few merry little rowan trees. The Norse Greenlanders gave this place the beautiful and descriptive name of Vatnahverfi (land of waters), and here lay the largest of the inland settlements.

The saga tells us that Hafgrim, who accompanied Eirik the Red, took possession of Hafgrimsfjord and Vatnahverfi. The fjord so named must be identified with the large inlet near the mouth of Einarsfjord, called by the Eskimoes Eqaluit (salmon-place). On a fertile plain near this same fjord-mouth are certain indistinct ruins of a large farmstead which may have been Hafgrim's home. Beside it C. L. Vebaek has found traces of a small church which, as I said earlier, I believe to be the church of Langanes where Einar of Brattalid slew Ossur, in 1132.[1]

It was Aaron Arctander who started research in Vatnahverfi, as early as the 1770s. In our own day many Danish archaeologists have followed his lead, the latest being C. L. Vebaek, who has added to our knowledge of Norse culture in this very distinctive area. Today we know of no fewer than fifty homesteads here, some of which have been excavated; and a wealth of material – partly new – has been brought to light.

The gateway to Vatnahverfi is Hafgrimsfjord. Here a fertile valley runs westward to great lakes and salmon rivers, and this was no doubt the route followed by the first settlers. But there is also a natural back

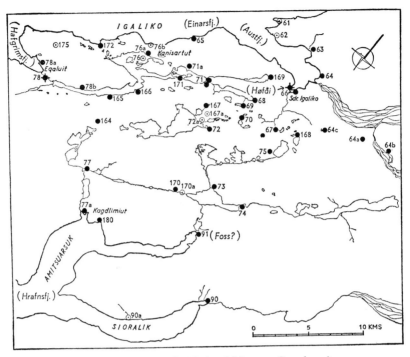

Map of Vatnahverfi. (National Museum, Copenhagen)

door, Austfjord, at the base of the peninsula; and for this we are now bound.

We swung into Austfjord and a wild landscape. To the north, mighty mountains soared to the sky, some of them with green vegetation at their base. The head of the fjord, farthest to the east, seemed ice-scoured and bleak: here the great river rolls out among gravel and stones. Waters from two valleys meet here; they rise from two spits of the inland ice, and glacier-water runs milk-white far down the fjord.

Southward the view is different. At the end of a bay lies a friendly land-scape of green slopes running up to a ridge: this is Undir Höfdi.[2]

Nowhere else in Greenland have I beheld such a wealth of flowers as on these slopes. An expanse of long-stemmed buttercups stretches yellow upon yellow into the distance. Elsewhere, beyond the ancient home-fields, grow angelica, horsetail, fragrant thyme and wild pink (*dianthus deltoides*). A glorious place on a sunny day. Little birds were everywhere, and were strangely tame: a snow-bunting even perched on my shoulder. Down by the shore two big ospreys had settled on a stone.

244

A river runs down the middle of the valley, and it was on the slope to the west of it that the Norse Greenlanders had their most important buildings. The eye is caught first by the ruins of the church, whose massive stone walls still reach a height of six or seven feet. It is rectangular in plan, with an outside measurement of 17 by 7 metres (about 56 by 23 ft.), and the west wall was presumably of timber.

The churchyard was surrounded by a wall in the usual manner. A number of skeletons and scraps of woollen cloth have been dug up here, most of them in poor condition. The main building projects from the church wall; it had eight rooms and was of a quite unusual design. Here lived the priest, who was also a smallholder, and scattered about near by are ten or twelve other ruins. Undir Höfdi was a good place for stock-raising, for across the hillsides we could see not only grass but also willow and birch.

Beneath the church floor the following interesting finds have been made by G. F. Holm[3] and others: seven skulls, fragments of soapstone dishes and pots, two pieces of stone from querns, charcoal, a few small bits of mica, and a fused lump of clay and glass. I should add that since then Mogens Clemmensen[4] has come upon a fused mass, no doubt of glass, outside the east end.

This indicates that the church had that precious rarity, glass windows, and that it was burnt.

Among the objects found in the main building[5] we may mention a piece of soapstone engraved with a human head, other pieces of the same bearing runes and personal marks, an amber bead, a padlock with the keyhole at the end, and part of a key, all of iron.

The padlock is surprising. Having regard to the conditions in which the Norse Greenlanders lived, one would have thought that no door would ever be locked – that the laws of hospitality prevailed everywhere, so that the wayfarer might walk in where he would and help himself even if no one were at home, just as he could in Norway at that time, and as he still can in the Arctic.

The same was surely true of the Norsemen in Greenland, so that the padlock found in the main building beside the church must have had a special purpose. Possibly it belonged to some chest in which the church valuables were kept.

Crossing the river we walked up to the grass and willow-thickets four or five hundred yards beyond. Here were numbers of strange hollows in the ground that seemed man-made. Some were small, others over twenty feet long by three deep. The object of these hollows is a mystery. Trial digs made by Daniel Bruun and C. L. Vebaek[6] revealed ashes, half-burnt animal bones, some soapstone and a few small pieces of iron. Had it not been for these finds I would have guessed that all these holes were a network of reindeer pitfalls, as the place is admirably suited to such a purpose.

*

We strolled for some time through this beautiful countryside, where the valleys leading to the many lakes and rivers of Vatnahverfi beckon so invitingly. A short distance to the south-east lay an interesting homestead (No. 64c on map) which had been excavated by C. L. Vebaek some years before.[7] It was so deeply buried in sand that nothing of the walls could be seen, and it was necessary to dig down from three to ten feet to find them. This shows the effect of the south-easterly föhn wind. Apparently the Norsemen had stripped away the near-by woods and thickets, then the boundary walls collapsed and laid all open to the storms.

The main building was a long-house, the byre being separate from it and connected with the bath-house. This is the first long-house ever found inland, which shows that one should be cautious in drawing up a chronological scheme of building-styles in Greenland. Some people had thought that the long-houses were the earliest, and were found only on the coast.

A little farther to the east and nearer the big river was a homestead (No. 64a) of a quite different type: the kind known as the central house. About fourteen rooms, including four for animals, were built together in an irregular cluster and connected by passages. A stone oven was found there, but the Norse Greenlanders never got as far as building a flue-pipe.

Among the objects found in these two houses we should mention a padlock made from the bone of a whale, soapstone moulds, chessmen of walrus tusk, part of a hand-quern, a fragment of an iron drill, a steel for kindling fire, of the same type as that used in the Viking period, and an ice-chisel of whalebone. A small piece of a church bell was also discovered, showing that there were Norsemen in Greenland after the bells were destroyed.

I may add here a few items from other digs in this extensive inland area of Vatnahverfi undertaken by C. L. Vebaek. On one farm (No. 71) the imprints of three great wooden barrels were found, the wood having rotted away. Where one of these barrels had stood lay the bones of about a hundred house-mice: they must have tumbled into the cask and been unable to get out again. This is the first evidence we have of the existence of mice in Greenland during the Middle Ages.

On another farm (No. 167 on map) the finds included half a pair of sheep-shears, two crucifixes carved from soapstone and a small piece of Rhenish pottery. This last is of especial interest, as imported goods are a rarity among the Norse ruins of Greenland.

The most remarkable discovery was made in the entrance-passage to this house, for there under stone and turf lay a human skull and a number of bones. The skeleton was in such a decayed condition as to prevent any positive identification of the skull, though the indications are that it is a Norse one. If so, it is the only example of a Norse Greenlander being found dead on a farm. If the Black Death had struck the people here one would suppose that many families died in their beds and remained there. But what happened to this solitary person who once, long ago, fell headlong in the passage?

The people of Vatnahverfi must have done well. The land offers good pasture and plentiful supplies of Arctic char in the rivers and lakes. Finds show that they kept horses, cattle, goats, sheep and possibly pigs, as well as dogs. An interesting feature is that the people of these inland farmsteads – like those of Vesterbygd – were very sea-minded; this is evident from the quantities of local bone-finds – bones of walrus, polar bear, seal, whale, etc. Nor were they content to hunt off Austerbygd, since for walrus they would have had to go far to the north.

Fresh-water fishing was the surest source of supply, both winter and summer. The great importance of this appears from Ivar Bårdsson's description, which incidentally gives us information of an unusual kind. Of a large lake which must undoubtedly have been in Vatnahverfi he says:[8]

' ... and down there lies a great fishing lake full of great fish, and when much water comes down and rain falls, and the waters then sink, countless fish are left lying upon the sand.'

It is quite possible that here and there along the rivers fish were left stranded when the water-level dropped; but it is strange that Ivar Bårdsson should speak of heavy rainfall in this connection. We may suppose that this somewhat obscure statement refers to events similar to those observed in Vatnahverfi by Sverri Dahl in 1949. He told me that once there was so violent a storm that in places one river was whipped almost dry and they could catch the fish in their hands.

One thing must have been of vital importance in Vatnahverfi, where many depended on the fishing from one piece of water, and that was the delimitation of fishing-rights, and rules to ensure that no one interfered with another's catch by netting off any vital part of the river. Here the usage mus have been that expressed so beautifully in the Gulating Law: 'The gifts of God shall wander freely to hill as to shore, if wander they will.'[9]

One was tempted to linger at Vatnahverfi, to roam at random with tent and fishing-rod in the place where the Norse Greenlanders had their homes. Fifty homesteads: many people in the course of time must have had their roots here. They knew every hill and watercourse, and named them all. The children hung over the gunwale peering down at the line, or caught fish in their hands from the little streams, and they set snares for ptarmigan and hare. This was a wonderful place to be young in.

On one of the farms a haft of whalebone was found, possibly belonging to a fish-spear. On it, in sure, bold runic characters, is engraved *Gunnar*. What sort of a man was he?

Handle of whalebone, with the runic inscription 'Gunnar'

We continued into the more southerly districts of Austerbygd, first via the mighty Einarsfjord, and came again into the strange world of drift-ice that glided north along the coast. Now white plains, now vast, blue-white mountains of fantastic shapes – a magnificent sight in sunny weather when the sea is calm: an everchanging picture that never loses its fascination.

We passed some small dwelling-places. The houses were built on the naked rock, and there the Greenlanders of today watched us pass. A kayak appeared, a bunch of cod lying on the foredeck, and the paddles flashed in the sun. To the west, the Davis Strait melted into blue distance; eastward lay the tip of Vatnahverfi promontory, where more homesteads face the sea than anywhere else in the settlements.

Next we headed into Hravnsfjord (Agdluitsoq), and cruised for a time up and down the northern shore trying to find the ruins of a church which according to the evidence once stood somewhere in this area: probably a small chapel-of-ease. We also made a long tour on foot northward along the peninsula and saw much fine country, but no new ruins.

About halfway up the fjord lies the outpost of Sletten, where today about two hundred Greenlanders live, some in wooden houses, others in earth huts. We were kindly received. The one pure-blooded Dane there was a pleasant fellow named Karl Andersen. He told us that fish were plentiful in that region: cod, halibut, rose-fish, herring, shrimps and capelan. The local people believe that a sea-monster lives in the deeps of the fjord, and several of them declare that they have seen it.

We went on up Amitsuarssuk, the northern arm of Hravnsfjord. Here are the falls of a river that rises in the great lakes of Vatnahverfi, and near by must have been the Norwegian King's House mentioned by Ivar Bårdsson. The name of the homestead is said to have been Foss (waterfall), and this gives us a good clue, for there is a fall down by the fjord and another bigger one higher up.

On a slope east of the river-mouth lie the ruins of a homestead and various outhouses, but they are so sunken and overgrown with willow that it is impossible to make out any details. Perhaps this was the King's House of Foss. It is not unlikely, for the salmon rights must have been of great value; and if the king's commissioner had to collect taxes or make purchases, he could leave the fjord either by sea or overland to Vatnahverfi, which was not far away.

Next we wanted to test the fishing in these waters. Some bare rocks provided a good place for casting with a spinner; below them the river foamed down into the fjord, making glorious eddies and swirls far and wide under flying spray. Conditions were exactly right, and it was not long before the fish began to bite. Anne Stine, bright-eyed with excitement, hauled in one glittering catch after another.

They were Arctic char, and weighed from two to six pounds. Now and then we hooked a big cod, but tossed it contemptuously back.

On going farther inland we soon came to a small lake, and here we beheld a landscape which in Greenland was entirely new to us. Along the side of the valley lay a birch wood, twisted and gnarled indeed, but something like a real wood. In the background a great waterfall foamed over a bare rock-face: these were the biggest falls in south Greenland. A superb scene – if it hadn't been for the midges, angry midges, that closed about us like a wall.

Towards evening we returned to the fjord and the boat. By the light of the sunset we caught a few more shining char in the pool below the falls, and agreed that we'd had a successful day. Back aboard the *Benedicte* I lay long in my sleeping-bag puffing at my pipe while the water lapped against the hull, and thought of the Norwegian King's House which may once have stood no more than a bowshot from where we lay.

XXVII SOUTHWARD: RELIGIOUS HOUSES AND HERJOLFSNES

OUR next fjord to the south was Siglufjördr (Unartoq). Near the entrance lies a small island named Unartoq, meaning 'the hot'; here we cast anchor and went ashore. It was somewhere in this neighbourhood that the famous hot springs were supposed to be. Ivar Bårdsson writes of them:[1]

' ... in these islands is very warm water which in winter is so hot that no one may come near it, but in summer it is of an agreeable warmth so that men may bathe in it and many restore their health thereby and become vigorous, and are healed of sickness.'

Steam was rising from a bare slope facing the sea, and soon we were standing beside the springs, three in all. Beside one of them a large round pool had been built, and here hot water bubbled up through blue-green weed.

To bathe or not to bathe? We hesitated at the brink of the pool, for the day was unusually dank and chilly, with a biting wind off the sea. In the end we took the plunge, and did not regret it: it was a rare delight to lie there in the warm water and watch the icebergs passing down the fjord in review order. When Ivar Bårdsson described the water as agreeably warm he was right: the temperature was 41° C. (105·8° F.).

When Aaron Arctander visited this place in 1778, a basin had been built round each of the three springs. Near the edge of the middle one he found ruins of an earth-and-stone house, rising about 18 inches above the ground (or, as he reckoned it, almost an ell), and measuring 8 ells in length (12 ft. 8 in.) and somewhat less in width. Of this we could find no trace. Most probably this house sheltered visitors; for in those days, as now, sick people would have spent some time at the springs, and may have come from far away. The marvel of the hot water that bubbled up from the depths of the earth and possessed healing powers would have been known in the remotest settlements.

Before we left the island I took a stroll, and came upon a small hut and a few Greenlanders. They were dark-skinned and markedly Eskimo in appearance, but of a different temperament from the Eskimoes I had met in Alaska, who welcomed strangers with a smile. These were intensely grave and taciturn. I tried to make contact with them – a thing I usually succeed in doing – but gave up the attempt. Just as I was going one of the women pointed to a bucket and removed the lid; inside was a young bird – a black guillemot, surely. It was sitting quite still. She looked at me, then suddenly replaced the lid and went into the hut.

South of the island near the mouth of the fjord Vebaek[2] has recently found traces of a church which is almost certainly that described in the texts as Vágar church. It was at the top of a near-by mountain that the Norwegian John Christian Mørch[3] found, at the end of the eighteenth century, a remarkable stone-built cross measuring 24 metres by 8 (80 ft. by 26 ft. 8 in.).

We continued halfway into the fjord, and came to a bay on the north-west side, where we cast anchor. Green meadowland stretched away inland; this was Narssarssuaq: i.e. The Great Plain. Here it was that the Benedictine convent of the holy sisters stood. Ivar Bårdsson tells us that it was dedicated to 'Sancti Oluff the King', and that it owned all the land along the fjord and the hot springs, jointly with Vágar church.

Its age we do not know, but Benedictine religious houses are among the oldest in Norway. That of Selja, for example, dates from the end of the eleventh century. Monastic life in Bergen and Nidarholm (Trondhjem) is barely more recent. In Iceland there were four Benedictine monasteries, three of them dating from the twelfth century. The Order of St Benedict was active not only on the Christian level: it exerted exceptional influence upon European medieval culture; and it may well be that the Greenland nunnery – on a more modest scale – played a similar part.

We rowed ashore. A family of Greenlanders – shepherds and fishermen – lived here in a small house. On the beach we came upon some women washing wool in two huge cauldrons, each over its own fire. As each batch was cleansed, young people ran up to carry it away and spread it out to dry on the grass. It looked like new-fallen snow on the green.

A kitten followed us across the plain to the ruins. The loveliness of that place! Level ground under lush grass, brushed with the bright colours of willow-herb, buttercups and mauve veronica. From there we had the view of the fjord and of curiously striated mountains on the opposite side.

Here, in the old days, was a sizeable settlement: about twenty-five ruins of various kinds testify to this. Two of the most important have been dug up by C. L. Vebaek,[4] and have yielded a number of interesting finds.

The church measured about 15 by 9 metres (50 ft. by 30 ft.). In the main, the building-materials consisted of stone, except for the west wall which must have been of timber. Inside the church were a score or so of graves, and a large number of skeletons have been dug up from the churchyard. In some cases there are indications of mass burials, which may mean that the population were visited by an epidemic.

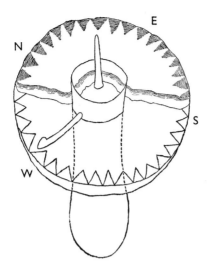

Bearing-dial. Shaded portion found by C. L. Vebaek at Siglufjord convent, Austerbygd.

Near the church was once a building on a plot of ground measuring about 80 by 25 metres (266 by 83 ft.); this was the site of the convent. It seems as if a number of houses were built together in a cluster, but they are in such a state of collapse that it is difficult to make out any clear plan. There may have been a small cloister among them.

Here a number of remarkable finds have been made. On one of the skeletons was a form of zip-fastener, consisting of flat rings attached to the edges of the garment and drawn together by a cord running through them. There were the remains of seven big wooden tubs for milk, etc., so farming must have been carried on on quite a large scale. There was also part of a wooden spoon decorated with fine 'band-runes'. Other discoveries include a wooden knife which to my way of thinking must have been what we call in Norwegian a *rennekniv*, and which was used to hold the cream back when pouring milk from a vessel. There was a pointed bone needle, probably a hair-pin. Threaded through the eye was a little shred of twisted yarn which may have been bound round the hair.

The most remarkable find was part of a small wooden disc with triangular marks carved round its edge. Carl Sølver[5] has devoted special study to this and believes it to be part of a bearing-dial, identical with what the sagas call a 'solar stone'.

Another link with seafaring was found at this monastery: a length of braided withies or roots, about 2½ inches thick. I had seen no explanation of this, and was puzzled by it until the most recent excavations of the German Quay in Bergen provided the answer. There I was shown many such pieces of 'rope', some of them quite long and from two to three inches thick. It appears that this material must have been in common use as ship's cables during the Middle Ages.

An Arctic nunnery. Here women walked in the black, voluminous habit and white coif of the Benedictine order. They attended Mass in the church, murmured Latin prayers to the Virgin Mary and bent their minds to piety. What sort of life did they lead? Did they help with milking and cheese-making on the farm? Did they weave and sew? Did they row out to the hot springs in the fjord, or to homes where the sick and dying needed help? What was the daily life, what were the thoughts of the women who dwelt here in the shadow of the inland ice?

We don't know. Women lived here for several hundred years, busy with their affairs, and we know nothing about them. We have found some ruins on the grassland, a few little objects handled by women, and a number of skeletons; no more.

A calm evening fell over the convent plain and steep mountains on the other side of the fjord. Then came a soft dusk and with it a mist that spread over the land. Shapes became blurred and shadows seemed alive. I saw them, those devout sisters, crossing the fields in their wide cloaks; they walked slowly with bent head. The bell of the little church was summoning them to vespers.

Austerbygd also had a monastery dedicated to St Olav and St Augustine, says Ivar Bårdsson. It lay somewhat farther to the south, up Ketilsfjord, one of the most beautiful fjords in Greenland. Here fantastic peaks soar into the sky; some parts are chill and bare, but others are more kindly, and there is a richer growth of birch here than anywhere else. The monks did not choose the smiling landscape for their house, but the wildest and bleakest, under steep mountains with scree at their foot and ice-scoured walls. It was in their shadow that they had built the little monastery of stone and turf.

Here are ruins of a main building and six or seven more modest structures, including a byre and a church. All have collapsed, and what remains to tell us of these pious men who chose a life of solitude is melting back into the landscape. The church is small: 12 metres by 9 in the nave (40 by 30 ft.), 6 metres (20 ft.) in the chancel. Only a tiny religious community can have lived under these mountains, and conditions were hard.

It is remarkable how all through the ages monks have sought out the farthest and often the bleakest corners of the wilds. Irish monks found their way to Iceland and the Faroes before the Norwegians arrived there in the ninth century. When people came with their worldly noise they moved from Iceland, leaving 'books, bells and pastoral staff', writes Are Frode.

'In the sea there is peace', says an old Irish record of the monastic life.

That was what the monks sought in their solitude and their communion with nature – they turned their minds to sea and mountain, stone and earth: a step on the stair to God.

We had seen most of Austerbygd by now and were nearing the southern tip of Greenland. But we had far to go to reach Vesterbygd in the north, and beyond. It was time to turn if we were to do all that we had planned before winter set in, and we had to give up the idea of seeing the great manor of Herjolfsnes. Nevertheless, I will mention some of its most interesting features.

Herjolfsnes is the only large homestead that faces the open sea. There is good pasture, and the game must have been abundant so far as seal, whale, polar bear and fish were concerned; and it is likely that the people here also made yearly expeditions to hunting-grounds on the east coast.

The place was called after Herjolf Bårdsson, who came over with Eirik the Red in 985. It was his son Bjarne who was storm-swept to North America and showed the way to the Vinland voyagers. Some years later Torbjørn the Icelander and his daughter Gudrid arrived at Herjolfsnes after a terrible voyage during which half the crew perished. At that time Torkel owned the homestead. In the eleventh century we hear that Skjegg the Stately was once the owner, and that Skald-Helge married his widow, the rich but dangerous Torunn. In the middle of the twelfth century three Icelanders who had been wrecked on the east coast tried to reach the settlement across the inland ice. Their bodies were found the following winter and were buried at Herjolfsnes.

Ivar Bårdsson tells us that near Herjolfsnes was a harbour 'called Sand, a common harbour for Norwegians and traders'. There is much to indicate that this was an important port of call for merchant ships.

The Eskimoes call Herjolfsnes Ikigait: that is, the place devastated by fire. It is interesting to note that the first detailed investigation of the church at the beginning of the last century revealed the presence of so much charcoal that Dr C. Pingel believed it to have burnt down.[6]

Today one may see the ruins of the main building and an added banqueting-hall, a few outhouses and a church. The church is the third largest in the settlements, ranking after Gardar and Brattalid. It has an inside length of 14·5 metres (47 ft. 6 in.), the nave being 6·5 metres (21 ft. 4 in.) wide and the chancel 4·3 (14 ft.). The west wall was presumably of timber. Traces of an older church have been found under the masonry. Subsidence of the land has caused part of the churchyard to sink beneath the sea.

In our time Herjolfsnes has become famous through the outstanding discoveries made by the Danish archaeologist Poul Nørlund,[7] on his dig in 1921, and especially during his examination of the church and churchyard. Close by the church he uncovered thirty coffins made of driftwood and

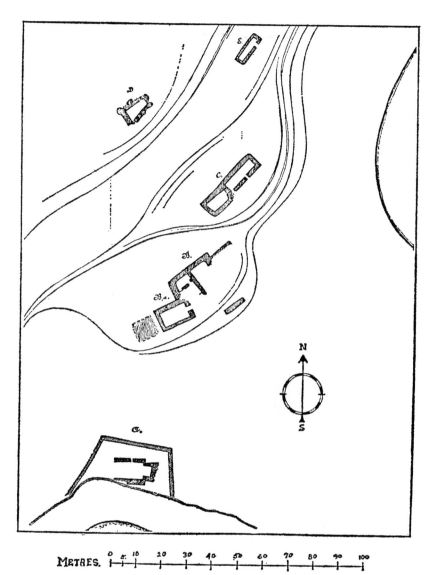

METRES.

0 5 10 20 30 40 50 60 70 80 90 100

Church and homestead of Herjolfsnes. A. church and churchyard. B. dwelling-house.
C. byre. D and E. outbuildings. (National Museum, Copenhagen)

pegged together with wooden nails or lashed with whalebone (baleen) cords. Little was found inside them, most of the dead having been most probably interred with little clothing on them. Farther out in the churchyard the case was different: here the dead had been wrapped in their own clothes and laid coffinless in the ground. Thanks to the permanently frozen soil many of these garments were preserved, and form a matchless collection of medieval costume.

The clothes were woven of wool and home-made, and they testify to skilled tailoring and good tools. The colour was brown or brownish black, and the style European; evidently the Norse Greenlanders were keen to keep up with the fashions of Paris and Burgundy.

We find that the ankle-length *cotte* of the thirteenth and fourteenth centuries found its way to Greenland. It was drawn over the head. Some were close-fitting at the waist and very full below, the greatest width being 4·25 metres (5 yards). The men's clothes were usually somewhat shorter than the women's, otherwise there was little difference. With these garments went long stockings suspended from the waist; some examples of these were found. A characteristic of this dress was the number of gores in it: as many as fourteen vertical seams may be found at the hem.

In about 1350 men's fashions in Europe changed and the *cotte hardie* came in; this was a tight-fitting jacket fastening down the front and reaching barely to the hips. Legs were revealed to their full length. It seems as if the Herjolfsnes folk did not quite venture to adopt this daring mode, though its influence is plainly to be seen.

The most remarkable garments found here were the numerous capuchons – hoods with a cape – characteristic of the fourteenth century. As Nørlund says, the headgear of Dante, Petrarch and Robin Hood was worn by all classes in Scandinavia in the time of Queen Margaret. A typical feature was the liripipe: a point or tail to the hood, worn exaggeratedly long by fashionable men in Europe.

There were also some quite simple round caps, fairly high in the crown, with a flat top. These were popular in the fifteenth century. Then there was a cap about ten inches high and somewhat pointed, rising steeply above the forehead but widening at the back of the neck. Nørlund points out that this is the kind seen in the paintings of Dirk and other Low Country artists, and worn in the days of Louis XI and Charles the Bold, during the second half of the fifteenth century. This garment proves that the Norse Greenlanders were in communication with Europe until about 1500.

Many of these garments were not worn by the common people of Europe, but only by the well-to-do middle class. Altogether the finds testify to a cultivated and fairly prosperous community; certainly not to a people on the brink of extinction. The conclusions drawn by F. C. C. Hansen from his

Aerial photograph of the Gardar plain. The site of cathedral and bishop's house is near the middle of the picture. (Cf. map on p. 184.) (Photograph: Geodetic Institute, Copenhagen.)

Crosier of walrus tusk found in a grave at Gardar. (Cf. Pl. 23.) (Photograph: National Museum of Copenhagen.)

above: Crosses from Herjolfsnes. The middle one bears a runic inscription. *below, left:* Gravestone from Gardar. 'Here lies Vigdis M[agnus] D[ottir]. God rejoice her soul.' *right:* Ingibjørg's grave, Brattalid churchyard. (Photographs: National Museum of Copenhagen.)

The inner end of Ketilsfjord. At the foot of these wild crags there once stood a little monastery dedicated to SS Olav and Augustine. (Photograph: National Museum of Copenhagen.)

Skeletons of man and woman each holding a child. Between them a little wooden cross. Sandnes churchyard, Vesterbygd. (Photograph: National Museum of Copenhagen.)

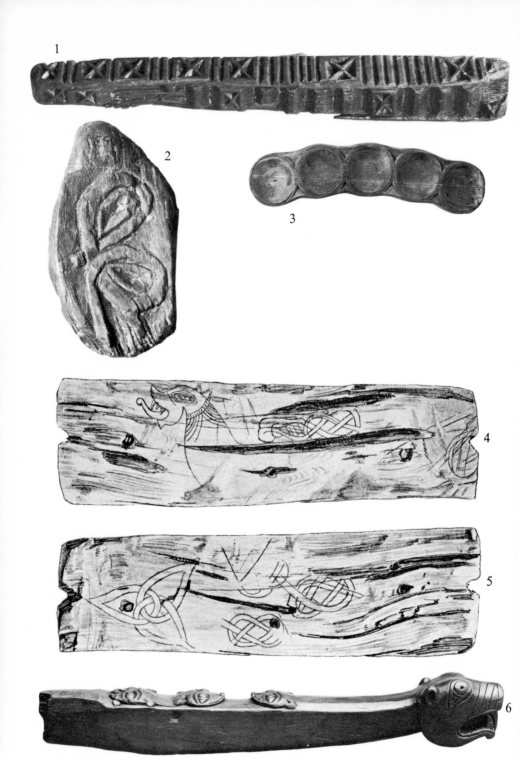

1. Runic calendar. 2. Decoration cut by Eskimo on the back of a carving (see Pl. 13, No. 4). 3. Saucers cut from a single piece of wood, Sandnes. 4 and 5. Carvings in boards from a chest, Herjolfsnes. 6. Chair-arm (?) with cats' heads carved on the upper side, Sandnes, Vesterbygd. (Photographs: National Museum of Copenhagen.)

Medieval chessmen used in the Norse territories. Reading from top to bottom. *first column:* Vesterbygd (Umiviarssuk), Vesterbygd (Umiviarssuk), Austerbygd (Vatnahverfi), Røst; *second column:* Vesterbygd (Umiviarssuk), Vesterbygd (Umiviarssuk), Vesterbygd (Sandnes), Hebrides (Norwegian chessmen from about 1200); *third column:* Vesterbygd (Umiviarssuk), Vesterbygd (Umiviarssuk), Marshall Bay (Eskimo site at approximately 79° N.), Hebrides (as left); *fourth column:* Svalbard (about 78° N.), Oslo (Gamlebyen), Vestfold (Tjøme), Hebrides (as left).

above: Three little girls from Gardar. *below:* Scene in Vesterbygd, photographed from the Sardloq site, now deserted.

examination of the Herjolfsnes skeletons are at variance with this view. He is of the opinion that the people were terribly degenerate; but this is not borne out by the more recent findings of a number of other scientists. I will return to this in more detail in a later chapter.

Nørlund emphasizes that the clothes found were of the everyday sort. In some instances this may be true, but to ignore exceptions might tend to present a misleading picture of conditions in Greenland; the more so as there is no certain evidence of short working-tunics having been discovered. For one thing, it is natural to assume that many would have buried their dead in their best clothes; for another, it is hard to believe that such practical people would have toiled on their farms wearing ankle-length, tight-waisted, voluminously skirted coats. One has only to think of the byres, that were so cramped that it was as much as a man could do to make his way between the rumps of the cattle. It is by no means certain that the everyday dress of civilization was everyday dress in the north.

Yet even if a certain number of farming-folk wore long garments – of the less encumbering sort – those who worked away from the homestead must have been dressed quite differently. And this is to say the majority; for here, as elsewhere in Greenland, fishing and hunting were the most important activities. No Greenlander would put on an ankle-length, flapping gown to chase polar bears, or to race for hours among the mountains in pursuit of reindeer, or to embark upon a perilous voyage to the north when in storms and ice swiftness and agility were essential.

No characteristic working-dress for the man of Greenland has yet been found. The reason for this is probably that leather clothes disintegrated, while wadmal survived. Nørlund gives illuminating examples of this from his work at Herjolfsnes. What did the men wear, then, for their most exacting physical labour?

At sea they must have worn clothing that repelled water and conserved warmth. This puts one in mind of the Norwegian fishermen's leather jerkin, worn from time immemorial not only in Norway but in Iceland and the Faroes too. Hide with the hair on was also used, especially in winter; and they undoubtedly wore seal- and reindeer-skin.

The eleventh-century Fosterbrothers' Saga tells us that Lodin, the bailiff at Brattalid, had jacket and breeches of sealskin.[8] We hear too of a combination of leather and wadmal. The man whom Jon Grønlending[9] found lying dead, face downward, some time at the beginning of the sixteenth century, 'had upon his head a well-sewn hood, and the rest of his clothes were partly of wadmal, partly of sealskin'. Since so many hoods have been found at Herjolfsnes, it may well be that the other garments were of leather which in the course of time have rotted away.

Among other finds at Herjolfsnes we may mention a gravestone with the inscription: *Here Lies Hro[ar] Kolgrim:s [on]*. Sixty wooden crosses of various sizes were discovered, often on the breast between the hands of the dead. A number of them bore runic inscriptions such as 'Jesus Christ help'; others had Christian magic invocations blended with Latin and Hebrew words (see pages 219–20). On one of the coffins is some bold ornamental carving, including that of a dragon's head dating probably from the twelfth century. On the shore, where part of the churchyard has been washed away by the sea, other objects were found, including a beaker of lead and a glass button.[10]

Herjolfsnes churchyard gives us more than dry, archaeological facts; from it we gain some notion of the people's way of thinking. There the bodies lay in rows, their heads to the west, so as to meet the rising sun when they rose from the dead. We see too how strong was their faith in the power emanating from the house of God, and how sharply defined their social ranks.

The noblest burial-place was in the church itself, where two graves were found. Exalted men must have lain there, with a reasonable hope of salvation. In one of these tombs was found the tooth of a polar bear: an amulet. Well, one wanted to be on the safe side: one never knew. Close by the church lay the other coffins, and these too must have been occupied by people of high birth. They had a safe resting place, especially those under the eaves.

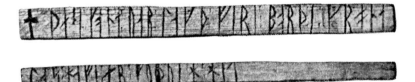

'*This woman whose name was Gudveig was lowered overboard in the Greenland Sea.*'
Rune-staff found in a coffin in Herjolfsnes churchyard.

Such a place had the coffin containing Gudveig's rune-staff: Gudveig, who perished at sea and was given symbolic burial, as was mentioned earlier. A further safeguard was a gigantic stone, weighing a ton and a half, laid over her grave. A protection against the powers of evil? Or to prevent her walking again?

Farther from the church lay the common folk, and they had to do without a coffin; it would be rather more of a struggle for them on resurrection day. But one man lay right in the east corner of the churchyard, in the wretchedest place of all, squeezed up against the wall. This must have been someone held in very low esteem: a quite insignificant person. His plight on the Day of Judgment would be pitiable indeed, for to win salvation when buried so far from the power of the holy house was no easy matter.

XXVIII NORTH TO
VESTERBYGD

WE had now visited the essential parts of Austerbygd. We had entered fjord after fjord and seen the more important ruins and other memorials of the Norse age, and our days had been filled with strange and wonderful impressions as we re-lived our ancient history in a setting of wild enchantment.

Now we were moving northward up the coast to Vesterbygd; before us lay a stretch equivalent to that from Bergen to Bodö (or from Land's End to the Isle of Man). An old manuscript, as we saw, states that from the most northerly part of Austerbygd to Vesterbygd was six days' rowing by a crew of six in a six-oared boat.

We had a certain amount to preoccupy us on such a trip with no guide, for a watchful eye was needed to navigate a tiny craft like ours through the outer fairways of Greenland. Uncharted rocks abounded, and ice drifted in from all directions to threaten our hull. At times a dense wall of fog confronted us; at others we met high winds from the Davis Strait.

There were some bad moments, but we got by – thanks chiefly to that fine seaman Harald. He was ever alert and alive to his responsibilities and he had lightning reactions. 'Herring-fishing teaches us to be quick off the mark,' he said. 'You've got to be there first, and get on with it.'

These men from south-west Norway have the sea in their blood; they come from places whence so many sailed to Iceland and Greenland in the old days, and young fellows like Harald carry on the ancient tradition of seamanship.

In many ways the coast reminds one of Norway. As we moved forward through an archipelago of bare rocks and isles, we glimpsed deep fjords flanked by mountains. Sometimes the open sea broke in and we were on our own. Sometimes on the islands we spied old, overgrown cairns, many of them with the green patina of vegetation born of the droppings of all the seabirds that have settled there. Now and again we passed some small modern settlement, where a group of today's Greenlanders live alone at the edge of the sea.

Then we reached Ivigtut and the well-known cryolite mine, which was started in the middle of last century and has proved most profitable. The people employed here welcomed us with boundless hospitality, and showed us the mine, which was open-cast: just a great hollow cut in the mountain-side.

We were now in a region once inhabited by the Norsemen of ancient days. Their homesteads lay about fifty miles from the northern part of the denser settlement, yet they formed a part of Austerbygd. It is possible that the following fjords enumerated in an old Icelandic manuscript allude to this region: Dýrafjörðr, Þorvaldsfjörðr, Arnlaugsfjörðr, Steinsfjörðr and Berg-þorsfjörðr. For practical reasons this settlement is known today as *Mellom-bygden*, or the Middle Settlement.

Here the ruins of twenty-two homesteads have been found, besides those of certain lesser buildings which probably belonged to them. Strangely enough no vestige of a church has been discovered, though the local in-habitants must certainly have had one of their own. Digs here have resulted in no positive conclusions, although, as I mentioned, a tombstone has been found on a little island of Ivigtut, with the inscription 'Ossur Asbjarnarson'. This is strange, when we remember how particular the people were about burying their dead in the churchyard, however laborious the journey.

We next came to Narssalik: a little outpost on an island facing the sea. Here we enjoyed a performance put on by a young Greenlander. He paddled out to us in his kayak, and rolled round and round in it, in the water. In the old days this was a common feat; today, not only is there a decline in skill, but there are fewer and fewer kayaks. To a large extent the modern popula-tion has adopted open, easily-rowed canvas boats; for the essential industry is no longer seal-hunting but fishing.

We met friendly people here at the edge of the sea, but hardly one of them understood Danish. This was the case wherever we went, and it is something which must greatly increase the difficulty of this period of transition.

Our toughest stretch was over the Frederikshåb Ice-blink, where there is a large expanse of open sea, and a mighty promontory of the inland ice runs down to the water. We advanced by fits and starts, meeting now with gales, now with fog, and were kept pretty busy. At last one night we completed the crossing: an unforgettable journey. We sensed the great glacier alongside us, but never saw it. Clouds raced overhead, and upon the waters glint upon glint of foam-white islets met our eyes.

We arrived at Bjørnefjord, where on the southern shore lie ruins of a Norse homestead. Here some family must have lived in complete isolation, for many days' sailing separated the place from both Auster- and Vesterbygd. One is tempted to believe that only an outlaw would settle in so remote a region.

At last we swung into Faeringehavn. People swarmed down to the landing-stage to welcome us, and it was a joyful meeting. Moored along the great

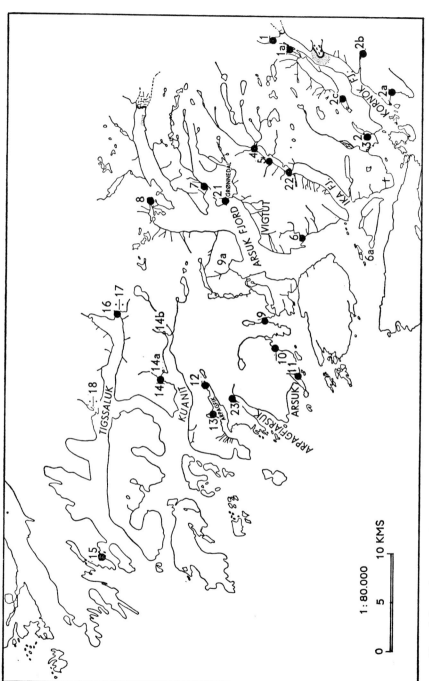

Map of the northern part of *Austerbygd*: the so-called *Mellombygd* or *Middle Settlement*. No trace of any church has been found here.

●: *ruins of Norse homesteads.*

quay and beyond it lay about twenty fishing-boats; inland, on the plain, was a freezing-plant and other modern buildings, besides bunk-houses and a large community-block provided by the Norwegian state. For us, fresh from the ocean and skerries, it was startling to come upon such activity in this stone-grey, silent land.

This whole installation is a Danish–Faroese–Norwegian enterprise, which was started in 1949 and acquired a definitive form with the founding in 1953 of the Nordafar Company. It presents an example of good Nordic co-operation, especially cheering in that it marks the solution of an old deadlock. For many years there had been bitterness in Norway because fishermen were denied the necessary harbourage in west Greenland. Fishing is carried on off the banks of the Davis Strait, where there is great abundance of cod. At times the catch is supplemented by halibut and other kinds of fish.

We greeted the head of the station, the Dane Jørgen Jørgensen, who offered us most generous hospitality. Norwegians have set their mark upon the place, and the drive and enterprise of those from Sunnmøre is very noticeable. Of those who have implemented the plans for this fishing-station, two men from Ålesund – Nils Skarbøvig and Olaf Holm – are among the foremost. Lars Øye, the Norwegian in charge, gave us much and varied support. He showed us his house-pet: a mighty sea-eagle. It seemed resigned to its existence, and just sat there looking regal. When things became too trying it flapped its wings, raising a gale about our ears. Being not quite full-grown it was still unaware of its own strength; unaware too that the blue expanse of heaven was its true domain.

In Godthåb, the capital of Greenland, the first thing that struck us was a fine statue of Hans Egede, the Norwegian who became the apostle of Greenland. It stands upon a crag facing the sea.

Godthåb has something over a thousand inhabitants, and is in a bustling state of transition. Earlier, Greenland was a colony under a state monopoly, and was closed to foreigners. The change came in 1952, when the Greenlanders became Danish citizens and were represented in the lower house of the Danish parliament.

There is much to be done, and the problems are not easy, particularly the psychological ones, such as the undercurrent of bitterness that is liable to make itself felt wherever there has been a monopoly of long duration. Then there are diseases, especially TB, which have ravaged the population. The Danes are doing much to improve the Greenlanders' living conditions and are taking vigorous measures to combat disease.

East of Godthåb lies a network of deep fjords, and it was in the inner part that Vesterbygd lay; chiefly along the fjords, though there were also home-steads some distance from the coast.

NORTH TO VESTERBYGD

According to Bjørn Jónsson's transcription of 'a most ancient' manuscript, Vesterbygd comprised ninety farms, and an old ecclesiastical list mentions four churches.[1] Seventy-four farms and three churches have actually been found, the latter being those of Sandnes, at the head of Lysefjord, Anavik, at the head of Ujaragssuit, and Andafjördr, on the north shore of Kapisigdlit fjord. The 'church at Hop' has not yet been found, and the same is true of sixteen homesteads. We also know a number of Vesterbygd fjord-names,[2] but only one or two of them can be located with any certainty.

The texts relate chiefly to Austerbygd, where the highest-ranking chieftains and later the bishop lived, and our information about Vesterbygd is very scanty. Bjørn Jónsson[3] mentions a few settlers of Vesterbygd, but they were people who returned to Iceland for good.

Eirik the Red's son Torstein had a place in Lysefjord with his wife Gudrid, and he died there. In about the year 1000 Audun was in Vesterbygd: the man who acquired the live polar bear and took it across the sea. He had arrived in Greenland aboard the Norwegian Torer's ship, and the story tells us that they 'arrived in Eiriksfjord, where all well-to-do men remained, but the others went on to Vesterbygd'.

The tale of Einar Sokkesson[4] gives interesting and presumably reliable information about two merchant ships that put in at Vesterbygd. The master of the Norwegian ship was Kolbein Torljotsson from Kinn and Sunnfjord, and the Hedmark chief, Ketil Kalvsson, was also there. It is understandable that traders should have been much interested in Vesterbygd. The people there must have been hunters to their finger-tips, and had easier access to the northern hunting-grounds where the more valuable sea-animals were to be found. The voyage was surely a difficult one for the Norwegians, and being unfamiliar with those waters they would no doubt have employed a pilot.

The Icelandic list of fjords mentions ten of these in Vesterbygd:

Lysufjørdr	Rangafjørdr
Hornsfjørdr	Leirufjørdr
Andafjørdr	Lodinsfjørdr
Svartifjørdr	Straunsfjørdr
Agnafjørdr	Eyarfjørdr

Rangafjørdr is apparently identifiable with Godthåbsfjord, but the others are more difficult to determine. The last four should probably be sought north of the Godthåb district.

It was a sunny day with a fresh breeze when we headed into Godthåbfjord, all agog to see what awaited us in this second great medieval Norse settlement. A tremendous landscape met our eyes: great distances, blue water and rolling hills, but above all wild mountains with a glint of glaciers beyond.

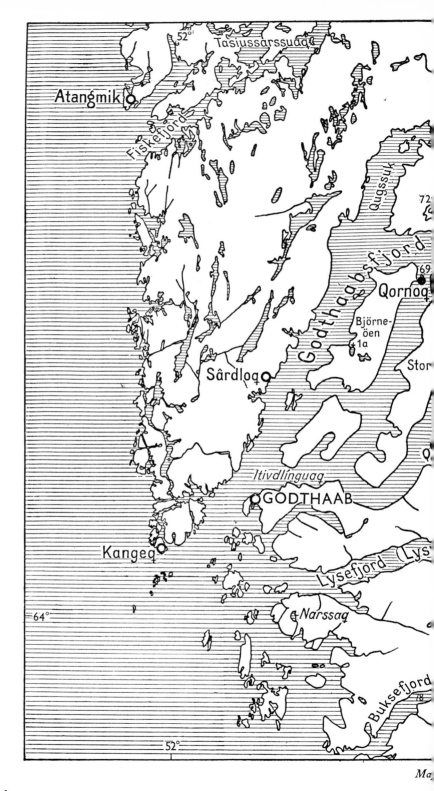

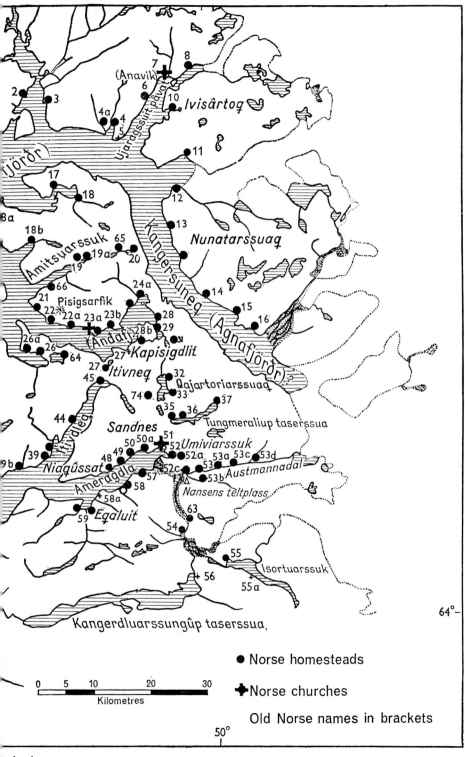

Norse homesteads ●

Norse churches ✚

Old Norse names in brackets

This was bleaker country than that of Austerbygd, though there was a wider horizon. Hunters must have liked these far-flung wilds; moreover the pressure exerted upon the community by the Church and the powerful chiefs cannot have been so intense here as elsewhere, and I imagine that the folk of Vesterbygd, though they may have been poorer, felt freer. We were now at about latitude 64° N., that is, on a level with Trøndelag in Norway, but the climate and vegetation were those of our mountains.

We come to the narrow, ice-filled straits at the outpost of Qornoq, one of the best fishing-grounds in Vesterbygd. Quite a number of modern Greenlanders live there. We cast anchor in the bay between mighty icebergs, went ashore and surveyed an old Norse home-field.

Towards evening a boat came alongside us, and a man swung himself aboard. He called my name and shook hands. He was a Danish fisherman named Kristian Nilsen, and it turned out that once, long ago, we had been neighbours on the other side of the inland ice. It was when I was Norwegian Governor of east Greenland;* he was fishing then in the same area. So we had things in common and found plenty to talk about as night came on and tobacco-smoke filled the little cabin. He was an amusing, carefree sort of fellow, and told me many interesting things about Vesterbygd, both on land and at sea.

First we tried to nose our way forward into Ujaragssuit, the innermost fjord in the area, as we wanted to see the ruins of Anavik church at the head of it. I would also have liked to examine some of the country to the west, for I believed that there were some ruins of homesteads there which are still unknown. But the ice was hopeless. We struggled a little way, and then stuck; the whole fjord was solid white and it was as much as we could do to edge our way out again. We agreed to make another attempt on our way back from the north.

Then we swung eastward over Kapisigdlit fjord, where the ice was not too bad. What a landscape that was! Steep mountainsides, gently rolling hills and sheltered valleys. Pisigsarfik – that is, the Bowman's mountain – dominated the whole countryside. The foot of the steep slopes was clad with the green of willow and grass, and here the ruins of a row of modest Norse farmsteads once lay; also a small church, presumably the one referred to in the texts as 'the church at Andafjord'.

It is easy to understand that Bowman's mountain should have stirred the imagination of the Eskimoes, towering as it does above fjord and drift-ice to pierce the clouds with its pointed peak. And indeed an ancient legend[5] is

* During a dispute with Denmark (1931–3) over the sovereignty of the east coast, which Norway had occupied. The case was brought before the International Court at The Hague. Norway lost.

connected with it. It tells of the first time that the Eskimoes encountered the Norse Greenlanders – Qavdlunât – and emphasizes that the Norsemen treated them well and that the two races were soon on good terms. Indeed, the Greenlanders even began to learn the Eskimoes' language. One Eskimo and one Greenlander in particular became inseparable friends; but they were for ever vying with each other at different sports, and one day the Norseman proposed that they should spread a hide out on the ground, on a small island, climb to the top of the great crag and compete in marksmanship. The man who failed to hit the hide should be cast from the summit. Naturally the Eskimo won, and the Norseman was hurled over the precipice. It is from this event that the crag is said to derive its name (see Plate 33).

We landed and looked at some of the old home-fields at the foot of the crag. Neither they nor the homesteads had been large. Beside two of them was a long row of 'hopping-stones': large stones laid down at intervals, close enough for the players to hop from one to the other. This is an Eskimo game, and similar rows of stones have been found in Newfoundland, northern Canada and on St Lawrence Island in Alaska.

In the pile of stones at the foot of Pisigsarfik there was thought to have been a 'mummy-cave' where the Eskimoes had buried their dead; and in time we came upon some passages roofed with massive stones. There were a number of tombs, one of them quite small: it was that of a child. From it projected portions of reindeer-hide and the skins of birds, so the youngster was well wrapped up for his last journey. Jørgen Meldgaard, who took some child-mummies from this burial-place, believes that they date from about 1600.[6]

It was evident that the Eskimoes buried the children alive. The custom of exposing children was once general among most Eskimoes, and in heathen times among Norsemen too. It is easy enough for people living in civilized lands to condemn this practice, but for primitive folk it was of vital importance to limit the population in proportion to available food-resources.

We went over the fjord to Itivneq – the crossing-place – which is only a few kilometres from the neighbouring fjord to the south: Lysefjord. Here I wanted to greet some animal-compatriots of ours: about three hundred domesticated reindeer that were brought over from north Norway in 1952. Two Norwegian Lapps helped with the herding.

A rowing-boat came to meet us, and the man aboard waved eagerly, shouting a welcome. This was Jens Rosing, a splendid fellow. He has about as much Eskimo blood in him as Knud Rasmussen, and something of the same artistic nature, with a deep sense of folk-tradition. He writes and draws and is absorbed by everything in nature, and he has also uncovered a number of important archaeological finds which have established the fact that the old Sarqaq Eskimo culture existed in the Godthåb district.

Rosing is now director of the reindeer enterprise, and is better qualified for this than anyone else in Greenland. Among other things he has lived with the herdsmen of Norway and learnt the business from the bottom up. So far the breeding of domesticated reindeer in Greenland has been very successful, and the animals thrive and multiply. Indeed they are larger than those of the mother country. The warble-fly larvae under the skin and in the nostrils, which in Norway cause such torment to the deer, disappear in these polar regions.

This enterprise may prove of far-reaching importance in a country where the native deer are almost extinct. There is no doubt that many modern Greenlanders could make an excellent profit by it: but here, as in Alaska, the great problem is the human factor. Hunters are not turned into herdsmen in five minutes.

Next day I walked over the narrow neck of land with Jens Rosing, his charming Danish wife, Aslak their little boy and the Lapp dog from Kautokeino. There was a clearly marked track across the dry terrain, presumably dating from the days of the Norse Greenlanders. It was an important thoroughfare. Jens pointed to great stones that had been rolled aside to make the going easier, adding that no Eskimo would have bothered to do such a thing.

Soon we came upon a Norse field, and then an ancient hide where the hunter lay in wait with bow and arrow for the wild reindeer. It was built of stones and lay in the most favourable position possible on this narrow neck of the peninsula.

After twenty minutes' walking an enchanting view opened out before us. Farthest out lay Itivdleq, an arm of Lysefjord, and just below us a small lake – a *hop* – into which the tide-water foamed through a narrow channel. From the water's edge grass-green slopes ran up to the ruins of an old Norse homestead, and behind this a mountain soared to the sky, surmounted by a cairn which is also said to date from the Norse period.

It is possible that this was the site of Hóp church, and that the building disappeared into the sea with the subsidence of the land. But we may question whether there was a *hop* here in the Norsemen's time, for the entrance to the little lake is so shallow that before the ground subsided there may have been dry land where now the tide-water flows in and out.

The homestead must have been one of the biggest in Vesterbygd. The main building is greatly sunken, and the earth covers it like a mysterious mantle. But at the highest point of the ridge, among the willows, stood a little house with walls reaching to my chin.

We went on farther up the fjord to Kapisigdlit: that is, the salmon. Here is an outpost inhabited by about three hundred Greenlanders, and their main livelihood is fishing for cod, which is exceptionally abundant in this area. We met Mr Holm, the manager, and his wife: most hospitable people.

A river runs into the head of the fjord, and here real salmon are to be found – not Arctic char as is usual elsewhere. The course of this river runs through a big valley of many lakes, where in the old days a number of Norse homesteads were situated. Later I intended to explore this part, but for the moment we kept to the lower reach of the river.

At the river-mouth stood a small house in which a small Greenlander lived with a crowd of little children, and his name was Jakob-by-the-River. As we cast anchor all the youngsters stood and stared, but when we landed they shot into the house like scared birds.

Jakob was standing out in the river, spearing fish. Quick as lightning he drove his weapon into the foaming eddies and splashed ashore with a struggling salmon. We marvelled how he could see the fish in these rapids, where the waters ran white. Harald, the fisherman from the west of Norway, shook his head, baffled.

It was a fair evening; first the rosy afterglow of sunset lay over the hills, and then a great, shining moon. We went upstream as far as the little lake Nagtoralinguit, or 'the water of little eagles', and enjoyed ourselves fishing for salmon.

The following day I walked north-eastward and came to the remarkable fjord of Kangersuneq. It was crammed full of ice, and remains so all the year round. At its farthest point I could see a great glacier. From here I had a good view of the shores on the opposite side and of the mighty Nunatarssuaq mountains beyond. Over there, along the ice-filled fjord, there were once five Norse homesteads. What a solitary hamlet! Yet these folk may have prospered, for there are seal in the fjord, and the neighbouring heights are known to be rich in reindeer.

But the way to other people's dwellings must have been a hard one. When they went to church at the head of Ujaragssuit fjord, their journey might be eventful indeed. There were precipices and glaciers to be negotiated, and the fjord ice might be too broken to cross, either on foot or by boat. More than one child would be tired by the time the wayfarers glimpsed Anavik church at the foot of the hills.

On my way back I came upon one of the Norse ruins in the inner part of Kapisigdlit fjord (No. 28). The home-fields are level and more fertile than in many other places. In the byre were six stalls divided by flat stones set on edge. On the whole, the homesteads of Vesterbygd are smaller than those of Austerbygd. Here too, no doubt, the sheep stayed in the open all the year round, as they do today. In 1956 there were about 1,200 head of sheep in the Godthåb district, some 850 of these on the state sheep-station of Korkut. From the sheriff's office I learned that the Vesterbygd area could support about 10,000 head if all the suitable pasture-land was properly exploited. This gives us an idea of conditions in the old days, when such pasture-land was tended, and the stock no doubt of a hardier type.

But to judge living conditions in medieval Vesterbygd by the size of its farms would be misleading. Fishing and hunting must have played an even greater part here than in Austerbygd. A great number of homesteads lay along the inner part of the fjord where cod have their spawning-grounds – Kapisigdlit. Here in the spring it was like a 'little Lofoten', a Dane told me. Fishermen come all the way from Holsteinsborg, and great quantities may be caught in a short time. Somewhat later the capelan surge in in their masses; for these the Eskimoes use landing-nets, and so no doubt did the Norse Greenlanders. Off Qornoq and elsewhere there are halibut. An important factor is that in some places fishing may be carried on even in winter.

Lastly I should mention that in the 1770s, when the Icelander E. Thor-hallesen [7] visited Kapisigdlit, he found a stone structure down by the shore. He believed this to have been a rack built by the Norse Greenlanders for drying fish. The structure has now disappeared.

Another local product of great importance to their existence was soap-stone. In a country so lacking in timber it provided an easily worked material which, as we have seen, was put to many uses: for cooking-pots, blubber-lamps, scoops, weaving-weights and much else. The soapstone culture of Greenland was at an advanced level, and it is in Vesterbygd in particular that many finely wrought objects have been found. At times they were of considerable size, such as the two-handled cauldron from Kapisigdlit fjord, which measures over three feet across. [8]

XXIX HOMES IN THE REINDEER COUNTRY

W E headed into Lysefjord, that deep inlet known to the Eskimoes as Ameralik, on our way to the other great district in Vesterbygd where Norsemen settled. It was not isolated: on the contrary, two well-marked tracks ran between this fjord and the ones we had just visited to the north. Along these tracks lay homesteads, and a messenger could swiftly cover the stretch between fjord and fjord.

At its head Lysefjord divides into two branches, and we followed the more southerly one, Ameragdla. From here we swung into Eqaluit, the 'salmon-place'. A strange landscape met our eyes; at the foot of the mountains rose great mounds of moraine cleft by a river. There were also kindly slopes covered with grass and scrub: a good place. Norsemen found their way here too, for down by the shore were several overgrown ruins.

Being in need of fresh food we lost no time in trying for some fish. Harald, who is one of the most passionate fishermen I have ever met, wandered away up the big river, to return late that evening, soaking wet and laden with fine fat char.

On the other side of the fjord and somewhat farther in we came to the place called by the Eskimoes Niaqûssat, or 'the headlike'. There was once a Norse homestead here. At the end of the last century some skulls are said to have been found on the shore, having been washed out of the ground by the sea; some of them had Eskimo arrow-heads sticking in them, says Daniel Bruun,[1] and it seems that a German missionary named Spindler, who afterwards went to Alaska, took possession of two such skulls. But this evidence is uncertain.

It is understandable that from time to time the Eskimoes should have found various objects in this homestead, for the sea is scouring away the steep bank, and on the shore we saw several fragments of soapstone. Up the slope where the main building stood is a thicket of osiers and other vegetation, while the old midden is covered with a sturdy growth of angelica. The Greenlanders of today come here to gather these plants.

At the head of Ameragdla the scenery changes in character. To the west the hills fall away and a low, undulating stretch of country runs down to a little bay. Beyond lie blue ridges and alluring heights which we guessed to be the haunt of reindeer. To the east is another inlet into which run two glacial rivers. These rise far away, and in the course of time have carried down so much silt that the fjord-bed shoals over a wide area.

We rowed to the western shore of the little bay and came to a Norse site that was among the loveliest of any I have ever seen in Greenland. Osiers had invaded the home-fields, but on the whole these were surprisingly well preserved, although the land had lain untended for so many hundred years. Here and there we waded through soft grass that reached to our thighs, and came upon little plots of gay flowers. In Austerbygd buttercups had predominated; here in Vesterbygd willow-herb, harebells, daisies and other flowers flourished together. Along the river bank tall-stemmed angelica raised its screens against the sun; and beyond, the fjord lay blue.

It is here that the great manor of Sandnes must have stood. The Eskimoes call the place Kilaersarfik: that is, 'the place where one mends holes [in the boat]'. Ruins of houses lie near the water's edge, among them a clearly identifiable long-house with an outside measurement of 28 by 8 metres (93 by 26 ft.). Near by was a forge: slag had been found there, no doubt from the smelting of bog-ore. Byre and barn had stood farther inland: two quite large buildings that told of a good-sized herd of cattle and other stock. There must certainly have been a number of outhouses, but they disappeared as the sea washed away outlying parts of this fine, level land.[2] E. Thorhallesen, who came here in the eighteenth century, counted over twenty house-sites, large and small, along the shore.

Opposite the main building was the church: one of the old type with the narrow chancel. Now little remains either of it or of the churchyard, for the subsidence of the land has caused most of both to be washed away by the sea. Part of the churchyard is still above water-level; and in a gully where the water has broken through, bones can be seen projecting from the sides: the bones of those who once walked the plain of Sandnes.

The name Sandnes occurs only in connection with an ancient register of churches, yet there is reason to believe that it was this manor that was owned by Torstein, Eirik the Red's son, somewhere about the year 1000. He moved here with his wife, the beautiful Gudrid. The saga[3] says, 'Torstein owned a farm in Vesterbygd on the estate called Lysufjörðd', and adds that he owned it jointly with another man, so the property must have been a large one; and it is difficult to imagine any other estate in Lysefjord large enough for Eirik the Red's son to be content with half.

In the winter, sickness struck the community. Torstein and many others died. The account given in the saga shows the terrible force of superstition in action: mysterious things happened, and the peril of ghosts – 'walkers-again' – loomed threateningly over the people. And no wonder. When the

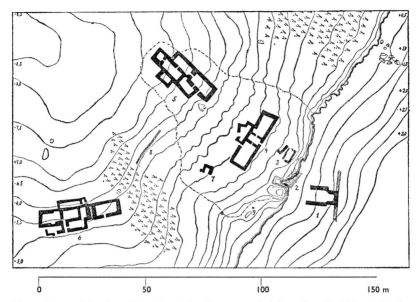

Manor-house of Sandnes, Vesterbygd. In about 1000 it belonged to Gudrid and Torfinn Karlsevne the great Vinland voyager. 1. church (now submerged). 4. main dwelling-house. 5 and 6. byre and barn. 7. forge. (National Museum, Copenhagen)

disaster swooped upon the inhabitants of this remote region, they felt small and puny indeed, and defenceless against the powers of evil.

Torstein requested that his body might be borne to church; he refused to be buried in unconsecrated ground. We learn that he was carried to Eiriks-fjord in Austerbygd, where priests chanted over his remains. It is evident from this that at that time there was no church in Lysefjord.

When Torstein's body was taken to Eiriksfjord, Gudrid accompanied it. She moved into the house of her father-in-law Eirik the Red at Brattalid, where she later met Torfinn Karlsevne, the great Vinland voyager, and mar-ried him. She sailed with him to Vinland, and the saga states that they first called at Vesterbygd. I have already mentioned this, but it is as well to emphasize it here, because through his marriage Torfinn Karlsevne acquired certain financial interests in his wife's estate in Vesterbygd; it was therefore only natural for them to call there, not only on their way to Vinland, but after their return.

These events are of particular interest in connection with the finds made at Sandnes – the Indian flint arrow-head and the lump of anthracite – which as we saw (pages 163–6) must have originated in North America.

We have also a note in Ivar Bårdsson's description:[4] ' ... in Vesterbygd stands a great church, called Stensnes church; this church was once a

273

cathedral and a bishop's seat ... ' As Finnur Jónsson has pointed out, the church in question must be that of Sandnes.

When we hear that this place was once a bishopric, we are reminded of Eirik Gnúpsson[5] who was consecrated bishop of Greenland, left Iceland in 1112 and sailed for Vinland in 1121. This was some years before the seat of Gardar was founded, and circumstances point to his having lived at Sandnes.

A curious find that was made in the deeper layers of the Sandnes homestead bears this out: it is a length of wood ending in the carved head of a dragon or a bear, and with cats' heads carved along the upper side. This is a fine piece of ornamental work in the Viking style, which suggests that it dates from the earliest days of the colonization of Greenland. Behind the dragon's left jaw runes have been cut, spelling Hael[k]i: that is, Helge.

It looks like the arm of a chair. Aage Roussell has compared it with chair-arms illustrated on episcopal seals and in medieval miniatures; and it does bear a most striking resemblance to them.

Sandnes was excavated by Poul Nørlund and Aage Roussell,[6] the latter having also carried out digs in the neighbouring homestead across the fjord – Umiviarssuk – and at some inland farms farther east. Valuable finds were made, the objects having for the most part lain in frozen ground and thus been well preserved; and they give us a fascinating picture of the medieval Norse way of life in this part of the world.

Most of the finds date presumably from the eleventh to the mid-fourteenth century, when, as we noted, most of the people seem to have emigrated to North America. It is possible that a few remained behind, or that other Norsemen succeeded them in this settlement. The human head carved from walrus-tusk that was found at Sandnes indicates this, for it wears the type of cap that came into use in Europe at the end of the fourteenth century. Roussell[7] believes it not to be a cap at all, but that the carving was never finished. Yet the work is carefully executed and gives the impression of a completed whole (see Plate 13, fig. 6).

I will mention some of the most interesting finds, chiefly from Sandnes, but also from neighbouring Umiviarssuk and the inland farms. An odd feature about Sandnes is that many objects pertaining to the dwelling-house were found in the frozen ground in the byre; as for example wooden platters, spindle-whorls, shoe-lasts, combs, etc.

Norse culture was preserved, as is shown by the tools and weapons. These are of the Norwegian–Icelandic type, whether axes, hunting-spears, sickles, smith's tongs, looms or spinning-wheels, etc. And although iron was smelted from bog-ore, it must have been on a small scale, as we saw, owing to the scarcity of fuel. For this reason bone was often substituted; arrow-heads and even an axe-head of bone have come to light.

In Vesterbygd too we find those almost incredibly primitive spades of wood and reindeer horn. It must have been laborious indeed to toil in stony ground with such implements.

The many small items discovered show that these people were orderly, and took good care of their simple possessions. They carved wooden cases for many of them, such as for instance the sheep-shears, which were of iron and no doubt greatly prized. They provided similar protection for their horn spoons. A surprising number of wooden platters have been discovered, some of them with a cross carved on them. Altogether it appears that the Norse Greenlanders did not dash at their food like Eskimoes or Indians, but that their meals were served in a seemly manner.

Toilet articles included bone combs and large wooden or bone pins used by women for their hair. A wooden bed was found at Umiviarssuk, and in the same homestead was a little bath-house with a furnace and a bench of roughly hewn planks. Beneath this lay a delightfully carved model boat, no doubt a copy of the craft used in the old days. Here perhaps a seafaring Greenlander sat in his steam-bath, whittling away at the little boat in leisurely fashion as the sweat poured off him. It is a four-oared boat, and the slender lines of Norwegian ships appear in miniature. Discoveries at Sandnes included the foot of a mast and planks from a small craft that was no doubt used on the fjord.

It is surprising to find wooden shoe-lasts and ordinary shoe-soles at a place like Sandnes; there is something urban about such things. But the footgear made on these lasts can hardly have been such as was worn at sea or in the hills. Not only are the soles extremely thin, but the stitching is so placed that water would penetrate it. Roussell is certainly right in saying that these shoes were for best – for parties and church-going. They form a parallel to some of the impractical garments found at Herjolfsnes.

What kind of footgear was worn every day on the farm, out hunting and at sea? We cannot say for certain, but in Skald-Helge's saga we hear that the son wore furry shoes,[8] and of the soothsayer Torbjørg, who in the eleventh century wove her spells at Herjolfsnes, it is reported that she wore 'shaggy calfskin shoes'.[9] Various types of furry hide shoes used in winter during the Viking age are known to us.[10] Those made of the skin from the hind-legs of reindeer, cattle or horses were known in Norway as *fitjar*, and were used in Telemark down to our own day. It would have been natural for the Norse Greenlanders to make similar use of reindeer-skin, but footgear that had to be watertight was surely made of sealskin.

These people kept count of the days, using a tally-stick. Other considerations apart, it was important to know the holy days and fast days. Similar ones were used to determine the rights of two parties to a deal: the marked stick was cut in half, and each received his share according to the notches. In Greenland money was hardly ever used, so we must suppose that in the give-and-take of barter some kind of record was kept.

Few traces remain of imported goods: some shreds of hemp from Sandnes, and from Umiviarssuk four shards of dark-red Rhenish pottery[11] which according to Roussell date from the fourteenth century. Similar shards have been found in Austerbygd, at Hvalsøy church in Vatnahverfi and at Herjolfsnes.

Something mysterious was found near the Sandnes smithy at a depth of about three feet. This was a small hearth surrounded by flat stones. The place was covered with an eight-inch layer of clay which had been exposed to fire and had a yellowish or russet tinge.[12] Might this have been a little workshop for the making of dyes?

Another remarkable discovery was that of five little round saucers carved side by side within a single piece of slightly curved wood, the whole having the appearance of a palette (see Plate 14, fig. 3). On the back of this is a runic inscription which reads: 'Ave Maria gratia plena'. Was this indeed a palette, and was a painter at work here? It was possible to obtain colours from plants, stones and earth, and someone might have been tempted to use his brush on an altar-picture or on tanned leather.

Sandnes churchyard has revealed a fine carving of Christ upon the cross, with two disciples below; the whole surrounded by an ornamental framework. A number of skeletons have also been uncovered, and examination has shown that these people were healthy and vigorous, and Norse to their fingertips.

Two of the graves have a special story to tell. Here lay the bones of a man and a woman, side by side. Their arms were crossed on their breasts, their heads turned away from one another, and upon each of them was laid the skeleton of a child. Between them lay a little wooden cross (see Plate 36). Near by the skeleton of a young person was found. These people must have been buried at the same time, perhaps as the result of an epidemic; and we are reminded of the saga's account of a sickness that raged here in the eleventh century, killing Eirik the Red's son Torstein and many with him.

The examination of animal bones, carried out by Magnus Degerbøl,[13] shows that the people here – and in Vesterbygd as a whole – raised the same stock as in Austerbygd: a small breed of cattle, sheep, goats, pigs and dogs. They also hunted and caught the same land- and sea-creatures, while reindeer-hunting seems to have played a larger part here in the north, as one might expect.

Two men appeared from behind an osier-bed: the Greenlanders Peder Josefson and Bernt Jakobsen. In Kapisigdlit we had arranged that they should come overland to meet me at Sandnes, after which we were to go north up the long valley with its salmon river and lakes as far as Kapisigdlit fjord. In this inland region a number of Norse ruins had been discovered, and I was eager to look at them. Moreover I had heard from the Greenlanders of a Norse boat lying submerged in one of the lakes. I did not expect to see it, but wanted to locate the site as accurately as possible.

We walked up the slope towards the watershed. At a place where angelica grew the Greenlanders paused and took time off to eat great quantities, for it is a plant they are very fond of. Bernt cut a flute from one of the stems, made four or five holes in it and played away merrily.

After half an hour's walk we came to undulating country where there were large areas of sand, and here we saw the remains of two mounds which had been excavated by Roussell, who believes them to have been Norse barrows from the heathen period.[14] In one of them little was found. The other revealed a stone structure about 7 metres in diameter (23 ft.). In the middle was another measuring some 7 ft. by 1 ft. 8 in., standing just over 1 ft. high. At the bottom of this lay flat stones; and here the following meagre finds were made: two split reindeer bones, the head of an iron nail, and three pieces of soapstone including a potsherd. There was a hole in one of the other two.

I cannot think that this was a burial-mound. For one thing it would be strange if the Sandnes people wanted to bury their dead away in the wilds at such a godforsaken spot. Yet from the finds one can only conclude that Norsemen had something to do with the mound, and my own opinion is that it was most probably a trap, and that in course of time gales have swept the sand up round the stones.

We soon entered some pleasant hill-country with a broad valley smelling of the wilds; and now the lakes came in sight. To the east we caught a glimpse of the great lake Tungmeraliup taserssua, beside which had been three Norse farms. We were at the source of the salmon-river, and northward appeared new waters.

The sun shone and the air was sparklingly clear, but there were swarms of midges. The vegetation resembled that of the high ranges in Norway. The path was clearly defined, partly by the modern Greenlanders who hunt reindeer in this region, but chiefly by the old Norsemen who with their livestock used this trail through long ages. The route was well marked with cairns, and no Eskimo would have troubled to do this in such terrain. Many of the cairns are so moss-grown that they may date from the Middle Ages; for moss grows slowly in these latitudes.

We arrived at the great salmon lake Qajartoriarssuaq – 'the great water where one can use a kayak': a sheet of azure among the hills. Near the southern end we took a short rest at the top of a ridge, and as I sat looking out over the landscape I spotted something that I was ever on the look-out for: a sharply-defined patch of rich vegetation. This is usually the sign of an old midden near a Norse homestead. But this patch, which lay high up at the foot of a sheer mountain wall, was in a place that surely no one would choose as a site for a farm.

The Greenlanders seemed to know what I had seen and guessed my thoughts. Bernt smiled, rose at once and walked ahead up the hillside under Aputitoq, that is, 'the mountain where there is snow'. When we reached the green patch I did indeed find the ruins of an unknown Norse homestead.* The walls still stood to a height of three feet or more, and the house had measured about 18 by 8 metres in area (60 by 26 ft.). There were traces of outbuildings behind the main structure and also farther down the slope, where two small rivers ran through the home-fields. The midden bore a lush growth of juicy green grass and glowing willow-herb.

The door of the main building faced south – and what a view it commanded! As the inhabitants stepped out they could see across the salmon lake to the mountains and far beyond. But what they first looked for must have been the reindeer herds; for no doubt, like Indians and Eskimoes, these men, women and children were instinctively on the look-out for game, even when busy with other things. And when the shout went up, the hunters grabbed bow, quiver and spear and dashed away.

We walked on round the great salmon lake and looked at the ruins of two other homesteads on the eastern shore, which were already known. One, lying in a valley about halfway along the lake, was of particular interest. The walls still attained a height of five feet or so, though the place was much overgrown and gave the impression of great age. In all there were three homesteads by the salmon lake; and for people here the presence of neighbours must have meant a good deal, few though they were, and distant.

Near the rocky outcrop not far away lay a big, flat stone, on which were two or three others. This was a primitive fox-trap of the type used by Eskimoes and Norwegian hunters. The stone is propped up aslant in such a way that it will fall when the animal snatches the bait.

We continued north alongside the lake to other waters, and put up some ptarmigan. They did not fly, just scurried off and squatted again. There were only a few, though some years they appear in great numbers.

We had now been on the move since early morning, and evening was coming on. It was heavy work tramping through bog and scrub. A loon cried from a lake we could not see, and a crescent moon swung up over the hills. When we stopped for a breather I told my Greenland companions what my friends among the Alaskan inland Eskimoes thought about such a moon: when it hung like a basket at the mountains' edge it was filled with reindeer, which pour out across the land. The Greenlanders laughed, plainly enjoying the tale; they are themselves passionate reindeer hunters.

Night was far advanced when at last we reached our destination: the

* No. 74 on the map, page 265.

place where the submerged Norse boat was said to lie. The Greenlanders call it Igdlorssuit, or the great house; and at the foot of a mountain not far off there were indeed the ruins of a Norse homestead. We were tired and wet. The tent was pitched on a good ledge just beside the water, and I lost no time in crawling into my sleeping-bag. The Greenlanders did not crawl into anything; they lay on the bare ground inside the tent, drenched as they were, without a scrap of covering. 'Is it cold?' I asked them, but they were already asleep.

Early next morning our fire crackled merrily in front of the tent and we ate a delicious breakfast of freshly cooked salmon. Now to see the site of the sunken boat. Immediately below the ruins of the homestead was a little cover with a narrow outlet to the lake: a suitable mooring. Pointing to this cove Bernt declared that the boat lay there about twenty yards from shore.

He told me that a generation before, part of the upper part of this craft could plainly be seen. By tradition the story of it was linked chiefly with that of a remarkable Greenland woman named Ane Janarssuaq. 'The Mother Earth of the Kapisgdlik people' is how she was afterwards described by the Greenlander Jens Rosing. She appears to have been a singular and marvellously strong woman.

How much truth there is in this story there is no knowing, but there is nothing intrinsically incredible in a Norse boat having sunk near the old homestead. At least I pinpointed the place.

We now returned to Sandnes, pausing at a small lake called by the Greenlanders Ataneq to try for salmon. A lively fish took the spinner, the reel whizzed round and I had an exciting time at the mouth of the river before a glittering salmon lay flapping on the stones.

The Greenlanders pointed out the evenness of the river bank from the mouth to about a hundred yards upstream; they believed that Norsemen had cleared the river in the old days. There is a tradition to this effect, and circumstances suggest that it is well founded. The bank is noticeably straight, and the stones along it are ranged almost like a wall. They had good reason for doing this: instead of a number of shallow streams running out into the lake the water is channelled into a single well-defined course where it was possible to set up fishing-gear.

By evening we had arrived at Sandnes and the boat, which lay anchored some way out. The Greenlanders came aboard with us and had a good meal; they were to sleep on the after deck. I turned in early, but for a long time I heard Harald's animated conversation: that is to say, he was talking his singsong Sunnmøre dialect, while the Greenlanders replied in Eskimo. Neither understood a word of what the other was saying, but the talk flowed no less freely for that.

*

It was not only the great explorer Torfinn Karlsevne who had visited these parts; in later days a Norwegian hardly less eminent came here: Fridtjof Nansen. In 1888, as we know, he crossed the ice cap together with Sverdrup, Dietrichson and Kristiansen and the Laplanders Balto and Ravna. On their way down towards the west coast they came to a fertile valley which they called Austmannadal, and followed it to the head of Lysefjord in the south. Here they built a rickety canvas boat in which Nansen and Sverdrup rowed the long way to Godthåb.

Austmannadal lies a little south of Sandnes. I wanted to see the places where my countrymen had walked and where they built their canvas boat, and also to take a stroll through Austmannadal, where some old Norse buildings had been found right up under the inland ice. It was a strange coincidence that Nansen should have happened upon a valley where people of his own race had lived in bygone times.

Early one morning, under dark, driving clouds, I set off to the east. On the other side of the bay I came upon the ruins of the big Norse homestead whose name is unknown to us, but which is now called Umiviarssuk. This is the Eskimo name for the land round the bay somewhat lower down, and means 'the place where the women's boats are beached'. The main building comprised no fewer than sixteen rooms built together in a cluster. I have already mentioned some of the interesting finds made here, such as the model boat, the bath-house, the wooden bed and the fragments of Rhenish pottery.

The situation is idyllic, being sheltered and lying somewhat back from the sea, with a view across the water. The home-fields are large, quite rich in grass, and divided by a river. In front of the main building stand the walls of the storehouse.

I went on then over hill and dale, enjoying my solitude in this wild landscape. In a small lake ducks were swimming, and I came to level stretches where there were masses of whortleberries. These berries were unusually sweet, and I wondered whether the Norse Greenlanders ever made wine from them.

A cliff blocked my way. I took a chance on a gully that led upwards, and was lucky, for above there was a clearly marked pass where I found a cairn. It was an ancient, moss-grown cairn which must have been built by the Norsemen, so I was presumably following the usual route between the settlements.

I went up to it, and from there beheld new country: Austmannadal. It was a narrow, wild valley, where a glacier river ran white, though a mist of green lay upon the hillsides to the west.

Having scrambled down the steep slope I set off up the valley to see something of the old buildings. A drenching rain began to fall, and never stopped; yet there was this to be said for it: I was soon so soaking wet that I hadn't to trouble about keeping anything dry.

It was peaceful in this remote valley, where Norse farmers and hunters had had a kingdom to themselves. The sides of the valley offered no level ground, but in places there was grass and heather, and the willows often grew to a good size. A hare skipped away and stopped again at a distance and I spied an occasional ptarmigan. But the most exciting encounter – the first of its kind that I had had – was with a Greenland reindeer: a big bull standing on an outcrop. Just standing. Then suddenly he swung round and was gone.

I came to the ruins of a homestead that had stood near the river. Here, some years ago, a fine pair of smith's tongs was found, showing that here too the people smelted bog-ore.

There had been four homesteads in this valley, and one in a side-valley high up near the edge of the inland ice. This last one is of exceptional interest because of its remote situation, its size, and the many interesting finds that have been made there.

It is a large building of no fewer than twenty-one rooms – living-rooms, storerooms, byre, barn, etc. – all built together in a single great complex. It housed a large number of people. One room must have been specially important in daily life: it had a fireplace in a corner near the door, and farther in, on each side of the long-fire, ran benches of roughly hewn drift-wood, about 13 ft. long, joined by a cross-bench – presumably the high seat, where the master sat. It was here that the remarkable carved wooden crucifix was found (see Plate 37).

In another room Aage Roussell[15] discovered as many as 147 objects, besides a quantity of soapstone, all well preserved in the frozen ground. Of particular interest is an iron hunting-spear of the type seen at Brattalid, but more carefully made. I believe this spear tells us something of reindeer-hunting; like Indians and Eskimoes these men probably drove the animals down to the lakes, where boats were lying ready, and speared them as they swam. This was an effective method by which a quantity of meat, fat and skins could be obtained at a single hunt. Most likely people from a number of homesteads joined in the drive, for this, like other activities, would have been a communal effort as it is among primitive peoples.

On a weaver's batten was a carved drawing of two men fighting with swords and shields. What does this tell us about the inhabitants of this most out-of-the-way of all inland farms? Since the artist chose combat as his theme, it may possibly relate to some tussle with the Eskimoes, or to one of the Norse tales or sagas, which surely had as strong a hold on people's minds in Greenland as in the mother-countries of Iceland and Norway; and we may imagine that in the long winter evenings some weatherbeaten

Ring marks the site of a lonely Norse farm; it lay high up at the edge of the inland ice in Vesterbygd, near Austmannadal where in 1888 Fridtjof Nansen came down after crossing the ice-cap (site No. 53d on map). It contained about 21 rooms (see plan on opposite page).

storyteller of Austmannadal, sitting on the fireside bench, would bring the past to life.

These inland folk no doubt used horses to carry driftwood, meat, blubber and other things up from the sea. A hame and part of a sled-runner have been found. In this terrain skis would have been an excellent means of travel, but no trace of any has been found.

These people were as active at sea as on land, and there were times when the hunters came down from the hills and set off in their big boats after whale, seal and walrus. Many bones found on inland farms testify to this. Blubber was necessary for food and lighting, and sealskin for waterproof boots.

There is nothing to suggest that this remote community was a persecuted remnant of the Norse people which had fled to the hills. Their life was a hard one, but they were seasoned to it from birth. Finds here show that they preserved their culture and even produced original carving of aesthetic merit.

They held fast by Christianity, and among them were men learned in the magic runes. On the remotest homestead was found a board bearing a

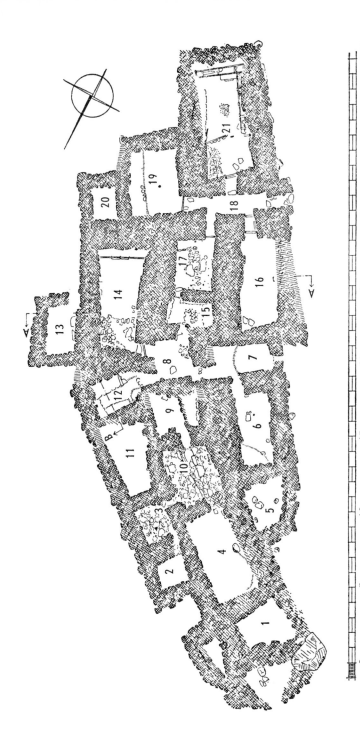

Plan of homestead, site 53d. A characteristic example of a 'central house'; it includes living-rooms, byres, etc., all grouped together in a single unit. 4. barn surrounded by stalls for livestock, sheds and storerooms. 10. byre. 12. cheese-cellar. 15. bath-house (?). 16–21. living-rooms.

(National Museum, Copenhagen)

Carvings on a loom-batten of whalebone (original size). Found on site 53d, Austmannadal, Vesterbygd.

fairly long Latin inscription:[16] a Christian magic formula. All that can be deciphered is ' ... my one God the Father of us all'.

I had come some way up Austmannadal, but now it was time to turn, for evening was drawing on. I walked down towards the head of the fjord, along the route followed by Fridtjof Nansen and his companions after crossing the ice-cap, and was now to see the place where they made their boat and set off down the fjord for Godthåb.

Near the mouth of the river were some great moraines. I searched about their foot and found at last the distinctive little pool by Nansen's camp. On the slope immediately behind it was a thicket of stout, crooked willows; it was from this they took the material for the framework. I spotted some black marks caused by axe or knife, possibly dating from that time. The Greenlanders call this spot Nansenip Tupeqarfia, Nansen's tent-place. I imagine they were astonished to see living men descending from the vast inland ice, which for them represented a mysterious boundless world high up beneath the sky.

I had made the tour as planned, and started on my way back. It was dark, and the rain still poured down. I climbed hills and splashed through bogs, but I was sure of my direction and about midnight I rounded the bay at Sandnes, and followed the shoreline, which was now far out, for the tide was at the ebb. Just below the old homestead I tripped over some stones and fell headlong. Looking more closely I found myself among the ruins of Sandnes church; for although the sea has taken it, at low water the foundations are uncovered. I paused for a little, my thoughts turning to this house of God that once stood so handsomely beside the fjord, and to the people who gathered there. Then I shouted for Harald, who soon appeared, and we pulled out to the boat.

XXX GLIMPSES OF THE LAST PERIOD

IT had not been a big place; just the home of an ordinary family. The ruined byre once held four or five cows, besides sheep and goats. Yet there was something about these ancient stones that evoked the past more vividly than many a chief's manor-house.

It was beautifully situated on a slope overlooking fjord and mountain, and the home-fields lay green on either side of the river. As elsewhere the stone and turf partition walls had collapsed, but the outer ones still stood to a height of three feet or so, and the living-room itself was relatively speaking in good repair. It was almost as if the family had only just left the long fire, for half-burnt logs still lay there. Close beside this hearth were two big flat stones, where people used to sit.

It was a lovely summer's day with a glittering sea. All round me lay the brightness of flowers: daisies, harebells and forget-me-nots. The scream of a gull sounded clearly, though the bird was no more than a dot far out in the blue. When the bronze bell of Gardar rang for Mass, that sound too must have carried as far as where we now stood.

This was just one of the close on three hundred homesteads of Greenland, and many of them were far larger. To these we may add the episcopal seat, sixteen parish churches and two religious houses, all serving a population of four or five thousand when the community was in its heyday. They had their laws and their poetry – all that is born when people gather together. From coast to ice-cap settlement lay by settlement, under the smoke of their fires.

For about five hundred years there was life here; then, mysteriously, every single Norse soul vanished from Greenland. What became of them?

The first and most natural question is: what was the reason for the decline and ultimate cessation of Norwegian sea-communications with Greenland? I have already touched briefly on this point, and will now deal with it in greater detail. It involves a number of political and economic factors which largely contributed to the downfall of Norwegian supremacy, and of which I will mention one of particular significance.

This was the sway exercised by the Hansa towns, including Bergen, towards the end of the fourteenth century. Norwegian foreign trade was paralysed and no doubt the Greenland trade as well. The art of shipbuilding stagnated; Norway clung far too long to the type of vessel modelled on those of the Viking age, while Germans and others went on to larger types – cogs and the like – which were superior both in commerce and in war.

The end of the fourteenth century saw the union with Denmark, which meant that the seat of government was moved to Copenhagen. The kings were now German, and the Danes themselves had no traditional links with the far north, so it was hardly to be expected that they should take any interest in Greenland. Norway was elbowed into the background. The Catholic Church, which had committed itself so deeply in Greenland, did nothing to keep in touch with its distant flock.

Norway was afflicted by other disasters too. In 1349–50 the Black Death ravaged the land. This was so appalling a catastrophe that it is hard for us to appreciate its full effect. More than a third of the population perished, farms were deserted, churches stood empty, and property values dropped. It was a crushing blow to many, especially landowners, of whom the king was one.

In 1393 Bergen was attacked by German privateers, the Vitalines. Many citizens were killed and their town sacked. In 1428–9 more German pirates appeared under the command of Bartolomaeus Voet, and were as ruthless as the others. Norway's largest seaport and the centre of the Greenland trade was put out of action for long periods, and the inhabitants had other things to think of than sending ships to the Arctic.

Another question suggests itself: were the Greenland products still of such value as to warrant the risk of sending a Norwegian merchant-ship to fetch them? Certain kinds of goods, such as walrus-tusks and furs, may have dropped in value, owing largely to the competition set up by mighty Novgorod, which had expanded its dominion to the White Sea and had the Russian wilds as its source of supply. Also, more ivory was now reaching Europe than ever before. The prices of Greenland wool and cloth may also have deteriorated.

Yet this does not mean that they were too low to make the goods worth fetching; there is no doubt that the Greenlanders had certain wares to offer for which there was a demand on the European market: notably whale- and seal-oil, butter, down, furs, skins and dried fish.

For the Greenland trade to endure, however, it was essential that its people should be numerous and robust enough to amass worthwhile cargoes for the ships when they did come. And if foreigners were plying their illegal trade on such a scale as to deplete the Greenlanders' stocks, Norwegian merchants may have been discouraged from making any further voyages to that country.

In deducing the fate of the Norse Greenlanders it is important to collate the most important of the known facts which have, or may have, some bearing on the final period of this Arctic community. Some items in the following summary have already been mentioned, but I repeat them for the sake of continuity.

1341 Ivar Bårdsson[1] is sent from Bergen to Greenland on ecclesiastical business. He is later appointed bishop's deputy at the episcopal seat of Gardar. Some years later, by order of the law-man, he undertakes the journey to Vesterbygd to drive out the Eskimoes, but finds no one there. Returns to Norway in 1364.

1342 Gisle Oddsson's seventeenth-century annals state that the Norse settlers had abandoned the true faith and turned to the people of America.[2]

1344 Tord Egilsson, the Norwegian, sails to Greenland and returns with many wares.[3]

1346 The Greenland *knarr* docks at Bergen with a valuable cargo.*

1347 A Greenland ship manned by a crew of eighteen arrives at Iceland from Markland (Labrador), and the following year sails to Norway.*

1349 The Black Death ravages Norway, including Bergen, as well as the
-50 Hebrides, Orkneys, Shetlands and Faroes.*

1354 King Magnus Eiriksson[4] commands that the *knarr* shall be fitted out under the leadership of Pål Knudsen in order that the Christian faith may be maintained in Greenland. (It is not known whether this expedition was ever made.)

1360 An English Franciscan and astronomer, presumably Nicholas of Lynne, arrives in Greenland, apparently aboard an English ship. He undertakes a voyage of discovery northward along the west coast – to the 'North Pole'[5] (see pages 91–4).

1368 A Greenland *knarr* is wrecked. Bishop Alf arrives in Greenland.*
-9

1377 Bishop Alf dies in Greenland.*

1379 The Skraelings (Eskimoes) kill eighteen Norse Greenlanders and take two boys prisoner.*

1381 The ship *Olavssuden* drifts to Greenland.*

1382 The ship *Torlakssuden* drifts to Greenland and is wrecked there.*

1383 *Olavssuden* arrives in Norway from Greenland, carrying the crew of the wrecked *Torlakssuden*.*

1385 Four Icelandic ships drift to Greenland, where the crews spend two winters. One of the men is Bjørn Einarsson Jorsalfare, who becomes district judge and revenue-officer in Eiriksfjord. Four years later the ship's company arrive at Bergen, are charged with unlawful trading with Greenland, but are acquitted (see page 241 et seq.).*

* From the Icelandic Annals.

1393 Privateers (the Vitalines) attack Bergen and sack the town. (The assault was repeated in 1428–9.)*

1406 A ship from Norway is blown off course to Greenland, where the
−10   crew remain for four years. This is the last known vessel to make port in Greenland. There is a wedding at Hvalsøy church. Kollgrim is burnt to death for exercising the black arts.*

1406 Bishop Anders is (possibly) sent to Greenland.[6]

1426 *Sira* Peder Grønlending[7] appends his seal with those of Bishop Bertold of Gardar and Jon Torersson to a transcript, in Nidaros (Norway). Peder Grønlending was presumably once resident in Greenland.

Much of this information has been derived from the Icelandic Annals – an essential source. But their later records include nothing about Greenland. The silence may have had specific causes. In the early fifteenth century Iceland was so violently afflicted by plague and other disasters that its literary activity was almost entirely in abeyance. Moreover communications with Norway were at times so bad that news never arrived. The Icelandic Annals of 1412, for example, report that no news from Norway reached Iceland that year.

The last word we hear, therefore, dates from 1410, and sounds convincing. A number of documents, as we have already seen, testify to the wedding celebrated in Hvalsøy church on September 16th, 1408, of a member of the Icelandic ship's company, Torstein Olavsson, and one Sigrid Bjørnsdatter. *Sira* Eindride Andresson, officiating priest of Greenland, and *Sira* Pål Hallvardsson testify in a letter dated April 19th, 1409, from Gardar,[8] that they had called the banns on three consecutive Sundays for the wedding of Sigrid and Torstein, and mentions that 'there were many people in church'. And this was an ordinary Sunday.

A papal letter of 1492–3[9] refers to conditions in Greenland eighty years earlier: that is, about the time that the afore-mentioned marriage took place. It also mentions that no ship is believed to have called there since. The letter concerns the nomination of the Benedictine monk Mathias as bishop of Greenland, and reveals that this man has declared himself willing to go there as missionary. The Pope further speaks of the hapless folk at the world's end, who live on nothing but milk and dried fish and lack both priest and bishop. Most members of the congregation are thought to have lapsed from the true Catholic faith, of which the only memorial is an altar-cloth that had been in use one hundred years before, when the last priest was there.

This account can hardly give a true picture of conditions in the Greenland settlements eighty years before the issue of the Pope's letter. It refers to about the year 1410, when the Hvalsøy marriage was celebrated. What reli-

* From the Icelandic Annals.

able documents we have about this suggest quite normal conditions: both bishop's deputy and a priest were functioning, and there was a large congregation. The papal letter must be based either on misleading information, or on such as was forthcoming some time later.

An event alleged to have taken place in Greenland is mentioned in a papal letter from Nicholas V in 1448, addressed to the two bishops of Iceland.[10] It is stated among other things that barbarians from the adjacent coasts of the heathen attacked the Norse Greenlanders in a fleet of ships, burned a number of churches and took prisoners who later returned to their homes. Opinions are divided on this letter, of which more will be said in the next chapter.

The Danish cartographer Claudius Clavus mentions in his description of the North, in the first half of the fifteenth century, that he has seen the infidel Karelians (Eskimoes) descending on Greenland with a numerous army from the other side of the North Pole.[11] This is largely fable. He also states that north-east of Greenland there are pygmies, only an ell in height. Of the Greenland settlements he knows nothing, and the place-names on his map are invented. His use of the term 'Karelians' suggests that he was influenced by the old belief in a continuous land-mass between Finnmark and Greenland.

Clavus can never have been in Greenland, but there can be no doubt that he had certain grounds for his statements. Thus he tells how Norwegians had caught Eskimoes 'on the sea in a skin boat which now hangs in the cathedral of Trondhjem, where there is a long boat of skin besides [a woman's boat] which was also captured with such pygmies in her'. This statement sounds credible; a similar one was made by Olaus Magnus, who relates that in 1505 he saw two skin boats over the west door of St Hallvard's church in Oslo.

According to a number of sources, some of them independent, the name of the Norwegian Jon Skolp was connected with an expedition which in the 1470s discovered new land in the north-western part of the ocean. Most probably it reached Labrador via Greenland. It emerges from this account that Skolp was a navigator. As Fridtjof Nansen has pointed out,[12] the name Jan Scolus appears in an English state document of about 1575, which gives a survey of the various attempts to find the North-west Passage. It is also included in a number of sixteenth-century maps. In one of the oldest texts, *Historia de las Indias* (i.e. America), written by the Spaniard Francesco Lopez de Gomara in the middle of the sixteenth century, is the statement in connection with the land he calls Labrador, ' ... hither are come men from Norway too, with the pilot Johannes Scolvus, and the English with Sebastian Cabot.'[13]

As Brøgger emphasizes,[14] it is natural to regard Jon Skolp's expedition against the background of the Vinland voyages. The old Norwegian-

Icelandic tradition was being carried on, and resulted in the rediscovery of North America.

Gustav Storm[15] assumes that Jon Skolp's expedition was the one in which the two famous pirates Pining and Pothorst took part. This cannot be proved, but it is possible. Pining, the Norwegian nobleman, was a gay, rackety but certainly able man, a story-book character in many ways. He had held a number of positions, but was especially well known as the king's admiral and privateer.

A letter dated March 3rd, 1551, addressed to King Christian III of Denmark, gives us some interesting information.[16] It records that the king's grandfather Christiern I, at the request of the Portuguese king, sent Admirals Pining and Pothorst to seek out new lands and islands in the North. It appears that the well-known Portuguese Joao Vaz Cortereal took part in this enterprise. It is further stated that Pining and Pothorst had erected a big seamark on the rock Kvitserk, off Greenland, because of the Greenland pirates who, in many little keelless craft (kayaks), attacked other ships in great numbers.

The expedition took place, it seems, in about 1474, which would make it quite possible for Jon Skolp to have been on it. In what concerns the Greenlanders' possible links with the outside world the voyage is of considerable interest. Evidently Pining must have been to Greenland before, since he had erected that big seamark. It is hardly likely that this would have helped in fights with the Eskimoes. It was on Kvitserk, which according to old navigational directions was the fixed landmark on the south-east coast for Norse seafarers on their way to the settlements. Pining probably built a cairn or something of the sort, to enable bearings to be taken on the right peak more easily and certainly from the sea.

This fits in with other information. On the Faroes discovery was made of an old account-book, Ivar Bårdsson's description of Greenland, and a note to the effect that Pining and Pothorst had lived in Iceland for several years 'and sometimes went to sea and traded in Greenland ... '[17] with whom we are not sure, but from Kvitserk, where he raised his seamark, to the Norse homestead of Herjolfsnes was not far.

This seamark is mentioned by Olaus Magnus too,[18] in his noted work on the Nordic people, dated 1555. He tells us that Pining and Pothorst lived on Kvitserk as outlaws and that on the summit of the rock they had constructed a great compass with lines and circles of lead, to make it easier for them to set their course when bound on plundering expeditions and so forth. This is something of a traveller's tale, but may have a core of truth; Olaus Magnus had possibly heard of a compass on a peak, and confused the two stories. When I was in Thorshavn, in the Faroes, I was shown a compass dial cut into the rock near the sea and the old *thingsted* or parliament-place. It is not

Kvitserk rock with its compass. Fight with a Greenland 'pygmy'.
(Olaus Magnus, 1480–1557)

mentioned in the literature, and no one seems to know why it is there. The Faroes were a port of call for the Greenland ships, and it was not unusual for pirates to put in there. Could this be the compass that Olaus Magnus had heard of?

In Peyrere's book *Relation du Groenland* of 1647, there is a story taken from a Danish source purporting to explain why the Greenland sailings ceased. It seems that in 1484 there were forty experienced Greenland voyagers in Bergen who refused to sell their wares to the Hanseatic traders. Angered by this, the merchants invited the seafarers to a feast and slew them all. An improbable story.

In 1500 Gaspar Cortereal, the Portuguese, sailed from Lisbon to the fairways off the east coast of Greenland and presumably some way up the west coast. The details of this voyage are meagre, but the map afterwards drawn in 1502 – the so-called Cantino map (see page 292) – was the best of its day. It is so great an improvement on earlier ones and is relatively so consistent with actual conditions that it must be based on more than Cortereal's observations on his voyage through the drift-ice.

Norwegian sources offer scanty information about Greenland for the relevant period. There must once have been records of these matters in both Bergen and Nidaros, but sacking and burning destroyed a great deal.

In 1516 Erik Valkendorf, the Archbishop of Nidaros, fitted out an expedition to Greenland.[19] Church matters seem to have played a secondary part

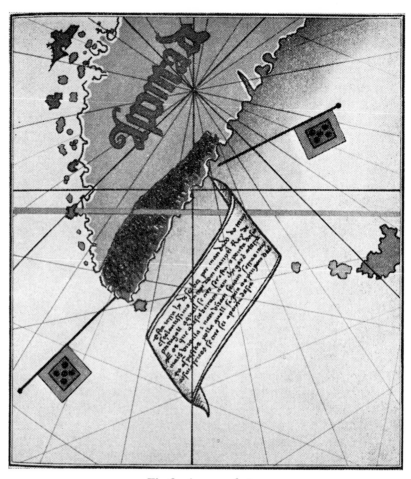

The Cantino map of 1502

in this enterprise: it was above all profitable business that he was after; which is to say that he was banking on the continued existence of the Greenland community. Valkendorf collected all available information about the country, but fell foul of King Christiern II and had to flee from Norway. The expedition never came off.

In 1567 Absalon Pederssøn, who lived in Bergen, describes the courageous exploits of Icelanders and Norwegians in Greenland through the ages, and is sharply critical of the failure to revisit the old Nordic lands.[20] He believes that the Norse Greenlanders had moved to other countries, and makes this interesting point: 'And many of the nobility have deeds of estates in Greenland, but of the properties and lands they know nought.'

*

Throughout the fifteenth and sixteenth centuries, shipping in northerly regions received a new and powerful impetus: the increased trade with Iceland. The commodity was dried fish. It was mainly the English who sailed north, after the Hanseatic merchants had shut them out of Bergen, the great staple port for the Norwegian tributary countries. The first English ship sailed to Iceland in 1412, and more soon followed. Germans and others joined the flow, little heeding the prohibition against trading with the Norwegian colony.

Most of the English came from Bristol, though some hailed from Lynn, Grimsby and elsewhere. There was a strong Norwegian element in these towns; their seamen were experienced, daring and often ruthless. English shipping was booming at this time, and an English poem written in 1437, entitled *The Englysh Policy to Keep the Seas*,[21] is illuminating. In it we read of trade with Iceland:

> Of Iseland to write is little nede
> Save of Stocke Fish. Yet forsooth in deed
> Out of Bristowe and costes many one
> Men have practised by nedle and stone
> Thiderwardes within a little while
> Within twelve year, and without peril
> Gon and come, as men were wont of old
> Of Scarborough unto the costes cold.

At first the Icelanders were not opposed to commerce with England, for after the Vitalines' attack on Bergen in 1393 Norway was unable to send six ships a year to Iceland as had been agreed. But every year the bad elements among the English became more violent: they behaved as in Viking days, slaying, sacking, burning and carrying off numbers of people, especially young boys and girls who were afterwards sold into slavery. We should remember too that this piracy affected Finnmark and the Faroes and no doubt other parts of the north. Seamen of other countries were no better: it was a rude, rough age.

The Danish-Norwegian king Erik of Pomerania protested time after time to the English king Henry VI, but to little effect. Then in 1432[22] a treaty was concluded between the two kings, by which it was agreed – among other things – that Englishmen should pay compensation for damage done, and restore to their homes all whom they had carried off. English trade with Norwegian tributaries should be forbidden. This treaty was to be valid until 1451. Yet unlawful trading must have continued among both Englishmen and Germans, for in 1450 King Christiern I issued *Den lange retterbot*:[23] a document decreeing outlawry for foreigners who abducted people from Iceland or traded there.

Towards the end of the fifteenth century trading with Iceland became freer; the Danish-Norwegian king had little authority over that remote island, and on the whole had to be content if his *ombudsmann* or commissioner succeeded in collecting the prescribed duty. Ships from Hamburg then began to arrive in increasing numbers, and Germans too acquired a position of power there. The gallant Icelanders were helpless, and suffered greatly, not only from assault but from plague and famine.

We know from earlier history that there was nothing unusual in vessels bound to or from Iceland being blown off course and arriving at the Norse settlements of Greenland. In the fifteenth and sixteenth centuries, when sea-traffic with Iceland was more active than it had ever been, this must have happened much oftener. As early as 1435 there were at least thirty-five English ships in Iceland; in 1419 twenty-five were wrecked, and at the end of the century a whole little fleet sailed north. In 1528 no fewer than one hundred and forty-nine English ships lay off the coasts of Iceland, besides Germans and others.[24]

With all this shipping it was inevitable that from time to time some English ships should touch at the Greenland settlements, which must have been quite familiar to British seafarers. It would be odd if no one thought of exploiting the possibilities of trade or plunder that existed here – as for instance in 1436, when so many English ships put in at Iceland that a number of them had to return without a cargo.[25]

This background is important when we come to deduce the fate of the Norse Greenlanders. There are few reports of vessels drifting to Greenland on their course to or from Iceland. It is said to have happened in 1537 and 1539 to vessels coming from Hamburg, but their crews did not go ashore. In 1542 a German expedition led by Gert Mestermaker is said to have sailed to Greenland to investigate; it is further stated that he found the country, but no people, and returned without making any stay.[26] Bjørn Jónsson gives the following interesting account, dating from about 1540:[27]

A man was called Jon Grønlending because he drifted to Greenland no fewer than three times and had much to tell of it. Once when he was sailing with German merchants from Hamburg, they entered a deep, still Greenland fjord where there were many islands. There were buildings both on these and on the mainland. Avoiding the places where there were people, they cast anchor off a small island. Upon going ashore they saw boat-houses, fish-sheds and stone houses for the drying of fish such as are in Iceland ... There they found a dead man lying face downwards. On his head was a well-sewn cap. The rest of his garments were partly of wadmal, partly of sealskin. Beside him lay a sheath-knife,

Carvings in soapstone from Undir Höfdi and Gardar

much worn from frequent whetting; this they brought away with them as a souvenir ...

This account rings true. Yet it does not appear whether the people living in these inhabited places were Eskimoes or Norse Greenlanders. The Germans appear to have avoided contact with them.

In the last chapter I shall return to the question of the significance of Iceland-bound or other vessels touching at the Norse settlements of Greenland.

Bjørn Jónsson[28] relates a story dating from the mid-sixteenth century which suggests that Englishmen were trading regularly with people living on Gunnbjørn Skerries. This can only mean that they were bartering with Eskimoes somewhere on the east coast of Greenland, presumably in the Angmagssalik district.

The first man whom we know with certainty to have arrived in Greenland in the sixteenth century was the English explorer Martin Frobisher. In 1578, on his third expedition, he landed on the west coast, which he believed to be the so-called Friesland. He saw no Norsemen, but a number of Eskimoes, who fled. In their tents he found a box containing nails, etc., which may have originated with other European ships.

In 1585 the eminent navigator John Davis set sail in search of the Northwest Passage, and entered Godthåb fjord, the site of old Vesterbygd. He too saw no Norsemen, but made contact with the Eskimoes. On one island the expedition came upon a grave made for several people; it was covered with sealskin and a cross lay upon it. This too may have originated with a European ship, and it adds to our general impression that a great deal happened in Greenland which will never come to light.

A letter written by the Icelandic bishop Gudbrand Torlaksson in 1595 to his colleague in Harwich[29] contains the passage:

' ... But now it is reported that your Englishmen (whom I may almost call the lordes of the ocean sea) make yeerely voyages unto Gronland: concerning which matter if you please to give me further advertisement, you shall do me an especial favour ... '

In general, there is evidence that English voyages to Greenland had become a tradition; one has only to remember the English 'North Pole' expedition which arrived at the Greenland settlements in 1360 (see page 91 et seq.). On his return the leader, Nicholas of Lynne, gave his account of the journey to the king. Greenland and the settlements, in other words, were known of and discussed in England. It is also interesting to read what the philosopher John Dee wrote in his diary for November 28th, 1577:[30] 'I spake with the Quene hora quinta: I spake with Mr Secretary Walsingham. I declared to the Quene her title to Greenland, Estetiland and Friseland.'

In the seventeenth century a number of expeditions were active in Greenland waters, some being led thither in the search for the North-west Passage. Among the most eminent names are those of the Englishmen James Hall, Hudson and Baffin, and of the Dutchman Joris Carolus. Some landed on west Greenland, but met only Eskimoes.

I shall not go into the history of the exploration of Greenland, beyond saying that throughout the ages it was commonly believed that Austerbygd and the old Norse families still existed, but that they were to be found on the barely accessible *east* coast.

Hans Egede the Norwegian, the 'apostle of Greenland', held the same view, and it was because he was convinced that he would find and preach to his own countrymen that he crossed the ocean. He sailed in 1721 and began his great work among the Eskimoes. In Bergen, his starting-point, some of the merchants traded with Eskimoes, and it was in conjunction with The Bergen Greenland Company that Hans Egede began his mission.

While in Greenland it was his constant hope to find Austerbygd and its people. He writes:

... I wished therefore in my heart that my situation had been otherwise, for then I would have held it my greatest Bliss and Joy to preach Christ unto them; and it appeared to me as the greater Obligation inasmuch as they, as I thought, both had been Christian and were of Norwegian Race and Extraction, their country being subject to the Norwegian Throne.[31]

After working in Greenland for many years and gaining detailed knowledge of the Eskimoes and of natural conditions, he remained to the last firmly convinced that Austerbygd and its inhabitants would be found:

> ... concerning the old Austerbygd of Greenland, I believe beyond a doubt that it survives and is inhabited by people of pure Norwegian Extraction, which by God's help in due Time and when Occasion offers, may be discovered ... [32]

☒☒☒☒☒☒☒☒☒☒☒☒☒☒☒☒☒☒☒☒☒☒☒☒☒☒☒☒☒☒☒☒

XXXI THE GREAT MYSTERY

How did it come about that a population of several thousands, resident in Greenland for some five hundred years, entirely disappeared? In the assessment of factors that may have determined the fate of these people, the point has often been made that in general they were at the social and cultural level of ordinary farmers: able in their own way, but inferior to the Eskimoes in much that concerned the Arctic, and hardly less handicapped in their struggle for existence there than most other civilized people would be.

This view may lead to a distorted judgment on a number of important questions, and I believe it essential to bear in mind the background of the Norse Greenlanders and the peculiar characteristics that developed and took shape in them through the years.

The people who emigrated to Greenland at the end of the Viking age were tough experienced folk, used to getting along in bleak conditions in Iceland and Norway. They did not start from scratch, but, as has been stressed, brought with them a traditional culture of seamanship, stock-raising, hunting and fishing, and they came from countries akin to Greenland. There indeed they were confronted with some new problems, yet these were not so very different from the ones they were used to; and in the course of generations they learned how to deal with them. They were not farmers in the ordinary sense, for hunting, trapping and fishing were a more important means of livelihood.

In their long period of isolation in the Arctic, old and new blended together to form a Greenland culture. I have already noted how this set its stamp on their legal system, their speech and poetry and their church architecture; but its effect was surely no less marked in all that concerned survival. They acquired a technique adapted to local demands, as well as greater hardiness through natural selection and training. Thus they were equipped to thrive where others might have gone under: they were Greenlanders.

Their society was based on self-sufficiency. In normal conditions they must have prospered, local resources being at least as good as those of Iceland: good pasture for their animals, reindeer in the hills, and all the game of coast and islands.

It has been said that the Eskimoes had the advantage of them in the fight

Man and horse on snowshoes in northern Scandinavia (Olaus Magnus)

for existence through a superior hunting-technique. We know nothing about this. It has come to be a generally accepted myth that no white man can ever equal an Indian or Eskimo at primitive hunting; yet I have known some who did. It would be strange if generations of Norse Greenlanders, whose forbears had also handled bow and arrow, harpoon and spear from time immemorial, did not attain adequate proficiency in hunting, whether by sea or land. Both races were hunters and fishermen, and the Norsemen had a resource which the Eskimoes lacked: stock-breeding.

The Norway ship was not essential to them, though the wares she brought certainly made life easier. As we have seen they could do without imported iron. Psychologically, no doubt, this link with the outside world was important, in that it saved them from feeling entirely isolated on their strip of land between drift-ice and inland ice.

If events had followed their normal course there is reason to believe that the Norse Greenlanders, like the Eskimoes, would have continued to win their struggle for existence. But something must have occurred to bring about a decisive change in their life.

Climate

Was there a deterioration in climate during the Middle Ages? This question has often been raised, both in our own century and the last, and has been vigorously debated.

Fridtjof Nansen[1] is among those who believe that in the main the climate of Greenland in medieval times has remained unchanged to this day. He bases his opinion not on scientific grounds alone, but maintains that it is borne out by historical sources.

Of recent years the eminent Swedish glaciologist Hans W. Ahlman[2] has presented a different case. He alleges that in all probability the climate of Iceland and Greenland did deteriorate 'between the latter half of the thirteenth century and the beginning of the fifteenth'. He deduces this from measurement of glaciers, especially those made by Sigurdur Thorarinsson in Iceland.

Other climatic researches seem to indicate a milder period around the year 1000, but an accurate assessment is difficult. The expression 'deterioration of climate' is often used, but is vague; it is precisely the *degree* of variation which is essential to the evaluation of human living-conditions. It is also important to bear in mind that in Arctic regions a lowering of temperature may be all to the good. It means more ice, colder waters and more favourable conditions for specifically Arctic animals such as seal, Greenland whale, narwhal, beluga, walrus, etc., and would have enabled the Norse Greenlanders to hunt these creatures near the settlements instead of having to seek them far to the north. Digs have revealed how important such game was to the people.

It would be helpful, when attempting to form an idea of the climate in medieval Greenland, if we knew more about the state of the fish at that time. We know that cod disappears from waters below a certain temperature, and that air- and sea-temperatures are closely related. Great abundance of fish, especially cod, off the coasts of Greenland would suggest a reasonable climate; and on this point we have some valuable information.

In the story of Einar Sokkesson,[3] from 1132, we read that the Norwegian merchants came upon an underground food-store at the head of Einarsfjord. Among the provisions was a great quantity of dried fish.

Ivar Bårdsson's fourteenth-century description[4] mentions, as we have seen, that all kinds of fish were to be found, and more of them than in any other country. Coming from a Bergen man these are strong words.

A papal letter of 1492[5] dealing with conditions in Greenland at the beginning of the century, states that the Norse Greenlanders lived chiefly on dried fish and milk.

From about the middle of the seventeenth century Bjørn Jónsson[6] tells of an Icelander named Clemens who arrived at Gunnbjørn Skerries and found a bay full of cod. He filled his boat with fish. This was probably in the Angmagssalik area off the east coast.

These scattered notes suggest an abundance of fish round the coasts of Greenland, at least at some periods, and this indicates a favourable climate. Naturally we would expect an occasional bad fish-year, as in our own day, but that does not imply any real deterioration in the climate as a whole. It tallies with notes we have of John Davis's voyages northward along the west coast in 1586 and 1587.[7] In the diary-entry for August 1st we find, with reference to the Sukkertopp district (63° 30′ N.), that there was no ice, that it was very warm and that the midges were a great torment. At 72° 12′ N. he could see no drift-ice, either to the north or to the west.

These records are hardly consistent with the theory of climatic deterioration in the late Middle Ages. Another important piece of evidence is that of the Danish geologist J. Iversen[8] who, basing his opinion on pollen-analysis performed at Vesterbygd, believes that there can have been no change in the climate towards the end of the Norse Greenlanders' period; indeed, he deduces that the summer temperature in Greenland has not altered essentially for the last thousand years. His study of vegetation down through the ages also indicates that towards the end of the Norse period the climate became drier and more continental in character.

In support of the climatic-change theory it is often pointed out that the old home-fields of the Norsemen are in many cases dry and impoverished; also that the byres show that the head of stock kept was disproportionate to the pastures seen today.

I think one should be wary of concluding too much from these facts. So far as these home-fields are concerned, they are today largely neglected. To make a proper assessment we should have to take into account all the regulations formulated by the Norsemen for the care and protection of their land – regulations which were abandoned several hundred years ago. They manured and irrigated their soil, and their fields were not only richer than they are now, but firmer, less eroded and more resistant to gales. The fields were also surrounded by walls which protected them from animals and the dreaded föhn winds. When manuring and watering ceased, when boundary walls collapsed and centuries of storms swept away the soil and brought in drifts of sand, what more natural than that the home-fields here and there should become somewhat barren? Added to this is the fact that on many homesteads along the coast the subsidence of the ground (15 to 20 ft.) has caused large areas of the home-fields to be flooded by the sea. Other fields, on the other hand, are surprisingly well preserved.

As for the relatively large number of cattle indicated by the byres – from four to eight head on a medium-sized farm – I repeat that this was governed by the available vegetation, for grazing or winter fodder, over wide areas. The beasts were small and hardy and in the winter were kept at starvation-level. As has been mentioned, they are now about 20,000 head of sheep in Austerbygd, and there is pasture for four times that number (see pages 60–1). All in all, conditions in Austerbygd today are so favourable that quite a large number of Norwegian smallholders would be able to make a profitable living there by stock-raising and fishing. If it is true that the climate since the latter part of the Norse period has become drier, this has not led to such a diminution of vegetation as to prevent the inhabitants from making a living.

Damaged Pasture

From time to time in the settlement areas there is an invasion, great or small, of caterpillars (*Agrotis oculta*) which may damage the vegetation. The question is whether they can have so stripped the grazing-grounds as to deal a serious – even a disastrous – blow to the Norse Greenlanders' livestock. I have never heard of these caterpillars doing any serious damage in Auster-bygd. On our way to Greenland I discussed the point with the late K. N. Christensen, a great authority who had lived in Greenland for many years. He had never known caterpillars to threaten the pasture-land in the Julianehåb district, and added that they attacked the osiers, leaving the grass alone.

From Vesterbygd we hear a different story. In 1932 J. Iversen[9] observed a massive onslaught of caterpillars in the area between Lysefjord and God-thåb fjord and at Ujaragssuit. In places the invaders had stripped almost all the greenery, not only osiers and dwarf birch, but grass as well.

Iversen thinks that such an invasion would have been disastrous for the Norse Greenlanders. His pollen-analysis shows that other severe attacks occurred at the end of the Norse period, and presumes that this was a contributory cause of the decline of the Vesterbygd people in the mid-fourteenth century.

Iversen's interesting observations relate to a fairly large area, but Vester-bygd is an extensive region of plains, valleys and hills, and many more facts are needed if we are to assess the effect of these caterpillar invasions on the Norsemen's livestock. Among other questions, we might ask this important one: were the attacks equally severe everywhere, or did some large grazing-areas escape – those at a greater altitude, for instance – so that the free-roving animals could maintain themselves there?

I have already mentioned the icing-over of grazing-land (page 65). Rain or snow-thaw may sometimes be followed by a cold spell, when vegetation is covered by sheet-ice. This makes it difficult – sometimes impossible – for stock to get at their food. If heavy snow follows, the situation is almost hopeless.

In Svalbard reindeer sometimes starve to death in these conditions, and in another book I have shown that icing-over was the cause of the disappearance of reindeer from east Greenland at the turn of the century.[10]

Greenland sheep were left in the open all the year round, so that ice and deep snow must have been a real danger. I have already spoken of the cala-mitous year 1948–9 when over 10,000 sheep perished in Austerbygd in similar circumstances. Yet it must be said that the Greenlanders of today have done very little to guard against these misfortunes. There are indications that the Norse people took better care of their stock and built refuges and shelters for them.

Such calamities are not peculiar to Greenland; all down the ages they have been frequent both in Norway and Iceland. Whether it was the snow or the ice that destroyed the sheep is not always easy to tell.

Deterioration of pasture-land from these causes may have hit the Norse Greenlanders hard, but they had other means of livelihood, and there is no reason to suppose that such a blow would have proved fatal.

Vegetation and Driftwood

In the southern parts of west Greenland there is a quantity of birch – gnarled mountain birch which in Norse times must have been far more plentiful. There is evidence that it became greatly depleted, much of it being used for domestic fuel and for the smelting of bog-ore. Moreover birchwood was precious material, useful for many different things in a country so poor in trees. As Werner Werenskiold [11] points out, grazing animals must also have contributed to the destruction of woodland. Trees were nibbled at and stunted, and saplings had no chance of maturing.

Wreckage and driftwood off the Greenland coast (Olaus Magnus)

These depredations must have led to the disappearance of woodland over quite large areas. As we saw, Ivar Bårdsson comments that at the head of Einarsfjord there was a large wood where the bishop kept all his stock; and this wood no longer exists.

Men took heavy toll, too, of heather, scrub and moss, great quantities being gathered yearly from the outer pastures and brought home by pack-horse or sled, some for forage, some for fuel.

Where wood and other growth had been harvested, the soil dried and rain washed away the turf and topsoil. Often it was either under the trees or to leeward of them that the lushest grass grew. Werenskiold[12] is undoubtedly right in emphasizing that the most serious consequence of spoilation was that it exposed the land to the full force of the winds. The effect of the föhn is noticeable in many places in Greenland; in some instances soil has been swept away, leaving only gravel and stones, while elsewhere sand has settled in drifts over the countryside.

The devastating effects of wind-erosion all over the world are well known. In Iceland, which in many respects resembles Greenland, we find a number of examples; there in the Middle Ages drifting sand began its invasion, and steadily continued. It was a disaster for the people, especially when combined with cold winters and lean years.

In Greenland the destruction of vegetation had less fatal consequences. The homesteads usually lay under the hills, and were sheltered by them. But here and there, especially in open country, great damage was done. In Vatnahverfi, as we noted, a ruin was found entirely buried in sand and surrounded by barren plains which in earlier days were quite certainly fertile.

Despoiling of woodland and other vegetation through the years certainly caused difficulties to some Norse Greenlanders, but on the whole the damage was not so great as to explain the disappearance of the entire population.

Driftwood was important material. At first there was a great deal of it piled up on the beaches, but as these stocks dwindled the settlers became dependent on what was washed up from day to day. Many kept watch for the Siberian timber that swept inshore with currents and ice after its long journey. A sound log was a precious thing.

Driftwood was put to many uses, including boat-building. For this it may have been difficult to collect enough material of the necessary quality. Yet we know that Greenlanders sailed to Markland,[13] where there were great forests; and there is much to indicate that these voyages were fairly common. Diminishing supplies of driftwood cannot therefore have been a decisive factor, although no doubt the material was greatly missed.

Hunting and Fishing

Hunting with such primitive gear as bow and arrow, spear, harpoon, trap, etc., does not as a rule cause a noticeable decline in a head of game, even though intensive and engaged in by many people. This is a common experience in northern regions. In Greenland there are two exceptions: the strange, flightless great auk, which is now extinct, and the walrus. The latter was much sought after by the Norse Greenlanders because of its tusks and the export value of its skin. These beasts were relatively easy to catch when they thronged up on land. They were not exterminated, but their numbers dwindled; in time they avoided the shore and had to be harpooned at sea, which was a more troublesome matter.

Both during this century and the last the annual migration of Greenland seal along the coast has been known to fail, either partially or entirely. This may have happened in the Middle Ages too, and would have been a serious blow to Norsemen and Eskimoes alike. But variations of this sort are a regular feature of the hunter's life.

Fishing is governed by special conditions already mentioned (page 73 et seq.). The most useful sort of fish was the cod which, since our present warm period set in, has greatly increased in numbers off the coasts of Greenland. There are enormous masses of them not only on the banks but in many of the fjords. Greenland waters, as we saw, represent the northern limit for cod, and the water temperature has only to drop a little below normal for these fish to disappear from the fjords and seek the banks, where the warmer waters of the Atlantic flow in.

No doubt in the Middle Ages there were 'black years' when the fishing failed. The saga mentions one, but in the course of centuries there must have been others, and I believe that such a season must have been among the worst misfortunes that could overtake the Norse Greenlanders. Yet on the other hand they came through many similar troubles, so we are not justified in thinking that a shortage of fish had a decisive influence on their fate.

Sickness and Health

From time to time vessels arriving in Greenland must have brought epidemics with them. The saga tells us of three separate instances. One was at Herjolfsnes, where we hear of Torbjørg the soothsayer[14] predicting that the sickness that has run through the settlements will pass off more quickly than expected. Of the Norwegian Torer and his ship's company who were rescued by Leiv Eiriksson and brought to Eiriksfjord it is said that many of them perished of the sickness and that Eirik the Red died that same winter.[15] Some sort of epidemic came to Vesterbygd too, where Eirik the Red's son Torstein died, with many of his men.[16]

At Siglufjord convent C. L. Vebaek[17] found what he believes to be mass-graves, which suggests a similar visitation.

Both Iceland and Greenland seem to have escaped the appalling Black Death which ravaged Norway, the Shetlands and the Faroes in 1349–50, but it was followed by other serious epidemics. The Icelandic Annals tell of fifteen such diseases that ran through Iceland between 1284 and 1404, and Norway was scarcely more fortunate. The 'sudden sickness' that swept Iceland from 1402 to 1404 was a disaster that is said to have claimed no fewer than 50,000 lives. But whether this and other scourges reached Greenland is unknown.

Probably the Norse Greenlanders were hard hit by these plagues, but there is no reason to suppose that they were wiped out by them. It is certain that they survived a number of epidemics before the fifteenth century, during which conditions in Greenland are reported as being normal.

A dangerous epidemic would have been worse for the Eskimoes than for the Norsemen. The former are so lacking in immunity from the diseases of civilization that even measles may be catastrophic.

THE SKELETONS OF HERJOLFSNES

After the sensational find in Herjolfsnes churchyard in 1921, F. C. C. Hansen the Dane made an anatomical examination of the skeletons uncovered there:[18] those of twenty-one adults and four children or young people.

On the basis of this material, which was in a poor state of preservation, he arrived at a most startling conclusion, and applied it to the whole settlement area in Greenland: namely, that the Norse Greenlanders had been degenerate and diseased to a quite incredible degree. They were stunted in growth, many of them having deformities of various kinds, and Hansen believed that he could demonstrate the presence of TB and rickets. The pelvises of the women were so narrow that childbirth represented a danger to life for both mother and child. The teeth were badly worn down, suggesting that diet presented great difficulties. The skull-capacity was small, and the death-rate among children and young people very high. And so forth. The causes of their miserable state, Hansen declared, were hard living-conditions and isolation.

This assessment by an expert has for the last forty years haunted all the literature relating to the Norse Greenlanders. It has been widely accepted as factual and as offering the only possible explanation of the fate of the Norse Greenlanders: degeneration and sickness finished them off.

Few have heeded the fact that certain eminent scientists reject this conclusion, among them Danish anatomists who of recent years have made an extensive study of both Norse and Eskimo skeletons.

K. Fischer-Møller[19] says concisely of the Herjolfsnes skeletons, '... but the material is very small and in such a poor state of preservation that it is difficult to judge with any certainty.' He is further of the opinion that it is impossible to use observations of so few skeletons from so remote a place as a yardstick for judging conditions in two far-flung settlements. He then considers one of Hansen's basic statements regarding the deformity of a female pelvis and the resulting difficulty in childbirth. Fischer-Møller points out that an important part of the skeleton (the *symphysis pubis*) is missing, which makes it difficult to pronounce upon the facts, and adds:[20] ' ... and on the whole the pelvis, like most of the skeletal material from Herjolfsnes, is in an extremely poor state of preservation. Nevertheless Hansen states that pelvic deformation of this kind in an isolated population like the Norsemen in the Middle Ages would be a considerable hindrance to any increase in the population.'

Having regard to Hansen's startling conclusions it is interesting that he himself on several occasions admits that the determination of both age and sex is uncertain. As will be shown below it also appears that the remarkably low stature alleged – men 157 cm. and women 143 cm. (5 ft. 1·6 in. and 4 ft. 8·1 in. respectively), is not consistent with the accepted method of measurement.

From his statement that some of the skulls were remarkably small, little can be deduced – and I base this on the pronouncements of eminent anatomists. The skull of Anatole France had a capacity of 1,100 cubic centimetres, that of Jonathan Swift 2,000.

He draws very sweeping conclusions from the 'enormously' worn-down teeth, but it is now clear that the wearing is no greater than that generally found among Eskimoes and Scandinavians of the Middle Ages.[21]

In what follows, the examination of a far greater number of skeletons from Auster- and Vesterbygd will be discussed. I submitted the question of the Herjolfsnes skeletons to Drs (in medicine) Johan Torgersen and Bernhard Getz (demonstrator in anatomy), of the Anatomical Institute of Oslo University. They were kind enough to study the matter and make the following pronouncement:

> So far as the published material relating to medieval Norse skeletons in Greenland allows of evaluation, we are in full agreement with K. Brøste and K. Fischer-Møller in their objections to the conclusions drawn by F. C. C. Hansen after his examination of the material in 1924.
>
> The most important point, as Fischer-Møller points out, is that the material in question is too scanty and defective to allow of such comprehensive and categorical pronouncements as those made by Hansen. Furthermore it does not appear that the material, where usable, gives grounds for believing that the people of Herjolfsnes were degenerate.
>
> One of us [Dr Getz] has calculated the stature of the bodies, on the basis of Hansen's measurement of the long bones of the extremities. According to the tables and formulae commonly used, and having regard to Hansen's reservations in the matter of sex-determination, he finds an average height of approximately 5 cm. (1·9 in.) in excess of the figure arrived at by Hansen. This is an important point in the assessment.

Today, therefore, we must set a question-mark after the horror-picture presented by F. C. C. Hansen, based on his examination of the Herjolfsnes skeletons and echoed by so many others. Later researches have made this abundantly clear.

THE SKELETONS OF AUSTER- AND VESTERBYGD

It is striking that the examination of bones from other parts of the settlements has produced the opposite result to that arrived at by Hansen at

Herjolfsnes. Most of them probably date from between about 1150 and 1350, so they are somewhat older than the ones at Herjolfsnes which are apparently fifteenth century.

In Austerbygd sixteen skeletons have been examined, of which eleven were from Gardar and five from Undir Höfdi; in Vesterbygd, about fifty, forty-five of these from Sandnes and the rest from Ujaragssuit. The results of these investigations[22] were briefly as follows: In a few cases arthritis was found, but no sign of degeneration or chronic disease. We might expect some degree of the debility to which Hansen attributed the crippled state of the Herjolfsnes people, yet there was no trace of it. The skeletons bear witness to a sound and vigorous people.

These conclusions are based on material which is not only more abundant than that at Herjolfsnes, but also in a far better state of preservation.

Examination of these Norse skeletons has revealed many interesting features. The skulls bear a distinct resemblance to those of west and south-west Norway (Sogn and Jaeren).[23] This was the region whence so many Norwegians emigrated during and after the Viking period. A Celtic element is also discernible among them.[24] As I said earlier, it is likely that the first settlers brought with them their thralls, who were often Irish prisoners of war, and it is interesting to find this borne out by anthropological research.

The race remained pure, for only a few skulls show Eskimo characteristics. Jørgen Balsev Jørgensen[25] has compared the cranial measurements of the Norse Greenlanders with those of the three most important Eskimo groups in Greenland, and the figures show that there is an extraordinary difference between them. He concludes:

'Thus nothing seems to indicate that a mingling, leaving lasting marks in the Eskimo population, took place between the Eskimoes and Norsemen.'

The average height for the people of Vesterbygd was: men, 162·9 cm.; women, 155 cm. (5 ft. 3·9 in. and 5 ft. 0·8 in. respectively). The few Gardar skeletons are slightly taller, the doubtful ones from Herjolfsnes somewhat shorter. In medieval Norway the average heights were about 167 cm. for men and 156 for women (5 ft. 5·9 in. and 5 ft. 1·2 in.): that is, slightly taller than in Greenland. Today Norwegian men average no less than 10 cm. (3·9 in.) more than in the Middle Ages.[26]

The teeth of the Norse Greenlanders were found to be free of caries; this applies both to those of Herjolfsnes and to 243 others originating in Auster- and Vesterbygd. Fischer-Møller[27] notes this fact as exceptional; even among primitive peoples 2 per cent is considered normal. Schreiner[28] found 17 per cent caries among sixteenth-century Oslo people, out of 840 skulls.

The Greenlanders' teeth showed much wear, but, as has been noted, no more than among Eskimoes and medieval Scandinavians. The wear indicates the tough consistency of the diet, perhaps especially meat. There are few minor fractures, such as are common among Eskimoes, showing that the Norsemen did not subject their teeth to as great a strain. They would have used them less in their daily work, and probably their diet was somewhat different. In shape and size, too, their teeth are distinct from those of the Eskimoes.

Another interesting feature of the skeletons is the peculiar bone-development within the mouth: three forms of *torus*.[29] This occurs frequently, often to a marked extent. *Torus mandibularis* predominates: it is a projecting ridge of bone running along within the teeth. Such bony growths are found mostly among Eskimoes, Lapps and others living in Arctic conditions. They are believed not to be hereditary, but promoted by external factors, including the energetic use of jaws and teeth.

Fridtjof Nansen[30] and others were of the opinion that the Norse Greenlanders' diet was not all it should have been, and that this affected their physique. Neither bones nor teeth show any evidence of this. They had to do without flour, but this was of minor importance; all necessary nourishment was available from meat, fish and milk-products, with the addition of angelica, berries and other vitamin-rich food, as for example liver, seaweed and the skin of the beluga whale. Surely through the centuries these people would – like the Eskimoes – have learnt to provide themselves with an appropriate, well-balanced diet.

It has been suggested that too much inbreeding undermined the race. This is unlikely, for several reasons. As we have seen, the Church banned marriage within seven degrees of consanguinity. Furthermore, we may take it that a fair proportion of new blood was introduced when Norwegian or Icelandic ships' companies spent from one to four consecutive years among them. For a time there was the repeated arrival of fresh immigrants. Both priests and bishops were replaced from time to time, and they were probably no chaster than the generality of medieval churchmen.

In any case examples from remote Norwegian hamlets show that the inhabitants remained healthy, despite the rarity of contact with people from outside. Adolf Steen's investigation of the Kautokeino Lapps[31] shows that intermarriage among kinsfolk is 20 per cent higher among them than among the rest of the population. Marriage between first cousins is usual, and has gone on for generations with no apparent ill effects.

Today endogamy is regarded somewhat differently. We know that any unfortunate results are caused primarily by hereditary weakness in father or mother. From this point of view the Norse Greenlanders were in a stronger position than most, for the weaklings among them must have gone under, and only the healthy and vigorous survived to carry on the race.

XXXII THE SKRAELINGS

FROM the west came black-haired Eskimoes with their dog-teams and kayaks, moving slowly along the northern coasts. From the east came Icelanders and Norwegians, sailing over the high seas in open ships. Both races landed on the same Arctic island, on a strip of coast at the foot of the mighty ice-cap.

At some time these people came face to face. When? How did they get on together through the centuries? The answer may be found in a number of sources, historical and archaeological, and in Eskimo tradition.

Historical information is scanty. I will mention the most important items, including some which I have already noted but which for the sake of the general survey I will repeat.

Are Frode's *Íslendingabók*,[1] dating from the early twelfth century, states that the first settlers who came to Greenland found no more than traces of such people as lived in Vinland, whom they called Skraelings; so they saw no Eskimoes in Greenland in the early days.

Torgils Orrabeinfostre's somewhat fanciful saga[2] (eleventh century) includes an account of two 'troll-women' or witches on the east coast of Greenland.

Historia Norvegiae,[3] written by a Norwegian at the end of the twelfth century, relates:

> Beyond the [Norse] Greenlanders to the north hunters have found some little people called Skraelings. They are such that when they are struck by weapons, but not mortally, their wounds whiten without bleeding, but then they are wounded to death the blood will scarcely cease to flow. They have no iron at all; they use walrus-tusks for their throwing spears and sharp stones for knives.

In 1266 Bjørn Jónsson[4] tells of the discovery of driftwood bearing adze-marks and with bone wedges in them. The same summer men returned from the northern hunting-grounds, having travelled farther than anyone before, but had seen only the dwellings of Skraelings, at Kroksfjardarheidr. Shortly after this the priests set off to the far north and Baffin Bay, where they found other Skraeling dwellings. This voyage, which was described more fully in connection with Nordrsetur (see page 86 et seq.), has a convincing ring.

310

Then from the fourteenth century we have that remarkable historical document, the runic inscription found in the neighbourhood of Upernavik at about 73° N.: the Kingigtorssuaq stone (see Plate 12). This is of special interest in that excavations at the neighbouring Eskimo habitation of Inugsuk show that there must have been communication between Eskimoes and Norse Greenlanders.

In Ivar Bårdsson's description we learn that by order of the law-man he went to Vesterbygd to drive out the Skraelings, that he found neither Christians nor heathen, but that he fetched away all the livestock that could be carried aboard the ships. This must have been in the middle of the fourteenth century.

Of 1379 the Icelandic Annals say:[5] 'The Skraelings harried the [Norse] Greenlanders, killing eighteen men and taking two boys as thralls.'

From 1385 to 1387 Bjørn Jorsalfare was in Austerbygd as district judge and revenue-officer.[6] At that time he had with him two young Eskimoes, brother and sister, who helped him in fishing, hunting, etc., and became so devoted to him that they committed suicide when he and his wife left the country.

In European literature we find, in the fifteenth century, Claudis Clavus's mention of the Eskimoes – whom he had never seen. He speaks of the infidel Karelians who continually descended on Greenland in great armies. Akin to this is Olaus Magnus's sixteenth-century account, which is also very imaginative. But their statements about the skin boats hanging in Nidaros Cathedral and St Hallvard's church in Oslo respectively seem credible and are of considerable interest.

On the whole it is surprising how seldom the Eskimoes are mentioned in old literature. It may be that in time the Icelanders and Norwegians became too familiar with them to think them worth writing about unless something special happened. They were also heathen; there is a derogatory undertone to the word Skraeling.

Archaeological finds show that there were Eskimoes in Greenland long before the Norsemen arrived there, but whether any of them inhabited the west coast is not known. Excavations so far indicate no contact between the two races earlier than about the thirteenth century.

Earlier I spoke of the Inugsuk culture[7] which Therkel Mathiassen identified near Upernavik at about 73° N. (see page 89 et seq.). It dates apparently from the beginning of the thirteenth century, and the Eskimoes concerned must have immigrated from Canada ata relatively late date. One of the characteristics is the marked development of everything to do with the kayak; it also shows a strong Norse influence. Examples have been found at a series of points southward along the west coast, and up the east coast as far as the Angmagssalik region. House-ruins and other signs mark the Eskimo

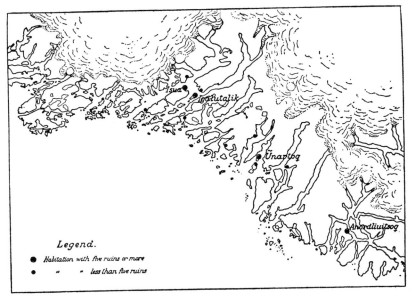

Sites of medieval Eskimo ruins, Julianehåb district (Austerbygd). After Therkel Mathiassen.

migration which during and after the fourteenth century moved on in the direction of the Norse settlements. These people would have come not in a steady stream but in isolated groups, which set off at various times as if wandering from hunting-ground to hunting-ground, at their leisure.

Some settled in Austerbygd and became the neighbours of the Norsemen. They built their stone huts about halfway along the fjords: a characteristic site for them, for the heads of the fjords were occupied. It was there as a rule that the densest Norse settlements were to be found. In Austerbygd Therkel Mathiassen[8] discovered sixty-nine Eskimo ruins which presumably date from between 1350 and 1650. The finds are related to those made at Inugsuk far to the north. He excavated forty-nine houses, and found in even the oldest of them many Norse objects. The Eskimoes may have acquired them by trade or by plundering deserted homesteads.

The number of medieval Eskimo dwelling-places discovered in the settlement area is not impressive when compared with the far-flung Norse ones, even allowing for the fact that it was the custom among the Eskimoes for several families to live in the same house, and that some of these buildings may have disappeared.

Further archaeological evidence is provided by the many Norse objects found at Eskimo dwellings along the west coast as far as 79° N., and along the east coast to Angmagssalik: pieces of church-bells, iron, knives, etc. They may have been taken from abandoned Norse farms or acquired by barter.

Long experience has shown that as a rule primitive Eskimoes are peaceable, hospitable people with a cheerful attitude to life. Yet there are sombre depths in their nature, and we cannot ignore the fact that they can be headstrong and may act brutally when insulted, either as individuals or as a race.

Of the Norse people it is commonly said that, in the Viking manner, they were from the outset arrogant in their demeanour towards the despicable Skraelings. I can hardly believe that this was so, even though in course of time certain clashes occurred. Vikings raiding foreign shores are one thing; the same folk fighting for existence in their own country is quite another. They would certainly avoid damaging their own interests, and to remain on a friendly footing with the Eskimoes was greatly to their advantage.

Might they not even have felt a certain fondness for those smiling kayak-folk, who were such masterly hunters? Bjørn Jorsalfare adopted two of them, and they became devoted to him. Eskimo legends tell of friendship between Eskimoes and Norsemen; in one story, retold by Niels Egede, and of particular interest because of its historical character, we hear that Eskimoes helped the Norsemen in a time of stress. I will speak of this more fully later.

The most important basis for good relations between the races was barter. In exchange for bits of iron, knives, wadmal and so on, the Norsemen could acquire valuable export goods such as walrus-tusks, furs, skins, blubber, down, etc. We should be underrating the Norsemen in supposing that they failed to exploit this most tempting opportunity. It seems probable, as we have seen, that they traded with Eskimoes as far north as 73° N., where the rune-stone was found, and there is reason to suppose that a regular system of barter was developed between them and became a feature of the Norse Greenlanders' life.

There are other indications that the two races were on friendly terms. We find that the Inugsuk Eskimo culture was influenced in various ways by that of the Norsemen; for example, the Eskimoes learned to make tubs in proper cooper's style. Such vessels or remains of them have been found in Angmagssalik, Inugsuk and even in Comer's midden right up in Thule. It is of particular interest that Therkel Matthiassen found similar tubs at the deepest layer of Inugsuk; which surely means that the Eskimoes had learnt to make them as early as the thirteenth century. It may be that other Eskimo implements were similarly influenced, such as knives, spoons, small whalebone saws and nets for seal-catching. Matthiassen[9] found such a net at an Eskimo dwelling in the Disko area; it was made of whalebone (baleen). Seal-hunting with nets must have been general among the Norsemen, for as we saw it is referred to in the old laws.

In the Eskimo language too we can trace Norse elements. Let me cite what Professor Knut Bergsland was so kind as to tell me about this important question:

> Hans Egede[10] believed that the Eskimo language in Greenland contained a few words of Norse origin, and mentioned among others *kona* (from old Norwegian *kona* – woman) and *qvaunnek* (old Norwegian *hvonn*, plural *hvannir* – *angelica officinalis*).
>
> The word *kona* first appears in a list of words noted down in the 1650s, and is based on information given by three Eskimo women abducted from Greenland and carried to Denmark. The word is also included in Paul Egede's lexicon of 1750 and in that of Otto Fabricius in 1804, but it is not certain to what extent it was actually used; therefore it is hard to pronounce upon its origin.
>
> The second word, now spelt *kuáneq*, is regarded – with good reason – as a Norse loan-word ...
>
> *Sava* (sheep) has been mentioned as a possible loan-word, but phonetically it does not fit the old Norwegian form *sauðr*, plural *sauðir*. We know that sheep were sent from Norway to Hans Egede in 1723; the indication is that the word was not added to the Eskimo language until that time.
>
> *Kaláleq*, plural *kalâtdlit*, is the name applied to themselves by the modern south Greenlanders. In north Greenland, as in Canada and Alaska, the Eskimoes call themselves *Inuit* – people. The southerners told Paul Egede that it was the old dwellers in the north who used the name *kaláleq*, and it is generally thought that it originated in the word Skraeling. That the word should be used in Labrador to denote Greenlanders is no valid counter-argument, for as Fridtjof Nansen pointed out, the term may have been taken to Labrador by missionaries.
>
> The conclusions to be drawn from the above are therefore that the Eskimoes of south Greenland have at least two words in their language – *kuáneq* and *kaláleq* – which can hardly be accounted for except as Norse loan-words.

To sum up: Trade by barter was so important to both Norse Greenlanders and Eskimoes that it was in their common interest to preserve good relations. There are signs of a closer understanding: the Eskimo culture was influenced by the Norse Greenlanders in the spheres of tools and language. Bearing in mind how conservative primitive people are, we must accept that the introduction of entirely new features into their culture can only be the result of peaceful contact with the Norse people over a very long period.

Some people insist that the Eskimoes exterminated the Norsemen.

We have already noted that in general Eskimoes are a peaceable folk, and nothing is more illustrative of this than the fact that Hans Egede lived among them, on a friendly footing, for sixteen years, although they were so numerous that they could easily have wiped out his little flock. Yet there are instances of fiercer behaviour. In Alaska and Canada Eskimoes and Indians have been at loggerheads, sometimes to the point of violence. Groups of Eskimoes have also been known to clash among themselves, and to put white men to death.

Unpremeditated killing is one thing, but for Eskimoes to attack in large numbers the provocation must be great indeed. Even then it can hardly be described as warfare: rather a wily incursion. In any event the struggle for existence is so demanding that Eskimoes are reluctant to leave their hunting-grounds for long enough to march off and do battle.

When white men were their victims it was usually a question of revenge. In 1612 the Englishman James Hall was killed in the same Greenland fjord where Danes had once abducted Eskimoes and carried them off to Copenhagen. Such kidnappings were not rare; they struck at the very nerve of the tribe and their effects must have been of long duration.

However, the Norsemen of Greenland were in a different position from those who put in from sea, ravaged as they pleased and set sail again, away from reprisals. They had lived side by side with the Eskimoes for a long time; they were concerned to maintain good relations with them and must therefore have learnt to understand them. The allegation that they were wiped out by these neighbours of theirs demands exceptionally strong supporting evidence.

With regard to Vesterbygd, holders of this theory point to Ivar Bårdsson's account of his journey about the middle of the fourteenth century, for the purpose of driving the Skraelings out of that region. The account contains not one word of fighting or slaying, but mentions circumstances that suggest emigration. This will be dealt with more fully in the next chapter.

The main basis for the emigration-theory is Eskimo oral tradition,[11] which is meagre. Some stories tell of attacks made on the Norsemen, yet just as often they record the friendship between the two races. Most of the tales were not written down until the nineteenth century. Here is a summary of the most important one, to which significance is often attached.

Ungortoq was chief of all Norsemen in the Qaqortoq-land, in the neighbourhood of Hvalsøy old church. There was an Eskimo dwelling-place near by, and for a long time there was peace between the two peoples. Then one day it chanced that an Eskimo went out in his kayak to test his bird-arrows. A Norseman on the shore teased him, screeching like an auk and calling to the Eskimo to shoot him. The Eskimo did so, and he fell dead.

Some time later another Norseman was killed, and in retaliation his men attacked the Eskimo village. One of the Eskimo survivors fled and sought refuge with fellow-tribesmen. First he learned strong medicine which would paralyse the enemy, then with his knife he hollowed out a great tree-trunk and covered it with a white hide. He set off with a party of men to Qaqortoq, launched the tree-trunk, hoisted sails of white skins and with a following wind glided forth towards the Norse homesteads. A number of kayaks followed in his wake. Seeing the approaching whiteness, the naive Norsemen believed it to be drift-ice, and, when the Eskimoes appeared, fled into their houses, some being burnt alive inside, others slain as they tried to get out. Ungortoq alone succeeded; he leaped through a window with his little son in his arms. Being pursued, he saw no alternative but to throw the child into a lake. He escaped for the time, but a wily Eskimo later transfixed him with his last arrow, which had magic power.

Another similar story is that of Norsemen who attacked an Eskimo dwelling-place and slew a woman. They then fled across the ice, which was so slippery that they continually fell. But the avenger, the brave Kalaleq, sped easily over the ice and stabbed them, one after the other, with his spear.

These tales are typical of all. We hear of the cunning and courageous Eskimo versus the foolish and ever-retreating Norseman. There is a convenient glossing-over of such practical objections as that the watch-dogs of Qaqortoq would have caught the scent of the Eskimoes who came ashore with a following wind. The story of Ungortoq is located sometimes in Austerbygd, sometimes in Vesterbygd. It is also worth noting that one of the chief episodes (that of the bird-arrow and the cry of the auk) also occurs in quite a different context: a story recounted by Hans Egede.

Such tales are familiar not only from Greenland, but from the Eskimoes of Canada and Alaska. They form an heroic folk-lore; the canvas is roughed in with a bold brush and adorned with the usual superstitious trimmings characteristic of this kind of Eskimo tradition. Possibly the tales grew from a factual core; a minor one perhaps, but often of an unusual nature. Then imagination got to work on it, and to such effect that the original element can no longer be distinguished.

But the Eskimoes have another kind of tradition: that of strictly historical narrative. As an example of this I may mention certain features of an account given me by a Nuniamiut, an inland Eskimo, in north Alaska. It concerned a clash that took place between Eskimoes and Indians more than two hundred years ago, and it was with meticulous detail that he described to me the Eskimoes' somewhat treacherous attack. Not only did he give me a precise indication of the place and full particulars of the battle, but also the names of many of the Eskimoes who took part and a description of them. The names of one or two Indians were also mentioned, and superstitious touches were kept to a minimum. Later the Eskimoes showed me where the Indian dead were buried.

If, then, the Eskimoes really had exterminated the Norsemen – even though gradually, by successive attacks, killings and plunderings – we should expect some historical tradition to have survived among them, as such events would have been of vital concern.

Again, had such a tradition existed, we would expect Hans Egede to have heard of it. He arrived about two hundred years after the Norse Greenlanders disappeared, and that is not long in terms of Eskimo tradition. Moreover Egede was intensely interested in discovering what had become of his 'countrymen', and believed that some of them still lived in Austerbygd. It was to find them that he had come to Greenland in the first place. We also know that he explored ruins and gathered what information he could from the Eskimoes.

And what did he discover? Practically nothing.[12] He writes: 'Of the Norwegians and the Decline of their Colony here on the Western Side of Greenland I can gain no sure Report from them [the Eskimoes].'

We are struck by the fact that most of the heroic tales are not heard of until the middle of the last century. The explanation may be that during and after Egede's day a series of Norwegians and Danes have been most eager to establish the fate of the Norse Greenlanders. They have travelled about the country with the Eskimoes, examining ruins, digging and asking questions, and in a sense training some of the Eskimoes to become 'Norse-minded'.

Many of these Eskimoes must have become very familiar with the theory that their ancestors wiped out the Norsemen. Eskimoes have a marked tendency to agree with any white man, and in this case they would have done so very readily, since the whole idea was in line with their wishful thinking. Thenceforward the superiority of their forbears in battle against the whites became an honourable page in the saga of their race. Imagination worked upon the theme in stories and drawings, to show how the valiant Eskimo stamped out the Norseman.

It is also possible that Eskimoes of the eighteenth century were not always clear in their own minds as to whether some tale of slaughter related to the ruthless days of the whalers or to an earlier period.

If we accept the theory that there was hostility between the two races, I believe we should be underrating the Norse Greenlanders in assuming their inferiority in battle. If peace prevailed in general, clashes must have occurred from time to time – especially, perhaps, when strange Eskimoes came south. We have only one record of such a clash, in the Icelandic Annals of 1379:[13] 'The Skraelings harried the [Norse] Greenlanders, killing eighteen men and taking two boys as thralls.'

We do not know where this happened; perhaps on one of the hunting-grounds, since no women are mentioned. It seems likely that a ship's company was taken by surprise, for we know that the Greenland boat from

Markland, for example, carried a crew of eighteen. If so, no doubt a couple of boys sailed with them to learn seamanship and hunting-technique, as is the custom to this day aboard Norwegian vessels plying in Arctic waters.

That this was just an incident and not part of a general and permanent hostility between the races is evident from the account – given in the Icelandic Annals and elsewhere – of the wedding in Hvalsøy church which took place about thirty years later. The ship from Norway lay in Austerbygd for four whole years. We hear of many people in church, but nothing of any danger.

If it was true that the Eskimoes were behaving aggressively and were a threat to the existence of the Arctic community, the records whether then or earlier would hardly have dealt exclusively with marriage, ships and bishops. The fate of Church and kinsmen would have been in the balance; yet we hear nothing of it.

The accounts written by Claudius Clavus and Olaus Magnus at a later date are so fanciful that we can deduce little from them. And we must demand hard facts if we are to believe that after remaining on a friendly footing with the Norsemen for about four hundred years the Eskimoes suddenly set about exterminating them.

Fridtjof Nansen and others go to the other extreme, alleging that the Norsemen interbred with the Eskimoes; which would explain their disappearance. But a number of facts refute this theory.

The skeletons found in Norse churchyards show that the Norse race remained pure and undiluted, and only in a very few cases is there any hint of mixed blood. Then although, as was mentioned earlier, the Eskimo culture was influenced by the Norse, there is no trace of the opposite having happened. The Norse culture was the stronger. A few Eskimo objects have been found on Norse sites, such as a kayak-scraper at Gardar, whalebone icepicks and a walrus-bone handle carved with the heads of bears at Vatnahverfi, an oval box made of whalebone (baleen) at Herjolfsnes, and some things at farms in Vesterbygd. These were all made by Eskimoes and presumably brought home by Norsemen.

If the Norsemen did indeed interbreed with Eskimoes we should expect to find, as Nørlund has pointed out, some trace of transitional styles in house-building; but no such trace has been found.

From time to time through the ages, of course, a Norseman might set up house with an Eskimo girl and go native, as happens today. Eskimo girls can be very attractive. And for outlaws to join an Eskimo group might have been a matter of bare survival.

Such incidents must have been the exception. In Catholic times it was a mortal sin to go over to the heathen, entailing eternal punishment, and we have already seen how strong a hold Christianity had on these people.

318

It is true that in a few texts we find complaints about the miserable state of Christianity in Greenland, and a weakening in faith, as in the papal letter of 1492,[14] but the grounds for this are uncertain. It may mean nothing more than that the Christian religion was passing through a difficult stage inasmuch as the people had so long been without a bishop or any guidance from the Pope.

Strong evidence that the people did not merge with the Eskimoes but kept to their own religion and culture is provided by the Herjolfsnes finds. These bring us right into the sixteenth century, the final Norse period. The dead were buried in the churchyard either in coffins or in clothes of European cut. On the graves were tombstones, crosses and religious inscriptions. In the coffins themselves, and on the breasts of the dead, lay simple little wooden crosses.

☒☒☒☒☒☒☒☒☒☒☒☒☒☒☒☒☒☒☒☒☒☒☒☒☒☒☒☒☒☒☒☒

XXXIII A RACE THAT VANISHED

IN the foregoing chapters we considered a number of theories as to what finally happened to the Norse Greenlanders. Some of the disasters that overtook them must have made life difficult at times, such as when a large number of sheep froze to death in winter, or during epidemics, or after the onslaught of caterpillars, or when fishing and seal-hunting failed. Others were of long-term character, like the spoliation of woodland. When a number of these disasters befell them at once they were naturally in an even worse plight. Yet none of these theories provides a satisfactory explanation for the disappearance of their entire race.

There is also a risk of distorting the picture by adding together all possible misfortunes. We must bear in mind that the country as a whole offered many and varied means of livelihood, and that the inhabitants were specialists in Arctic conditions. Moreover famine and epidemics scourged most northern countries in the Middle Ages; no people can have endured greater sufferings than the Icelanders, yet they survived. And the Herjolfsnes finds tell us that Norse Greenlanders inhabited the country up to the beginning of the fifteenth century.

Are there then other factors which may provide a key to the riddle? We have good reason to think so. The reasons for the disappearance seem to have differed in Vester- and Austerbygd, and will be examined separately.

Vesterbygd

As we saw, there has been a widespread belief that the Norsemen were wiped out by the Eskimoes. This belief is to a great extent based on Eskimo stories, which, as has been shown, are suspect. Where Vesterbygd is concerned another source has been relied upon: an extract from Ivar Bårdsson's *Description of Greenland*.[1] In this it is stated that in Vesterbygd there is a large church called Stensnes church, once a cathedral and episcopal seat; that horses, goats, cattle and sheep run wild there, but no people are to be found, whether Christian or heathen. Bårdsson goes on to state that he, the bishop's deputy at Gardar, saw all this with his own eyes, having been one of those appointed by the law-man to journey to Vesterbygd against the Skraelings and drive them out, and that on finding neither Christian nor

above: The wild valley of Austmannadal, where Fridtjof Nansen and his five companions came down after crossing the ice-cap in 1888. The moss-grown cairn was erected by Norse Greenlanders. *below:* In the foreground the pool where Nansen built his canvas boat. He and Sverdrup then rowed down the fjord.

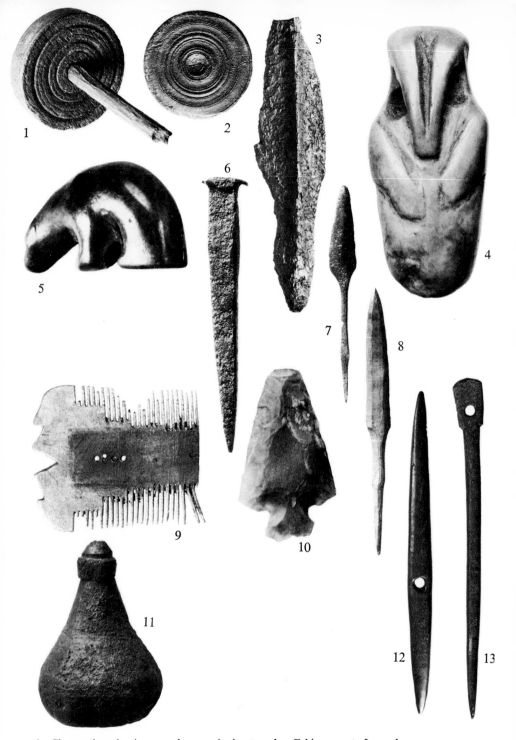

1. Chequer-board piece used as spinning-top by Eskimoes at Inugsuk.
2. Chequer-board piece from Sandnes. 3. Spearhead from Brattalid. 4. Walrus
carved from back tooth of walrus, Umiviarssuk. 5. Polar bear carved from
walrus tusk, Sandnes. 6. Iron wedge, Umiviarssuk. 7 and 8. Arrowheads of iron
and bone, Vesterbygd. 9. Bone comb from Brattalid. 10. Flint arrowhead from
Sandnes, probably of North American Indian origin (see p. 166). 11. Bone
chequer-board piece from Brattalid. 12 and 13. Bone needles. (Photographs:
National Museum of Copenhagen.)

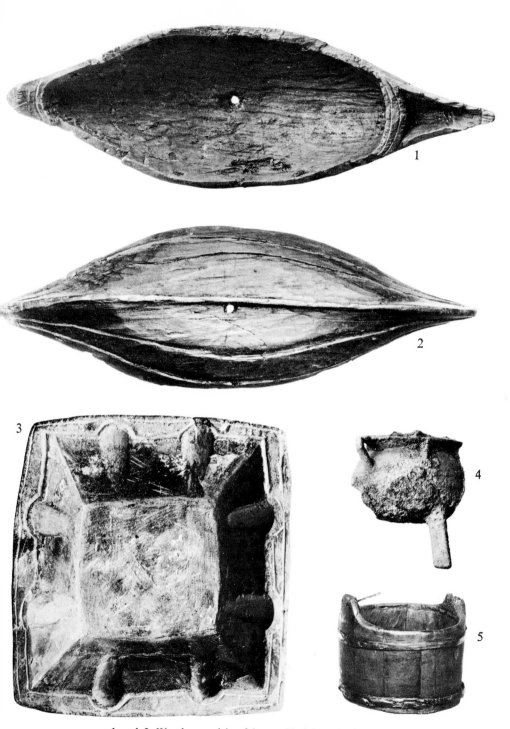

1 and 2. Wooden models of boats, Umiviarssuk. 3. Soapstone blubber-lamp, Umiviarssuk. 4. Metal cooking-pot, found on an Eskimo site in Disko Bay. 5. Wooden tub found on the Eskimo site of Inugsuk, about 73° N. (Photographs: National Museum of Copenhagen.)

Pisigsarfik, the Bowman's Crag, Vesterbygd. According to the saga, an Eskimo and a Norse Greenlander climbed to the top for a shooting match. The loser was to be hurled over the precipice.

above: Just below the inland ice east of south Strømfjord we brought down a reindeer. The country here was beautiful, with rolling hills and little lakes set like blue eyes in the autumn landscape. *below:* Into south Strømfjord, which is over 100 miles long and about 2½ miles wide. The tide-race runs like a torrent.

East of south Strømfjord. Barnabas the Greenlander with the mighty reindeer antlers. Behind him the inland ice.

Return to south Strømfjord with a cheerful party of Greenlanders heavily burdened with reindeer meat

Arrival at Angmalortoq – the round lake – east of south Strømfjord. An old Norse hunting-lodge is said to have stood here. To our surprise we came upon a camp of reindeer hunters.

heathen there, members of his expedition helped themselves to as much of the stock as the ships could carry and returned home.

When did this expedition take place? We know that in 1341 the bishop of Bjørgvin issued a pass to Ivar Bårdsson for a voyage to Greenland on Church business, and that he was back in Norway in 1364. It seems likely, therefore, that the Vesterbygd expedition took place between 1348 and 1363. This tallies with the statement that he was deputy at Gardar, which indeed at that time was without a bishop.

Asgaut Steinnes[2] has an interesting theory that the law-man who sent Ivar to Vesterbygd was Pål Knutsson. We have already seen that King Magnus Eiriksson sent him a letter dated 1354 authorizing him to fit out an expedition to Greenland (see page 167). Steinnes believes that the reason for the journey may have been a rumour that the Eskimoes were making life difficult for the people of Vesterbygd. Pål Knutsson had been law-man of the Gulating and may well have been appointed to a similar office in Greenland. But, as we said, we know no more of the expedition than is mentioned in the brief letter from the king.

In studying the content of Ivar Bårdsson's account, we note that the wild horses, cattle and small stock are specifically mentioned, in some cases twice, as something of essential importance. There are said to be 'enough' of them, which we may translate as plenty. Fridtjof Nansen[3] has emphasized that this is quite inconsistent with the statement that the Eskimoes had wiped out the people of Vesterbygd, for had they done so they would never have spared the animals. I believe that anyone who knows anything of the Eskimo mentality would agree. Indeed I would go so far as to say that it is almost unthinkable that such passionate hunters would leave the stock alone and fail to take advantage of all the meat that had fallen into their hands. They would have slaughtered the beasts en masse, in the primitive manner. They must have known that the Norsemen had domesticated animals; and in any case if they had advanced up the fjords and killed off the owners they could not have failed to observe a fair proportion of the stock in that bare, unwooded landscape.

Ivar Bårdsson met not a soul in Vesterbygd; he states categorically, twice over, that neither Christian nor heathen was to be seen. When in the same sentence he declares that the Skraelings 'owned all Vesterbygd' he must mean that the Eskimoes had the whole area at their disposal; but there is no hint that this was the result of slaughter; no word of battle or of people killed. Yet when he gave an account of his journey afterwards it would have lain uppermost in his mind to tell how his countrymen of Vesterbygd had been – or appeared to have been – slain, if indeed this had been the fact.

Fridtjof Nansen takes it that the people were out on some temporary hunting-trip along the sea coast, but it is hardly reasonable to suppose that every single person would have gone, leaving the cows unmilked. And since Ivar Bårdsson declares so emphatically that the whole place was deserted, we must assume that he had made due search. It would have taken no more than a few days to sail into the two main fjords and visit a number of the most important homesteads.

In weighing up these matters we should be careful to set them in their proper context. Ivar Bårdsson undertook this long journey to the north at the law-man's order; therefore he held a responsible position. The expedition comprised several ships manned by experienced men who were well able to judge from the look of a farm whether its inhabitants were temporarily absent or had left it for good. As the man in charge of the bishop's seat, Ivar Bårdsson would never have returned to Austerbygd without having done his best; far less would he have loaded his vessels with as many cattle and other stock as they could hold, and carry them south, unless he was perfectly certain that the Vesterbygders had gone, never to return; for that would have been to rob the very people he had come to help. The crews would have seen to it that the matter became known in Austerbygd, and his prestige as leader of the Church would have been destroyed.

In Ivar Bårdsson's remarks about the wild horses, cattle, goats and sheep we seem to detect a note of surprise. At any rate he has no explanation to offer, and gives us the impression that he simply does not know what has become of the people of Vesterbygd.

Well, what did become of them? For a number of reasons, to be examined later, it seems likely that they emigrated. Such a conclusion fits in with Ivar Bårdsson's mention of all the livestock running wild about the place, for if their owners had left the country they could have taken no more than a minute percentage of stock, etc., aboard their ships. Nor had it been long since they sailed, for the abandoned cattle could not have survived many winters in the open.

It is difficult to say for certain why the people should have emigrated. The invasion of caterpillars noted by J. Iversen (see page 302) towards the end of the Norse period may have destroyed much of the grazing, yet the cause seems more likely to be found in Ivar Bårdsson's reference to the Skraelings who were to be driven out. This need not imply any great hostility, but occasional episodes may have occurred, possibly through the Eskimoes having encroached upon old Norse hunting- or fishing-grounds. It was at this period that the Inugsuk people moved south. Thus the people of Vesterbygd may have been living under a certain pressure. They were few and scattered, and would not have been able to put up so firm a resistance as the people of Austerbygd. If in addition to this their living-conditions were deteriorating, they may well have been tempted to try their luck in some other country.

Which country? An interesting point is that of all the Greenlanders they lay nearest to the old Vinland route which crossed the Davis Strait and followed the coasts of Baffin Land and Labrador southward. The saga tells us that when Torfinn Karlsevne sailed on his great expedition he went first to Vesterbygd before putting out to the open sea; and it was also the only place where objects that must have originated with the America voyages were discovered: namely the flint arrow-head and the lump of anthracite (Sandnes).

In all probability the hunters and fishermen of Vesterbygd had not only sighted Baffin Land many a time, but had good knowledge of the southward coastal route, either from tradition or from their own experience. I have already mentioned the sources indicating that sailings to North America were continued after Leiv Eiriksson's day (see page 167 et seq.). We also have the record of Bishop Eirik Gnúpsson who sailed for Vinland in 1121.

When therefore life in the home-fjords of Vesterbygd became too difficult it would have been a natural – even a tempting – course to seek the far more fertile land in the south-west. They loaded the ships and set sail, but most of their livestock had to be left behind.

Much else belonging to dwelling, byre and barn had to be abandoned, and a striking number of serviceable things have been uncovered on the excavated farms of Vesterbygd. Shipping-space was limited and only essentials were taken.

There are other indications that the Vesterbygders emigrated to North America.

Bishop Gisle Oddsson was for a long time resident at the Icelandic seat of Skálholt, where he had access to books and archives. In his annals for the year 1342 he writes:

> The settlers of Greenland lapsed of their own free will from the true faith and the Christian religion; having abandoned all good conduct and true virtues they turned to the people of America [*ad Americae populos se converterunt*]. Some people believe that Greenland lies very near to the westerly countries of the world. In consequence, Christians began to abstain from the Greenland voyage.

Opinions have been divided on this text. Gustav Storm[4] thinks that the expression *ad Americae populos se converterunt* was intended to suggest that the Norse Greenlanders emigrated to America, but was invented to account for their disappearance. Nansen's interpretation[5] is that the Norsemen began to interbreed with the Eskimoes. P. A. Munch, like Storm, believes that the Latin phrase indicates emigration to America, but that such an emigration did actually take place.

P. A. Munch's[6] interpretation is in line with the facts already mentioned. Moreover the fateful event concerning Vesterbygd took place in the mid-fourteenth century, presumably a few years before Ivar Bårdsson's expedition.

At about the same period – 1347 [7] – the Icelandic Annals mention the ship from Greenland that had been to Markland, was storm-driven to Iceland and later sailed for Norway. This vessel may have crossed the Davis Strait to fetch a load of timber; yet there is another possibility. The event so exactly fits in with the time of Ivar Bårdsson's journey to Vesterbygd and the postulated emigration that it may be more than a coincidence; the ship may well have been one of the emigrant vessels which reached the coasts of Labrador but was caught in a storm and swept eastwards.

Hans Egede, after surveying the ruins of the church at the head of Godthåb fjord (Ujaragssuit), in 1723, wrote: 'I inquired of the Savages whether they had thus destroyed the Stone Building, but they replied that the Norwegians did it when they left this Country. Of this I have no more to relate.'

To sum up: there is much to indicate that the Norse Greenlanders had knowledge of North America and that they made journeys to it in the period following the Vinland voyages. We know for certain that a Greenland vessel was there in 1347. Ivar Bårdsson's description and Gisle Oddsson's annals strongly suggest that the Vesterbygd people emigrated at about this time, and there is reason to think that they followed Bishop Eirik Gnúpsson's example and went to North America.

Where they settled and what afterwards befell them is unknown, but from the account of the Vinland voyages we remember that it was a perilous thing for a small community to land on Indian shores.

Austerbygd

There were still Norse people in Greenland in the early 1500s, but we should remember that by that time their community had dwindled. The Herjolfsnes folk wore clothes of European pattern, so that in one way or another they must still have been in communication with the outside world.

Norwegian ships may have called at the settlements later than we think, and there could be a number of reasons why we find no mention of them in the records, as for instance that the seamen were trading illegally, without royal consent. The boom in English trade with Iceland from the beginning of the fifteenth century onwards – chiefly in dried fish – has already been mentioned. Some of these trading vessels must almost certainly have been blown across to the Greenland settlements, and possibly German ships as well.

What would have been the effect of such arrivals?

First and foremost they would have led to trade. The Herjolfsnes clothing also makes it clear that for a period the local inhabitants were on a peaceful footing with foreign seafarers; and the fact that they adopted foreign fashions and copied them so exactly shows that such visitors cannot have been so very rare.

This in turn suggests that the Norse Greenlanders could still offer wares that had a value in the European markets, such as blubber, skins, downs, furs, etc. To this we may add dried fish. Though the Greenlanders may not have produced this on a large scale up to that time, they would certainly have been encouraged to do so now.

Their stock-in-trade was at their very door, if fish were as abundant in the fjords as they are today. And at that particular period the production of dried fish would have been more profitable than ever before. Until the middle of the sixteenth century it fetched a high price, and in Iceland we find that fish, to a large extent, superseded wadmal as a unit of measurement. In the Middle Ages a larger proportion of the daily diet all over Europe consisted of fish than we can readily imagine today, partly because of the many fast-days observed by the Catholic Church. The demand, by kings and commoners alike, was very great.

Nearly all the fish was caught within the Norwegian dominions, and for a long time the sale was restricted to Bergen, the staple town. As we saw, the English were excluded and were forced to seek other sources of supply, such as Iceland. But here competition rapidly increased, and owners who made contact with the Greenland community found a profitable opening – so long as it could be kept secret – for the Greenlanders could produce only a limited supply.

No distance was too great, it seemed, when there was a chance of bringing this precious fish to Europe. Numbers of vessels crossed perilous seas to Iceland and north Norway; and after the discovery of Newfoundland in 1492 a surprisingly short time elapsed before whole fleets made their way across the Atlantic. In 1517[8] we hear of a hundred French ships in those parts, besides some from other countries. This shows that not even the Greenland route was too arduous so long as dried fish and other valuable goods were to be picked up there.

There is another element to be reckoned with: pirates. The fifteenth and sixteenth centuries were the pirate age; then it was that the scum of England, Germany, Norway, Denmark, Portugal, Spain and other lands roamed all the seas for prey. Sometimes their activities formed part of the political game of kings and were given a gloss of legality. Privateering at sea and assault on land were often no less outrageous than the wild forays of the Vikings, and it was common practice to take prisoners and later sell them. This happened time and again in north Norway, the Faroes, Iceland and elsewhere.

The activities of the English pirates in Iceland are of special interest. Their vessels may have drifted to the Greenland settlements, or, if they had heard of them, they deliberately sailed there in hopes of plunder. Their procedure in Iceland illustrates what they may have done in Greenland, and I will give a few scattered instances.[9]

In 1420 Englishmen attacked Bessastaðir (Iceland), took the royal commissioner and a chaplain prisoner and killed the latter's deputy. At Skagafjord, in the north, the crews of three ships advanced in battle-order with trumpets and banners, killed the king's official, beat up the steward of Holar bishopric in the presence of the bishop himself, and committed other misdeeds. In 1422 Rawlin Beck and John Percy attacked Bessastaðir again, killed an official in the churchyard and sacked the King's House and the church. In 1423 British pirates harried the north of the country, burning the churches of Husøy and Husavik, and from the only church on Grinsøy they stole the chalice, vestments and sacred books. In this area they also drove off a great number of cattle and sheep and took so many people prisoner that the countryside seemed deserted. They spared neither grown people nor children, but carried them all away into slavery.

Such incidents were all too frequent. In 1450 the king of Denmark–Norway issued the decree called 'den lange retterbot',[10] which strictly forbade the abduction of young and old from the country; so common had this practice become.

Turning now to Greenland we find, as we noted earlier (page 293 et seq.), indications that pirates may have found their way to that country too. The important question is whether there is anything in the records to corroborate this. In what follows I shall mention two passages that dovetail remarkably neatly into the piratical activity in Iceland and the kind of thing we might expect to happen in Greenland.

In a letter from Pope Nicholas V, written in 1448 and addressed to the two bishops of Iceland, we read:[11]

> Thirty years ago, from the adjacent coasts of the heathen, the barbarians came with a fleet, attacked the inhabitants of Greenland most cruelly, and so devastated the mother-country and the holy buildings with fire and sword that there remained on that island [Greenland] no more than nine parish churches which are said to lie farthest away and which they could not attain because of the steep mountains. The pitiable inhabitants of both sexes, and especially those whom they deemed strong and fit for continual burdens of slavery such as their tyranny imposed, they carried away prisoner to their own country. But, as is added to the same complaint, because the greater number have since returned from this captivity to their own homes and have here and there repaired the ruins of their dwellings, they most earnestly desire to restore and extend divine service ...

*

We learn too that the victims had been unable to support bishop or priests for the last thirty years. Those who wished to attend divine service had to make a journey of several days to reach such churches as the barbarians had not destroyed. They implore the Pope's assistance, and the Pope instructs the bishops of Iceland to help the Norse Greenlanders in their spiritual need.

Gustav Storm[12] points out that this papal letter is addressed to the two traitors, the Germans Marcellus and his confederate Matheus, who on false pretences had induced the Pope to consecrate them bishops of Iceland. For this reason he maintains that no credence should be given to the complaint to which the Pope's letter is a reply. Fridtjof Nansen goes even further, and holds that the papal letter should be rejected as an historical document.

It is true that Marcellus practised various kinds of fraud: an activity not altogether unknown in exalted circles of the day. Yet he was a man who by virtue of his eminent appointments had received and issued a long series of documents all of which are perfectly in order. The fact that from time to time he proved unreliable hardly entitles us to dismiss the whole of his correspondence as deceptive.

Moreover the letter in question is not one that we know to have been written by him, but one addressed to him by the Pope. Nansen assumes that the complaint replied to by the Pope was invented by Marcellus, but for this there is no shadow of evidence. Had he or his friends gone to the trouble of fabricating such a complaint, it could only have been because Marcellus had something to gain by it. But what? There could have been no pecuniary advantage, and that he should have taken such curious action for the sake of prestige alone seems most improbable.

Lars Hamre the archivist has drawn my attention to circumstances which seem to indicate very clearly that the letter from the Pope was not based on any communication from Marcellus. Marcellus was a south German, and at the time the letter was sent he had never yet been in the North. His knowledge of Greenland can hardly have been extensive, and it is improbable that he knew as much about Greenland as the Pope supposed. Not until 1450 – that is, two years after the letter was written – is he known to have been in the North (Norway).

It would be strange indeed if this south German, bound to the North for the first time – and as bishop – should begin his work there by giving the Pope false information about an Arctic country that was entirely alien to most of Europe.

It seems most probable that the information dealt with in the letter originated with the Greenlanders themselves. Lars Hamre believes that their messenger may have been Marcellus' predecessor in the Icelandic bishopric of Skálholt, the Carthusian from the Low Countries, Godwin Comhaer. In 1445 he was in England and in 1446 in Holland, where he died in 1447.[13]

The events referred to in the papal letter tally with those known to us from piratical attacks on Iceland: murder, plunder, burning of churches and abduction.

The letter also contains one passage that applies to a historical fact: namely, that most of the Norse Greenlanders who had been taken prisoner were later returned to their homes. The eminent Danish student of the Arctic, W. H. Graah,[14] pointed this out in 1823, but his opinion has been almost entirely disregarded. He refers to the peace treaty of 1432 between the Norwegian King Erik of Pomerania and Henry VI of England.[15] Among the terms of this treaty are those relating to payment of compensation and to penalties to be imposed on English subjects who have committed crimes in Iceland and north Norway, and demanding that the men and women who have been carried off to England as prisoners should be taken back to their homeland. The papal letter mentions that most of the prisoners have returned to their homes, and this may be in compliance with the treaty.

There is much to be said for this solution. How then were the prisoners brought back? Only a limited part of the settlement was affected by the attack, and the Norse Greenlanders must still have been able to collect enough goods for export. Here as elsewhere, no doubt, peaceful trading and piracy went on at the same time; thus the transport of prisoners northward from Bristol, Lynn, Grimsby, etc., may not have presented great difficulties, for they would have travelled aboard the merchant ships. Or again, Englishmen who wanted to trade or fish in the north may have felt it an advantage to take with them people who were familiar with the region and its possibilities. The captured Greenlanders may even have joined forces and built their own ships.

The pirates' attack is said to have been made thirty years before the date of the papal letter, that is, in 1418. This was only eight years after the Norway ship wintered in Austerbygd and the wedding was celebrated in Hvalsøy church: the last events in the Arctic community of which we have certain knowledge. The letter tells us that nine parish churches in the remoter parts were spared, and it is reasonable to suppose that the assailants concentrated on the rich, central regions, and did not stay to go in and out of all the long, ice-filled fjords of Austerbygd.

We also learn that the areas ravaged by the pirates had had no church leader at the episcopal seat nor any priests for thirty years. Our thoughts turn to Gardar. We know that eight years before the attack there was an *officialis* in Austerbygd: that is, a man who had full authority from the bishop to act for him in legal matters. His name was *Sira* Eindride Andresson. It seems likely that the worst-hit places were Einars- and Eiriksfjord, and later I will speak of certain signs suggesting that the cathedral at Gardar and other churches in these fjords were destroyed by fire. This would tally with the passage already quoted from the papal letter: ' ... they devastated the mother-country and the holy buildings with fire and sword ... '

I have already mentioned that Eskimo legends are too unreliable to be considered in connection with the fate of the Norse Greenlanders. What I sought were the historical tales which preserve traditions through long periods with extraordinary accuracy and detail.

There does indeed exist such an historical account which is directly linked with the Norse Greenlanders and throws light on their last period. The interesting point about it is that it records events of the kind mentioned in the papal letter: a pirate attack on Austerbygd.

The story is found in the diary of Niels Egede,[16] Hans Egede's son, who lived between 1710 and 1782. He grew up in Greenland, spoke Eskimo like a native, and was deeply interested in the country and its people, especially anything relating to the Norse Greenlanders. It is a sober, unpretentious diary; he does not claim to solve any problems, and ends by saying that if it is thought worth reading it should be copied out fair and its style improved. It bears all the marks of truth.

The passage that is significant in this connection has had little attention paid to it, so far as I know. It deals with things told him by an *angagok* (medicine-man) who lived 'south by the hot baths', that is, the hot springs in Unartoq fjord. While journeying north he tells Niels Egede about the country down there in the south (Austerbygd), and about the pirate attack on the Norsemen in the old days. Egede writes:

> He told me too that his forefathers had related that when their fore-fathers came from north America and advanced southward upon this Western Side of Greenland to settle, some desired to live among the Norwegians, who forbade them, and would permit them only to trade with them. They [the Eskimoes] were afraid of them, since they had many kinds of firearms. But when a number of families had gathered and come upon a more cordial footing with them, there came from the south-west three small ships, and plundered and killed some of the Norwegians; yet as the Norwegians overmastered them, the second ship sailed away and the third they took as prize, but we Greenlanders [Eskimoes] having no fixed dwelling at that time, were afraid and fled far into the country. But the following year there came a whole fleet and fought with them, plundering and slaying wantonly, carrying off their Cattle and Furniture and then sailed away. Those who remained shoved out their open boats and went aboard, and sailed to the southerly part of the country, leaving some behind. Our Greenlanders [Eskimoes] promised to stand by them in support if more such evils should occur.

329

But the following year those wicked pirates came again and when we saw them we fled and took some of the Norwegian women and children with us up the fjord, leaving the others in the lurch; but when in the autumn we returned, thinking to find some of them, we saw with horror that everything had been carried off, Houses and farms burnt and laid waste, so that everything was lacking. At this sight we took the women and children back with us and fled far up the fjord, and there we remained at peace for many years. We married the Norwegian women, five in number, with some children. When in time we became numerous we travelled about and settled down along the Land, and for many years saw no more of the pirates. At last one came, which was one of the English privateers, and when they saw that we possessed but little and that we were many they did not venture to come against us, but traded only. This same kind of people still come here from time to time to trade with the Greenlanders [Eskimoes] and when they find an Opportunity to do it they rob everywhere, so it is likely that these sea-rovers were the same; and they now have colonies over against us in the American settlements.

This remarkable account, related with such restraint and in such detail, appears genuine. There is no hint of the superstition or Eskimo hero-worship that characterizes so many of the folk-tales. Certain words, such as America and American, are of course Niels Egede's own, but they are of minor importance. It is of especial interest that this story was told as early as the eighteenth century: that is, little more than two hundred years after the Norse Greenlanders disappeared. Moreover, as the narrator had come north from areas where at the time the Eskimoes had little contact with white men, the traditional account cannot have become blurred or confused with others.

To start with it is interesting to hear of the Eskimo southward migration along the coast towards the settlements at so late a period; which migration is borne out by the archaeological finds (the Inugsuk culture). We learn too that Eskimoes were not allowed to live with Norwegians, as is consistent with Catholic teaching, which forbade close association with heathen; but the Norwegians traded with them, which must have been lawful here as in Finnmark. This confirms what I emphasized earlier: that trade with the Eskimoes must have been of great importance.

At first the Eskimoes were afraid of the Norsemen because they had 'many kinds of firearms'. This is Egede's translation of an Eskimo word which may have meant weapons. It is possible that the Norse Greenlanders used the cross-bow, which reached Scandinavia in the fourteenth century, though no trace of such a weapon has been found in Greenland.

Then we learn that a number of families formed a group and that they 'came upon a more cordial footing' with the Norse Greenlanders. Further evidence of their friendly relations is revealed later, when the Eskimoes saved the lives of some of them.

We next have the description of the two pirate attacks and their consequences. The story is sober and matter-of-fact, and nowhere can we detect any false interpolation. In simple words we are told of the two horrible events, which clearly made a deep impression on the Eskimoes.

It seems as if the pirates made a fairly clean sweep of the place they came to, which was probably the richest part of Austerbygd. After the first attack 'those who remained' went south. After the last we hear nothing certain of the remainder of the Norsemen; it is said that the Eskimoes left them 'in the lurch'. All we know is that the Eskimoes saved five women and some children and took them to the inner end of the fjords, and that they later married the women. This isolated case cannot of course be counted in support of the theory that the Norse Greenlanders disappeared through interbreeding.

The statement that the assailants were English privateers may be coloured by Niels Egede's own views; yet on the other hand the old-time Eskimoes may well have learnt as much from the Norse Greenlanders. In any case it is only to be expected that English pirates harrying Iceland would sooner or later find their way to the Greenland settlements.

I may mention here that the Eskimoes have an unusual word for Englishman, namely *tuluk*, plural *tuluit*. Philologists are baffled by it. It is in another category altogether from other words denoting a foreign race. These follow a common Eskimo pattern. The word for Dutchman for instance (from the whaling-period) is *qardlikaq*, meaning one who wears big trousers. I shall say no more about this now, but perhaps one day the riddle of the word for Englishman may be solved.

Is there any further evidence, archaeological or other, of piratical invasion? The destruction of churches by fire is interesting in this connection. Latterly it has been difficult to form an opinion, owing to the number of digs made at the best-known places. Earlier investigations are more reliable, and some of these I will now mention.

Pastor Esmand undertook excavations at the cathedral of Gardar in 1832 and declared that so much charcoal was found that both he and the Eskimoes believed the church to have been destroyed by fire.[17] In 1842 Dr C. Pingel[18] tells us: 'Nothing else was found in the church [Herjolfsnes] but some dressed stone from the walls and some small pieces of charcoal, the latter seeming to show that this church, like a number of the old Norsemen's buildings in south Greenland, was burnt to the ground.'

In Brattalid church some partly melted fragments of bell-metal were found; at the church of Undir Höfdi there were charcoal, slag and a fused lump of clay and glass.[19] In addition there were many pieces of church-bells, partly melted, indicating destruction by fire. A farm at Singitsoq,[20] six miles west of Julianehåb, was apparently also burnt. There are indications that future digs in the central areas will reveal that a number of homesteads suffered the same fate. Gustav Holm[21] makes the general comment: ' ... layers of charcoal, as also slag and drops of metal, suggest that a large proportion of the buildings, at the least, were destroyed by fire.'

Daniel Bruun[22] states that so much charcoal was found in Gardar church as to make it probable that the building was burnt down. This is borne out by the Eskimoes' name for Herjolfsnes: Ikigait, which means 'the place destroyed by fire'.

The Norse Greenlanders may have had open fires in their churches, and later perhaps the Eskimoes too lit them there, but this would not account for the melted glass, the drops of once-molten metal or the fact that considerable quantities of charcoal cover the whole site. A number of the men quoted above are authorities on the Norse buildings of Greenland.

It is also remarkable that no vestige of church vessels or other valuables has been discovered in Norse or Eskimo ruins. The invaders would have secured these things first, as we know was done in Iceland; and indeed we are struck by the meagreness – in quantity, quality and usefulness – of the finds in central Austerbygd (Gardar, Brattalid and elsewhere) compared with those of Vesterbygd. No doubt this was because Austerbygd was so situated as to be more easily accessible to plundering Eskimoes; also the frozen soil of Vesterbygd was a better preservative. Yet this is hardly the full explanation.

It is always possible that the Eskimoes may have set fire to the churches; yet as we saw there is good reason to believe that the two races were on good terms. And when historical evidence of sacking and burning by pirates is forthcoming it seems natural to attribute the gutting of the churches to these foreign marauders.

We have examined several important facts indicating that Austerbygd was subjected to attack by pirates. Yet such assaults did not lead to the extinction of the Norse Greenlanders. According to the papal letters, nine parish churches remained intact. The Eskimo account expressly tells us that some of the people 'shoved out their open boats and went aboard, and sailed to the southerly part of the country'. We may assume that the pirates did not reach all the settlements.

What happened afterwards?

The repeated assaults must have shaken the little community; and the devastation of Gardar and Brattalid, the centres of their religion, must have been a hideous blow. The survivors, surveying the ruins, were surely in despair, knowing that no unaided effort of theirs could ever restore all that had been destroyed; and always they were haunted by the dread of fresh onslaughts.

It is also possible that economic pressure was increasing, especially as the demand for dried fish was falling off. The great quantities of fish now being caught on the Newfoundland banks and elsewhere broke the monopoly of the Hanseatic League and caused a sharp drop in the price of dried fish at the turn of the sixteenth century.[23]

Such conditions would force the inhabitants to consider emigration. It is reasonable to think of this move as being accomplished gradually, over a period during which difficulties increased and while there was a good chance of getting away from Greenland. Just when the last of the Norse Greenlanders went we do not know for certain, but there is much to suggest that it was at the beginning of the sixteenth century. It was about then that Jon Grønlending found a dead man wearing cloak and hood lying face-downward with a worn sheath-knife at his side.

Where did the people go?

Norse Greenlanders may have sailed to Norway during the fifteenth century, but hardly later. As we saw, Erik Valkendorf prepared to launch an expedition to Greenland in 1516, and collected what information he could about the country. In the main he relied on Ivar Bårdsson's description, and he does not seem to have learnt much that was new. Had he talked to men who had been in Greenland his information on certain points would have been more accurate.

Absalon Pederssøn[24] writes in 1567 – and from Bergen, the town which for centuries had been the starting-point of the Greenland run:

> And many of the nobility hold the deeds of estates in Greenland yet of the country and properties they know nothing ... and because we so negligently fail in our sailings to Greenland it is likely that the Russian or some other lord now rules over the country, for it is impossible but that the inhabitants of Greenland have sought other lands adjacent, there to obtain what they need of iron, salt and other goods.

Such a percipient man as Absalon Pederssøn would not have written thus if there had been fresh news of Greenland in Bergen, far less talked of its 'mighty forests', stags, sables and marten-skins.

But the Norse Greenlanders had the chance of emigrating to more than one place; a chance that in the last period of the Arctic community would have seemed very natural.

We know that they sailed to Markland, probably to fetch timber. I mentioned earlier that the inhabitants of Vesterbygd appear to have made for North America, and for a time at least a Norse colony must have existed there; so that it is reasonable to suppose that some people from Austerbygd as well were tempted to set sail for the new, thickly wooded country and settle there with their countrymen. That crossing was shorter than the voyage to Norway.

There was another possibility. Not only pirates touched at the Greenland settlements, but presumably also friendly English ships that came to trade. These trips seem to have been so profitable that they were maintained regularly over a long period.

It could not have been difficult for Norse Greenlanders to buy a passage to the British Isles aboard a homeward-bound ship, in return for furs, blubber, skins, dried fish, etc. The same thing had been done in the days when the Norway ship maintained communications with Greenland, and there seems no reason why the Norse Greenlanders could not have come to an understanding with seafarers from Lynn, Grimsby, Bristol, etc.: towns where in course of time so many Norse families had settled.

At the end of the sixteenth century Hakluyt tells us of an event dating from 1501–2, and reported in Fabyan's Chronicle. He says that

> three men were brought to the king, having been captured on the new-found island which I [Fabyan] spoke of earlier in the time of William Purchas when he was mayor. They were clad in the skins of animals and they ate raw meat, and their speech was such that none could understand them, while in their manners they were like wild beasts. The king kept them for a time, and when I saw them in Westminster Palace two years later they were dressed in the English fashion, nor could I distinguish them from Englishmen until I was told who they were. But as for speech, I never heard one of them utter a word.

These men seem to have been brought back from a voyage made by Bristol merchants in 1501 or 1502. The king's accounts[25] show that men from Bristol 'who found the island' were given five pounds reward. Hakluyt's heading declares that it was Sebastian Cabot who brought the three wild men back, but as Fridtjof Nansen[26] points out, this must be a later and suspect addition, as Cabot would hardly have been on that voyage.

It is possible that the island the three wild men came from was Greenland. Though they are described as very primitive, one must remember that in civilized and especially court circles, a little primitiveness went a long way. The mere fact of people coming from the far north and wearing skins was enough to set the imagination working.

An important point about the story is that the three men stayed at Henry VII's court for two years, dressed like Englishmen and indistinguishable from them. Nansen thinks it possible that they may have come from Greenland, and that they were descendants of Norsemen who had interbred with Eskimoes. There are indeed many indications that they came from Greenland, but I can hardly think that they were of mixed race. They may simply have been emigrant Norse Greenlanders. Members of the ancient families of Herjolfsnes, Brattalid and the like would soon have been able to adopt the habits and manners of the Palace of Westminster.

At any rate there came a day when the last of the Norse Greenlanders put to sea. Men, women and children stood by the rail gazing at the receding land below the ice-cap, which for five hundred years their people had called home.

XXXIV   THE END OF A SAGA

W E were bound for Nordrsetur. To complete our picture of the Norse Greenlanders' life we had to gain some idea of the distant hunting-grounds in the north, to which the people made regular trips for walrus-tusks, skins, blubber, down and driftwood. Behind us lay Vesterbygd, where we had lately explored the greater part of the settlement. Some investigation remained to be made, and that we were able to do on our way back.

In Nordrsetur, as was mentioned earlier, some traces of the Norse Greenlanders had been found. The most certain of these was the rune-stone at Kingigtorssuaq. The texts mention Karlsbuðir, which consisted presumably of hunting-lodges, but neither they nor others have been found, apart from the so-called 'bear-trap'. Where can they have been?

Another question arose here: was Vesterbygd limited to the Godthåb district, or were there more homesteads farther to the north? Our sources state that Vesterbygd comprised ninety dwellings, but of these sixteen had yet to be found, despite comprehensive researches over a period of many years. Certain known place-names too are hard to fit within the limits of Godthåb, such as Leirufjörðr, Lodinsfjörðr, Straumfjörðr (where there is said to have been a church at Straumsnes), and Eyarfjörðr.

Our time was short, for winter was approaching. There could be no question of undertaking any thorough investigation, and we did not expect to come upon any new traces of the Nordrsetur folk in that vast region. Yet we did hope to gain some knowledge of these remote hunting-grounds which meant so much in the old times.

We chugged along the coast through sea-spray and wind. Autumn weather had set in, so in navigating these northern waters without a pilot we had to keep our wits about us. Reefs and ice were plentiful, and at times we met stormy weather.

We headed into the larger fjords, going right to the inner end to spy out the land, and then out and on again. It was like a moving picture in which a mighty landscape passed in review: now bare islands, surf and surging seas, now deep fjords flanked with ice-clad peaks, steep valleys and rolling hills. From time to time amid this world of waters and wilderness people would appear: little flocks of Greenlanders whose homes stood on the bare rocks at the sea's edge.

We arrived at Atangmik, where some of the most highly skilled kayak folk were said to live; but no men were to be seen, only women, children and a tame eagle that stood majestically by a mud hut. At last I found the men; they had gathered on some boulders that commanded a wide view out to sea, some sitting, others standing. They said little, and merely gazed out over the waters that glittered with broken seas and drifting ice.

They have stone-age man in them, and a profound nostalgia for what was once the Eskimo life. They mourn the days when there were seal enough and all was as it had ever been; when, softly as a breath, the hunter swept his kayak towards his quarry, flung the harpoon and made for home towing the seal, with his heart full of joy; when before him he beheld the stone huts and the people on the shore ...

Head of raven in soapstone, from Gardar

All day long the old hunters now sat on their boulders, looking out to sea.

I got into conversation with these people and they told me some interesting things about the old days. Then three of them shoved off in their kayaks and showed that some of them at least were masters in the old skills. Over and over they rolled in their canoes as if it were the easiest trick in the world.

Atangmik lies near the mouth of Fiskefjord which in Eskimo is called Niaqúngunaq: i.e., 'the one that gives one a headache'. The vegetation in the inner parts of this deep fjord was reputed to be surprisingly rich, so we felt it worth while to go in and have a look at it, and judge whether Norse Greenlanders might have settled there.

Taking a local man as guide we set off eastward in the motor-boat. Little by little a landscape was revealed that was a delight to the eye, and very different from the usual fjord scenery of Greenland. Not only had a mighty glacier ground its way from the ice-cap to the ocean, and in the course of ages ploughed a deep furrow through the mountains where the sea now ran in; nature in playful mood had formed minor fjords, narrow straits and idyllic corners, and as a finishing touch had strewn islands over the water with a lavish hand.

We came to two narrow sounds where the tide-water ran like a swift river, and we had to wait for some time before even thinking of driving the boat forward. On the surface of one backwater was a milling swarm of something black, which turned out to be the dorsal fins of a close-packed shoal of cod.

First we went to the inner end of Tasiussarssuaq, the beautiful great side-fjord to the north, where in places there was good pasture. Next we continued to the eastern end of Fiskefjord itself, and found ourselves in surroundings that fell little short of the Godthåb fjord. Here there was an abundance of tall willow, alder, mountain birch, heather and moss, and scattered patches of grass.

A little way north of the bay is a minor ridge, and here our Greenland guide showed us something strange. Almost at the top of the hill a block of soapstone some thirty inches high stuck up like the continuation of the vein in the rock. It had been shaped into a little obelisk, and measured about twenty inches across at the foot. Evidently it was once considerably taller, the top having been sawn or cut off.

Our Greenland friend told us that it was the Eskimoes who in times past had taken the upper part to make blubber-lamps of, adding that on it had been the drawing of a human head, a cross and an inscription in pointed characters.

The character of the countryside at the inner end of Fiskefjord was favourable enough for Norsemen to have settled there. There was pasture for their animals, cod in the sea and salmon in the rivers, while eastward among the hills lay what must have been excellent reindeer country. A native of Atangmik told me that a Norse arrow-head had been found there.

It seems likely that the Straumfjörðr (fjord of the stream or current) of the texts should be identified with Fiskefjord, where in places the current is exceptionally strong; while the great northern arm that contains so many beautiful islands may well be ancient Eyjarfjord (fjord of islands).

We were tempted to explore farther, but we had to go on; so leaving the fjord we headed north again. We then arrived at the little outpost of Napassoq. Not far east of this were ruins of the dwelling-place called Iglutalik, where during the winter of 1856–7 nearly all the Eskimoes starved to death. This was no exceptional occurrence: all through the ages famine and death by starvation have been the scourge of their race.

Nevertheless few people have such zest for life as the Eskimoes when they live like their forefathers, in stone or mud huts, hunting seal with a harpoon from a kayak and roaming the hills with bow and arrow. Little is needed to bring out their smiles and laughter.

The Canadian Eskimo Sâmik gave some explanation of how people who lead so hard and dangerous a life can be so joyous, when he said to Knud Rasmussen:[1]

' ... Ah, you strangers see us only when we're gay and carefree! But if you knew the terrors we so often have to face you would understand why we love laughter, why we love food and song and dancing. There is not one of us who has not known a winter when hunting failed, when people were dying of hunger all round us and when we ourselves survived only by some chance. But how should a man who is healthy and well-fed understand the madness of hunger? All we know is that we long to live.'

We made a detour into Sukkertoppen, the colony founded by Anders Olsen in 1775. It is pleasantly situated in a setting of mountain and sea. Here too there has been a great increase in fishing and the people have almost all become fishermen.

An amusing object dating from the Norse period was discovered here in Sukkertoppen; it was a brass weight in the shape of a little horse, and weighed 46·97 grammes, or about 1½ oz. It was the Norwegian King Håkon V who had this type of weight made, so this horse came from Norway, though how it arrived so far north is unknown.

Next we entered the wild Hamburger Sound, familiar from the whaling-period, and arrived at the dwelling-place of Agpamiut. Here an old woman told us very solemnly that on a slope at the head of the fjord she had once seen something that must have been a sunken roof. Strange noises came from under the earth and it was down there in the house that the *qavdlunat* – the Norse Greenlanders – must have their dwelling. It is significant that to this very day new tales are being woven round the Norsemen.

As soon as we dropped anchor off any village, tiny craft packed with children swarmed out to us. The youngsters poured over the deck like a pack of hounds, black-haired, dirty, funny little creatures with running noses. They were everywhere at once and as quick as animals. Relations between these little ruffians and Harald were of a special kind. As a seaman his thoughts were for his boat and gear, and not for a second did he lose sight of the children. He sat there puffing at his pipe watching their every move with a mistrustful eye.

When they grew too turbulent he would suddenly spring up and shout at them in his ringing Sunnmøre dialect. The youngsters vanished with incredible speed; but it was not long before one grinning little face after another popped up over the rail. Poor Harald.

After visiting a large number of fjords we at last reached Holsteinsborg, where for the time we met Arctic dogs. Herds of these massive beasts roamed among the houses, streamed over the quay or splashed about in the water. From time to time a fight broke out among them and the din of it rose to high heaven. Human beings are tolerated here, but it is clear that the dogs rule Holsteinsborg as their own domain.

In the eighteenth century H. C. Glahn, the missionary, and E. Thorhalle-sen[2] stated that inland, far to the east of Holsteinsborg, there was said to have

339

been a Norse house and that beside it some iron and bone spades had been found. The house was now thought to have disappeared, probably buried by drifting sand. To reach the place one had first to enter Amerdloq, the deep fjord immediately south of Holsteinsborg, and then from Maligiaq up a narrow river barely navigable even for small craft.

Even if the house had disappeared it would be interesting to see its surroundings, and we set off. On a dark evening with a fresh breeze and head sea we arrived at Sarfánguaq, a little outpost by some swift narrows. Here we met the man in charge, Ulrik Linnert, an interesting and unusually frank and forthcoming Greenlander. He told us that the year before, on a little island in Ikertoq fjord, a sickle had been found and also the carved figure of a woman sitting in a chair. It was not an island where people lived, but a place where salmon-fishers and reindeer-hunters usually camped.

Taking with us Noa, a man with local knowledge, we sailed on into the northern end of the fjord, where there was a wide plain crossed by a winding river, and with the high tide we made our way upstream. We could barely manage it, the river being so narrow, but Noa was a skilled pilot.

It was not a long trip, and just below some rapids we drew alongside the bank. The place was lovely. Beside the rapids a stone salmon ladder had been built and near by was a little plain on which grew sturdy osiers, flowers and some grass. If there was ever a Norse house by this river it must have stood somewhere here, but there was no sign of any building. There may be ruins under the sand, but the land here was unsuitable for stock-raising, so the house may have been a hut for salmon-fishers and reindeer-hunters.

Back to Holsteinsborg and on again northward. We were now in a part of Nordrsetur that was of great importance in the old days, for there were quantities of walrus. Krogh, who was manager here, and showed us great kindness, told us that walrus were still hunted in these parts, but mostly right out on the ice to the west. The journey to the hunting-grounds took six or seven hours, and the previous year about a hundred and fifty had been shot, most of them females.

We were approaching the mouth of Nordre Strømfjord, where up to the beginning of this century quantities of walrus were to be found near the coast. As was mentioned earlier, the animals swarmed up on to certain islands. As their numbers remained fairly constant down to our own day, despite the use of modern weapons, we may imagine what masses there must have been here in the days when Norse Greenlanders sailed to Nordrsetur.

Greenland whale were plentiful too. The many whaling-ships that operated here during the eighteenth and nineteenth centuries bear witness to this. The animal is so sluggish by nature that it can be harpooned without much difficulty, and the Norsemen undoubtedly hunted it. It is now almost extinct.

Sea-creatures were not their only quarry; they went after reindeer as well, and in the old days there must have been enormous numbers of them in the region.

One evening we were caught in a storm off the coast, and our little boat had a rough time of it. Then the engine failed. Hastily we hoisted sail and ran before the wind. We had to negotiate some seething breakers and get under the lee of an island. It was a nasty moment, but we made it, and breathed again. We cast anchor in a small cove, flanked by steep cliffs, with a little beach at the inner end.

There, off that beach, I spied an unusually big piece of driftwood rocking in the waters. It had reached the end of its long journey from the forests of Siberia, where it started down one of the mighty rivers, then drifted northward across the Arctic Ocean, southward along the coast of east Greenland, round the southern tip and northward along the west coast: a voyage that must have taken some years. If a Nordrsetur man had caught sight of this tree-trunk he would have rejoiced, for the gathering of driftwood was almost as vital as hunting and fishing.

The vegetation here was meagre: there was coarse grass, bog-cotton and other plants that thrive in the colder regions. It was a wild landscape of riven coasts and deep fjords: the kingdom of the hunter. And though much may have altered since the Norse Greenlanders sailed hither in their open boats, one could see that this country had a great deal to offer them. Farther away inland were endless hunting-grounds which in the old days were even richer in game.

Here was a vast land that tempted one to explore more thoroughly, and in the north lay dim, alluring coasts. But one morning when we came on deck and looked inland we saw that the mountains were a fine white veil: a veil of fresh snow. This was a signal to us to head south. There were still a few things to be done, so we had to get busy before winter set in.

In changeable weather we headed south along the coast and came at last to the dwelling-place known as Kangamiut. From here we wanted to take a trip eastward through Søndre Strømfjord, and then farther inland to a small lake near the edge of the ice-cap named Agnmalortoq: that is, the round lake. Near this sheet of water there was said to be a little plain which by Eskimo tradition was called 'the Norsemen's summer place'. Louis Bobé,[3] writing in 1921, tells us that the foundations of a big Norse building had been visible here until a few years earlier, but were now entirely buried in sand-drifts. He also mentions a rune-stone which had fallen down and been shattered.

This presumably meant that the old hunting-lodge had vanished for ever, for the föhn wind can heap the sand up in mighty mounds; yet it was interesting to learn something of these remote inland areas to which the Norse

Greenlanders had made their way. For it appears that on their Nordrsetur expeditions they not only went on short hunting-trips after reindeer, as an incidental variation of their pursuit of sea-creatures; they had huts far inland, where they must have stayed for considerable periods at a time.

It was also of great interest to look more closely at the country round Søndre Strømfjord. Finnur Jónsson identifies this with the Straumfjörðr of the texts, where there is thought to have been a church.

We took two Greenlanders with us as guides: cheerful Filimon and the older, more sedate Barnabas – two good-humoured men, hunters to their finger-tips. We entered Søndre Strømfjord, the third-longest fjord in the world: about 110 miles. It averages no more than $2\frac{1}{2}$ miles across and runs like a canal straight in among the mountains with no bays or harbours worth mentioning. Here the difference between high and low tide is about 17 feet, so that at flood and ebb the water races through the narrow channel like a river. We came in on the rising tide, and little *Benedicte* went faster than ever in her life before.

We had gone some way in when a squall burst upon us and we only just reached shelter behind a promontory. It was fascinating to sail along this narrow fjord, which is flanked with steep, sometimes snow-capped heights.

At last we reached the end of the southern arm, where the water shoals for some way as a big glacial river runs out here. Filimon, Barnabas and I were rowed ashore, and slinging our packs on our shoulders we set off westward over the hills for Agnmalortoq.

The path was plain to follow, for this has been the reindeer-hunters' trail through countless ages. It was late autumn: a glorious season in the mountains. The air was clear and chill, the carpet of heather had turned a fine rust-red, which was broken here and there by the wine-red leaves of the dwarf birch. The osiers alone had put up some resistance to the night frosts, for among the yellow there remained a few stubborn green leaves. Beyond the marshes lay a haze of bog-whortleberry.

Towards evening we pitched the tent by a spring. At dusk an Arctic fox came to greet us, and stood for some time in surprise on a hillock. Then with an ugly, shrill bark it padded away. There was a keen chill in the air, but Filimon and Barnabas lay down on the bare ground just as they were, and fell asleep.

At noon next day we caught our first sight of Agnmalortoq: a small lake fringed with white beaches, lying among gently sloping ridges. But what was that? Something was moving over there by the river-mouth. My companions hallooed eagerly, and a woman came running towards us so fast that her skirts flew in the wind. She stopped in front of us, smiling and chatting away in Eskimo while she got her breath back. She was a Greenlander of about fifty with kindly wrinkles in her quaint face.

Norse Greenlander stalking reindeer from a bogastille (*hide*)

Then she went on ahead to lead the way. When we came out from the osier thicket we had a full and delightful view. On a green slope near lake and river four tents were pitched. Men, women and children moved among them, and from a camp fire smoke rose into the sky. Round about lay magnificent reindeer antlers; meat was hanging up to dry and on the ground hides were being stretched.

Three families shared this reindeer-hunters' camp, and all had shot a great many animals. The gay, cheerful atmosphere so familiar to me from the primitive reindeer people of north Canada and Alaska came to meet me. Smiles and kindliness everywhere. It is extraordinary to see the change wrought in the Greenlanders when in the wilds; those at the outposts often seem to have been tinged with the drabness of civilization. Hunting their deer here at the edge of the ice-cap they were completely happy and found outlet for the primitive and still essential element in their nature.

We met with the old-fashioned hospitality too. Fresh wood was at once thrown on the fire, which blazed up, and a huge cooking-pot cram full of reindeer meat was set over it. Soon the exhilarating fragrance of game reached our nostrils, and we could settle down to eating as much as we could hold of the best that the wilds have to offer: tongue, kidney, liver, meat and the most luscious marrow-bones. Filimon and Barnabas grinned blissfully.

There we sat on 'the Norsemen's summer place', for it was this very plain that was linked by tradition with their memory. They found an ideal site. Even in our own day there is a good head of reindeer in this region, so what numbers there must have been in the past!

As for the Norse hunting-lodge, there was little point in searching for it.

343

The Greenlanders believed it had stood on the western side of the lake, where there was now a vast sand-dune. This may be so, yet at the lower end of the plain where we had our camp there was a mound covered with strikingly rich vegetation which might be worth closer investigation.

Norsemen would have been unlikely to winter so far from the sea, and I imagine that they followed some such routine as this: when the shipload of hunters arrived at Nordrsetur in the spring, single parties were landed in promising areas. Most of them went after sea-creatures, though some hunted reindeer. Those camping at Agnmalortoq would have to start back in good time, carrying their meat and hides to the head of the fjord to have everything ready for loading.

Next day we walked eastward over the hills towards the edge of the ice-cap, and arrived in one of the most beautiful pieces of country I have seen in Greenland. The sun sparkled; in the east the inland ice soared glittering to the sky. From within that mighty wall a crag was emerging; it was like a foetus. Before long the mountain will be born, and rear its head proudly in the sun and wind after thousands of years beneath the ice.

Between us and the eternal ice lay an undulating expanse of country strewn with little lakes like deep blue eyes in the autumn landscape.

Filimon and Barnabas had just one idea: to shoot reindeer. We needed meat, and I said, 'Get one, but no more.' They were all excitement, and before long they brought one down. In no time they had the entrails out, and sitting down to the stomach as to a dinner-table they gulped down its contents together with bits of the stomach itself. This is the favourite delicacy of the Eskimoes.

It was interesting to watch them flay and quarter the animal, for with minor exceptions their technique was that of the Eskimoes of Alaska.

A herd of reindeer swept over the hill close by, led by a bull with mighty antlers. They were somewhat larger than the Norwegian breed. Later we came upon two other animals. I wanted to try my old dodge, and after they had sighted us we sat down on a stone and simply waited. Yes, reindeer are the same the world over, and it was not long before they zig-zagged up to us in a perfect fever of curiosity.

I had to frown my fiercest at Filimon and Barnabas to prevent them shooting. They were sitting, finger on trigger, gazing fixedly at the reindeer, which were only twenty-five yards away; it was almost more than a Greenland hunter could stand. Then the animals swung round and disappeared.

Back we went to the camp with our substantial burden of meat. On the way we came upon the bones of a bull reindeer with an unusually handsome pair of antlers which I had not the heart to leave. I perched it on top of my pack. It was later to embitter my existence; nevertheless in the end it came safely to Norway.

It was late when we regained the camp, where the fire glowed through the dusk. The hunters came smilingly to meet us; the eldest said he was glad of our luck, and I believe he meant what he said.

We sat long by the fire that evening, and much was told me of the land of reindeer. But beyond the 'Norsemen's summer place' boys and girls were playing in the twilight, and all was as it should be.

Next day was the day of departure. The Greenlanders, who had been hunting for some time and shot many deer, were to return to their homes on the coast. But first they had to carry meat and skins down to the fjord by stages. Hunters, women, boys, girls and children set off on their journey.

It was a strange procession. All were laden with meat. No Greenlander uses a rucksack; meat and hides are bound with straps slung from the shoulders, and the weight is taken by a broad brow-band. They carry huge burdens in this way. Even quite young children walk bowed under loads of meat. Little Margrete, who cannot have been more than thirteen winters old, carried a weight of at least forty pounds. In a long, bowed file we set off.

At last we reached the head of Strømfjord, and far away on the opposite side the *Benedicte* lay at anchor. I lit a beacon on the nearest crag, and it was not long before the vigilant Harald pulled across and took us on board. Then, on the ebb, we sped away down that long, strange fjord.

Southward again to Vesterbygd, where something more remained to be done. We wanted above all to explore an area inland where I believed there must be several undiscovered Norse ruins.

Once more, therefore, we headed into Godthåb fjord, where blue water and wild hills melted into remote distance. The place had an atmosphere all its own in that chilly autumn weather. This time we wanted to take a guide with us, for last time we found that drift-ice at the inner end of the fjords could present a problem. We put in at Qôrnoq, the fishing-place by the narrow sound, and found the Greenlander Pavia: a first-class man with whom we were soon on the best of terms.

There was now more ice in the inner part of Godthåb fjord than before. Once we got stuck, and were squeezed by the ice, yet we managed to withdraw our frail craft safely into open water, and breathed again. To the north the Ujaragssuit fjord was entirely blocked.

Pavia told us of the Norse hunting-lodges built of stone, far inland northwest of Anavik, the ancient ruined church. They were familiar to Greenland hunters, and he had seen them several times. Thus when the men of Nordrsetur built a hut for reindeer-hunters beside Agnmalortoq, near the edge of the inland ice, they were merely following a settlement custom.

He also spoke of a strange animal-trap near the western headland at the mouth of Ujaragssuit fjord. It was built of stone, with a trap-door, was about seven feet long and two feet wide. Pointed reindeer antlers are fixed inside in such a way that the trapped creature would impale itself if it tried to break out.

This is of especial interest, in that even in Hans Egede's day[4] we hear of no fewer than four similar large stone traps in the same fjord area. One of these was 2½ ells long, one ell in width and 1½ ells high. No hunter would make so large a trap for foxes. They must have been intended for wolves.

We now set about exploring part of the western shore at the head of Godthåb fjord. Somewhere here, I believed, there were more Norse home-steads than those we know. Pavia was at once interested by this, and told us things that proved of great importance.

We made for the eastern shore of the peninsula that projects due north of Bjorneøya. Near the southern tip and just north of Niaqornánguaq mountain we entered a bay and dropped anchor by some big icebergs that had run aground. Then we landed to survey the area, which looked promising.

Seven or eight hundred yards north from the end of the bay, to my delight, we came upon a Norse ruin* hitherto unknown. The main building was about 66 feet by 33, free-standing, with its long side to the sea. Near by were the ruins of at least five outbuildings, one being a storehouse built on a rock.

The evenly sloping ground in front of the house had been the home-field; even now there were patches of grass between tall willows. Fifty yards east of the main building ran a river which might easily have been used for irrigation. A little way to the west we found a stone structure: a *bogastille* or hide for reindeer-hunters.

Next day we made a tour towards the west, and after half an hour's walk we came to a big lake beautifully situated among the mountains. Pavia called this Tasiussaq. It was a *hop*: the tide-water ran in and out of it through a narrow channel that opened into the bay where our boat was anchored. We went forward along the north side of it, over a sunny hillside where a river foamed over a rock ledge and on to the sea through a copse of tall willows.

Near the mouth of the river was a promontory, and just above this we found another unknown ruin. It was quite big – about 80 feet by 60 – widen-ing noticeably towards the east. The walls had collapsed in chaos, so digging will be necessary before we can establish the building-plan, but there is no doubt at all that it comprised many rooms. Below the main building and nearer the headland were the remains of three small outhouses and a little structure built up against a large rock (see sketch on page 347).

In the same area was a long, clearly marked depression in the ground, apparently the course of an old ditch. Part of an irrigation-scheme? We could find no ditches leading to the river, but the water may have been carried across in wooden gutters.

* See map of Vesterbygd on pages 264–5, Nos. 72 and 73.

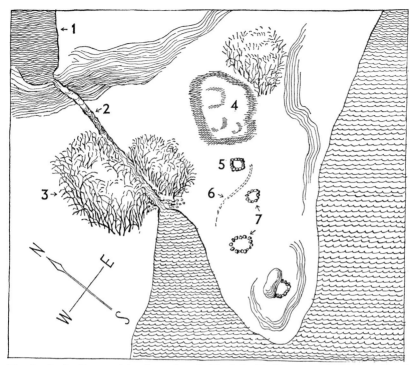

Sketch of ruin discovered by the author, beside Lake Tasiussaq on the western side of Godthåbfjord. 1. lake. 2. river. 3. osier-beds. 4. main building. 5 and 7. outbuildings. 6. ditch. (See map pages 264–5, No. 72)

In places we waded through tall grass, and the osiers were of sturdy growth, especially on the western side of the river. They formed an absolute jungle. Up the hill and along beside the lake the pasture was good.

There was something enchanting about this out-of-the-way place. What an atmosphere there must have been here in the days when the great house of stone and turf brooded at the foot of the sunlit hillside, with the river glittering close by and the sea beyond, ringed in by the high mountains. A world on its own.

I spent a long time examining the crumbled walls to discover how the house had been planned, reflecting at the same time how different the picture had once been, when the building stood firm, with smoke rising from the roof-vent; when generation after generation lived there, when cattle grazed on the slope and by the lake, and children played on the headland.

But at some time in the course of centuries something must have happened – something that cut so deep into the lives of these people that they had to leave their home. There, on the height, where the path dropped down

towards the sea, they looked back for the last time, and left the homestead to live its own life. In time the walls leaned this way and that, and one by one collapsed. Grass and flowers sprang up. No one broke this peace, and today all is as nature intended.

But the river rushing by sings its unchanging song.

When we awoke next morning there was new ice round the boat and it was time to leave this strange Arctic country. A week later we were out at sea, and slowly the coast of Greenland sank below the horizon.

NOTES

I EIRIK THE RED

1. *Íslendingabók*, ch. 6.
2. *Det norske folks liv og historie*, I, p. 348.
3. Eirik the Red, relevant sources: *Landnámabók, Eiríks saga rauða, Groenlendinga saga.*
4. *Landnámabók*, in *Íslendinga sögur*, I (Copenhagen, 1843), pp. 106–7.

II THE PEOPLE STRIKE ROOT

1. *Konungs Skuggsiá*, ed. L. Holm-Olsen (Oslo, 1945), p. 29.
2. *Íslenzk Fornrit*, 4 (*Eiríks saga rauða*) (Reykjavik, 1935), pp. 210–12.
3. Ibid. (*Groenlendinga saga*), pp. 253–4.
4. Ibid. (*Eiríks saga*), p. 210.
5. *Grønlands Historiske Mindesmaerker*, III, p. 229.
6. Ibid.
7. Finnur Jónsson: *Grønlands gamle Topografi efter Kilderne. Meddelelser om Grønland*, 20, IV (1899), p. 297.
8. *Beiträge zur Vorgeschichte der Ost-Eskimo* (Christiania, 1907).
9. *Paleo-Eskimo Cultures in Disko Bugt, West Greenland. Medd. om Grønl.*, 161, II (1958).
10. Ch. 6.
11. *Historia Norvegiae* (*Den eldste Noregs historia*), trans. H. Koht (Oslo, 1950), p. 13.
12. *Medd. om Grøn.*, 77, IV (1931), pp. 145 ff.

III LANDFALL

1. Ivar Bárðarson: *Det gamle Grønlands Beskrivelse*, ed. Finnur Jónsson (Copenhagen, 1930).
2. Ibid., p. 28.
3. *Ísl. Fornr.*, 6 (Fosterbrothers' Saga), p. 224.

IV BRATTALID

1. *Rímnasafn*, I, ed. Finnur Jónsson (Copenhagen, 1905), p. 161.
2. *Íls. Fornr.*, 4, p. 273.
3. *Det gamle Grønl. Beskr.*, p. 28.
4. *Grønlands Hist. Mindesm.*, III, pp. 437–9.
5. *Flóamanna saga*, ed. Finnur Jónsson (Copenhagen, 1932), pp. 52–3.
6. *Ísl. Fornr.*, 4 (*Eiríks saga*), pp. 219 ff.
7. *Medd. om Grønl.*, 88, I (1934).
8. Ibid., p. 60.

NOTES

V GREEN HILLSIDES BEYOND THE ICE
1. *Medd. om Grønl.*, 88, I, pp. 106–17.
2. Ibid., pp. 149 ff. (Appendices).
3. *Ísl. Fornr.*, 6 (Fosterbrothers' Saga), pp. 237–8.
4. G. F. Holm: *Beskrivelser af Ruiner i Julianehaabs Distrikt. Medd. om Grønl.*, 6, IV (1883), p. 79.
5. *Venetianeren Querini paa Røst i Helland*: Norges Land og Folk, XVIII. Nordlands Amt. 2, p. 888.
6. *Gulatingsloven*, ch. 23, trans. Knut Robberstad.
7. *Medd. om. Grønl.*, 6, III (1883), p. 79.
8. *Grágás: Islaendernes Lovbog i Fristatens Tid*, ed. and trans. V. Finsen. 1–4 (Copenhagen, 1870–82). Kristenretten, dept. 3.
9. *Medd. om Grønl.*, 88, I, p. 15.
10. H. Ostermann: *Dagbøker av nordmenn på Grønland før 1814* (Oslo, 1944), pp. 75–7. For Aron Arctander, see H. Ostermann: *Nordmaend paa Grønland 1721–1814*, 1 (Oslo, 1940), pp. 96 ff.
11. M. P. Porsild: *Alien Plants and Apophytes of Greenland. Medd. om Grønl.*, 92, I.
12. *Árbok hins íslenzka fornleifafélags* (Fylgirit, 1958). *Þridji víkingafundur* (Reykjavik, 1956). (Topographical and archaeological investigations in the Norse settlements in Greenland.)
13. *Grønlandsposten* Nos. 24–5 (1954), p. 18.

VI OF HOMES AND MEN
1. *Ísl. Fornr.*, 5 (Reykjavik, 1934), p. 60.
2. *Flóamanna saga*, p. 34.
3. K. Brøste and K. Fischer-Møller: *The Mediaeval Norsemen at Gardar. Medd. om Grønl.*, 89, III (1944), p. 67.
4. O. Stv. Hansen: *Bygdefortelling. Optegnelser fra Tydalen* (Tromsø, 1873), p. 109.

VII PASTURE BELOW THE INLAND ICE
1. *De gamle Nordbobygder ved Verdens Ende* (Copenhagen, 1942), p. 58.

VIII LIVING OFF THE COUNTRY
1. *Ísl. Fornr.*, 4 (*Eiríks saga*), p. 290.
2. Sigurður Sigurðsson: *Landbrug og Landforhold i Island* (Copenhagen, 1940), p. 73.
3. Eggert Olafsen and Bjarne Povelsen: *Reise igiennem Island*, I (Sørøe, 1772), p. 28.
4. 'Om Norgis rige', in *Historiske-topografiske Skrifter om Norge*, ed. G. Storm (Christiania, 1895), p. 70.
5. Ove Arbo Høeg in *Våre Nyttevaekster* 36 (1941), pp. 134–5.
6. *Tromsø Museums Skrifter*, II (1928), p. 139.
7. *Riese igiennem Island*, II, p. 943.
8. Ibid., pp. 829–32.

NOTES

9. Sigurðsson: *Landbrug og Landforhold*, pp. 68–9.
10. Jens Holmboe: 'Norske matplanter', treatise (published by Det Norske Videnskaps-akademi, Oslo, 1929) in *Matem-naturv*, 2, p. 19.
11. *Biskupa sögur* I (Copenhagen, 1958), p. 135.
12. *Ísl. Fornr.*
13. Niels Nielsen in *Medd. om Grønl.*, 76, IV (1929), pp. 191 ff.
14. Alexander Bugge: *Den norske sjøfarts historie*, I, pp. 212, 222, 230, 233, 265.
15. *Islandske Annaler*, ed. G. Storm (Christiania, 1888), p. 120.
16. *Ísl. Fornr.*, 4 (*Eiríks saga*), p. 234.

IX FISHING AND HUNTING

1. Paul M. Hansen: *Oversigt over Fiskeriundersøgelse ved Grønland:* Det grønlandske Selskabs Aarskrift (1931), pp. 19 ff. *Studies on the Biology of the Cod in Greenland Waters: Rapports et procès-verbaux des réunions*, vol. 123 (1949). P. M. Hansen and Frede Hermann: *Fiskene og havet ved Grønland:* Skrifter fra Danmarks fiskeri- og havundersøgelser, No. 15 (Copenhagen, 1953).
2. *Det gamle Grønl. Beskr.*, p. 31.
3. *Ísl. Fornr.*, 4 (*Eiríks saga*), p. 206.
4. *Det gamle Grønl. Beskr.*, p. 26.
5. Robberstad, *Gulatingsloven*, ch. 20, p. 91.
6. *Grágás*, section 212.
7. *Gulatingsloven*, chs. 150–1 (Norges gamle love I, p. 59).
8. *Konungs Skuggsiá*, pp. 15–17.
9. *Ísl. Fornr.*, 6 (Fosterbrothers' Saga), p. 230. Cf. F. Nansen: *Nord i tåkeheimen* (Christiania, 1911), pp. 95–7.
10. *Ísl. Fornr.*, 4 (*Eiríks saga*), p. 275.
11. Ibid., p. 291.
12. *Ísl. Fornr.*, 6 (*Auðunar þáttr. Vestfirzka*), pp. 361–3.
13. *Grønl. Hist. Mindes.*, III, p. 816.
14. *Grágás*, section 243.
15. *Danish Greenland, its people and its products* (London, 1811), p. 102.
16. Ibid., p. 104.
17. Helge Ingstad: *Pelsjegerliv blant Nord-Kanadas indianere* (Oslo, 1957), pp. 110–16.
18. Ingstad: *Nunamiut* (Oslo, 1952), pp. 164–9.
19. Aage Roussell: *Medd. om Grønl.*, 88, II (1936), pp. 105–7.
20. Ørnulf Vorren: *Dyregraver og rengj. i Varanger*, Nord-norske samlinger VI, 2, i (1944).
21. Bugge: *Det norske sjøfarts historie*, I, p. 156.
22. *Konungs Skuggsiá*, p. 30.

X VOYAGES TO NORDRSETUR

1. *Håkon Håkonsson's saga*, ch. 311.
2. *Grønl. Hist. Mindesm.*, III, pp. 242–3.
3. Ibid., III, pp. 228–9.

4. *Communication from the Danish Geological Association*, B 9, part 5 (1940), pp. 653–63 (Den danske Nugssuaq Ekspedisjon 1939).
5. *Grønland i Tohundredaaret*, etc., I, p. 30.

XI FARTHEST NORTH

1. *Grønl. Hist. Mindesm.*, III, pp. 238–43.
2. *Antiquitates Americanae* (Hafniae, 1845), p. 450.
3. *Kringsjaa*, vol. XI, part 7 (1898).
4. Gunnar Isachsen and Fridtjof Isachsen: *Norsk geografiske tidsskrift*, vol. 4, parts 1–3 (1932).
5. *Nord i tåkeheimen*, p. 236.
6. *Hvor lå Vinland?* (Oslo, 1954), p. 125.
7. *Naturen*, VII (Christiania, 1883), p. 177 (the first Polar expedition).
8. M. Olsen: 'Kingingtorssuaq-stenen og sproget i de grønlandske runeinnskrifter', *Norsk tidsskrift for sprogvidenskap*, 5 (1932), pp. 189 ff.
9. Ibid., p. 229.
10. *Medd. om Grønl.*, 77, IV (1930).
11. *Syn og Segn*, 1958 (*Ein Nordpolsekspedisjon år* 1360).
12. *Fra Nationalmuseets Arbeidsmark* (1945), pp. 78–84.
13. *Norsk geografisk tidsskrift*, 4, parts 1–3.
14. *Geografisk tidsskrift* 41, 2nd half-vol. (December, 1938).

XII THE WASTE PLACES OF EAST GREENLAND

1. *Grønl. Hist. Mindesm.*, III, pp. 524–5.
2. Ibid., I, pp. 71–134; cf. *Íslendinga sögur* I, pp. 86, 105, 150 and 163.
3. *Flóamanna saga*, pp. 33 ff.
4. *Grønl. Hist. Mindesm.*, II, pp. 656–7.
5. Ibid., pp. 662–3.
6. *Det gamle Grønl. Beskr.*, p. 21.
7. *Ísl. Fornr.*, 4 (*Eiríks saga*), pp. 277–9.
8. *Sturlunga saga*, I (Copenhagen, 1906), pp. 15 ff. *Islandske Annaler*, p. 120.
9. *Biskupa sögur*, I, p. 408.
10. *Islandske Annaler*, p. 120.
11. Ibid., pp. 142 and 196.
12. *Grønl. Hist. Mindesm.*, I, pp. 110–13.
13. Olaus Magnus: *Historia om de nordiska folken*, Sw. trans., I, p. 94 (Stockholm, 1916).
14. Louis Bobé: 'Aktstykker til Oplysning om Grønlands Beseiling', *Danske Magasin*, 5th series, VI (Copenhagen, 1909), p. 310.
15. *Ísl. Fornr.*, 4 (*Eiríks saga*), p. 200.
16. *Det gamle Grønl. Beskr.*, pp. 20–2.
17. *Íslendinga sögur*, I, p. 26.
18. *Medd. om Grønl.*, 28, VI (1909), pp. 472–6.
19. *Grønl. Hist. Mindesm.*, III, pp. 222–5.
20. Ibid., pp. 360–1.
21. Oluf Kolsrud: *Olavskyrka i Trondheim* (Oslo, 1914), p. 60.

NOTES

22. G. Storm in *Ymer*, 9th year, 1899, p. 140 ('The Danish Geographer Claudius Clavus or Nicolaus Niger').
23. Olaus Magnus: *Historia om de nordiska folken*, I, p. 92.

XIII THE SAGA TELLS OF THE EARLIEST TIMES

1. *Flóamanna saga*, pp. 13 ff.
2. *Skald-Helga rímur*, in *Rímnasafn*, I (Copenhagen, 1905–12).
3. *Fóstbroeðra saga*, in *Ísl. Fornr.*, 6.
4. *Ísl. Fornr.*, 6, *Auðunar páttr vestfirʒka*.

XIV NEW LAND IN THE WEST

1. Magnus Andersen: *Vikingefaerden* (Oslo, 1895).
2. C. V. Sølver: *Vestervejen. Om vikingernes seilads* (Copenhagen, 1954), pp. 83 ff.
3. Adam of Bremen: *Gesta Hamburgensis* IV (*Descriptio insularum aquilonis*), 38. Norwegian trans. of section relating to Vinland is to be found in *Den eldste Noregs historia* (Oslo, 1950), p. 88.
4. *Íslendingabók*, ch. 6.
5. *Islandske Annaler*, p. 112.
6. *Íslendínga sögur*, I, p. 46.
7. *Ísl. Fornr.*, 4, p. 135.
8. *Islandske Annaler*, p. 213.
9. *Grønl. Hist. Mindesm.*, III, pp. 218 ff.
10. Ibid., p. 225.
11. *Norges Indskrifter med de yngre runer. Hønen-Runerne fra Ringerike* (separate section) (Christiania, 1902).
12. *Norges Indskrifter med de yngre runer*, ed. Magnus Olsen, 2 (Oslo, 1951), pp. 42 ff.
13. Following up a certain clue the author undertook extensive investigations in Ringerike, but without result. An account of this is to be found in the collection *Oldsakssamlingen* in Oslo. There is still a chance that the rune-stone may turn up, perhaps in some old wall or the like.
14. *Den norsk-islandsk skjaldedigtning*, ed. Finnur Jónsson, A, 1 (Copenhagen, 1912), p. 358.

XV THE SAGAS TELL OF THE VINLAND EXPEDITIONS. HELLULAND AND MARKLAND

1. *Studier over Vinlandsreiserne. Vinlands geografi og Ethnografi.* Yearbooks of *Nordisk Oldkyndighed og Historie*, 2nd series, II, 1887.

XVI WHY VINLAND?

1. *De gamle nordbornas Helluland, Markland og Vinland.* No. 1, 1941.
2. The text of a lecture given by Sven Söderberg at Lund in 1888 in which this point is discussed appeared in the newspaper *Sydsvenska Dagbladet Snällposten* of Oct. 30th, 1910.
3. M. Olsen: *Aettegård og helligdom*, p. 164; Valter Jansen: *Nordiska vin-namn* (Lund, 1951).

353

4. *Aettegård og helligdom*, pp. 167–9.
5. *Den eldste Noregs historia*, p. 88.
6. C. V. Sølver: *Vestervejen*, pp. 62 ff.

XVII WHERE WAS VINLAND?

1. *Vestervejen*, p. 66.
2. *Vinland og tidevannet*. Det kongelige norske videnskapsselskap. Museet. Yearbook for 1955.
3. *Medd. om Grønl.*, 88, II, pp. 34–5.

XVIII LATER VOYAGES TO NORTH AMERICA. WHAT CLUES?

1. *Islandske Annaler*, p. 112.
2. *Det gamle Grønl. Beskr.*, pp. 29–30.
3. *Annalium in Islandia Farrago* and *De mirabilibus Islandiae*, by Gísli Oddsson, in *Islandica*, vol. 10 (Ithaca, 1917), pp. 2 ff.
4. *Islandske Annaler*, p. 403.
5. *Grøn. Hist. Mindesm.* III, pp. 120–3.
6. Ibid., p. 243.
7. *Hist.-topogr. Skrifter om Norge* (Christiania, 1895).
8. *Medd. om Grønl.*, 21, II, pp. 322–3.
9. *Ísl. Fornr.*, 4 (Groenlendinga saga), pp. 261–2.
10. G. Storm: *Columbus på Island og vår forfaedres opdagelser i det nordvestlige Atlanterhav*. Det norske geografiske selskaps yearbook IV, 1892–3, pp. 67–75.
11. G. Storm in *Historisk tidsskrift*, 2nd series, V (Christiania, 1886), pp. 385 ff.
12. W. G. Gosling: *Labrador* (London, 1910).
13. Hjalmar R. Holand: *Explorations in America before Columbus* (New York, 1956), pp. 161–76.
14. Ibid., pp. 207–10.
15. *American Anthropologist*, vol. 57 (1955), pp. 35–43 ('Vikings in America – Theories and Evidence').
16. *Explorations*, etc., pp. 231 ff.

XIX TO HVALSØY CHURCH

1. *Medd. om Grønl.*, 118.
2. *Det gamle Grønl. Beskr.*, pp. 26 and 28.
3. Ostermann: *Nordmaend på Grønland*, 2, pp. 657–69.
4. Sources relating to Hvalsøy:

> G. F. Holm: *Beskrivelser af Ruiner i Julianehaabs Distrikt, undersøkt i året 1880. Medd. om Grønl.*, 6, III.
> M. Clemmensen: *Kirkeruiner i Julianehaab Distrikt. Medd. om Grønl.*, 47 (1911).
> Aage Roussell: *Farms and Churches in the mediaeval Norse Settlements*, etc. *Medd. om Grønl.*, 89, I (1941).

5. *Islandske Annaler*, p. 288.
6. Ibid., p. 296.
7. Ibid., pp. 289 and 291.
8. Roussell: *Medd. om Grønl.*, 89.
9. *Det gamle Grønl. Beskr.*, pp. 26–7.
10. *Íslendinga sögur*, I, p. 107.

XX GARDAR

1. *Ísl. Fornr.*, 4 (Groenl. Þ.), p. 282.
2. Ostermann: *Dagbøker av nordmenn på Grønland før 1814*, p. 104.
3. *Historisk tidsskrift*, 2nd series, I (Christiania, 1886), pp. 412 ff.
4. *Medd. om Grønl.*, 76, 1930.
5. *Grønl. Hist. Mindesm.* III, 116.
6. S. Grieg: *Middelalderske byfund fra Bergen og Oslo* (Oslo, 1933), pp. 380–5.
7. *Medd. om Grønl.*, 76, p. 149.
8. Ibid., p. 109.
9. *Ísl. Fornr.* 6, p. 229.
10. *Medd. om Grønl.*, 47, pp. 334 ff.
11. *Grønl. Hist. Mindesm.*, III, p. 813. Holm in *Medd. om Grønl.*, 6. D. Bruun: *Arkeologiske Undersøgelser i Julianehaab Distrikt. Medd. om Grønl.*, 16 (1896).

XXI FROM THOR TO WHITE CHRIST

1. *Ísl. Fornr.*, 4 (*Eiríks saga*), p. 210.
2. F. Paasche: *Landet med de mørke skibene* (Oslo, 1938), p. 40.
3. *Ísl. Fornr.*, 6 (Fosterbrothers' Saga), pp. 245 and 247.
4. Ibid., 4 (*Eiríks saga*), pp. 206 ff.
5. Ibid., p. 217.
6. *Grønl. Hist. Mindesm.*, III, p. 446; cf. *Heimskringla*, St Olav's saga, ch. 124.
7. *Dipl. Norv.*, XVII, No. 850.
8. Cf. *Den eldste Noregs historia*, p. 88.
9. *Ísl. Fornr.*, 4 (Groenl. Þ.), p. 273.

XXII THE CHURCH FLOURISHES – AND FAILS

1. Bishops of Greenland include:

   Eirik Gnúpsson of Upsi: went to Greenland 1112 (or 1113); to Vinland 1121.

   Arnald: appointed by King Sigurd, consecrated in Lund 1124. Later returned to King Sigurd. Was in Iceland 1125–6. In summer 1126 went to Greenland and took up residence at Gardar. Shortly before 1150 retired from bishopric of Greenland and in 1152 was appointed bishop of Hamar.

   Jon (Knutr), consecrated 1150, d. 1187.

   Jon Smyrill, consecrated 1188; was in Iceland 1189 and 1202–3. Went to Norway and Rome 1203, d. 1209.

   Helge succeeded Jon Smyrill as bishop; in 1212 moved from Iceland to Greenland; d. 1220.

   Nikolas, consecrated 1234, went to Greenland 1239; d. 1242.

Olaf, consecrated 1246, went to Greenland summer 1247. Was in Iceland from 1262–4 and in Norway until 1271, when he returned to Greenland; d. 1280.

Tord, consecrated in Nidaros 1288, moved to Greenland 1289 and to Norway 1309 (he was still there in 1311); d. 1314.

Arne, consecrated 1314, went to Greenland 1315, transferred to Faroes 1348.

Jon Skalle, consecrated 1343 when Bishop Arne was believed to be dead. Jon never went to Greenland, and in 1357 was appointed bishop of Holar.

Alf, consecrated 1365, was in Bergen 1366; to Greenland 1368; d. 1376 or 1377. Of the other bishops who succeeded Alf only one, Anders, went to Greenland, where he seems to have arrived in 1406.

Vincens Pedersson Kampe was the last bishop of Greenland. He was appointed its titular bishop in 1519, consecrated 1520, d. 1537.

2. *Dipl. Norv.* Supplement to 17th collection (XVII B), p. 284.
3. *Grønl. Hist. Mindesm.,* III, pp. 94–100.
4. *Håkon Håkonsson's saga,* ch. 257; *Islandske Annaler,* pp. 132, 136 and 193.
5. *Dipl. Norv.,* X, No. 9.
6. Ibid., I, No. 16.
7. *Pavelige Nuntiers Regnskabs- og Dagbøger,* ed. P. A. Munch (Christiania 1864), pp. 25 and 28.
8. *Dipl. Norv.,* VI, No. 36.
9. Ibid., I, No. 66.
10. Munch: *Det norsk Folks Historia,* IV, 2, p. 37.
11. *Dipl. Norv.,* I, No. 71.
12. Sigurður Sigurðsson: *Landbrug og Landboforhold i Island,* p. 73.
13. *Reise igiennem Island,* I, p. 28.
14. O. A. Johnsen: *Norgesveldets undergang* (Oslo, 1944), p. 60.
15. *Frå gamal og ny rett,* I (Oslo, 1950), pp. 35–6. Cf. Odd Nordland: *Øya med giftarmålsvanskene,* in *Viking* 1953, p. 87.
16. *Norgesveldets undergang,* p. 69.

XXIII GLIMPSES OF AN ARCTIC COMMUNITY
1. Erik Holtved: 'Har Nordboerne vaeret i Thuledistriktet?' From *Nationalmuseets Arbeidsmark,* 1945, p. 79.
2. *Grønl. Hist. Mindesm.,* III, pp. 436–9.
3. Roussell, *Medd. om Grønl.,* 88, I.
4. *Grønl. Hist. Mindesm.,* III, p. 243.
5. *Sturlunga saga,* I, p. 121.
6. *Medd. om Grønl.,* 88, I, pp. 21, 28 and 208.
7. *Ísl. Fornr.,* 6 (Fosterbrothers' Saga), p. 230; cf. *Grønl. Hist. Mindesm.,* II, p. 411, note 42.
8. *Norges Innskrifter med de yngre runer,* ed. M. Olsen, 4 (1957), pp. 112 ff.
9. M. Olsen: 'De norrøne runeinnskrifter', *Nordisk kultur,* 6 (1933), p. 104.
10. Ibid., p. 110.

11. *Grønl. Hist. Mindesm.*, II, p. 657.

12. *Sturlunga saga*, I, p. 153.

13. Basic literature dealing with the runic inscriptions of Greenland and of which use has been made here:

> Finnur Jónsson: 'Runestenen fra Kingigtorsoak'. *Det grønlandske selskabs* yearbook for 1914, pp. 89–99.
>
> Finnur Jónsson: 'Grønlandske runestene'. *Det grønl. selsk.*, yearbook for 1916, pp. 63–4.
>
> Finnur Jónsson: 'Interpretation of the Runic Inscriptions from Herjolfsnes'. *Medd. om Grønl.*, 67 (1924), pp. 271–90.
>
> Finnur Jónsson: 'Rune Inscriptions from Gardar', 1929. *Medd. om Grønl.*, 76, pp. 171–9.
>
> Magnus Olsen: 'Kingigtorsoak; Stenen og sproget i de grønlandske runeinnskrifter'. *Norsk tidsskrift for sprogvidenskap*, V, 1932.
>
> Magnus Olsen: 'Runar er ristu rynastir menn'. *Norsk tidsskr. for sprogvidenskap*, V, 1932.
>
> Erik Moltke: 'Greenland runic Inscriptions. Sandnes and the neighbouring farms', *Medd. om Grønl.*, 88, II, 1936. Appendix.

14. *Det grønl. selsk.*, yearbook for 1916, p. 66.

15. Roussell, *Medd. om Grønl.*, 89, I, p. 249.

16. *Norsk tidsskr. for sprogvidenskap*, V, pp. 237 and 248, 1932.

17. Magnus Olsen, *Nordisk kultur*, 5, p. 19.

XXIV THE LAW OF THE LAND

1. *Grágás: Islaendernes Lovbog i Fristatens Tid* (Copenhagen, 1852–70).

2. *Ísl. Fornr.*, 6, p. 229.

3. Ibid., 4, pp. 279 ff.

4. 'Skáld-Helga rímur', in *Rímnasafn*, I (Copenhagen, 1905–12).

5. *Det gamle Grønl. Beskr.*, p. 28.

6. *Ísl. Fornr.*, 4, pp. 279 ff.

7. This view is held by most authorities, including Bjørn Magnússon Olsen, Finnur Jónsson, Einar Arnórsson, Olafur Lárusson, Knut Robberstad and others.

8. *Håkon Håkonssons saga*, ch. 257.

9. *Grønl. Hist. Mindesm.*, III, p. 200.

10. Ibid., p. 458.

11. Ibid., I, pp. 111 ff. Cf. *Islandske Annaler*, p. 365.

12. *Grønl. Hist. Mindesm.*, III, pp. 139–40.

XXV PERILOUS SEAS AND RICH CARGOES

1. *Ísl. Fornr.*, 4 (*Eiríks saga*), p. 204.

2. *Konungs skuggsiá*, p. 28.

3. *Hauksbok* (Copenhagen, 1892–6), p. 4.

4. *Vestervejen*, pp. 83 ff.

5. *Dipl. Norv.*, I, No. 71.

6. *Islandske Annaler*, pp. 22, 63 and elsewhere.
7. *Pavelige Nuntiers Regnskabs- og Dagbøger*, ed. P. A. Munch (Christiania, 1864), pp. 25 and 28.
8. *Dipl. Norv.*, XIX, No. 167.
9. *Den norske sjøfarts historie*, I, p. 153.
10. Ibid., p. 156.
11. *Ísl. Fornr.*, 4 (*Eiríks saga*), p. 210.
12. Ibid., p. 206, and *Groenl. þ.*, p. 290.
13. Finn Magnussen: 'Om de Engelskes Handel og Faerd pa Island i det 15de Aarhundrede'. *Nordisk tidsskrift for Oldkyndighed*, 2 (Copenhagen, 1833), p. 151.
14. *Om Norgis rige*, in Hist.-topogr. Skrifter om Norge, p. 70.
15. *Den norske sjøfarts historie*, I, p. 186.
16. *Dipl. Norv.*, XVIII, No. 33.
17. Cf. *Ísl. Fornr.*, 6 (*Auðunar þ.*), p. 321.
18. Ibid., 4 (*Groenl. þ.*), pp. 281 ff.
19. *Norges Innskrifter med de yngre runer*, ed. Magnus Olsen, 2 (Oslo, 1951), pp. 48–59.
20. *Ísl. Fornr.*, 4 (*Groenl. þ.*), p. 287.
21. *Medd. om Grønl.*, 20, p. 307.
22. *Isl. Fornr.*, 4 (*Groenl. þ.*), p. 279.
23. *Dipl. Norv.*, VII, Nos. 103 and 104.
24. *Islandske Annaler*, pp. 212–13, 228.
25. O. A. Johnson in *Nordisk kultur* 16 (1934), p. 133.
26. *Scriptores minores historiae Danicae medii aevi*, ed. M. Cl. Gertz, II (Copenhagen, 1922), pp. 75–6. Cf. translation by Bjarne Svare: *Jorsal-ferda åt danene* (Oslo, 1934), Norrøne bokverk, No. 31.
27. Munch: *Det norsk folks historie*, V, 1, p. 616.
28. *Norges gamle Love*, III, No. 93.
29. *Dipl. Norv.*, XVIII, No. 33.
30. *Islandske Annaler*, p. 414.
31. Ibid., p. 288.

XXVI TO VATNAHVERFI AND KONGSGÅRDEN

1. *Ísl. Fornr.*, 4 (*Groenl. þ.*), p. 282.
2. F. Jónsson in *Medd. om Grønl.*, 20, IV, p. 291.
3. *Medd. om Grønl.*, 6, III, pp. 119 and 139.
4. Ibid., 8 (1889), p. 344.
5. Daniel Bruun in *Medd. om Grønl.*, 16, III (1896), pp. 455 ff.
6. Ibid., p. 387.
7. *Fra Nationalmuseets Arbeidsmark 1952*, pp. 101 ff ('Vatnahverfi: en middelalders bondebygd i Grønland').
8. *Det gamle Grønl. Beskr.*, pp. 24–5.
9. *Gulatingsloven*, ch. 14.

NOTES

XXVII SOUTHWARD: RELIGIOUS HOUSES AND HERJOLFSNES

1. *Det gamle Grønl. Beskr.*, p. 24.
2. 'Nordbobygdernes Kirker': *Grønland. Tidsskrift for dansk-grønlandsk samvirke*, part 8 (1952), p. 300.
3. *Grønl. Hist. Mindesm.*, III, p. 806, note 2.
4. *Klostre i de grønlandske nordbobygder: Grønland. Tidsskr. for dansk-grønl. samv.*, Part 5 (1953), p. 195.
5. *Vestervejen*, p. 83.
6. C. Pingel: 'Antiquariske Efterretninger fra Grønland', *Annaler for nordisk Oldkyndighed* 1842–3 (Copenhagen, 1943), p. 332.
7. Nørlund: *Buried Norsemen at Herjolfsnes. Medd. om Grønl.*, 67, I (Copenhagen, 1924).
8. *Ísl. Fornr.*, 6 (Fosterbrothers' Saga), p. 227.
9. *Grønl. Hist. Mindesm.*, III, p. 514.
10. G. F. Holm in *Medd. om Grønl.*, 6, III, p. 143.

XXVIII NORTH TO VESTERBYGD

1. *Grønl. Hist. Mindesm.*, III, p. 228.
2. Finnur Jónsson in *Medd. om Grønl.*
3. *Grønl. Hist Mindesm.*, I, p. 191, note 35.
4. *Ísl. Fornr.*, 4, pp. 279–81.
5. Rink: *Eskimoiske Eventyr og Sagn* (Copenhagen, 1866), pp. 205–6.
6. Meldgaard: 'Fra en grønlandsk Mumiehule', *Nationalmuseets Arbeidsmark 1953*, p. 17.
7. Egil Thorhallesen: *Efterretning om Rudera eller Levninger av de gamle Nordmaends og Islaenderes Bygninger paa Grønlands Vester-Side* (Copenhagen, 1776), p. 29.
8. *Grønl. Hist. Mindesm.*, III, p. 841.

XXIX HOMES IN THE REINDEER COUNTRY

1. *Oversikt over Nordboruiner i Godthaab- og Fredrikshaab-Distriktet. Medd. om Grønl.*, 56 (1918), pp. 92–3.
2. Thorhallesen: *Efterretning om Rudera eller Levninger*, etc., p. 36.
3. *Ísl. Fornr.*, 4 (*Eiriks saga*), p. 214.
4. *Det gamle Grønl. Beskr.*, p. 29.
5. *Islandske Annaler*, pp. 112 and 251.
6. Roussell: *Farms and Churches*, etc. *Medd. om Grønl.*, 89, I, 1941, p. 243. See *Sandnes and the Neighbouring Farms, Medd. om Grønl.*, 88, II.
7. Ibid., p. 124.
8. *Rímnasafn*, I, p. 160.
9. *Ísl. Fornr.*, 4 (*Eiriks saga*), pp. 206–7.
10. Hjalmar Falk: *Litt om sagatidens sko. Maal og minne*, 1917, p. 51.
11. Roussell: *Farms and Churches*, etc., *Medd. om Grønl.*, 89, I, p. 243; ibid., 88, II, p. 205; and Nørlund: *Buried Norsemen, Medd. om Grønl.*, 67, I, p. 221.

12. *Medd. om Grønl.*, 88, II, p. 124.
13. *Animal Remains from the West Settlements in Greenland*, 88, III (Copenhagen, 1936).
14. *Medd. om Grønl.*, 89, I, pp. 95–6.
15. Roussell: *Utgravninger i en avsides grønlandsk nordbobygd*. From *Nationalmuseets Arbeidsmark 1938*, p. 55.
16. *Medd. om Grønl.*, 89, I, p. 249.

XXX GLIMPSES OF THE LAST PERIOD

1. *Det gamle Grønl. Beskr.*, *Dipl. Norv.*, V, No. 152.
2. 'Annalium in Islandia Farrago' and 'De mirabilibus Islandiae', by Gisli Oddsson, in *Islandica*, vol. 10 (Ithaca, 1917), pp. 2 ff.
3. *Grønl. Hist. Mindesm.*, III, pp. 52 and 463. Cf. P. C. Friis, *Samlede Skrifter* (1881), p. 209.
4. Ibid., pp. 120–3.
5. A. Steinnes: 'Ein nordpolsekpedisjon ar 1360', *Syn og Segn* 1958, p. 415.
6. *Dipl. Norv.*, XVII, No. 759, part 6, p. 284.
7. Ibid., XIII, No. 91.
8. *Grønl. Hist. Mindesm.*, III, pp. 148–9.
9. *Dipl. Norv.*, XVII, No. 759; G. Storm: 'Nye Efterretninger fra det gamle Grønland, *Hist. tidsskrift*, 3rd series, II (Christiania, 1892), p. 407.
10. *Dipl. Norv.*, XX, pp. 165–74.
11. G. Storm in *Ymer*, 9th year (1899), p. 91.
12. *Nord i takeheimen*, pp. 385 ff.
13. Brøgger: *Vinlandsferdene*, p. 176.
14. Ibid., p. 182.
15. G. Storm: 'Søfareren Johannes Scolvus og hans Reise til Labrador eller Grønland', *Hist. tidsskr.*, 2nd series, pp. 385–400.
16. Louis Bobé: 'Aktstykker til Oplysning om Grønlands Beseiling', *Dansk Magasin*, 5th series, VI (Copenhagen, 1909).
17. *Hakluytus Posthumus or Purchas his Pilgrims*, etc., vol. XIII (Glasgow, 1906), p. 168.
18. *Historia om de nordiska folken*, I, pp. 94–5.
19. *Grønl. Hist. Mindesm.*, III, pp. 482–3.
20. *Om Norgis rige*, in *Hist.-topogr. Skrifter om Norge*, p. 50.
21. Gosling: *Labrador*, p. 19. *Dipl. Norv.* XX, No. 813.
22. *Norges gamle Love*, 2nd series, No. 72.
23. *Dipl. Norv.*, XX, No. 865.
24. *Den norske sjøfartshistorie*, I, p. 306.
25. *Dipl. Norv.*, XX, No. 831.
26. *Hansische Geschichtsblätter*, pub. by the *Hansischen Geschichtsverein* 65/66, for the year 1940–1, p. 199.
27. *Grønl. Hist. Mindesm.*, III, p. 513.
28. Ibid., I, pp. 125 ff.
29. Gudbrandus Thorlacius: *A Letter written by G. Th. concerning the Ancient State of Iceland and Greenland*, 1595.

30. *The Private Diary of Dr John Dee, and the Catalogue of his Library of Manuscripts*, Camden Society 19 (London, 1842), p. 4.
31. Hans Egede: *Relationer fra Grønland*, etc. in *Medd. om Grønl.*, 54 (Copenhagen, 1925), p. 3.
32. Ibid., p. 65.

XXXI THE GREAT MYSTERY

1. *Klimat-vekslinger i Nordens Historie*. Det Norske Videnskaps-akademi Oslo, I. Matem. nat. kl. 1925, III. *Klimat-vekslinger i historisk og post-glacial tid.* Det Norske Videnskaps-akademi (Oslo, 1926), III.
2. 'Glaciarer och klimat i Norden under de senaste tusentalen ar', *Norsk geografisk tidsskrift*, XIII, parts 3–8, 1951–2. 'Den nutida klimafluktuationen och dess utforskande', ibid., XI, parts 7 and 8.
3. *Ísl. Fornr.*, 4 (*Groenl. þ.*), p. 290.
4. *Det gamle Grønl. Beskr.*, p. 31.
5. *Dipl. Norv.*, XVII, No. 759.
6. *Grønl. Hist. Mindesm.*, I, p. 31.
7. Albert Hastings Markham: *Voyages and Works of John Davis* (London, 1880), XXIX, pp. 24–6.
8. 'Nordboernes Undergang på Grønland i geologisk Belysning', *Det grønlandske selskaps*, yearbook 1935, p. 12.
9. Ibid., pp. 5–16.
10. Helge Ingstad: *Øst for den store bre* (Oslo, 1935), pp. 130–45.
11. 'De norske bygders undergang pa Grønland', *Norsk geogr. tidsskr.*, X, part 4, 1944.
12. Ibid.
13. *Islandske Annaler*, pp. 213 and 403.
14. *Ísl. Fornr.*, 4 (*Eiríks saga*), p. 208.
15. Ibid. (*Groenlendinga saga*), p. 254.
16. Ibid. (*Eiríks saga*), pp. 215–16.
17. *Klostre i de grønlandske nordbobygder. Grønland. Tidsskrift for dansk-grønl. samvirke.* Part 3 (1953), p. 198.
18. *Anthropologica medici: historica Grønlandiae antiquae. Medd. om Grønl.*, 67, III, pp. 291 ff.
19. *The Mediaeval Norse Settlements in Greenland. Anthropological Investigations. Medd. om Grønl.*, 89, II (1942), p. 81.
20. Ibid., p. 58.
21. Ibid., p. 60. See also *Medd. om Grønl.*, 89, III, p. 43. (Brøste, Fischer-Møller and P. O. Pedersen: *The Mediaeval Norsemen at Gardar.*)
22. *Medd. om Grønl.*, 89, II, pp. 78 ff.
23. K. E. Schreiner: *Crania Norwegia* (Oslo, 1939).
24. *Medd. om Grønl.*, 89, II, p. 78, and III, p. 57.
25. *The Eskimo Skeleton. Medd. om Grønl.*, 146, II (1953), p. 85.
26. K. Wagner: *Mittelalter-Knochen aus Oslo*, pub. by Det Norske Vidensk.-akad. of Oslo, I (1926), VII. W. Kiil: *Statures and Growth of Norwegian Men*, pub. by Det Norske Vidensk.-akad. of Oslo (1939), VI.

27. *Medd. om Grønl.*, 89, II, p. 60.
28. 'Kariesprofylakse', paper read to the Norwegian Medical Association. *Norsk Magasin for laegevidenskap* 1936, pp. 109 and 139.
29. *Medd. om Grønl.*, 89, II, pp. 61 ff.; ibid., III, pp. 48 ff.; and *Medd. om Grønl.*, 146, II, pp. 127 ff.
30. *Nord i tåkeheimen*, p. 361.
31. *Samiske samlinger*, III (Oslo, 1956), pp. 36–7.

XXXII THE SKRAELINGS
1. *Íslendingabók*, ch. 6.
2. *Flóamanna saga*, pp. 32 ff.
3. Cf. *Den eldste Noregs historia*, p. 13.
4. *Grønl. Hist. Mindesm.*, III, pp. 435–41.
5. *Islandske Annaler*, p. 364.
6. *Grønl. Hist. Mindesm.*, III, pp. 435–41.
7. T. Mathiassen: *Inugsuk. Medd. om Grønl.*, 77, IV, 1930.
8. *Medd. om Grønl.*, 118, I (1936), and Mathiassen: *Skraelingene i Grønland* (Copenhagen, 1935).
9. *Medd. om Grønl.*, 93, II (1934), pp. 96–7.
10. Ibid., 54, p. 36.
11. Rink: *Eskimoiske Eventyr og Sagn*, pp. 198 ff.
12. *Medd. om Grønl.*, 54, p. 65.
13. *Islandske Annaler*, p. 364.
14. *Dipl. Norv.*, XVII, No. 759.

XXXIII A RACE THAT VANISHED
1. *Det gamle Grønl. Beskr.*, pp. 29–30.
2. *Syn og Segn* (1958), p. 7.
3. *Nord i tåkeheimen*, p. 370.
4. *Arkiv for nord. Filologi*, VI (1890), p. 355.
5. *Nord i tåkeheimen*, pp. 364 ff.
6. *Det norske folks historie*, V, 1, pp. 314–15.
7. *Islandske Annaler*, p. 213.
8. Gosling: *Labrador*, p. 36.
9. Cf. Finn Magnussen in *Nordisk tidsskr. for Oldkyndighed*, 2 (1813), pp. 112 ff.
10. *Dipl. Norv.*, XX, No. 865.
11. Ibid., VI, No. 527.
12. *Hist. Tidsskr.*, 3rd series, III, pp. 399 ff.
13. *Dipl. Norv.*, XVII, part 6, p. 267.
14. Graah: *Undersøgelser-Reise til Ostkysten af Grønland, 1828–31* (Copenhagen, 1832), p. 7.
15. *Norges gamle Love*, 2nd series, 1, No. 72.
16. Ostermann: *Niels Egedes Beskrivelse over Grønland*, pp. 48–9.
17. *Antiqvariske Efterretninger. Grønland. Nordisk tidsskr. for Landkyndighed*, II (1833), p. 319. *Grønl. Hist. Mindesm.*, III, p. 813.
18. *Annaler for nord. Olkyndighed*, 1842–3, p. 332.

NOTES

19. *Medd. om Grønl.*, 6, III (1883), pp. 120 and 139.
20. Pingel: *Annaler for nord. Oldkyndighed*, 1842–3, p. 332.
21. *Medd. om Grønl.*, 6, III, p. 72.
22. Ibid., 16, p. 392.
23. *Kulturhistorisk leksikon for nord. middelalder*, IV, 369 (Fiskehandel).
24. *Om Norgis rige*, p. 70.
25. H. Harisse: *John Cabot the Discoverer of North America and Sebastian his Son* (London, 1896), p. 147.
26. *Nord i tåkeheimen*, p. 538.

XXXIV THE END OF A SAGA
1. Knud Rasmussen: *Fra Grønland til Stillehavet*, 2 (Copenhagen, 1926), pp. 129–31.
2. *Rudera eller Levninger*, etc., p. 22.
3. *Grønland i Tohundredaaret*, etc., II, p. 100.
4. *Grønl. Hist. Mindesm.*, III, p. 841.

BIBLIOGRAPHY

Ahlmann, Hans W. 'Den nutida klimatfluktuationen och dess utforskande', *Norsk geogr. tidsskr.*, XI (Oslo 1947), pp. 290–326.
— 'Glaciärer och klimat i Norden under de senaste tusentalen år' *Norsk geogr. tidsskr.*, XIII (Oslo 1952), pp. 56–77.
— 'Is och eld', *Polarboken 1957* (Oslo 1957), pp. 50–5.
Allen, J.: *Early Christian Monuments of Scotland*, I–III (Edinburgh 1903).
Bårdssøn, Ivar (Ivar Bardarson): *Det gamle Grønlands beskrivelse. Af ... Udgiven efter håndskrifterne af Finnur Jónsson* (Copenhagen 1930).
Benskulptur og hornarbeider i Norge og på Island, Ca. 500–1850 (Oslo 1930).
Beyer, Absalon Pedersøn: *Om Norgis Rige* (Bergen 1928).
Birket-Smith, Kaj: *Ethnography of the Egedesminde District with aspects of the general culture of West Greenland* (Copenhagen 1924). *Med. om Grønl.*, 66.
Bjørnbo, Axel Anthon: *Carthographia Groenlandica* (Copenhagen 1912). *Med. om Grønl.*, 48.
Bobé, Louis: 'Hollænderne paa Grønland', *De danske Atlanterhavsøer* (Copenhagen 1915), pp. 257–84.
— *Opdagelsesrejser til Grønland, 1473–1806* (Copenhagen 1936). *Med. om Grønl.*, 55. No. 1.
Brøgger, A. W.: De gamle nordmenns seilaser i Norskehavet', *Norge. Tidsskr. om vårt land.* 2. (1926), pp. 225–42.
— *Den norske bosetningen på Shetland–Orknøyene. Studier og resultater* (Oslo 1930).
— 'Vinlandsferdene', *Norsk geogr. tidsskr.*, 6 (Oslo 1937), pp. 65–85.
— *Vinlandsferdene* (Oslo 1937).
— *Kongespeilet* (Oslo 1947).
Brøgger, A. W., and Haakon Shetelig: *Vikingeskipene deres forgjengere og etterfølgere* (Oslo 1950).
Brøndsted, Johannes: 'Norsemen in North America before Columbus', *Smithsonian Institution* (Washington 1954), pp. 367–405.
Bruun, Daniel: *Arkæologiske Undersøgelser i Julianehaabs Distrikt, 1895* (Copenhagen 1896), pp. 173–495. *Med. om Grønl.*, 16.
— *Nordboruiner i Godthaabs og Frederikshaabs Distrikter* (Copenhagen 1916). *Med. om Grønl.*, 56.
— *The Icelandic colonization of Greenland, and the finding of Vineland* (Copenhagen 1918). *Med. om Grønl.*, 57.
— *Oversigt over Nordboruiner i Godthaab- og Frederikshaab-Distrikter* (Copenhagen 1918), pp. 55–147. *Med. om Grønl.*, 56.
— *Fortidsminder og nutidshjem paa Island. Med et tillæg om Nordbogaardene i Grønland* (Copenhagen 1928).

BIBLIOGRAPHY

Bruun, *Fra de færøske Bygder. Samlede Afhandlinger om gammeldags Sæd og Skik.* (Copenhagen 1928).

— *Erik den Røde og Nordbokolonierne i Grønland* (Copenhagen 1931).

Bugge, Alexander: 'Skibsfarten fra de ældste tider til omkring aar 1600', *Den norske sjøfarts historie*, I (Christiania 1923), pp. 8–369.

Christensen, K. N.: 'Grønlands jord under kultur', *Grønland*, 11 (1953), pp. 407–13.

— 'Husdyrenes tilpasning til det grønlandske klima', *Grønland*, 9 (1953), pp. 356–60.

Clemmensen, Mogens: 'Undersøgelsesrejse i sommeren 1910. Kirkeruiner m. m. i Julianehaab Distrikt' (Copenhagen 1911), pp. 285–358. *Med. om Grønl.*, 47.

Cluness, Andrew T.: *The Shetland Isles* (London 1951).

Collins, Henry B.: *Arctic Area. Indigenous Period* (Mexico 1954).

Davis, John: *The voyages and works of ... the navigator.* Ed. with an introduction and notes by A. H. Markham (London 1880).

Debes, Lucas Jacobsøn: *Færoæ et Færoa Reserata. Det er: Færøernis og Færøeske Indbyggeris Beskrifvelse ... udi hvilket føris til liuset adskillige Naturens Hemeligheder ...* (Copenhagen 1673).

Dee, John: *The private diary of ..., and a catalogue of his library of manuscripts.* Ed. James O. Halliwell (London 1842).

Degerbøl, Magnus: 'Animal bones from the Norse ruins at Gardar' (Copenhagen 1930), pp. 183–92. *Med. om Grønl.*, 76.

— *Animal remains from the West Settlement in Greenland with special reference to livestock* (Copenhagen 1936). *Med. om Grønl.*, 88. No. 3.

Den Islandske Lov, Jóns Bogen, udgiven af Kong Magnus Lagabætir, Anno 1280 ... (Copenhagen 1763).

Det Norske folks liv og historie gjennem tidene, I–III (Oslo 1930–4).

Devold, Finn: 'Klimaforandringer', *Polarboken 1954* (Oslo 1954), pp. 33–41.

Diplomatarium Norvegicum, XVII, 6. Oldbreve til Kundskab om Norges indre og ydre forhold, sprog, slægter, sæder, lovgivning og rettergang i Middelalderen. Tillæg til syttende samling (Christiania 1913).

Edda-Kvæde: *Norrøne fornsongar. Paa Nynorsk ved Ivar Mortensen-Egnund* (Oslo 1928).

Egede, Hans: *Omstændelig og udførlig Relation, angaaende den Grønlandske Missions Begyndelse og Fortsættelse, samt hvad ellers mere der ved Landets Recognoscering, dets Beskaffenhed, og Ingbyggernes Væsen og Leve-Maade vedkommende, er befunden* (Copenhagen 1738).

— *Relationer fra Grønland 1721–36, og Det gamle Grønlands ny Perlustration 1741* (Copenhagen 1925). *Med. om Grønl.*, 54.

— *Det gamle Grønlands nye Perlustration, eller Naturel-Historie og Beskrivelse over det gamle Grønlands Situation, Luft, Temperament og Beskaffenhed, de gamle norske Coloniers Begyndelse og Undergang der Samme-Steds* (Oslo 1926). *Norge og Grønland*, I.

Egede, Poul and Niels: *Continuation af Hans Egedes Relationer fra Grønland, samt*

Egede, Niels: *Beskrivelse over Grønland* (Copenhagen 1939). *Med. om Grønl.*, vol. 120.

BIBLIOGRAPHY

Eidnes, Hans: *Hålogalands historie* (Trondheim 1954).

Eskeland, Severin: *Soga um Eirik Raude* (Oslo 1924).

Fabricius, Otto: *Fauna Groenlandica. Pattedyr og fugle.* With introduction and commentary by O. Helms (Copenhagen 1929).

Fægri, Knut: 'Omkring de norrøne grønlandsbygders undergang', *Naturen 1957* (Bergen 1957), pp. 432–6.

Fischer-Møller, K.: *The mediaeval Norse settlements in Greenland* (Copenhagen 1942). *Med. om Grønl.*, 89. No. 2.

— *Skeletons from Ancient Greenland graves* (Copenhagen 1938). *Med. om Grønl.*, 119. No. 4.

— *The mediaeval Norse settlements in Greenland* (Copenhagen 1942). *Med. om Grønl.*, 89. No. 2.

[Frobisher, Martin.] *The three voyages of M. F. in search of a passage to Cathaia and India by the North-West* ... (London 1867).

Gathorne-Hardy, G. M.: *The Norse Discoverers of America.* The Wineland Sagas translated and discussed by G. M. G.-H. (Oxford 1921).

Gini, Corrado: *On the extinction of the Norse settlements in Greenland* (Bergen 1958). The Institute of Economics. Paper No. 10.

Gjessing, Gutorm: *Fangstfolk, et streiftog gjennom Nord-Norsk forhistorie* (Oslo 1941).

Godfrey, William S.: 'Vikings in America. Theories and Evidence', *American Anthropologist,* 57 (1955), pp. 35–43.

Gosling, W. G.: *Labrador: its discovery, exploration and development* (London 1910).

Grágás: *Islændernes Lovbog i Fristatens Tid. Oversat af Vilhjalmur Finsen* (Copenhagen 1852–70).

Gray, Edward F.: *Leif Eriksson, discoverer of America a.d. 1003* (London 1930).

Greenland, I–III (Copenhagen 1928–9).

Grieg, Sigurd: *Middelalderske byfund fra Bergen og Oslo* (Oslo 1933).

Grønlandsbogen, I–II (Copenhagen 1950).

Grønlands Historiske Mindesmærker, I–III (Copenhagen 1838–45).

Grønland i tohundredaaret for Hans Egedes landing, I–II (Copenhagen 1921).

Graah, W. A.: *Undersøgelses-Reise til Østkysten af Grønland* (Copenhagen 1832). Narrative of Expedition to the East Coast of Greenland, sent by Order of the King of Denmark in search of the Lost Colonies. Transl. from Danish (London 1837).

Gudmundsson, Valtyr: *Privatboligen paa Island i Sagatiden* (Copenhagen 1889).

Hansen, Paul M. og Frede Hermann: 'Fisken og Havet Grønland' (Copenhagen 1953).

Hasund, S.: *Vårt landbruks historie* (Oslo 1932).

Hermannsson, Halldór: *The Norsemen in America (982–c. 1500)* (Ithaca, N.Y. 1909). *Islandica,* II.

— *The problem of Wineland* (New York 1936). *Islandica,* XXV.

Holand, Hj. R.: *Explorations in America before Columbus* (New York 1956).

Holm, Gustav F.: 'Beskrivelse af Ruiner i Julianehaabs Distrikt, undersøgte i Aaret 1880' (Copenhagen 1883), pp. 57–145. *Med. om Grønl.,* 6.

BIBLIOGRAPHY

Holm, Gustav: *Gunbjørns-Skær og Korsøer* (Copenhagen 1918), pp. 291–308. *Med. om Grønl.*, 56.

Holtved, Erik: 'Har Nordboerne været i Thule Distriktet?' *Fra Nationalmuseets Arbejdsmark, 1945* (Copenhagen 1945), pp. 79–84.

Hovgaard, William: *The Voyages of the Norsemen to America* (New York 1914).

Ingstad, Helge: *Øst for den store bre* (Oslo 1935).

— *Landet med de kalde kyster* (Oslo 1948).

— *Nunamiut. Blant Alaskas innlands-eskimoer* (Oslo 1951).

Isachsen, Gunnar: *Grønland og Grønlandsisen* (Oslo 1925).

Islandske Ættesagaer, I–III (Oslo 1951–3). Ed. Hallvard Lie.

Islenʒkt Fornbrefasafn ... Diplomatarium Islandicum, XVI, 1–2 (Reykjavik 1952–4).

Iversen, Johs: *Moorgeologische Untersuchungen auf Grönland* (Copenhagen 1934). *Med. fra Dansk geol. Foren.*, 8.

— 'Nordboernes Undergang paa Grønland i geologisk Belysning', *Det grønl. Selskabs Aarsskr., 1935* (Copenhagen 1935), pp. 5–18.

Jansson, Valter: *Nordiska vin-namn. En ortnamstyp och dess historia* (Lund 1951).

Jensen, Ad. S.: *Concerning a change of climate during recent decades in the Arctic and Subarctic regions, from Greenland in the west to Eurasia in the east, and contemporary biological and geophysical changes* (Copenhagen 1939). *Biologiske Meddelelser*, XIV. 8.

Johnsen, Oscar Albert: *Noregsveldets undergang. Et utsyn og et oppgjør. Nedgangstiden* (Oslo 1944).

— 'Norges handel og Skibsfart i middelalderen', *Nordisk Kultur*, 16 (Oslo 1934), pp. 128–47.

Jónsson, Finnur: 'Grønlands gamle Topografi efter Kilderne. Østerbygden og Vesterbygden' (Copenhagen 1899), pp. 265–329. *Med. om Grønl.*, 20.

— 'On the Icelandic colonization of Greenland' (Copenhagen 1928), pp. 331–61. *Greenland*, II.

— 'Rune inscriptions from Gardar' (Copenhagen 1930), pp. 171–9. *Med. om Grønl.*, 76.

Jørgensen, Jørgen Balslev: *The Eskimo skeleton* (Copenhagen 1953). *Med. om Grønl.*, 146.

— 'De første eskimoer på Grønland', *Grønland*, No. 7 (Charlottenlund 1954), pp. 265–71.

Keyser, R., and P. A. Munch: *Lovgivningen efter Kong Magnus Haakonsøns Død 1280 indtil 1387*, 3 (Christiania 1849).

Kiil, Vilhelm: *Stature and growth of Norwegian men during the past two hundred years*, I (Oslo 1939).

Koht, Halvdan: *Den eldste Noregs-historia. Frå latin ved H. K. Med tilleg: Meldingane frå Noreg hos Adam av Bremen* (Oslo 1950).

Kolsrud, Oluf: *Olavskyrkja i Trondheim* (Oslo 1914). *Norske Folkeskrifter*, No. 63.

— 'Den norske Kirkes Erkebiskoper og Biskoper indtil Reformasjonen', *Diplomatarium Norvegicum*, XVII, pp. 177–366.

Kulturhistorisk Leksikon for nordisk Middelalder fra vikingtid til reformasjondsti (Oslo 1956–).

Landnámabók Islands (Copenhagen 1925).

BIBLIOGRAPHY

Larsen, Helge, and Jørgen Meldgaard: *Paleo-eskimo cultures in Disko Bugt, West Greenland* (Copenhagen 1958). *Med. om Grønl.*, 161. No. 2.

Laursen, Dan: 'Klimasvingninger i Grønland efter istiden', *Grønland*, 7 (1954), pp. 241–6.

— 'Nivåforandringer i Grønland siden istiden,' *Grønland*, 4.

Lethbridge, T. C.: *Merlin's Island*. Essays on Britain in the Dark Ages (London 1948).

— *Herdsmen & Hermits*. Celtic Seafarers in the Northern Seas (Cambridge 1950).

Lorentzen, Bernt: *Bergen og sjøfarten*, I. Fra Olav Kyrres tid til året 1814 (Bergen 1959).

Madden, F.: 'Historical Remarks on the Introduction of the Game of Chess into Europe', *Archaeologia*, 24 (London 1932).

Magnussen, Finn: 'Om de Engelskes Handel og Færd paa Island i det 15de Aarhundrede især med Hensyn til Columbus' formeentlige Reise dertil i Aaret 1477, og hans Beretninger desangaaende', *Nordisk Tidsskrift for Oldkyndighed*, 2 (Copenhagen 1833), pp. 112–69.

Marwick, Hugh: *Orkney* (London 1951).

Mathiassen, Th.: 'Inugsuk. A mediaeval Eskimo settlement in Upernivik district, West Greenland' (Copenhagen 1931), pp. 145–339. *Med. om Grønl.*, 77.

— *Ancient Eskimo settlements in the Kangamiut Area* (Copenhagen 1931). *Med. om Grønl.*, 91.

— *Contribution to the Archaeology of Disko Bay* (Copenhagen 1934). *Med. om Grønl.*, 93. No. 2.

— *Skrælingerne i Grønland* (Copenhagen 1935).

— 'Nordboernes sammentræf med Eskimoene i Grønland', *Grønland*, 4.

— *The Sermermiut excavations, 1955* (Copenhagen 1958). *Med. om Grønl.*, 161. No. 3.

Mathiassen, Th., in collaboration with Erik Holtved: 'The Eskimo archaeology of Julianehaab District. With a brief summary of the prehistory of the Greenlanders' (Copenhagen 1936), pp. 1–138. *Med. om Grønl.*, 118.

Meldgaard, Jørgen: 'Grønlændere i tre tusinde år', I–II, *Grønland*, Nos. 4 and 5 (Copenhagen 1958), pp. 121–9; pp. 170–8.

Mohn, Henrik: *Vindene i den nordlige del av Nordsjøen og vikingetogene* (Christiania 1914).

Moltke, Erik: *Greenland Runic Inscriptions*, IV (Copenhagen 1936), pp. 223–32.

Munch, P. A.: *Det norske Folks Historie* (Christiania 1852–63).

Næss, Almar: *Hvor lå Vinland?* En studie over solobservasjoner i de norrøne sagaer (Oslo 1954).

Nansen, Fridtjof: *Nord i taakeheimen. Utforskningen av jordens nordlige strøk i tidlige tider* (Christiania 1911), vii.

— 'The Norsemen in America', *Geographical journal*, 38 (London 1911), pp. 557–80.

— *Klima-vekslinger i Nordens historie* (Oslo 1925).

— *Klima-vekslinger i historisk og postglacial tid* (Oslo 1926).

Nielsen, Niels: 'Evidence on the extraction of iron in Greenland by the Norsemen' (Copenhagen 1930), pp. 195–210. *Med. om Grønl.*, 76.

BIBLIOGRAPHY

Nielsen, *Evidence of iron extraction at Sandnes, in Greenland's west settlement* (Copenhagen 1936). *Med. om Grønl.*, 88. No. 4.

Nørlund, Poul: *Buried Norsemen at Herjolfsnes* (Copenhagen 1924). *Med. om Grønl.*, 67.

— 'Kirkegaarden paa Herjolfsnæs. Et bidrag til diskussionen om klimateorien', *Historisk tidsskr.*, Ser. 5. Vol. 6 (Oslo 1927), pp. 385–402.

— 'En Bispestav af Hvalrostand fra Grønland', *Fra Nationalmuseets Arbejdsmark 1928* (Copenhagen 1928), pp. 61–6.

— *De gamle Nordbobygder ved Verdens Ende* (Copenhagen 1934).

— *De gamle Nordbobygder ved verdens ende. Skildringer fra Grønlands Middelalder* (Copenhagen 1942).

Nørlund, Poul, in collaboration with Aage Roussell: *Norse ruins at Gardar, the episcopal Seat of Mediaeval Greenland* (Copenhagen 1930), pp. 1–170. *Med. om Grønl.*, 76.

Nørlund, Poul, and Mårten Stenberger: *Brattahlid* (Copenhagen 1934). Appendices: A. 'Animal bones from the Norse ruins at Brattahlid', by Magnus Degerbøl. B. 'Samples of Slag from Brattahlid', examined by Niels Nielsen. C. 'List of ruins'. *Med. om Grønl.*, 88.

Norsk biografisk leksikon (Oslo 1923–).

Norsk Kulturhistorie. Billeder av folkets dagligliv gjennem årtusener, 1–5. Ed. Anders Bugge and Sverre Steen (Oslo 1938).

Oesau, Wanda: *Hamburgs Grönlandsfahrt auf Walfischfang und Robbenschlag vom 17.–19. Jahrhundert* (Hamburg 1955).

Olafsen, Eggert: *Vice-Lavmand Eggert Olafsen og Land-Physici Biarne Povelsens Reise igiennem Island ... Deel 1–2* (Sorøe 1772).

Olsen, Magnus: *Farms and fanes of ancient Norway* (Oslo 1928). *Instituttet for sammenlignende kulturforskning*.

— 'Runebudskapet i Atlamál', *Arkiv för Nordisk Filologi*, 46. 3. F. 2. B. (Lund 1930), pp. 161–70.

— 'Rúnar er ristu rýnastir menn', *Norsk tidsskrift for sprogvidenskap*, V (1932), pp. 167–88.

— *Sigtuna-Amuletten. Nogen tolkningsbidrag* (Oslo 1940).

— 'Hønen', *Norges innskrifter med de yngre runer* (Oslo 1951), pp. 23–68.

— 'Gáreksey og andre orknøske stedsnavne', *Maal og Minne 1955*, pp. 54–64.

— 'Runic Inscriptions in Great Britain, Ireland and The Isle of Man' (Bergen n.d.), pp. 153–232. Reprint from *Viking Antiquities in Great Britain and Ireland.* 'Norge', Särtryck ur Nordisk Kultur, V, *Ortnamn*.

— 'De Norrøne Runeinnskrifter', Särtryck ur Nordisk Kultur, VI, *Runoran*, pp. 83–113.

Ostenfeld, C. H.: *The Flora of Greenland and its origin* (Copenhagen 1926). *Det Kgl. Danske Videnskabernes Selskab. Biologiske Meddelelser*, VI, 3.

Osterman, H.: *Nordmænd paa Grønland 1721–1814*, I. 2 (Oslo 1940).

Paasche, Fredrik: *Norges og Islands litteratur indtil utgangen av Middelalderen* (Christiania 1924). Norsk litteratur-historie, I.

— *Landet med de mørke skibene* (Oslo 1938).

Petersen, Jan: *Vikingetidens redskaper* (Oslo 1951).

BIBLIOGRAPHY

Pingel, C.: 'Antiquariske Efterretninger fra Grønland; redigerede af Dr C. Pingel', *Annaler for Nordisk Oldkyndighet* (Copenhagen 1838–9), pp. 122–41.

Rafn, Carl Chr.: *Antiquitates Americanae*. Ed. Societas regia antiquariorum septentrionalium (Hafniæ 1837).

Rasmussen, Knud: *Myter og sagn fra Grønland*, III (Copenhagen 1925).

Reynolds, Hans: *Vestré Bygdi* (Oslo 1926).

Rink, Henry: *Tales and traditions of the Eskimo with a sketch of their habits, religion, language and other peculiarities* (Edinburgh 1875).

— *Danish Greenland, its people and its products* (London 1877).

Robberstad, Knut: *Gulatings Lovi*. Umsett frå gamalnorsk av K. R. (Oslo 1937).

Rogers, J. D.: *Newfoundland*. A historical geography of the British colonies, vol. V, part iv (Oxford 1911).

Roussell, Aage: *Farms and churches in the mediaeval Norse settlements of Greenland*. Appendix: M. Degerbøl. 'The osseous material from Austmannadal and Tungmeralik' (Copenhagen 1941), pp. 1–342, 343–54. *Med. om Grønl.*, 89. No. 1.

— *Sandnes and the neighbouring farms*. Appendix: 'Greenland runic inscriptions', by Erik Moltke (Copenhagen 1936). *Med. om Grønl.*, 88. No. 2.

Shetelig, Haakon: *Vikingeminner i Vest-Europa* (Oslo 1933). *Instituttet for sammenlignende kulturforskning*, Ser. A. 16.

Schreiner, Johan: *Pest og prisfall i Sen-middelalderen. Et problem i norsk historie* (Oslo 1948).

Schreiner, Kristian E.: *Norske skjelettfunn fra folkevandringstid og yngre jernalder* (Oslo 1927).

Sigurðson, Sigurður: *Landbrug og landboforhold i Island* (Copenhagen 1940).

Snorre Sturlesens Norske Kongers Krønike, oversat paa Dansk af Herr Peder Clausen ... (Copenhagen 1757).

Solberg, Ole: 'Ivar Bårdssøns Grønlandsbeskrivelse', *Norsk geografisk tidsskrift.*, 3 (Oslo 1931), pp. 314–21.

Sølver, Carl V.: *Vestervejen. Om vikingernes sejlads* (Copenhagen 1954).

Steen, Sverre: 'Fartøier i Norden i Middelalderen', *Nordisk Kultur*, XVI (Copenhagen 1934), pp. 282–300.

— *Ferd og fest. Reiseliv i norsk sagatid og middelalder* (Oslo 1942).

Steensby, H. P.: *The Norsemen's route from Greenland to Wineland* (Copenhagen 1918). *Med. om Grønl.*, 56.

— 'Uddrag af Prof. dr. phil. H. P. Steensby's Dagbog om Rejsen til "Vinland"' (Copenhagen 1931), pp. 45–116. *Med. om Grønl.*, 77.

Steinnes, Asgaut: 'Ein Nordpolsekspedisjon år 1360', *Syn og Segn 1958*.

Stenberger, Mårten: 'Island och Grönland som nordisk bygd under vikingetid och medeltid', *Ymer*, 61 (Stockholm 1941), pp. 241–63.

Stephensen, K.: 'Nye fund af Nordboruiner i Østerbygden og bemærkninger om nogle af de gammelkjendte, 1913' (Copenhagen 1914), pp. 79–101. *Med. om Grønl.*, 51.

Storm, Gustav: 'Søfareren Johannes Scolvus og hans reise til Labrador eller Grønland', *Historisk Tidsskr.*, Ser. 2 Vol. 5 (Christiania 1886).

— *Islandske Annaler indtil 1578* (Christiania 1888).

BIBLIOGRAPHY

Storm, 'Om kilderne til Lyschanders "Grönlandske Chronica",' *Aarbog for Nordisk Oldkyndighed og Historie, 1888* (Copenhagen 1888), pp. 197–218.

— *Studier over Vinlandsreiserne, Vinlands geografi og ethnografi* (Copenhagen 1888).

— 'Nye Efterretninger om det gamle Grønland', *Historisk tidsskr.*, Ser. 3. Vol. 2 (Christiania 1892), pp. 392–408.

Svare, Bjarne (tr.): *Jorsal-ferda åt Danene* (Oslo 1934).

Tanner, V.: *De gamla Nordbornas Helluland, Markland och Vinland. Ett försök att lokalisera Vinlands-resornas huvudetapper i de isländska sagorna* (Åbo 1941).

— 'Outlines of the geography, life and customs of Newfoundland–Labrador', *Acta Geographica Fenniae*, 8. No. 1 (Helsinki 1944).

Taranger, Absalon: *Udsigt over Den norske rets historie*, I–II (Christiania 1898–1904).

Thalbitzer, W.: 'Ethnological description of the Amdrup collection from East Greenland comprising objects found in Eskimo house-ruins and graves north of Angmagsalik between 68° and 75° lat. N. 1909' (Copenhagen 1910), pp. 329–542. *Med. om Grønl.*, 28.

Thorarinsson, Sigurdur: 'Vinlandsproblemet. Några reflexioner med anledning av Tanners skrift', *Ymer*, 62 (Stockholm 1942), pp. 39–46.

Thórdarson, Matthias: *The Vinland Voyages* (New York 1930).

Thorhallesen, E.: *Efterretning om Rudera eller Levninger av de gamle Nordmænds og Islænderes Bygninger paa Grønlands Vester-Side, tilligemed et Anhang om deres Undergang sammesteds* (Copenhagen 1776).

Vebæk, Christen L.: 'Inland farms in the Norse East Settlement' (Copenhagen 1943), pp. 1–109. Appendix by M. Degerbøl: 'Animal bones from inland farms in the East Settlement', pp. 113–19. *Med. om Grønl.*, Vol. 90. No. 1.

— *Klostre i de grønlandske Nordbobygder. Grønland*, 5 (Copenhagen).

— 'Middelalderlige bondegaarde paa Grønland. En sommers udgravninger i Nordboernes Østerbygd', *Fra Nationalmuseets arbeidsmark 1941* (Copenhagen 1942), pp. 39–48.

— 'Nordboforskningen i Grønland. Resultater og fremtidsoppgaver', *Geografisk Tidsskrift*, 46 (Copenhagen 1943), pp. 101–28.

— 'Nordbobygdernes kirker', *Grønland*, 8] (Copenhagen 1953), pp. 300–4.

— 'Vatnahverfi', *Fra Nationalmuseets Arbeidsmark, 1952* (Copenhagen 1952), pp. 101–14.

— 'Mellembygden', *Grønland*, 3 (Copenhagen 1956), pp. 92–8.

— 'Topographical and archaeological Investigations in the Norse Settlements in Greenland. A survey of the work of the last 10 years', Third Viking Congress, 1958.

Visted, Kristoffer, og Hilmar Stigum: *Vår gamle bondekultur*, I (Oslo 1951).

Wagner, K.: *Mittelalter-Knochen aus Oslo* (Oslo 1927).

Wahlgren, Erik: *The Kensington stone, a mystery solved* (Madison 1958).

Werenskiold, Werner: 'De norske bygders undergang på Grønland', *Norsk geografisk tidsskrift*, X (Oslo 1945), pp. 157–63.

Yearbooks for 1954 and 1957, Norsk Polarklubb, Oslo.

INDEX

INDEX